WORLDS WITHIN

Children's Fantasy from
the Middle Ages to Today

WORLDS
WITHIN

*Children's Fantasy from
the Middle Ages to Today*

Sheila A. Egoff

AMERICAN LIBRARY ASSOCIATION

Chicago and London 1988

Designed by Charles Bozett

Composed by Ampersand, Inc.
    in Itek Perpetua and
    Delphian on a Digitek
    typesetting system

Printed on 50-pound Glatfelter,
    a pH-neutral stock, and bound
    in C-grade Holliston cover stock
    by Braun-Brumfield, Inc.

The paper used in this publication meets the minimum requirements of American National Standard for Information Sciences—Permanence of Paper for Printed Library Materials, ANSI Z39.48-1984. ∞

Library of Congress Cataloging-in-Publication Data
Egoff, Sheila A.
    Worlds within: children's fantasy from the Middle Ages to today /
    Sheila A. Egoff.
        p.   cm.
    Bibliography: p.
    Includes index.
    ISBN 0-8389-0494-7
    1. Fantastic fiction, English—History and criticism.
    2. Children's stories, English—History and criticism. 3. Fantastic
    fiction, American—History and criticism. 4. Children's stories,
    American—History and criticism. 5. Fantasy in literature.
    6. Children—Books and reading—History. I. Title.
    PR830.F3E43   1988
    823'.0876—dc19   88-10058

Perhaps there has never been a dedication to a
sister-in-law before, but then perhaps, there has never
been a sister-in-law like Lou Egoff

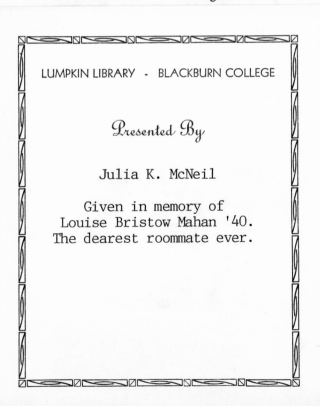

Contents

Preface

I began this exploration of fantasy by reading (or rereading) the major fantasies of the 1970's and early 1980's. Although they certainly are not all cut from the same cloth, I noticed strong trends and patterns emerging that were notably different from those of the past, that is, before the 1960's.

Change itself does not surprise me. Literature written for the young has always been strongly social. It reflects, although in miniature, the manners and mores of a given period in society and, in particular, those values society deems worthy of transmitting to the next generation. I expected that modern fantasists would reflect something of their own times. In strong contrast to the past, however, today's adults do not share a common view of childhood. The diversity shown by modern writers in their messages to the young was therefore also not surprising.

It was the altered concept of fantasy itself that intrigued me. Unlike other genres such as realistic fiction which, despite its new social and psychological candor continues to mirrot contemporary child and family life as it did in the past, fantasy has chiefly become the property of writers who explore new territory or who discover new vistas in old territory. Most importantly, it appeared to me that such writers were experimenting with fantasy's inner core, breaking many of its conventions and so changing its purpose and values.

Although, thankfully, it is never possible to come to an end in literature, I determined to follow at least part of the Red King's advice to the White Rabbit in *Alice's Adventures in Wonderland* and to "begin at the beginning." This advice has dictated my format. After a first chapter dealing with the roots, substance, types, and value of fantasy, the book proceeds chronologically from the first separate stream-of-writing for children in the seventeenth century into the 1980's. This approach allows for the perception of change and for some background on the social climate in which these books were written, in addition to dealing with the central issue of how the various components of the supernatural have been used in fantasy for the young.

The chronological arrangement has for the most part been divided into decades. Except for the long Victorian period, changes in fantasy have come rather quickly. In order that the principal types of fantasy (epic, animal, etc.) may easily be located within the time divisions, subheadings are provided. This arrangement allows for a quick comparison of the various subgenres of fantasy. The subheadings also show more clearly than a thousand words how the direction of fantasy has shifted (some headings had to be invented for the modern periods). However, the price of such helpful organization would be too great if the reader were to think that I feel comfortable with a rigid categorization of every work described. A fine work of literature can never be fitted into one sterile slot. Predictably then, Kenneth Grahame's *The Wind in the Willows* falls under the heading of "Animal Fantasy," although I do indicate its role as a social document concerning some of the effects of the Industrial Revolution. In every case, it is the total purpose and effect of a work that must be judged, and I hope that this aspect shines through the organizational pattern imposed on this study to make it a more usable reference book.

Over 375 titles are discussed or mentioned in this study, but still, choosing them from among hundreds of others was difficult. The past was easier to deal with than the present, for time did most of the winnowing out for me. However, some forgotten or almost forgotten early works have been included because they are typical of their period. From the 1960's on, with the exception of the few writers who garnered a considerable following, such as Lloyd Alexander, Ursula Le Guin, or Susan Cooper, my choices were chiefly based on critical reviews and library holdings. With one exception in each case, fantasy picture-books and translations from other languages have been excluded. This study is confined to fantasy written in English.

Biographical information about the writers is included only in those few cases when such facts bear directly upon the works under discussion. For example, George MacDonald's or C.S. Lewis's religious beliefs were fundamental to their writings and could not be ignored. There is also little or no attempt at an interpretation of the symbolism that is so much a part of fantasy. I realize that such revelations can be illuminating to the adult reader or critic, but overall I felt that the meaning of particular symbols had little to do with a writer's concept of fantasy as a form of literature.

The bibliographies are designed as a showcase, as it were, of each time period under discussion. Older works, although frequently mentioned, are listed only at the date of their first publication; however, all references to them are brought together in the index. Naturally, some writers span several decades. When the works of such writers are in essence a continuum, such as Ursula Le Guin's *Earthsea* trilogy, they are listed under the period during which their first part was published. Works by authors who changed or developed throughout their writing careers have been assigned each to its own decade. Only fantasies written for the young or those few that the young have co-opted are included in the bibliographies.

The index is similarly selective, omitting references to adult works, stories of realism, and proper names that only slightly impinge on my thesis.

Whatever its faults, this study has not been accomplished without help and encouragement. I would like here to thank Margaret Burke, Corinne Durston, Sarah Ellis, Ronald Hagler, Helen Jones, Kit Pearson, Samuel Rothstein and Judith Saltman. However, the theories propounded and any errors of fact are mine own.

Chapter 1

The Matter of Fantasy

The study of fantasy presents an intriguing set of paradoxes. Disdained, even denigrated throughout the ages as a literature of escape, fantasy has also been praised for its true reflection of reality and for its power to illuminate life's mysteries far beyond purportedly "realistic" novels. It can (and this is the generally accepted view of fantasy) transport us to another world, another time, or another dimension clearly separate and different from our own, or it can project the supernatural into the natural world. It can evoke a mood or an atmosphere that places a work slightly beyond the bounds of everyday reality, or it can wrench that reality out of shape. Like allegory or satire or parody, fantasy can infiltrate many types of literature, but it does so with more subtlety than these more discernible literary forms. It has served purposes ranging from moral instruction to the creation of a universal order of morality. Fantasy has been a vehicle used by writers to express their dissatisfaction with society, to comment on human nature, or to bridge the gap between the visible and invisible worlds. In all these various forms, fantasy exacts a discipline from its practitioners far beyond the constraints of realism. However, despite all its contradictions, range, and complexities, fantasy literature does form cohesive patterns and is best understood as a genre in its own right.

Much of early fantastic literature combined satire with a kind of tall-tale element. Journeys to the moon by means of various impossible mechanisms gave writers such as Lucian of Samosata (*True Historie*, A.D. 200), Bishop Godwin (*The Man in the Moone*, 1684) and Cyrano de Bergerac (*The State and Empires of the Moon and the Sun*, 1657) the opportunity to comment, savagely as well as humorously, on the people, customs, and science of their own times. H.G. Wells's *The War of the Worlds*, in which Martians invade earth, or C.S. Lewis's *That Hideous Strength*, in which King Arthur is brought back to life, are freighted with didactic ore. Other types of fantasy novels take steps, and sometimes leaps, beyond the probable. One thinks here of the symbolism of Herman Melville's *Moby Dick*, the impressionism of Emily Bronte's *Wuthering Heights*, or, more particularly, the aura (rather than the actual presence) of the supernatural in the short stories of Nathaniel Hawthorne and Edgar Allan Poe and in the *Gormanghast* trilogy by Mervyn Peake. John Bunyan's *Pilgrim's Progress*, with its dream journey to the Celestial City, and George Orwell's *Animal Farm*, with its talking barnyard animals as misled victims of a dictatorship, are considered allegory. Then there is the host of works, which is increasing in modern times, that take us to Other Worlds—to James Branch Cabell's realm of Poictisme, to J.R.R. Tolkien's Middle-earth, or to Stephen Donaldson's dark lands of Lord Foul in his recent *Thomas the Covenant* series.

Turning from adult literature to that written for the young, we find almost as wide a range of what is also generally described as fantasy. There are Lewis Carroll's daydream sequences, *Alice's Adventures in Wonderland* and *Through the Looking-Glass*; there is Lucy Boston's *The Children of Green Knowe* in which the happenings *may* be wholly in the mind of the protagonist; there are stories in which the only invention is that animals talk or dolls talk or time is suspended or wishes are granted. In Mary Norton's *The Borrowers* we are asked to believe only that people can be six inches tall and that friendship between a miniature girl and an ordinary boy is plausible. By contrast, the friendship between a great ape and a boy in Lucy Boston's *A Stranger at Green Knowe*, while probable, is touched with a mystic feeling that brings the story to the verge of fantasy. Peter Dickinson's *The Blue Hawk* and Elizabeth Pope's *The Perilous Gard* have only an aura of the supernatural, one that could be swept away under a microscopic eye. Young readers, like their elders, can also travel to Other Worlds—to C.S. Lewis's Narnia, J.M. Barrie's Never-land, Ursula Le Guin's Earthsea, or Alan Garner's Elidor.

At first glance, then, there seem to be no fixed boundaries enclosing the territory of fantasy, but there are some guideposts that can direct our footsteps, faltering though our steps may be. In speaking of the fairy tale and by extension fantasy, J.R.R. Tolkien declared that "Faerie cannot be caught in a net of words; for it is one of its qualities to be indescribable, though not imperceptible."[1] Any exploration or investigation of fantasy must therefore begin with its roots, which are deeper than those of any other literary genre, for they lie in the oldest literature of all—myth, legend, and folklore.

The Roots of Fantasy

Myths can now be seen as a dim vision of a reality that our ancestors saw very clearly—the true and fixed nature of things that made for a more orderly world. At their deepest level, myths comprise pre-literate humanity's philosophy, religion, history, and class structure; at their simplest, they are explanations of natural phenomena. Thus, for example, the god Prometheus felt sorrow for the poor shivering mortals on earth who were deprived of the joys of Olympus. He brought comfort to them in the form of fire, thereby incurring for himself a dreadful punishment. In another myth, daylight was provided by the god Apollo, who daily drove his fiery chariot across the sky.

Legends are less supernatural than myth. The heroes of legend—King Arthur, Charlemagne, Roland, Robin Hood, Grettir—lived in the arena of history. Their exploits were doubtless embellished as retellers, for reasons as varied as flattery and caution, altered events and incidents that actually occurred, to those that fell more pleasantly on the ears of their contemporary audiences.

Unlike myths, which are a connected series of stories, folktales are "nomadic" (Northrop Frye's word); versions of the same story are found in different parts of the world with local coloration added. Furthermore, while myths are set in a specific culture and so have not changed at all, folktales have been constantly revised by anonymous storytellers. Aristottle pointed out: "The marvellous . . . is a cause of pleasure, as is shown by the fact that we all tell a story with additions, in the belief that

1. J. R. R. Tolkien, "On Fairy-Stories," in *Tree and Leaf* (London: Unwin Bks., 1964), 16.

we are giving pleasure."[2] Folktales most of all embody our ancestors' love of giving this pleasure. Thus, they served a different social function rrom that of myths or legends, being conceived primarily for entertainment rather than instruction. Their very beginning, "Once upon a time," can still hold "children from play, and old men from the chimney corner."

More than any other form of literature, folktales are products of the pure imagination. But while their plots are filled with wonder, their observations of life are imbued with shrewdness and wisdom. Although their basic morality is simple enough—wisdom contrasted with foolishness, generosity with selfishness, the beautiful with the ugly, the true with the false—they are often subtle and psychological in their interpretation of human nature. All good folktales have more than just a page-turning plot, as is shown by "Puss in Boots" and "Bluebeard."

While myth, legend, and folklore can be differentiated in the above ways, they also share a common ground in their "matter," that is, in their elements of composition. They are filled with marvelous events engaged in by gods and goddesses, kings and queens, princes and princesses, heroes and warriors, wise men, seers and magicians, dwarves and giants, fauns and centaurs, as well as by ordinary mortals, whether they be brave, cowardly, kind, or cruel. Arthur and Sigurd have miraculous swords; Beowulf and St. George slay dragons; Merlin performs transformations; birds, fish, and animals converse with humans; and the real world and the world of the supernatural are as one.

There is, however, a significant distinction between works that have descended to us through the oral tradition and those to which we apply the word *fantasy*. Fantasists shape their stories through artifice rather than through cultural belief. Theirs is a private and metaphorical vision rather than a public dream, and the reader is asked to have faith in that artifice rather than in the events that lie behind it. For instance, the appearance of the Holy Grail in Malory's *La Morte D'Arthure* was not, in the fifteenth century, to be taken as fantasy. The story of the chalice and its miraculous appearance would have been received as a report of actual events. On the other hand, the Holy Grail found by three modern children in Susan Cooper's *Over Sea, Under Stone* is a fantasy device.

2. Aristotle, "On Poetics," in vol. 9 of *Great Books of the Western World* (Chicago: Ency. Brit., 1952), 696.

Many modern fantasists have made use of the "matter" of myth, legend, and folklore. They have also used the structural patterns of the imagination found in the oral tradition. The Mesopotamian hero Gilgamesh (*The Epic of Gilgamesh,* 3000 B.C.) goes on a quest that turns out differently from what he expected, and he returns home a different person; so do Bilbo Baggins in Tolkien's *The Hobbit* and Ged in Ursula Le Guin's *Earthsea* trilogy. But there is a difference; the story of Gilgamesh grew out of a specific culture, whereas Tolkien and Le Guin had to create the backgrounds that would give credence to the adventures of their heroes.

These basic differences between the old and the new literature provide only one guidepost toward a definition of fantasy; others may be found in a discussion of fantasy's major subgenres. Among these subgenres, two remain very close to their roots and are therefore the most perceptible as fantasy—the literary fairy tale and epic fantasy.

The Literary Fairy Tale

The literary fairy tale is a deliberate imitation of the traditional form. However, in selectively making use of the folk imagination, a new whole is created, stamped with the writer's individual personality. Frances Browne's stories in *Granny's Wonderful Chair and Its Tales of Fairy Times* have a softness of style and a strong moral cast that separate them sharply from "Cinderella" or "The Sleeping Beauty." Browne's tales are obviously the works of a writer who wished to instill goodness into children while giving them some pleasure. Hans Christian Andersen, the true originator and master of this special genre of fantasy, imbued his tales with his own observations of life and with his own experiences, and they are more often than not recounted with wit and sophistication. In comparing the works of Andersen with the "Märchen," or folktales, Walter de la Mare gave an apt description of a literary fairy tale:

> The folk-tales are of a universal, human sentiment. Andersen's are peculiarly personal; their nature, human and otherwise, has been distilled and etherealized. There is almost as curious a difference between the two as there is between a flint arrow-head and a Vic-

torian sampler. The wild bird of the folk-tales sings, in Andersen's, in an exquisite cage.[3]

In the English language, the taming of the folktale into a literary fairy tale is best seen in John Ruskin's *The King of the Golden River*. This tale is infused with a Germanic tone, but, for all its excellence, it lacks the earthiness of the collected tales of the Brothers Grimm.

Epic Fantasy

Epic, or heroic, fantasies are also distinguished by their close relationship to a branch of the oral tradition—the legend. While the Arthurian legends and the Welsh tales of the Mabinogion form the largest cauldron of story into which modern fantasists have dipped, one can also find various echoes from such sources as *Beowulf* and other English tales, Weland the Smith, Childe Roland of the Dark Tower, and Thomas the Rhymer, as well as from Scandinavian myths and legends. Fantasies with such components are not retellings of the original. Writers such as J.R.R. Tolkien, Susan Cooper, Alan Garner, Lloyd Alexander, William Mayne, Mollie Hunter, and others have used both the matter and structure of legend to infuse their works with the epic quality of the original—its emotional impact and grand design. Like their prototypes, modern epic fantasies are chiefly concerned with the unending battle between Good and Evil that is fought out in wide but well-defined landscapes. This type of fantasy is not to be confused with "sword and sorcery"—those action-packed pulps with their muscular barbarians luridly drawn, as in Robert Howard's *Conan*. Epic fantasy, like its forebears, is dominated by high purpose. There are worlds to be won or lost, and the protagonists engage in a deeply personal and almost religious battle for the common good.

In order to recreate the aura of times past in which the legends were developed, writers of epic fantasy frequently devise a kind of medieval Other World, such as Lloyd Alexander's Prydain, C.S. Lewis's Narnia,

3. Walter de la Mare, *Pleasures and Speculations* (Freeport, New York: Books for Libraries Pr., 1969), 21.

or Tolkien's Middle-earth. But even when the setting is real and geographically identifiable as part of our known world, as in Susan Cooper's *The Dark Is Rising* or Alan Garner's *The Weirdstone of Brisingamen,* the atmosphere resonates with mythic themes and symbols as legendary figures battle with modern protagonists.

Enchanted Realism

Other fantasists explore the strange, the uncanny, the eerie, or the dreamlike aspects of reality rather than the completely fantastic. The success of such works as Lucy Boston's *Green Knowe* series, Wiliam Mayne's *A Year and a Day,* Philippa Pearce's *Tom's Midnight Garden,* and Natalie Babbitt's *Tuck Everlasting* depends on only a delicate alteration of the everyday world. These works somewhat resemble the art form known as "magic realism." Magic realism, which appears to be a contradiction in terms, refers to a style or school of painting that is basically realistic but that has something contradictory to it, a slight intrusion of something unreal. It is this magic quality that allows us to see more realistic detail than we would in real life. The Canadian author Keith Maillard has applied the concept of magic realism to literature. He sees it as consisting of three parts:

> The first is the acceptance of most or all of the realistic conventions of fiction. The second is the introduction of a "something else" which is not realistic—the "magic" of the genre. . . . The magic element is not juxtaposed with the realistic for shock value, as in surrealism, but woven in seamlessly. The third characteristic is that the impulse for the writing of magic realism arises out of the desire to transcend the realistic novel, not as a *form* but as an expression. . . . The spirit of magic realism . . . is: "Something tremendously important must be said, something that doesn't fit easily into traditional structures, so how can I find a way to say it?"[4]

Since the books of magic realism in children's literature do not have the coldness or the static quality of the works of such artists as Alex

4. Keith Maillard, "'Middlewatch' as Magic Realism," *Canadian Literature* 92 (Spring 1982): 12.

Colville or Andrew Wyeth, and since they do have elements of the supernatural that are not always obvious in adult stories of magic realism, such as those by the Latin American writers Jorge Luis Borges and Julio Cortazar, the softer phrase "enchanted realism" seems more appropriate. While the settings in these books are real, they do have an aura of enchantment about them. There is the old house in Lucy Boston's *Green Knowe* stories and the garden that changes with the seasons in Philippa Pearce's *Tom's Midnight Garden*. Both William Mayne's *A Year and a Day* and Natalie Babbitt's *Tuck Everlasting* are set in times gone by, a distancing that gives the illusion of a dream.

Such books stand in strong contrast to epic fantasy. The protagonists are not called upon to participate in great events nor to test themselves against seemingly overwhelming odds. The children of enchanted realism do not change the world; instead they themselves are changed by their heightened concept of reality. Tom in *Tom's Midnight Garden* comes to an understanding of time and friendship; Becca and Sara in *A Year and a Day,* of the rituals of life and death; Tolly in *The Children of Green Knowe,* of the link between the past and the present; and Winnie in *Tuck Everlasting,* of the burdens of immortality. Books of enchanted realism generally cover only a short time span, almost only a brief moment, at most a season or a year but one that will never be forgotten since, for a while, the children themselves seem enchanted.

Stories of Magic

Another branch of children's fantasy might well be called stories of magic. Edith Nesbit, who brought this type of fantasy to its full flowering, has commented on it in her book *The Enchanted Castle:*

> There is a curtain, thin as gossamer, clear as glass, strong as iron, that hangs for ever between the world of magic and the world that seems to us to be real. And when once people have found one of the little weak spots in that curtain which are marked by magic rings, and amulets, and the like, almost anything can happen.

Indeed, the discovery of talismans and their use is the motivating force in such stories, but faith and belief in magic and an understanding of how magic works are also needed before the children can break through the vulnerable spots in the curtain. Stories of magic are never set in other fully created worlds, and they have less of the matter of fantasy than either the epic form or the literary fairy tale. The settings are real, whether a talisman takes the children to other places or times, or performs wonders in the children's own day-to-day environment. In Nesbit's *The Story of the Amulet,* a brief sketch of an idyllic future London is given, but its clean environment and social and educational advances may be seen as part of the hopeful philosophy of the Fabian society of which Nesbit was a member. In Hilda Lewis's *The Ship That Flew* (where magic is contained in a flying Norse ship), there is a visit to Asgard, which merely reflects the author's knowledge of Norse mythology. In Nesbit's *The Enchanted Castle,* Greek gods come alive and play a mystical part. However, these are all brief episodes. It is almost a characteristic of this type of fantasy to be episodic, with a talisman and whatever it can do providing the narrative link.

The chief strength of the magic story lies in its contrast between the ordinary and the fabulous—Nesbit's children in *Five Children and It* receive a wish a day, those in Edward Eager's *Half Magic,* half a wish. Thus, the children's everyday doings are as important as their magical ones, and such books show us much of the social structure of the time in which they were written, particularly as it affected children. Earlier ones have now become almost period pieces, much like realistic stories of child and family life. They do not have the timeless quality of epic fantasy, the literary fairy tale, or enchanted realism.

Animal Fantasies and Beast Tales

Tales of talking animals constitute another large branch of fantasy. Some critics, such as Tolkien, would, however, deny entrance here to the beast tales, those descendants of Aesop's *Fables* in which animal speech is used simply as a disguise for satire or for homily. But certainly the beast tale has taken on a new dimension since the times of Aesop and La Fontaine. In modern versions, such as John Donovan's *Family* or Richard Adams's *Watership Down,* the animals are endowed with human intelligence and emotions as well as with language, and their authors' diatribes are contained within a plot. It is a tenet of such stories that the animals must keep their animal characteristics even when appearing as mouthpieces for humans. Yet the more the animals are anthropomorphized, the more an aura of fantasy surrounds them.

There is a world of difference, for example, between *Watership Down* and Kenneth Grahame's *The Wind in the Willows*. Adams's rabbits are completely natural; they live in burrows and warrens, eat only what real rabbits eat, and do nothing physically that their kind could not do, given a measure of human intelligence beyond their natural instincts. Adams provides them with their own language (not human speech) and a kind of *lingua franca* for their converse with birds and other animals. In contrast, Grahame's Rat, Mole, Badger, and Toad wear the clothes of Edwardian country gentlemen, have household goods, and consume human food and drink ranging from cold ham to lemonade. All beast tales and animal fantasies are played out in the real world and often in a specific landscape (such as the Sussex of *Watership Down*), but the riverbank setting of *The Wind in the Willows,* although real, is an enclosed space where the human world only lightly intrudes. Thus, the aura of an Other World is sustained.

Past-Time Fantasy

Perhaps the most realistic of all types of fantasy is that in which the only magical premise is an entry into the past from the present—the present being the time at which the plot action begins in the real world. The entry may be made through a talisman such as Dicky Harding's bauble in Edith Nesbit's *Harding's Luck;* a piece of old lace, as in Ruth Park's *Playing Beattie Bow;* or through a door opening in the mind of the protagonist, as in Alison Uttley's *A Traveller in Time.* Whatever the method of entry to the past, the result is the same: the novel becomes historical fiction. The writers of past-time fantasy, however, have more license than do the writers of historical fiction, just as these writers, in turn, have more license than do historians. With time travelers as protagonists, contrasts can be made between modern periods and their precursors and may even be commented upon, as in Ruth Park's *Playing Beattie Bow.* The use of such knowledge is forbidden to the writer of historical fiction; whatever contrasts are to be made, readers must make them for themselves. Both types of fiction, however, operate under the same restriction: the past cannot be changed. In Alison Uttley's *A Traveller in Time,* Penelope Taberner's foreknowledge of the failure of the Babington Plot to rescue Mary, Queen of Scots, from the hands of the English adds a depth of pathos to an already moving story. But above all, past-time fantasy, with its controlled breadth of vision, can emphasize the universality of human needs and emotions, as Janet Lunn so clearly shows in *The Root Cellar.*

Some fantasies are completely set in more or less identifiable historical times or at least allude in part to historical eras. Katharine Briggs's *Hobberdy Dick,* for example, dwells in Cromwell's England; the landscape and time of Robin McKinley's *The Blue Sword* share elements with the early India of the British Raj; and Joan Aiken's *Night Birds on Nantucket* is set in a period that never was, that of James III of England, but it is faithful to its non-period (and to its literary antecedent, *Moby Dick*). Of course, such books have fantasy components, more or less intense, that separate them from stories that incorporate time traveling as well as from historical novels. An interesting example of past-time fiction that contains surely the least possible touch of fantasy is Joan Aiken's *The Wolves of Willoughby Chase,* which is a deliberate anachronism because there were no wolves in England in Victorian times.

Science Fiction Fantasy

Writers of time fantasies that involve the future have more freedom of movement, of course, than do those who take us into a known historical past. The future, as Walter de la Mare notes in his fantasy *The Three Mullah Mulgars,* is "easier to manage than the past." The variety of future-time novels is great indeed. Anne McCaffrey's *Dragonsong* and Jane Yolen's *Dragon's Blood* are set in future feudal ages and are rife with dragon-lore, as their titles indicate. The protagonist in William Sleator's *The Green Futures of Tycho* travels into his own future, and King Arthur makes an appearance in Peter Dickinson's future England in *The Weathermonger.* Since such books are not extrapolations of known scientific facts but are premised on the supernatural or contain elements of folklore and legend, they find a more natural niche in fantasy than in science fiction. Still, this special genre, now called science fiction fantasy, has not yet produced the shining examples that the past-time novel has. One explanation may be that science fiction fantasy suffers from having too wide a perimeter.

Ghost Stories

The ghost story forms another branch of fantasy, and, like its parent body, it does not conform to any theoretical model. Its range may be deduced from the varied words that are used to describe it: the tale of terror, the tale of horror, the weird tale, and, most commonly, the tale of the supernatural. The chief characteristic of the ghost story is that someone or something that should be dead, or that has escaped the realm of the demonic, invades the living and the present. These beings may be ghouls, apparitions, specters, poltergeists, vampires, werewolves, and, generally, "things that go bump in the night." Uneasy-resting spirits range from Banquo's ghost in *Macbeth* to the vampire in Bram Stoker's *Dracula* to the unseen horror from the grave in W.W. Jacob's short story "The Monkey's Paw."

The ghost story also differs from other types of fantasy in its intent. It is principally written to make the flesh creep and the hair stand on end. In English literature, it rose to prominence in the late eighteenth and early nineteenth centuries with the appearance of the first "gothic" novel, Horace Walpole's *The Castle of Otranto* (1764). However, it soon became apparent that the "spooky" tale lends itself best to the short story format. If sustained for too long, the tale loses its impact as well as its credibility, hence the short stories or the long short stories by the masters of the genre—Sheridan Le Fanu, Edgar Allen Poe, M.R. James, Algernon Blackwood, and many others.

Traditionally, ghosts do not flourish in the clear light of day. Therefore, in the telling of such stories, one turns down the lights and moves closer to the fire. In the classic ghost story, atmosphere is almost everything; it creeps, it steals, it permeates; it invades the reader as it does the protagonist. Most frequently, the terrors are within the range of human imagination. The characters are often older, generally recluses who are drawn to arcane matters by interest or propinquity, and who are often accidental victims of their fate. Most importantly, the supernatural forces win the battle; they are *supra*—above and beyond the natural; the humans thus go down before them.

Many earlier writers introduced into such tales personality disorders that were then being categorized (and popularized) by the new "black art" of psychoanalysis. Sheridan Le Fanu's "Green Tea," for example, can be interpreted as a case history of a split personality. Basically, however, the classic ghost stories are based on the psychology of fear as expressed by H.P. Lovecraft: "The oldest and strongest emotion of mankind is fear, and the oldest and strongest kind of fear is fear of the unknown."[5]

The ghost tale became part of children's literature via the oral tradition with such folktales as "The Golden Arm" and "The Teeny Tiny Woman." But it was not until the 1920's that Walter de la Mare included several ghost stories in his collection of short stories for children, *Broomsticks and Other Tales*. With the exception of "Alice's Godmother," he does not transform his specters into tangible figures. In such stories as "Miss Jemima," "Broomsticks," and "Lucy," de la Mare is saying that although this world is our principal concern, we do find ourselves subject to incursions from another. The spirit forces are close to us, but we can never turn our head quite quickly enough to see them plainly. Leon Garfield writes the more typical, sturdy kind of ghost tale in *Mr. Corbett's Ghost,* set as it is on a wild and stormy New Year's Eve in the eighteenth century and with the forces of the supernatural felt hovering in the air from the very first paragraph.

Light Fantasy

Humor and wit are the identifying marks of light fantasy, whose authors often poke fun at the very form they are using. Whether the humor is broadly cartoon-like, child-simple, or sophisticatedly adult, its presence removes the stories from the threatening struggles and the profound meanings of serious fantasy. The wide range of light fantasy extends from the cruel slapstick of Roald Dahl's *Charlie and the Chocolate Factory* to Robert McCloskey's playful *Centerburg Tales* to Helen Cresswell's larger-than-life story of the making of a gigantic pie in *The*

5. H.P. Lovecraft, *Supernatural Horror in Literature* (New York: Ben Abramson, 1945), 12.

Piemakers to the comic melodrama of Joan Aiken's *Night Birds on Nan-tucket* to the black humor of John Gardner's *Gudgekin the Thistle Girl.* It is another paradox of the genre that even light fantasy can have so many purposes and levels of meaning. Light fantasy is perhaps at its best and most memorable when it can fit into various slots and work for audiences of both children and adults, as does A.A. Milne's *Winnie-the-Pooh.*

Fantasists on Fantasy

Fantasists themselves have had a good deal to say about fantasy and have brought enlightenment to the subject, if not definitions. They have felt impelled to do so, probably, in order to give substance, in their own minds, to their own elusive art. In so doing, fantasists have often articulated their readers' feelings as well as their own. William Taylor Coleridge's phrase "the willing suspension of disbelief" has rung down the ages as almost the first law in dealing with the literature of the fantastic. Taken out of context, as it so frequently is, the phrase seems to imply that the reader must be ready and even eager to enter the gateway to the unreal. However, such is not its intent. In composing his famous phrase, Coleridge was indeed referring to the supernatural, specifically to his poems, such as "The Rime of the Ancient Mariner," which were to appear as opposites to William Wordsworth's poems of ordinary life to be published in their joint effort *Lyrical Ballads.* "It was agreed," says Coleridge,

> that my endeavours should be directed to persons and characters supernatural, or at least romantic; yet so as to translate from our inward nature a human interest and a semblance of truth sufficient to procure for these shadows of imagination that willing suspension of disbelief for the moment, which constitutes poetic faith.[6]

It is "a semblance of truth . . . for . . . shadows of the imagination" that is at the core of Coleridge's thought, and his view of the basis of fantasy is

6. William Taylor Coleridge, *Biographia Literaria* (London: J.M. Dent, 1975), 168–69.

certainly supported by other fantasists. For example, Ursula Le Guin writes:

> ... in fantasy, which, instead of imitating the perceived confusion and complexity of existence, tries to hint at an order and clarity underlying existence. . . . A fantasy is a journey. It is a journey into the subconscious mind. . . . [7]

It is also important to note that Coleridge calls for a "willing suspension of disbelief" only "for the moment"—that is, only for as long as one is reading the book. Fantasy is not meant to keep us in a never-land of the unreal but to return us to reality with a fresh vision of our own world and of ourselves. Some modern fantasists have disobeyed the axiom "for the moment" and leave the supernatural as a real presence in the real world when the story is over. Such an extension of fantasy may herald a new concept of it. Perhaps such modern authors as Margaret Mahy in *The Haunting* and *The Changeover* really believe in modern witchcraft, or perhaps they are trying to create a new mythology or a new metaphorical language to describe psychological states.

J.R.R. Tolkien also puts the onus for "the willing suspension of disbelief" on the writer. He sees the storyteller as a successful "subcreator":

> What really happens is that the story-maker proves a successful "sub-creator". He makes a Secondary World which your mind can enter. Inside it, what he relates is "true"; it accords with the laws of that world. You therefore believe it, while you are, as it were, inside. The moment disbelief arises, the spell is broken; the magic, or rather art, has failed. You are then out in the Primary World again, looking at the little abortive Secondary World from outside. [8]

Tolkien's insistence on the fantasist as a "sub-creator" is the chief point of his essay and is in essence a plea for literary art:

> Anyone inheriting the fantastic device of human language can say *the green sun*. Many can then imagine it or picture it. But that is not enough . . . .

7. Ursula Le Guin, "From Elfland to Poughkeepsie," in *The Language of the Night* (New York: Perigee, 1979), 87, 93.
8. Tolkien, 36.

> To make a Secondary World inside which the green sun will be credible, commanding Secondary Belief, will probably require labour and thought, and will certainly demand a special skill, a kind of elvish craft. Few attempt such difficult tasks. But when they are attempted and in any degree accomplished then we have a rare achievement of Art; indeed narrative art; story-making in its primary and potent mode.[9]

It is, of course, this "Art," both in its sense of skill and artifice, that separates fantasy from the traditional fairy story, a point that Tolkien never really makes clear until his epilogue, when he writes:

> Probably every writer making a secondary world, a fantasy, every sub-creator, wishes in some measure to be a real maker, or hopes that he is drawing on reality: hopes that the peculiar quality of this secondary world (if not all the details) are derived from Reality, or are flowing into it.[10]

Tolkien formulated his theories on fantasy in 1939, two years after he had written *The Hobbit* and after he had begun his saga of Middle-earth, *The Lord of the Rings*.[11] He therefore presupposes only one type of fantasy—that premised on a fully created Other World. Such a construct may provide (and fine fantasies usually do) analogies for and insights into the Primary World, but, once devised, it is basically an ecosystem, fully self-contained and drawing whatever new sustenance it needs from within itself. However, many fantasists do not form an absolute construct, nor do they intend to do so. They may introduce the supernatural into ordinary life, they may only slightly adapt the normal, or they may commingle the real and the unreal. But whatever they do, they must, to use Tolkien's phrase, command Secondary Belief. It would seem, then, that a Secondary Belief is a far more potent force than the creation of a Secondary World, since its presence is vital to all types of fantasy.

9. Tolkien, 45.
10. Tolkien, 61.
11. Humphrey Carpenter, *Tolkien* (Boston: Houghton, 1977), 191.

Defining Fantasy

Where have our various guideposts led us in developing a working definition of fantasy? Perhaps all that can be said with conviction is that fantasy is a story in which the sustaining pleasure is that created by the deliberate abrogation of any natural law, no matter how slight, or by the taking of a step beyond it. Such ventures, of course, imply the supernatural—that is, something or someone above and beyond the natural—whether this takes the form of the creation of a world that never was (a Secondary World) or of some unnatural intrusion into or effect in the real world (a Secondary Belief).

Now that we have reached this point, there are several caveats. As E.M. Forster has pointed out, fantasy "implies the supernatural, but need not express it."[12] Moreover, if the author's message takes precedence over the supernatural, as so frequently happens in the beast tale, for example, the result may be more allegory than fantasy. Consideration must also be given to the author's intent. It may well be that some authors, especially modern ones, really believe in second sight, extrasensory perception, or witchcraft. In such cases, a final decision must be left to the judgment of the reader.

The Value of Fantasy

Perhaps it is because E. M. Forster did not himself write fantasy that he felt it asked "something extra" of the reader:

> The general tone of novels is so literal that when the fantastic is introduced it produces a special effect: some readers are thrilled, others choked off: it demands an additional adjustment because of the oddness of its method or subject matter—like a sideshow in an exhibition where you have to pay sixpence as well as the original fee.[13]

12. E. M. Forster, *Aspects of the Novel* (New York: Harcourt, Brace & World, 1954), 160.

13. Forster, 160.

Here Forster appears to be envisioning only two types of readers—those who are open to fantasy and those who are not. But there are divisions among readers in any genre. On a very superficial level, fantasy offers what much of fiction in general offers—escape, romance, and exotic adventure. Many readers may stop at this level, thinking that this is what the fair is all about. However, for those readers who, like many protagonists in fantasy, pay all they have, and a little more, to embark on an odyssey of the imagination, the rewards are immeasurable.

Fantasy, first of all, returns to us what once belonged to us: a consciousness of the unity of the natural and supernatural worlds, a view of our universe that was wrenched apart with the coming of the "Age of Reason." Whatever seemingly strange figures we meet in fantasy— sibyls or seers, gods or godesses, earth spirits or witches, dragons or centaurs—the essential truth is that they were there before; they are the archetypes that touch the universal in the human condition and so are reminders of continuity, solace against the void, and redemption from despair. While we may have lost our belief in the validity of myth, we have not lost our craving for the eternal.

At the same time that fantasy roots us in universals, it also speaks to us of our place in our own world. Whether we wander in a Perilous Realm or sense a new dimension from the vantage point of our own backyard, whether we are portrayed as kings and queens or as rabbits or hobbits, we are at the center of things; and yet—and what is really at the heart of fantasy—this subtle distancing from ourselves saves us from egocentricity. To this end, fine fantasists almost invariably endow their main protagonists with generosity of spirit and concern for others, but in a way that reflects our own world. These fantasists do not present their versions of Eden, but rather worlds in conflict or disintegration that must be put right through struggle and sacrifice. Even Russell Hoban's dystopia in *The Mouse and His Child* offers hope to the individuals who fight for the survival of others as well as for their own survival. Here writers of fantasy show themselves as participants in the great tradition of liberal humanism; and because fine fantasists are masters of method as well as of message, their values are presented obliquely and delicately, not blatantly. The morals are implicit; the best fantasy does not preach.

Above all, fantasy offers its readers a true sense of story, that is, something beyond the urge to find out "what happens next." Admirable though a page-turning quality is, we pass on to something else. Fantasy's

THE MATTER OF FANTASY 19

plot is not simply a net for entrapment; more importantly, it is one in which we can catch the author's vision of life. The marvels of fantasy are not mere interjections for the sake of excitement or sensationalism; they are there as an expression of the writer's "third eye," the vision that draws from the imagination to create images that bond our psychological existence to the real world. It is this special quality of fantasy that makes a rereading of it so rewarding. It is a quality particularly appealing to and understood by children, as when they say of a story, "tell it again." They know the events of "Jack the Giant-killer" or "Cinderella," but it is the quality of the weak overthrowing the strong, littleness victorious against bigness, goodness surpassing selfishness (i.e., the journey itself, rather than the ending) that proves to have staying power. It is all better, the second time around.

Still, one must go gently and even circumspectly in praise of fantasy. In one way or another, all good literature seeks to impose some kind of order and meaning on the myriad experiences of life. What distinguishes fine fantasy from other fine literature is not merely its framework or its view of life, but its inner core. The writer of fantasy goes beyond realism to disclose that we do not live entirely in a world of the perceived senses, that we also inhabit an inner world of the mind and spirit where the creative imagination is permanently struggling to expand vision and perception. "Truth," Ursula Le Guin has written, "is a matter of imagination. Facts are about the outside. Truth is about the inside."[14] It is from the "worlds within" created by fantasists that the faculty of the imagination can be seen at its most powerful and stimulating.

An instinctive link exists between children and fantasy. Fantasy's wellsprings—myth, legend and folklore—were seized upon by children as their natural right long before special versions were written for them. The literature of the beginning of things thus appealed to those individuals who were in the first stages of life itself—children. This coexistence can be seen even more powerfully by default, as it were, during the long period of the Puritan ethos when such stirrings of the imagination could not be defeated even by adult fiat. It is no accident that many fantasies were first *told* as stories to delight an individual child and then

14. Jane Yolen, review of *The Language of the Night,* by Ursula Le Guin, *Book World* (12 May 1985): 13.

spread to others across the boundaries of time and space, as compelling narratives generally do.

Fantasists themselves have a childlike quality. They have a natural love of storytelling. Most importantly, however, they respect the qualities of children—curiosity, a sense of wonder, a love of the fabulous, and an ability to see to the heart of things with courage and honesty. Fantasists recognize that such assets should not be lost with the ending of childhood but are ones that are necessary for all mature and sensitive human beings. One of the world's greatest scientists might have been speaking of fantasy when he said:

> The fairest thing we can experience is the mysterious. It is the fundamental emotion that stands at the cradle of science. He who knows it not and can no longer wonder, no longer feel amazement is as good as dead.[15]

Thus, across a hundred years, Albert Einstein, a scientist, and Lewis Carroll, a mathematician and fantasist, join hands. For it was Alice who, in moving across a landscape as rich in conundrums and relativity as is Einstein's concept of the universe, remarked: "Curiouser and curiouser."

15. "The Talk of the Town," *The New Yorker* (28 May 1979): 27.

Chapter 2

The Fairies Underground:
Fantasy from the Middle Ages
to Victorian Times

I n Geoffrey Chaucer's *Canterbury Tales,* Dame Alison, the Wife of
Bath, begins her story by lamenting the disappearance of the fairies;
"No one sees an elf now, as you know. " She attributes this sad state of
affairs to the influence of the friars:

> For where you might have come upon an elf
> There now you find the holy friar himself.

In one respect, Dame Alison is correct: the friars were everywhere. They
were the ubiquitous, peripatetic clergy of the Middle Ages in a society in
which the Church (Catholic) dominated. As the creators and pop-
ularizers of "devotional lyrics and didactic poems, as well as ordinary
sermons,"[1] friars, it may be assumed, did not favorably regard any diver-
sion from spiritual matters. We know from evidence in the *Canterbury
Tales* that Chaucer disliked friars; his literary attack on them reaches
venemous proportions, and Dame Alison's accusation may be seen as
merely one more nail in their coffin. We also know that the fourteenth
century, given the accumulation of works in the oral tradition and their
lack of transmission by other than oral means, was an age as great for
stories and storytelling as the world has ever known. In addition, it was

1. Boris Ford, ed., *The Age of Chaucer* (London: Cassell, 1964), 1:99.

an age in which belief in the miraculous was still sometimes the only means for explaining nature's more mysterious processes and one in which pagan and Christian beliefs coexisted in considerable comfort. So it seems unlikely that elves and their ilk, whether in concept or in literature, were banished at this time for any reason.

Writers after Chaucer, however, continued to castigate aspects of religion for the disappearance of the fairies from England. Sixteenth century cleric and poet Richard Corbet blamed the Puritans in his witty poem *The Faeryes Farewell,* which begins, "Farewell, Rewards & Faeries." Much later, Rudyard Kipling in his short story "Dymchurch Flit" from *Puck of Pook's Hill* (1906) gives the cruel religious wars occasioned by the Reformation of Henry VIII as the reason for the fairies' disappearance:

> . . . for Good-will among Flesh an' Blood is
> meat an' drink to em' [the fairies] an'
> ill-will is poison.

In her own time, however, the Wife of Bath turned out to be something of a prophetess, for eventually religion was to send the literature of romance and faerie underground.

It is of more significance that Chaucer puts a folktale into Dame Alison's mouth. She bends the tale to her own purpose, but in its broad outline, the tale of the "loathly lady" was well known in the late fifteenth century. Dame Alison tells it to a group of adults; she would not have dreamed of addressing her story to children for two reasons. First, the notion that fairy tales were fit fare only for the young came much later, when they were put into print. It is a notion that has persisted into our own time despite protestations to the contrary by such afficionados of the fairy tale as G.K. Chesterton, C.S. Lewis, and J.R.R. Tolkien. Second, just as tales were not separated by age groupings, neither were children, for in the minds of medieval people the idea of a unique state called "childhood" simply did not exist.

As Philippe Aries points out in *Centuries of Childhood,* most children were not expected to live; if they survived the illnesses and dangers of infancy and early childhood, they were quickly drawn into adult life, both by participation and observation. Nothing was hidden from them.[2] This

2. Phillipe Aries, *Centuries of Childhood* (New York: Knopf, 1962).

view of children as "little adults" is, to the modern mind, most poignantly seen in paintings of the period. In these, children are depicted in gay abandon, joining in adult pleasures and lechery, as shown in Pieter Breugel's "Peasant Wedding," and identifiable only by their size. In portraiture, we see children in the stiff, heavy clothes of their parents, their faces devoid of expression—old heads on young shoulders. Few children were taught to read or write unless they belonged to the nobility or were destined for the priesthood or government service; and since there were no children, why provide anything special for them such as books? The Middle Ages, by default as it were, show the link between what a society thinks of its young and what it provides (or does not provide) for them in reading material. There were a few schoolbooks and books of manners and courtesy, but these were only preparations for adult life. *The Babees Book* (c. 1475), for example, directs a child how to wait upon his Lord, and Hugh Rhodes's *The Boke of Nurture* (1554) is subtitled: "for men, servants and children."

However, in the shared storytelling of the pre-literate oral tradition, which knew neither age nor hierarchical distinctions, children had their place, if only by oversight. What would children have heard during those several hundred years that we conveniently call the Middle Ages? We can only deduce what came from the Cauldron of Story from what remains in manuscript and from what later appeared anonymously in print. Certainly there would have been tales from the *Gesta Romanorum* (stories mixing the myth, history, and religion of the classical Greek and Roman heroes), Aesop's *Fables, Reynard the Fox,* tales of King Arthur and his knights, Charlemagne, Robin Hood, King Horn, Valentine and Orson, Havelok the Dane, Beowulf, St. George and the Dragon, Tom Hickathrift, Guy of Warwick, and Jack the Giant-killer, as well as tales that now form the *Mabinogion*—a rich fare indeed.

William Caxton, the first English printer, and his successor Wynken de Worde, put much of this oral tradition into print, thus spreading it even farther, contributing to literacy, and eventually arousing the wrath of the guardians of education. The cleric Hugh Rhodes, in his *Boke of Nurture,* warned parents to keep their children from the reading of "feigned fables or vain fantasies."[3] In 1570, Roger Ascham, the otherwise enlightened tutor of Elizabeth I, condemned *La Morte d'Arthure* as

3. Hugh Rhodes, *The Boke of Nurture* (microfilm).

reading for the young in his famous treatise, *The Schoolmaster,* on the value of a classical education:

> In our forefathers' time, when Papistry, as a standing pool, covered and overflowed all England, few books were read in our tongue, saving certain books of Chivalry, as they said, for pastime and pleasure, which, as some say, were made in monasteries by idle monks or wanton canons: as one for example *Morte Arthure:* the whole pleasure of which book standeth in two special points, in open manslaughter and bold bawdry . . . Yet I know, when God's Bible was banished the Court, and *Morte Arthure* received into the Prince's chamber. What toys the daily reading of such a book may work in the will of a young gentleman or a young maid, that liveth wealthily and idly, wise men can judge and honest men do pity.[4]

It is doubtful that these keepers of the public conscience would have cried "fire" without evidence of some smoke, and so we can assume that at least some of the young of England had access to the Romances.

It is impossible to judge the influence of Rhodes and Ascham or whether they were the only critics of "feigned fables" and "vain fantasies." However, within a few decades, a whole society was to excoriate such reading for children and to push aside any book that contained "the matter of fantasy." This viewpoint was to produce the dreariest era in all of children's literature, and it was to last for about a hundred and fifty years.

In the seventeenth century, with infant and early childhood mortality as pervasive as in the Middle Ages and with plagues and other diseases widespread, the Puritans felt it their duty to prepare their children for death. In so doing, they began the first separate stream-of-writing for children, complete with child characters. In book after book of the period, we see children dying (chiefly between the ages of three and eight) and happy at the thought of going to a better world. The apotheosis of such literature can be seen in a work by James Janeway, a Nonconformist preacher, one that has survived in historical collections in various editions. Its title lays out its contents: *A Token for Children:*

---

4. Roger Ascham, *The Schoolmaster* (Westminster, England: A. Constable and Co., 1903), 80.

being an Exact Account of the Conversion, Holy and Exemplary Lives and Joyful Deaths of several young Children . . . (1671). In his preface, Janeway lectures all who "have any hand in the education of children." The whole thrust of books for the young during this period can be seen in the author's questions and injunctions to them:

> Are the souls of your Children of no Value?
> Are you willing that they should be brands
> of hell? . . . They are not too little to die;
> they are not too little to go to Hell.

As much as we may now denigrate such offerings for children, it must be remembered that they were meant to give pleasure, the greatest pleasure that life could offer: that of going prepared and happy to God's beneficence.

Paradoxically, it was the greatest Puritan of them all, John Bunyan, who gave the children of his period and later a book that contained elements of fantasy. It was a book that even their elders approved of and who, it can be conjectured, had little idea of *how* their children were reading it. Bunyan's *The Pilgrim's Progress* (1671), a dream allegory of religious conversion, is one of the great books of the English language. Its message is a harsh one but was not unfamiliar to the Puritan child: the road to heaven—the Celestial City—is long, laborious, and filled with traps and pitfalls for the unwary. The evidence has long been in (from biographies, autobiographies, and from books such as Edith Nesbit's stories of the Bastable children) that children did read *The Pilgrim's Progress* and even played at being pilgrims until the early part of the twentieth century. However, there is equally no doubt that children took out of this book exactly what *they* wanted; it was rich enough for them to do so, for it contains fable, romance, dream, and satire as well as allegory. Children saw its hero, Christian, as a hero in the folk- and fairy tale tradition, for the story had all the appurtenances of faerie—monsters, giants and giantesses, dragons and hobgoblins, and other characters made familiar through oral tradition. There also were the place names to be rolled around on the tongue—the Slough of Despond, the Delectable Mountains, Doubting Castle, Vanity Fair. The book even had some humor, as when "Talkative" is outtalked by Christian. As in real play, there was also the serious fun of preparing for a quest or journey—the staffs, the hats, the scripts, and the emergency supplies. Bunyan may have thought he was writing an allegory, but as George MacDonald has said, "He must be an artist indeed who can, in any mode, produce a strict allegory that is not a weariness to the spirit."[5] Bunyan was such an artist.

However, when he turned his pen to writing strictly for children in *A Book for Boys and Girls* (1686), the full weight of the "brand of hell" school of writing can be felt once again. Bunyan makes his purpose clear:

> I do't to show them how each fingle-fangle,
> On which they doting are, their souls entangle,
> As with a web, a trap, a gin, a snare,
> And will destroy them, they have not a care.

Such a warning in the introduction was mild in comparison with the actual contents of the verses:

> And as I was born naked,
> I was with filth bespaked,
> At which when I awaked,
> My Soul and Spirit shaked.

Gradually, this religious tone softened in children's literature, although it lingered up to the end of the nineteenth century, and became melded into a somewhat more social literature that came to be known as the "moral tale." In it, children were exhorted to be good, generous, kind to the poor, strictly obedient to their parents, and assiduous in acquiring facts. In this latter aspect of their reading, children were frequently fed slanted and even incorrect information. Moral tales also stressed that badness or lack of thought brought dire consequences; if not death, at least some physical disaster would result (the mental problems of children do not surface until Freud). As a reversal of the coin, these tales emphasized that goodness led to praise, esteem, and material success. Certainly, virtue was not seen as its own reward. The result for

5. George MacDonald, "The Fantastic Imagination," in *Fantasists on Fantasy*, eds. Robert H. Boyer and Kenneth J. Zahorske (New York: Avon, 1984), 17.

children's literature was chiefly a gallery of priggish children who dominated the fictional scene for at least 150 years.

Nevertheless, real children fought back. They continued to fall with delight upon books intended for their elders—Daniel Defoe's *Robinson Crusoe*, which they read as a romantic adventure, and Jonathan Swift's *Gulliver's Travels* (1726), a book that combined the realism of *Robinson Crusoe* with the wonders of "Jack the Giant-killer" and "Sinbad the Sailor" and with the tall-tale quality of early travel tales such as Lucian of Samosata's *True Historie*. Swift, of course, wrote his book as a violent and even vicious satire on humanity, particularly the last three parts, in which the Houyhnhnms (a race of horses) are seen as noble and virtuous, and the Yahoos are seen as the embodiment of the bestial in man. With their usual acumen, children seized on the first two parts of the book— "The Voyage to Lilliput" and "The Voyage to Brobdingnag," in which the strain of misanthropy is muted (the last parts of *Gulliver* were written years after the first two).

It was the Lilliputians and the Brobdingnagians who captured children's imaginations; children were, after all, familiar with dwarves and giants. In this aspect, Swift does not even strain his reader's credulity. All he asks is: "why not creatures in human form taller or shorter than the normal?" Once he gives us these creatures' proportions—one of our linear feet representing an inch, or one of our inches representing a foot—he works out the consequences almost as mathematical problems. Swift wrote during the Enlightenment, and it can be presumed that, like Rabelais and Voltaire, he used the fantastic to escape the consequences of criticizing his own kind. Unlike his predecessors, however, Swift does not make fun of his own fantasy; he treats it with the utmost gravity, thus compelling belief. It was a quality emulated by his successors in their portrayal of a miniature world, such as that of T.H. White's *Mistress Masham's Repose* and Mary Norton's *The Borrowers*. Swift is more of a fantasist than they, however, because he does create the countries of Lilliput and Brobdingnag—that is, Other Worlds. However, it is not fair to compare a book written for adults with one for the young; Swift did not have to contemplate the problems of writing for children. He was an arrogant man, by all accounts, one who deemed himself far above "the madding crowd," and one can imagine his fury had he known that his bitter satire would become the property (at least in part) of children who have, in essence, destroyed its original purpose.

Still, there was little for children to feed their imaginations upon in the early part of the eighteenth century except for such borrowings as Swift and except for what gradually became evident as their own subculture of fiction. The latter was to become as resilient as children themselves and to survive the fiercest criticism ever directed against the literature of faerie.

The origin of chapbooks—a fairly modern corruption of cheapbook—is lost in the mists of time, but certainly they were printed as early as the sixteenth century along with broadsides, ballads, and newssheets. This printed material was part of the stock (as were ribbons, pins, and baubles) of the cheap-men (chapmen), the peripatetic salesmen of the sixteenth to early nineteenth centuries who traveled the length and breadth of England (indeed of the British Isles), stopping at inns and cottages and castles to peddle their wares. These miniature paper booklets that were sold for a penny became the reading matter of the common people. Their contents consisted chiefly of old tales and medieval romances cut to a minimum and sometimes enlivened by crude woodcuts. In the extant copies, it can be seen that these tales have life and vitality, the plots so compelling and their air of wonder so pervasive that the bare bones are clothed in the mind's eye. Thus, throughout this dreary age, children still had "Tom Thumb," "Jack the Giant-killer," "The Children in the Woods," "The Death and Burial of Cock Robin," "Valentine and Orson," and Perrault's French tales after they were translated into English in the early part of the eighteenth century. *Pilgrim's Progress, Robinson Crusoe,* and *Gulliver's Travels* were also compressed into chapbook form (twelve to twenty-four pages). Judging from the numbers that have survived, these frail little pamphlets must have been printed into the hundreds of thousands and distributed so widely that their influence could not be contravened.

Neither could that of servants and nurses and members of the lower classes in general, who were seen (and quite rightly) as oral purveyors of idle tales. The seventeenth century educationalist, John Locke, in his otherwise generous book of child-rearing, adjured parents to keep their children away from the depraving influence of servants, who were inclined to give them "Playthings and other such Matters"[6]—other mat-

6. John Locke, *Some Thoughts Concerning Education* (1690; reprint, England: Cambridge Univ. Pr., 1899), 45.

ters, no doubt, included stories that did not distinguish satisfactorily between truth and falsehood. Isaac Watts, who wrote moral verses for
children, was more specific in condemning the idle chatter of servants:

> Let not Nurses or Servants be suffered to fill their minds with *silly*
> *Tales and with senseless Rimes,* . . .
>   LET not Persons that are near them terrify their tender Minds
> with dismal *Stories of Witches and Ghosts, of Devils and Evil Spirits, of*
> *Fairies and Bugbears in the Dark.*[7]

The public view of children's reading matter was therefore at variance
with what constituted an effective underground movement of the literature of Romance and Faerie. Oddly enough, there seems to have been no
condemnation of writers for adults who made use of the same material.
For instance, Spenser borrowed Titania to praise *Elizabeth I* in his *The*
Faerie Queen in the sixteenth century; witches and elves and Puck himself
help to form the plots of some of Shakespeare's plays; and the poet
Richard Corbet could playfully introduce such creatures in his "The
Faeryes Farewell" in the seventeenth century. But so stringent were the
views expressed against such literature for children that even John New-
bery, that commercial dynamo in children's book publishing and one
who certainly had children's interests at heart (he published attractive
little books and sold them along with toys), trod carefully with Jack the
Giant-killer in *A Little Pretty Pocket Book* (1744). In this work the hero of
the folktale is reduced to explaining the use of a ball and a pincushion.
   The same caution in the use of fairy tales is observable in Sarah
Fielding's *The Governess; or, Little Female Academy* (1749), considered the
first children's novel. It included two fairy tales; but they were so
tedious, feebly plotted, moralistic, and crammed with the superficial
matter of Faerie that they cannot really be described as literary fairy
tales, although their origins certainly lie here. Mrs. Teachum, the
children's benevolent and intelligent governess, uses the tales themselves
as a warning against the genre. She would have her pupils know that

> " . . . Giants, Magic, Fairies and all sorts of supernatural assis-
> tances in a Story, are only introduced to amuse and divert: . . . For

---

7. Geoffery Summerfield, *Fantasy and Reason: Children's Literature in the Eighteenth*
Century (London: Methuen, 1984), 79.

if the story is well written, the common Course of Things would produce the same Incidents, without the Help of Fairies."

Even this apologia, however, was not enough for those who considered such literature harmful. Seventy-one years later, Mrs. Mary Sherwood, herself a writer for children, rewrote *The Governess* (she had enjoyed it as a child) and suppressed the tales, "substituting in their place such appropriate relations as seemed more likely to conduce to juvenile edification." Her own tales are even more moralistic and devoid of sparkle than those of Sarah Fielding, but their presence indicates the strong hold that the *form* of the fairy tale had taken even on its detractors. Mrs. Sherwood used the convention again in her separately published *The Rose: A Fairy Tale* (1824) in which a fairy is rewarded for spending her time in the proper rearing of her children.

Also accepted was the concept of talking animals. Here was an egregious violation of a natural law, but one that, like the fairy tale, the moralists were able to turn to their own advantage. Such a tale did have some cachet. John Locke ignored the fancifulness of beasts and birds talking and recommended Aesop's *Fables* as excellent fare for enticing children to read. There also seems to have been no outcry against the fables of La Fontaine and John Gay, which were probably read by children as well as adults.

Mrs. Sarah Trimmer was on fairly safe grounds, therefore, when she had a family of robins indulge in human speech in her *Fabulous Histories* published in 1798 and subsequently republished as *The History of the Robins*. The bird family is paralleled to the human family, and both are models for rearing the young. Feathers are no more a defense against homilies, advice on the proper regulation of the passions, and illustrations of folly and vice than is human skin. The young robins respond appropriately. When one is shot by a marksman, it falls dying to the ground. In a deathbed scene straight out of James Janeway, the felled robin manages to cry to its father: "Oh! my dear father, why did I not listen to your kind admonitions, which I now find too late, were the dictates of tenderness!" Like Sarah Fielding's Mrs. Teachum, Mrs. Trimmer feels that she has gone too far in granting speech to the feathered species; thus, in the introduction to her book she warns children against believing this aspect of her story in deference to the view that no child should really be encouraged to believe in artifice. Mice, dogs, cats, and horses were also used to mirror the manners, mores, and religious views of the time, but none were as lengthily tedious as Father and Mother Robin. The long life and numerous editions of *The Robins* can surely be attributed more to parental control of children's reading matter than to children's own delight.

It is as a critic of children's books that Mrs. Trimmer is now best remembered. Although her magazine, *The Guardian of Education* (certainly well-named), ran for only five years (1802–06), in her editorializing and reviews of children's books, she became the arbiter of their reading material. Nothing escaped her eye: "The expensiveness of children's books," she notes, "is a growing evil"—one comment that should endear her to the modern reader.

There is an echo of the convert in Mrs. Trimmer's writing. She recalls her own childhood reading of Perrault, Aesop, Gay's *Fables,* and Sarah Fielding's *The Governess* with pleasure, but as an adult she deems them "mostly calculated to entertain the imagination rather than to improve the heart, or cultivate the understanding." Even *The Governess* has to go, she says, because it contains fairy tales. Like any magazine editor, she is swayed by the opinions of her readers. The mention of Perrault was too much for one of them: "Cinderella," wrote a correspondent, "is perhaps one of the most exceptionable books that was ever written for children. . . . It paints some of the worst passions that can enter into the human heart, and of which little children should, if possible, be totally ignorant; such as envy, jealousy, a dislike to mothers-in-law and half-sisters, vanity, a love of dress," etc., etc. It should be remembered that Mrs. Trimmer wrote during the stormy days of the French Revolution, whose influence was greatly feared in England. Mrs. Trimmer was all for the status quo. It can be presumed that to her, fairy tales had an anarchistic element—the lowly could rise, and the poor peasant could outwit the king. Such a disruption of the social system was not to be tolerated; she therefore swung her axe quite widely. *Robinson Crusoe* was not fit reading for the young because it promoted "an early taste for a rambling life, and a desire of adventure"—and she had an example from real life to prove her point. She had heard of two boys who had actually run away in emulation of Robinson Crusoe. Even the Edgeworths (both father and daughter), considered the most careful educators of children in their time, met with Mrs. Trimmer's displeasure; they stressed utility and science at the expense of religion. "There is nothing to study," she declared, "but what is already known."[8]

It is as well for children that *The Guardian of Education* ceased publication in 1806, for there is little doubt that she would have honed a knife particularly sharp to eradicate William Roscoe's *The Butterfly's Ball and the Grasshopper's Feast* (1807). Its only purpose was to "entertain the imagination"; there is not a moral to be found in its few pages of verse that decribe a group of insects and small animals having a party that is watched by a small boy:

> Come take up your Hats, and away let us haste
> To the Butterfly's Ball, and the Grasshopper's Feast.
> The Trumpeter, Gadfly, has summon'd the Crew
> And the Revels are now only waiting for you.
>   . . .
> Then Home let us hasten, while yet we can see,
> For no Watchman is waiting for you and for me.
> So said little Robert, and pacing along,
> His merry Companions returned in a Throng.

With its pictures of a snail who wanted to dance a minuet and a mushroom with a water dock leaf spread for a tablecloth, *The Butterfly's Ball* is animal fantasy in verse. Although it barely survived into the twentieth century, it shows remarkable spontaneity for its time. Imitation being the sincerest form of flattery, it was quickly followed by such other animal verses as Mrs. Dorset's *The Peacock at Home* and many others. Along with nursery rhymes and some early limericks, such as *The History of Sixteen Wonderful Old Women* (1821), these selections were the only notes of levity—and fantasy—that broke the stranglehold of the moral tale.

Fairy tales were gradually becoming respectable. Aside from their hold on children through chapbooks, other influences were at work on their behalf. All the great writers of this long period, ranging from Shakespeare and Spenser through Henry Fielding, Samuel Johnson (and his Boswell), Addison, Steele, Charles Lamb, Coleridge, Wordsworth,

8. Mrs. Sarah Trimmer. *The Guardian of Education.* All references are taken from the Readex Microprint Edition of Early American Imprints (Worcester, Mass.: American Antiquarian Society, 1956–).

and Dickens, showed a knowledge of fairy tales and in many cases remarked on their love of them as children. Most of these writers discovered the fairy tale in chapbook form. Shakespeare comes into this pantheon because he quotes from two tales in his plays—"Mr. Fox" and "Childe Roland." Influences from abroad also added to the spread and popularity of fairy tales, mostly due to Charles Perrault, who put France's oral tradition into a form sufficiently sophisticated to amuse the courtiers of Louis XIV. It was only after his *Histoires ou Contes du Temps passé* (1697) was translated in the early seventeenth century, however, that fairy tales became fare for children only. Even before the work of the Brothers Grimm, the German Romanticists—Goethe, E.T.A. Hoffman, Novalis (the pseudonym of Friedrich von Hardenberg), and the Baron de la Motte Fouqué (his *Undine* [1811], the story of a water spirit who loved a mortal, pre-dates H.C. Andersen's "The Little Mermaid")—used various strands of fairy tales in their works of the supernatural and fantastic. These authors appreciated the "folk" imagination, recognizing its power to see truly below the surface of conscious belief. Novalis declared: "Everything is a fairy tale."

Reinforcing this influence was the appearance in Berlin of the Brothers Grimm's *Kinder-und-Hausmärchen* (1812–15), which, in turn, set off a wave of scholarly research into the folktale. The first English translation, by Edward Taylor, appeared from 1823 to 1826 and was to influence later English writers of fantasy as much as the German Romanticists did. In England, other works followed quickly. There were, for example, T. Crofton Croker's *Fairy Legends and Traditions of the South of Ireland* (1825–28) and Thomas Keightley's *The Fairy Mythology: Illustrative of the Romance and Superstition of Various Countries* (1828). These were scholarly works, source material, but soon fairy tales were collected or translated especially for children: Joseph Ritson's *Fairy Tales* (1831), Rev. H.C. Keene's *Persian Fables for Young and Old* (1833), E.W. Lane's *Arabian Nights* (1839–41)—the latter an example of how real wonder tales cannot be destroyed by even the heaviest of moralizing. Other important retellings were to help spark the rise of fantasy as a genre in the Victorian Age. But on the eve of this awakening, it can be seen that the fairies were back in England in full force. The Wife of Bath would have been delighted.

Chapter 3

The Golden Key:
Fantasy of the Victorian Era

Mrs. Sherwood's *The Fairchild Family* (Part I) was published in 1818. It was a popular book of its time and considerably above average in literary skill—Mrs. Sherwood had an ear for spontaneous childlike dialogue and a feeling for childish pleasures, especially those of eating and dressing up. However, her Evangelical zeal overcame her natural love of children, and such delights as hot buttered toast and feathered hats became lessons in greed and vanity, amply supported by Biblical quotations. The first edition of *The Fairchild Family* is of special significance. One long incident sets forth Mrs. Sherwood's belief that children are "by nature evil" and that "pious and prudent parents must check their naughty passions in any way that they have in their power, and force them into decent and proper behavior. . . ." Mr. Fairchild's way, after his children have quarreled among themselves, is to take them through a dark and gloomy wood to see a criminal mouldering on a gibbet. The man who is hung upon it is a murderer—"one who first hated, and afterwards killed his brother!" Mr. Fairchild's peroration on the subject, that death and perhaps hell await children who turn to fighting in their play, proved too strong even for the moralists of the day, and the passage was deleted from later editions.

In 1839, Catherine Sinclair, in the introduction to *Holiday House,* complained about the Sherwood-type school of writing and tried to avoid its endless moralizing in her own work. She was only partially successful, but she did loosen the first lace in the straitjacket then encasing the children's novel. Her children are allowed to be noisy, frolicsome, and mischievous without dire consequences and even without sermons on their misbehavior. What gentle chiding there is comes from the "goody-goody" older brother, who fades to his death in typical Victorian fashion. Catherine Sinclair could not bring herself to break all the conventions of the period, but she tried to live up to her stated beliefs by including in her episodic plot an original fairy tale, "Uncle David's Nonsensical Story of Giants and Fairies." This tale owes something to the giant in "Jack and the Beanstalk," and it has an unescapable moral; but its humorous exaggerations and convincing details make it the first literary fairy tale in the English language, an achievement of some substance. To many critics, Holiday House represents the true beginning of children's literature.

In the deletion of the "gibbet" passage from The Fairchild Family and in Catherine Sinclair's presentation of more natural children along with her injection of an imaginative story into a realistic novel, the indications of a softer attitude toward childhood and children's reading material were apparent. From these indications, one might have eventually expected an English version of Louisa May Alcott's Little Women (1868), a book of family life that in an American context combined the manners and mores of the period but with a striking leap forward in the delineation of the character of Jo March—the most memorable of the "little women." What emerged in England in 1865 instead was a perfect piece of nonsensical fantasy—Lewis Carroll's Alice's Adventures in Wonderland. It was to change the face of children's literature.

Considering the emphasis on information, didacticism, piety, and the daily routine of youthful life presented in the children's novel, it is astounding that Alice could have been written only twenty-six years after Holiday House or even forty-nine years after The Fairchild Family. This fact is so astounding that it might be considered as only the ordinary madness of a mathematician (that compulsion to play with figures and games and puzzles), combined with its author's love of children and, indeed, for one particular child. The word "mad" occurs in Alice more than once: "We're all mad here," says the Cheshire Cat. Forces at work in England before 1865 may somewhat explain this unique work.

Social and Literary Influences

Probably no past society has been so examined and criticized—for good or for ill—than that which existed during the period of Queen Victoria's reign, from 1837 to 1901. In the popular mind, this period is remembered chiefly for its tightly laced moral standards, and, indeed, many diaries, letters, biographies, and autobiographies of the period attest to a rigidity in the lives of middle-class, well-to-do, well-educated Victorians. As Leonard Woolf has written:

> People who were born too late to experience in boyhood and adolescence the intellectual and moral pressure of Victorianism have no idea of the feeling of fog and fetters which weighted one down.[1]

Paradoxically, the Victorians managed to maintain a solidly grounded code of duty, self-restraint, faith in goodness, and respectability despite an age of swift change almost as great as our own transition into the nuclear age. It was therefore shown that progress and discipline could go together.

By the time Lewis Carroll wrote *Alice's Adventures in Wonderland,* the Industrial Revolution was at its peak. Much of the unprecedented growth in human knowledge had already been backed up by a matching technology. To a people who had never been out of their villages in their lives, the walk from a haywain to a train must have seemed more magical than a flight into space, and the opportunities made available to the burgeoning middle-class must have seemed like a fairy tale come true.

Social reforms were not neglected, although many were "more honoured in the breach than in the observance." The Chimney Sweep Act of 1788, for example, was not enforced until after Charles Kingsley's story of a chimney sweep, *The Water-Babies,* was published in 1863. Among many others, there were acts to limit the labor of children and women in the mines and factories, the Education Act, and an act to abolish slavery, all of which affected children and eventually children's literature. The dangers inherent in the Industrial Revolution also were not ignored.

1. Leonard Woolf, *Beginning Again: An Autobiography of the Years 1911 to 1918* (New York: HBJ, 1963), 34.

Charles Dickens roused the conscience of a nation over the plight of the poor—especially poor and oppressed children—with such novels as *Oliver Twist* (1838), *The Old Curiosity Shop* (1841), *A Christmas Carol* (1843), and *David Copperfield* (1850). In art, the Pre-Raphaelites turned away from the growing materialism of industrialized England and sought refuge in what they interpreted as the simplicity of the medieval world.

The main thrust of Victorian literature was still the realistic novel, as exemplified by Charles Dickens, George Eliot, and Anthony Trollope. The Pre-Raphaelites (Christina Rossetti and William Morris, for example) eventually came to be accepted, as did Samuel Taylor Coleridge with his dream-poems, *The Rime of the Ancient Mariner, Christabel,* and *Kubla Khan*. Above all, there was Wordsworth with his mystical view of nature and his equally mystical view of the child, which was expressed in his "Intimations of Immortality from Recollections of Early Childhood":

> Our birth is but a sleep and a forgetting:
> The Soul that rises with us, our life's Start
>   Hath had elsewhere its setting,
>   And cometh from afar:
>   Not in entire forgetfulness,
>   And not in utter nakedness,
> But trailing clouds of glory do we come
>   From God, who is our home:
> Heaven lies about us in our infancy!
> Shades of the prison-house begin to close
>   Upon the growing Boy,
> But he beholds the light, and whence it flows,
>   He sees it in his joy;

These famous lines were written in 1789, but by 1865 Wordsworth's view of the child as a product of heaven rather than a natural prey of the devil had sifted into the popular imagination.

If children were lucky enough to be born into a well-to-do or middle-class family, and if they survived the diseases that still plagued children in those times, they were in a favored position. As Victorian families tended to be large, the Victorian child most likely had brothers and sisters with whom to play. Even the less wealthy families probably had a nursery and a nanny for the children. The discipline of a well-conducted household was quite strict and was taken very seriously. A child was brought up with a well-defined code of morals, manners, and behavior that included truth, obedience, punctuality, respect for one's elders, fear of God, and honor to Queen and country. All in all, though, the rearing of children had lost its previous thrust of saving them from damnation; it became less a process of conquering their will and more a responsibility of training them, guiding them into proper paths, socializing them, and teaching them to conform. As the Victorian age progressed, children were allowed one great freedom that had been denied to children of previous generations—the release of the imagination through books written specifically for them.

On the other hand, if children were born into a poor, lower-class (especially urban) family, their lot was typically a bad one. They lived in the poverty, disease, and squalor of slum life and had to work at an early age. If, for any reason, they were coerced into going to Sunday school, they probably learned to read, but they also were taught to accept their lot in life through such hymns as the following:

> The rich man in his castle,
>   The poor man at his gate,
> God made them, high or lowly,
>   And ordered their estate.

This particular verse is omitted today as congregations thunder out the hymn "All Things Bright and Beautiful, " but in Victorian times a relentless stream of books and booklets poured from such organizations as the Religious Tract Society and the Society for Promoting Christian Knowledge, exhorting the children of the poor to be slavishly pious in order to meet the approval of God, society, and parents. Kindness to the poor was the prerogative of more fortunate children, as can be seen from the title of Maria Charlesworth's *Ministering Children,* which was published in 1865, the same year as *Alice,* and which went into numerous editions before the turn of the century. The paradoxes of the Victorian Age also applied to children's literature, as the stern moral tale flourished alongside the new fantasy. Even the major writers of the realistic school of fiction for the young—R.M. Ballantyne, Frederick

Marryat, Charlotte Yonge, Mrs. Ewing, and Mrs. Molesworth—imbued their works with the conventional moral cast.

Nevertheless, the rigid attitude toward children had changed. How else can one explain the calm tone of the reviewers on the appearance of such an unpiestic handling of childhood as *Alice's Adventures in Wonderland?*[2] Carroll was not seen at the time for what he actually was—as great a revolutionary in children's literature as Giotto de Bodone in art or Beethoven in music—and it was probably to the advantage of children's literature that he was not.

In seeking actual literary precursors to Carroll, one can turn only to Edward Lear, whose limericks were first published as *A Book of Nonsense* in 1846. There is no evidence in their letters and diaries (and both were prolific recorders) that the two men had ever read each other's works. However, it is difficult to believe that Carroll was not aware of *A Book of Nonsense,* since it was immediately popular with adults as well as children. One cannot compare a book of limericks with a full-fledged fantasy (Lear's longer story-poems were not published until after *Alice*), but the two men could almost be considered consanguineous in their approach to childhood and nonsense. They wanted to amuse children rather than make them good, and they managed to do so with laughter and love and an invitation to Topsyturveydom that children of the period were more than happy to accept.

Lear illustrated his verses himself, and the title page to *A Book of Nonsense* most clearly illustrates his liberation of childhood. In this illustration, the children are pudgy and natural, and jumping and dancing with joy. Previous artwork often showed them as charming but more frequently as decorous, quiet, and rather dull. Here Lear shows himself most clearly to be the forerunner of such modern picture-book artists as Maurice Sendak and Mercer Mayer.

Early Victorian Literary Fairy Tales

As Lear built on an older form of verse, so John Ruskin, when challenged by a child to write a children's book, turned to an existing

2. Review of *Alice's Adventures in Wonderland,* by Lewis Carroll, *Illustrated London News* (16 Dec. 1865): 59.

form of story—the popular and influential German Hausmärchen. Ruskin's *The King of the Golden River,* written in 1841 but not published until 1851, might be a tale out of the Brothers Grimm.

Hans, Schwartz, and Gluck live in a fruitful Alpine valley. The two older brothers, in true folktale style, are mean and grasping and treat their younger brother like a servant, with "a wholesome quantity of dry blows, by way of education." One day, they refuse shelter to an irascible old gentleman who takes his revenge by reducing Treasure Valley to a desert and the brothers to destitution. After numerous ill-conceived attempts to earn a livelihood, they order Gluck to melt down his only treasure, a large drinking mug, the front of it in the form of a face with flowing golden hair and whiskers—"a fierce little face of the reddest gold imaginable"—and a pair of sharp eyes. The mug is metamorphosed into the King of the Golden River, who tells Gluck that three drops of holy water cast into the river will turn it into gold. The King's promise is delivered with the usual folktale caveat: "If anyone shall cast unholy water into the river, it will overwhelm him, and he will become a black stone." The two brothers try and fail because they refuse water to the thirsty and dying. Gluck succeeds, of course, and the river, while not becoming gold in the literal sense, is directed into the valley, which becomes fertile once again.

While the German folktale is the obvious source of its inspiration, this story also has a touch of Dickens in its portrayal of the South Wind, Esquire, and a parable from the Bible—the story of the Good Samaritan. Most of all, it is imbued with Ruskin's mystical feeling for nature and his sensibility as an art critic. The sky participates in the story and is described in word-chiaroscuro. When Hans refuses water to a dying old man, " . . . a flash of blue lightning rose out of the East, shaped like a sword; it shook thrice over the whole heaven, and left it dark with one heavy impenetrable shade." And when Schwartz passes by a parched child, " . . . a dark gray cloud came over the sun, and long snake-like shadows crept up along the mountain sides." *The King of the Golden River* suggests some of the ideas that Ruskin was later to develop into a body of social criticism: his antagonism toward a greed that destroyed the environment and his belief that the most important law of life is helping others. First and foremost, however, it is a wonderful story; and its style, with its touches of humor and irony, makes it the first of the great literary fairy tales to emanate from England.

There is no moral or message in William Makepeace Thackeray's *The Rose and the Ring* (1855), although poetic justice is dispensed at the end. This story was written as a Christmas pantomime, following the tradition of Charles Dickens's Christmas books, but it has no transformations, magical or otherwise, brought about by holiday cheer as does *A Christmas Carol*. It is simply a fairy tale romp, far too gentle and humorous to be considered a burlesque or a satire. Thackeray knew his fairy tales; there is hardly an aspect of them that he does not play with. For instance, the good fairy godmother wishes the hero and heroine a little *misfortune*, and her gifts pass from hand to hand, causing the utmost confusion. The villains perform in larger-than-life style, and love conquers all. Talismans include a magical bag and a fairy sword and the princess is left in the woods to be eaten by the lions. One can almost hear Thackeray chuckling as he wrote, but he still used the novelist's craft in making small details authentic in the midst of the hilarity. In the last chapter, the princess's true identity is established in Cinderella-like fashion by her little shoe, which has "Hopkins, Maker to the Royal Family" stamped inside it.

By 1855, therefore, Thackeray could count on a youthful audience so familiar with fairy lore that such lore could be appreciated even when it was turned upside down. Much of this influence was due to the new "prince" of Denmark, Hans Christian Andersen, whose tales were first published in English as *Wonderful Stories for Children* (1846). Andersen bridged two worlds. He was both a reteller and a creator, breathing life into the oral tradition with "Hans Clodhopper," and weaving new magic with such tales as "The Little Mermaid," "The Tinder-box," and "The Constant Tin-Soldier." No English writer achieved the skeptical irony evident in so many of Andersen's stories, and there is no doubt that he helped spark the English literary fairy tale, although it developed its own very English characteristics. It has been suggested by several critics that Ruskin, whose manuscript of *The King of the Golden River* lay dormant for ten years, decided to publish it only after the enthusiastic reception of *Wonderful Stories for Children*.

The King of the Golden River has a certain ecstasy to it due to Ruskin's passionate belief in the synthesis of the natural world with the material. In general, though, the English literary fairy tale of the period (as opposed to the fantasies that were to come) have a soft, moral quality to them that is alien both to the indigenous English folktale ("The Babes in the Wood," "Jack the Giant-killer," etc.) and certainly to Hans Christian Andersen. In *Granny's Wonderful Chair* (1857), Frances Browne salutes Andersen and laments the dearth of fairies:

> . . . the fairies dance no more. Some say it was the hum of schools—some think it was the din of factories that frightened them; but nobody has been known to have seen them for many a year, except, it is said, one Hans Christian Andersen in Denmark, whose tales of the fairies are so good that they must have been heard from themselves.

Her own stories have an inventive touch but are marred greatly by the use of personification to indicate her characters' traits—Sour and Civil, Childe Charity, Princess Greedalind, etc. The repetitive phrase "Chair of my grandmother, tell me a story" is a charming entrance to Browne's "once upon a time" worlds. She was wrong about the fairies, however; they were not as far away as she thought, and they were soon to inundate children's literature.

The Great Victorians: Charles Kingsley, Lewis Carroll, George MacDonald

The subtitle of Charles Kingsley's *The Water-Babies* (1863) is "A Fairy Tale for a Land-baby," a sure sign that the fairy tale was entrenched in the psyche of Victorian children's writers. Kingsley was an Anglican minister, a social reformer, and an amateur scientist, all pursuits that might have been expected to preclude fantasy. However, to Kingsley belongs the honor of creating the first partial "Other World" fantasy as opposed to a literary fairy tale. Although his waterscape lies beneath a real English river, it is peopled with fairies and water-babies, talking fish and fairy godmother figures, while Tom, the chimney sweep, becomes an eft—3.879002 inches long; Kingsley believed in accuracy in the midst of fantasy.

The Water-Babies is also the first of the multi-level fantasies that are now such familiar fare. On the surface, it is a simple, delightful tale and can be read as such. Tom is a chimney sweep who wants no more of life than to grow up and be like his cruel master, Grimes, have his own chimney sweep business, and do in turn as he has been done by. One day, in a wealthy country home, he takes a wrong turn while cleaning the flues and lands in a beautiful white bedroom in which an angelic-looking child is sleeping. In a mirror Tom sees his sooty self for the first time. Interrupted by the nurse, he turns and flees and is chased by the whole household in a humorous, cumulative scene on the order of Grimm's "The Golden Goose." After an unprecedented climb down a cliff, Tom plunges into a stream crying, "I want to be clean." Through a series of fantastic, underwater adventures, he does become clean, in body, mind, and soul. On this level, cleanliness becomes a parable of spiritual regeneration, Kingsley's basic philosophy, and on another it embodies the author's dislikes—the Irish, the Welsh, the Catholics, the anti-Darwinians, and all who were cruel to children, in ascending order of denigration. A key figure in the story is an Irishwoman (however, she does not speak with an Irish accent), a focus for the mythic sense of the story. She first falls in with Tom on the road to the country house, puts Mr. Grimes in his vulgar place, and, unknown to Tom, impels him to his flight to the river. She appears as part of the earth itself. In the water, she is queen of the water-fairies, Mrs. Doasyouwouldbedoneby (the personification of Mother Nature) and at the end is a glorious and mysterious being, the promise of an ecstatic spirituality to come.

The Water-Babies is an example of genuine storytelling (the opening paragraph is one of the finest in children's literature)—a combination of accurate information, playfulness, and exuberance. But above and beyond these literary traits are Kingsley's beliefs and personality, which eventually dominate the story. This aspect makes him the first of the confessional writers for children, those who incorporate their own philosophy of life into their works. Such writers may use only a slice of their philosophy, but they use it honestly, and it in no way contravenes what they have written elsewhere. Their aim in writing is to give of themselves, and this, in turn, gives their writing a passion and a sincerity that calls forth literary skills. Kingsley did not betray his adult ideas to entertain the young; for the most part, he was able to present them in images appealing to children. Certainly, Victorian children responded to the book's honest, blunt, and sometimes puzzling picture of the adult world, since it outsold *Alice* for several years after its publication.

It is Kingsley's view of the adult Victorian world that modern editors try to eliminate in their cut versions. They want the "Tom-foolery" (as Kingsley himself described *The Water-Babies*), but they want it without his major thesis concerning the link between divine and physical nature, without his personal jibes against his critics or his long, word-loving lists (one takes over four pages), and without his moral asides. These shortened versions never work. In the attempt to take out the moralistic pill, somehow the fun goes too. Much of the middle part of the book *can* strain the reader's patience, but it includes Professor Ptthmllnsprts—a professor of Necrobioneopalaeonthydrochthonanthropopithekology (the word is pronounceable if one works at it) who does not believe in water-babies—and Tom's adventure with the lobster, which was reprinted for years in Canadian readers.

There are many literary echoes in *The Water-Babies*. John Bunyan is there in the persons of Mrs. Bedonebyasyoudid and Mrs. Doasyouwould-bedoneby. So is William Blake. Kingsley's love of the natural landscape is expressed in his lines:

> Clear and cool, clear and cool,
> By laughing shallow and dreaming pool;

which are reminiscent of Blake's:

> When the green woods laugh with the voice of joy,
> And the dimpling stream runs laughing by;

Blake's picture of England "among those dark Satanic mills" is echoed in Kingsley's portrayal:

> Dank and foul, dank and foul,
> By the smoky town in its murky cowl;
>   Foul and dank, foul and dank,
> By wharf and sewer and slimy bank;

Blake's poetry is filled with references to child chimney sweepers and their lot in life. When Kingsley began *The Water-Babies,* it is hard to believe that he did not recall Blake's little sweep, Tom, who dreamed he was

> . . . locked up in coffins of black,
> And by came an angel, who had a bright key,

And he opened the coffins, and set them all free.
Then down a green plain, leaping, laughing, they run
And wash in a river, and shine in the sun.[3]

Kingsley's poetry is inferior to that of Blake, but his reforming zeal was greater. As mentioned earlier, *The Water-Babies* was the chief force in the revision of the Chimney-Sweep Act the year after the book's publication.

There are inconsistencies in the actual plot. If Tom's plunge into the cleansing river is, as has been argued, a metaphor for death, how can he turn out to be "a great man of science, and can plan railroads, and steam engines, and electric telegraphs, and rifled guns, and so forth"? Furthermore, if Tom is not to marry Ellie, why does she play such a strong part in the story? Can these two characters really ever forget one another after Ellie has waited for the Biblical seven years? In a fantasy, things are not always as they seem. At the end, Kinsley says:

> But remember always, as I told you at first, that this is all a fairy tale, and only fun and pretence; and, therefore, you are not to believe a word of it, even if it is true.

What was true to Kingsley was a mingling of the spiritual and the physical and even something beyond. He expressed these feelings at age twenty-three when he wrote:

> . . . All day, glimpses from the other world—floating motes from that inner transcendental life, have been flitting across me, just as they used to in childhood, when the seen and the unseen were one, an indistinguishable twin mystery; the one not yet forgotten, the other not yet learnt so perfectly as to dazzle, by its coarse glare, the spirit-perceptions which the soul learned to feel in another world . . . [4]

Through his watery Other World and its inhabitants, Kingsley hoped that Victorian children would see that an imaginative vision of the

3. William Blake, "The Chimney-Sweeper," in *Songs of Innocence.*
4. Charles Kingsley, *His Letters and Memories of His Life* (London: Macmillan, 1901), 81–82.

material and scientific world would open to them a spiritual reality not perceptible by the senses alone.

In contrast, Lewis Carroll had no such avowed purpose, and in his lack of an authorial stance lies the uniqueness of the *Alice* books. Contrary to the Duchess, who maintained that "Everything has a moral," . . . "if one can only find it," it is impossible to find one in either *Alice's Adventures in Wonderland* (1865) or *Through the Looking-Glass and What Alice Found There* (1871). That Carroll intended to give only pleasure to children can be deduced from the last verse in the prefatory poem to *Alice:*

> Alice! A childish story take,
>   And with a gentle hand
> Lay it where Childhood's dreams are twined
>   In Memory's mystic band,
> Like pilgrim's withered wreath of flowers
>   Pluck'd in a far-off land.

The story of how *Alice* came to be is too well known to be more than briefly noted here. It was written for a particular child, Alice Liddell, just as Ruskin wrote *The King of the Golden River* for twelve-year-old Effie Gray; Kingsley, *The Water-Babies* for his youngest child, Grenville; and Thackeray, *The Rose and the Ring* for his children. One would have liked to have known these children who could spark such storytelling. From his letters to children filled with puns, nonsense, and invented anecdotes,[5] it can be seen that Carroll was already a great storyteller when "all in a golden afternoon" in 1863, he and a friend took the three Liddell children for a boat ride and a picnic up the river Thames. When a story was demanded, he told them of

> The dream child moving through a land
>   Of wonders wild and new,
> In friendly chat with bird or beast—
>   And half believe it true.

5. Once when a small girl sent him "sacks full of love and baskets full of kisses," he wrote back and said she must have meant "a sack full of gloves and a basket full of kittens." Lewis Carroll, *The Selected Letters of Lewis Carroll,* ed. Morton N. Cohen (London: Macmillan, 1982), 242.

When Alice Liddell pestered Carroll to write the story down, he complied, rewriting much of the first part, which was later published in *Alice's Adventures Underground.*

That Carroll was in affinity with the child mind can be seen from the opening paragraph of Alice, now the most famous in children's literature:

> Alice was beginning to get very tired of sitting by her sister on the
> bank, and of having nothing to do: once or twice she had peeped
> into the book her sister was reading, but it had no pictures or con-
> versations in it, "and what is the use of a book," thought Alice,
> "without pictures or conversations?"

When Alice sees a white rabbit, she does not think much of it; but when the Rabbit actually "took a watch out of its waist-coat pocket," her curiosity gets the better of her and she follows it. When it plunges down a rabbit hole, down she goes too, "never once considering how in the world she was to get out again." Alice, as a true child of fantasy, is willing to take the first plunge, but she finds the underground world most perplexing and herself ill-prepared to cope with it. Her size keeps changing, a baby turns into a pig, a Cheshire cat keeps appearing and disappearing, and a tea party is not what she is used to at home. She is very polite to all the strange creatures she meets and is astonished when they are rude to her. However, when she has to appear at the trial of the Jack of Hearts, who is accused of stealing the tarts, and the Queen says, "Sentence first—verdict afterwards," Alice's patience is at an end. "Stuff and nonsense!" she says, "You're nothing but a pack of cards!"

Lewis Carroll was the pseudonym of Charles Lutwidge Dodgson, lecturer and tutor in mathematics at Christ Church, Oxford. It has been suggested by some critics that Dodgson's use of "Lewis Carroll" as a pseudonym for his children's books represented a split in his personality—the Oxford don, cleric, mathematician, and bachelor who was fussy, pious, and conventional, as opposed to the man who created a host of fantastic characters whose names have become part of the English language.

It is true that Dodgson cannot be found in the *Alice* books to the extent that Kingsley can be found in *The Water-Babies,* but then Dodgson/ Carroll had no moral axe to grind. However, his books do reflect him:

his logical mind; his knowledge of mathematics; his love of puns, jokes, games, and puzzles, and even his obsession with photography (the *Alice* books move as a series of pictures and would do so even without John Tenniel's famous illustrations). His childhood reading is in them too. Only someone completely familiar with the typical, moralistic poems for children of the late eighteenth century could satirize them as " 'Tis the Voice of the Lobster," "Twinkle, Twinkle Little Bat," and "You are Old, Father William." According to Martin Gardner's well-known book, *The Annotated Alice,* Carroll makes many references to political and academic figures of the time, to personal friends, and to both public and academic controversies.[6] These allusions are unimportant to a modern reader, however; and since they are punned, parodied, and played with, they become part of the dream and are no awakening from it. In contrast, Kingsley's asides frequently break the spell of his Other World.

Carroll also put a real child into his books. Of all the little girls he loved in an innocent way, Alice Liddell was his favorite. By all accounts, she was a beautiful child and, as the daughter of a Dean, would be mannerly, intelligent, well-schooled, and not used to having her way all the time. She was probably the quintessence of the favored, middle-class, Victorian child. So she is too in wonderland. But Carroll was on the side of children. He valued childhood for its own sake. Thus, when Harvey Darton speaks of *Alice* as "the spiritual volcano of children's literature,"[7] he does not use the phrase in a moral sense, but rather as one of liberation, referring to the complete release of the imaginative spirit of childhood. Children thus could choose to enjoy a book for no other reason than sheer pleasure. Through such books, children were also given stature. To the child readers (especially girls) of Victorian realistic fiction, in which the young were placed at the bottom of the social hierarchy, Alice must have seemed a most appealing heroine. She may be dreaming, but she is in command of the dream. In *Through the Looking-Glass,* Alice gets her wish and becomes a queen, and in *Alice* she is the one who upsets the adult world.

Alice's Adventures in Wonderland is the first dream fantasy in children's

6. Martin Gardner, *The Annotated Alice* (New York: Clarkson N. Potter, 1960).
7. Harvey Darton, *Children's Books in England* (Cambridge, England: Cambridge Univ. Pr., 1960), 267.

literature, springing almost full-blown from Carroll's mind because of a dreamy afternoon on the river Thames. *Through the Looking-Glass,* on the other hand, has a more sophisticated entry into a reverse world and is a less spontaneous piece of craftsmanship. The use of a game of chess as a *modus operandi* imposes a more tightly controlled scenario. However, one does not need to know the game in order to enjoy the book. In spite of its complex concepts of time, space, and dreams—who did the dreaming, Alice or the Red King?—it is filled with unforgettable characters. There is the White Knight, modeled on Carroll himself, with his gentleness, his topsy-turvy view of the world, and his delight in tricks and gadgets. There is sadness when Alice and the White Knight part, as there was in the real world when Dodgson saw no more of Alice Liddell:

> Years afterwards she could bring the whole scene back again, as if it had been only yesterday—the mild blue eyes and kindly smile of the Knight—the setting sun gleaming through his hair, and shining on his armour in a blaze of light that dazzled her . . . all this she took in like a picture.

There is Humpty-Dumpty, who pedantically explains to Alice the portmanteau words in "Jabberwocky" because he "can explain all the poems that ever were invented—and a good many that haven't been invented just yet." He takes all the mystery out of the poem for Alice (like poems that are taught in school), for although she does not understand it, she has pondered on it: "Somehow it seems to fill my head with ideas." There are nursery rhyme characters as well—Tweedledum and Tweedledee, the Lion and the Unicorn—other familiar characters from Wonderland, and more nonsense verses. But above all, both books are filled with a delight in language, its logicality and its illogicality. Lines from the two *Alices* can be made to fit almost any situation, and it is this quality that draws adults back to them time and time again. After the Bible and Shakespeare, they are the most quoted books in the English language.

The *Alice* books do not appear to be popular with modern children, however, who are apt to be more in tune with the simple wordplay in Norton Juster's *The Phantom Tollbooth* than with Carroll's more sophisticated and sustained verbal wit. But they have become the preserve of psychologists and psychiatrists (both Jungian and Freudian), academics, mathematicians, and logicians, and they have been combed for symbols that might have a bearing on Dodgson's life. We learn from Dodgson's diaries that he used to entertain children by showing them how to produce fun pictures by blotting their names on creased paper. Had he realized that *he* would become the object of Rorschach tests, he would have popped down the nearest rabbit hole, taking his manuscripts with him. It is surely more sensible to listen to Carroll himself as he begins *Through the Looking-Glass:*

> Enough that now thou wilt not fail
> To listen to my fairy-tale.

If modern children listen to Carroll, they will find what could be an appropriate wish for them: to learn self-control, to acquire a sense of identity, and to think logically without ceasing to be sensitive and imaginative. Perhaps the Duchess was right after all. There is a moral in everything.

There were attempts to emulate Carroll (imitation being the sincerest form of flattery); but although his theme of a journey to another dimension lent itself to variations, his talent for parody and his perfect sense of inverted logic could not be copied, and even the most popular of his imitators did not last beyond the turn of the century. Edward A. Parry's *Butterscotia: or A Cheap Trip to Fairyland* (1896) is well subtitled because in comparison to *Alice,* the fare is third-class. Most of the cast of characters is drawn from folk- and fairy tales, and the book ends with a weak emulation of the trial scene in *Alice's Adventures in Wonderland.* The attempts at puns are equally feeble: "It's terribly long. That's why it's called a brief," which is a far cry from Carroll's "That's the reason they're called lessons . . . because they lessen from day to day." Similarly, in G.E. Farrow's *The Wallypug of Why* (1896), Girlie falls asleep and goes to the land of Why "where all the questions and answers come from." She meets a medley of strange creatures and humans, including Wallypug himself—a king who has to obey his subjects rather than the other way around. There is an attempt to include Carroll's playfulness with time, "I don't want a watch that will *go,* I want one that will stay," but such lines are dropped in only haphazardly.

Although Carroll was to influence the whole of children's literature in a broad sense, his talents proved inimitable; and so his influence on fantasy, significant though it was, was chiefly confined to his own time. It was George MacDonald, although a lesser stylist, who left a legacy of fantasy that was to inspire writers up until the 1980's. Unlike Carroll, MacDonald was a myth-maker. In myth, words do not count as much as the pattern of events, the concepts, and the feelings they arouse—those sensations that are not readily describable. The stories of "Baldur" or "Prometheus" cannot be destroyed, no matter how poor the version, because the core of the story is itself a set of indelible images. So, although MacDonald was not a word-maker, his three most important children's books—*At the Back of the North Wind* (1871), *The Princess and the Goblin* (1872), and its sequel, *The Princess and Curdie* (1883)—are charged with emotion and reveal a mythopoeic imagination. They are also infused with his Christian beliefs, principally the need for all people to struggle to a higher level of existence. There is also the message of redemption for those who had failed, if they learned to have faith and trust in God and in his surrogates on earth. MacDonald's philosophy is tied into his plots, and so any one of his books is a more unified whole than *The Water-Babies,* where Kingsley frequently stops the action to deliver his homilies (a somewhat jarring experience even though most of his asides are delightful and playful). By contrast, MacDonald's authorial interventions are not only few, but when they do occur, they are couched in childlike terms. They say no more than what a loving parent of the time would say to a child, and MacDonald was the father of thirteen children.

George MacDonald was a Highland Scot and an ordained minister of the Scottish Congregational Church. However, he gave up the ministry under pressure from his congregation, who disliked his mysticism and his intellectual and spiritual independence, and devoted himself to literature. His first children's stories appeared in a feebly plotted adult novel, *Adela Cathcart,* and were reprinted, with additions, as *Dealings with the Fairies* (1867). Of these stories, the two most memorable are *The Light Princess* and *The Golden Key.* They are short stories, opposites in plot and tone, but both are harbingers of his later works.

The Light Princess begins with a fairy tale motif, but one with a twist. At the princess's christening, the wicked witch deprives her of her gravity and so also of gravity in her character. A Carroll-like punning continues throughout and is especially noticeable in the play on the word "light"—the princess is light in body and so in mind. She redeems herself, however, when she saves the prince, who is sacrificing his life for hers. Thus, the witch's spell is broken; and when the princess weeps for the prince, she obtains gravity. Humorous scenes, such as the servants playing ball with the weightless baby, are balanced by dramatic ones, such as the wicked witch drying up the lake, and poignant ones, such as the bittersweet musings of the love-sick prince as the returning water reaches his nose. The moral is two-fold—one has to consider other people, and one has "to cry a little" in order to reach goodness. These morals were to become full-fledged philosophies in MacDonald's later books. *The Light Princess* is the most lighthearted of all his stories and, along with *The Princess and the Goblin,* the one most likely to appeal to the modern child.

In his works, as in his life, MacDonald combined mysticism and orthodoxy. Like many English writers of his generation, he was influenced by the German romantic mystics E.T.A. Hoffmann (the author of *The Nutcracker*) and Novalis (the pseudonym of Friedrich von Hardenberg), both of whom expressed their philosophies through their fairy tales. *The Light Princess,* for instance, owes something to Hoffmann's *The Princess Brambilla,* with its basis in laughter without depth and in the healing power of water; and all MacDonald's work is an echo of Hoffmann's *The Fairy Child,* in which the fairy tells the children that they can have anything if they use their imaginations.[8] Even the little, light mind of "the light princess" had to be touched by imagination before she could recognize the sufferings of another person. However, MacDonald was orthodox in his view of childhood and in the basic tenets of Christianity. He therefore believed that as innocent and perceptive as children were in the Wordsworthian sense, they still needed a mentor and guide to raise their spiritual sights. "As the twig is bent, so grows the tree" is the constant theme of Victorian realistic fiction for children, and MacDonald avoided its monotonous voice only because he could translate the adage into images and into joyful beliefs rather than prohibitions. It was thus that he dealt with the concept of death as opposed to the pious, lingering deathbed scenes that were the norm at the time in stories of everyday life.

8. E.T.A. Hoffmann, *The Fairy Tales of Hoffmann,* retold by Marjorie L. Watson (London: Harrap, 1960), 16.

That he was preoccupied with death can be seen in MacDonald's adult fantasies *Phantastes* and *Lillith*. Both owe much to Novalis, who saw death as a joyful experience in which all the manifestations of life were fused into a glorious and mystical surrender to the Supreme Being. *The Golden Key* seems almost to embody Novalis's explanation of death for children, but one in which the nuances and images are so subtle and so delicately woven together that even a slender outline of the plot tends to destroy the nameless feeling that it arouses. It is basically a quest story. The boy, Mossy, finds a golden key at the end of the rainbow, but

> Where was the lock to which the key belonged? It must be some-
> where, for how could anybody be so silly as to make a key for
> which there was no lock? Where should he go to look for it?

On his journey, he is joined by the girl, Tangle; and mostly together, sometimes apart, and often with difficulty, they reach the country of the rainbow, which is death:

> "You have tasted of death, now," said the Old Man.
> "Is it good?"
> "It is good," said Mossy. "It is better than life."
> "No," said the Old Man: "it is only more life."

There is much in *The Golden Key* that reappears and is developed in MacDonald's later children's books. There is the "wise woman" who is the great-great-grandmother in the *Princess* books and the *deus ex machina* in his novelette *The Wise Woman* (1875). There is the marvelous child (also the Old Man of Fire) who can help everybody and who is transformed into Diamond in *At the Back of the North Wind* and into Irene in *The Princess and the Goblin*. MacDonald's belief that people could evolve into a higher state of being is hinted at in the aeranths (angel-messengers) who were once only air-fish. Above all, MacDonald's ability to create scenes and landscapes can be seen, especially "the land where the shadows fall," a land that fills Mossy and Tangle and the reader with a tearful joy.

George MacDonald has said that

> A fairytale is not an allegory. There may be allegory in it, but it
> is not an allegory. He must be an artist indeed who can, in any

mode, produce a strict allegory that is not a weariness to the spirit.[9]

Indeed, *The Golden Key* is not a teaching vehicle in the strict sense of Bunyan's *The Pilgrim's Progress* or of Spenser's *Faerie Queen*. In spite of its references to death, the story can be read on different levels. "The golden key" may unlock many doors—those of the poetic imagination, love, kindness, faith, or trust.

At the Back of the North Wind is set in two worlds: the Victorian London of the poorer classes (with episodes at seaside and in the countryside), and in little Diamond's dream world as he adventures with North Wind. However, unlike the *Alice* books, which are strictly dream narratives, the two worlds here sometimes become fused, not a welding together but as if one were in a long moment between sleeping and waking. Young Diamond is the son of a coachman, and he sleeps in a loft over his father's stable where the horse Old Diamond is kept. North Wind enters the story almost immediately, and the meeting between the little boy and the goddess-like figure of North Wind is one of the most memorable in children's literature. It is also touched with considerable humor as Diamond converses with her, with his head beneath the covers. Finally, a feeling of awe supersedes the banter:

> "Will you take your head out of the bedclothes?" said the voice, just a little angrily.
> "No!" answered Diamond, half peevish, half frightened.
> The instant he said the word, a tremendous blast of wind crashed in a board of the wall, and swept the clothes off Diamond. He started up in terror. Leaning over him was the large, beautiful, pale face of a woman. Her dark eyes looked a little angry, for they had just begun to flash; but a quivering in her sweet upper lip made her look as if she were going to cry. What was the most strange was that away from her head streamed out her black hair in every direction, so that the darkness in the hay-loft looked as if it were made of her hair; . . . the boy was entranced with her mighty beauty . . . .

In the real world, Diamond is a preternaturally good child (he has

9. George MacDonald, "The Fantastic Imagination," in *Fantasists on Fantasy*, eds. Robert H. Boyer and Kenneth J. Zahorski (New York: Avon, 1984), 17.

been called a prig), so good that even his mother comments upon it. He wins friends all around him, including his father's wealthy employer and family. He befriends Nanny, the little crossing-sweeper; looks after his new baby sister; and brings a drunken father to a better way of life. When economic disaster falls upon his own family, Diamond drives his father's cab, with old Diamond between the shafts, and even the rough London cabbies guard their speech in his presence. Nanny—the tough, experienced street gamin who is indebted to Diamond but who, of course, does not believe any stories about North Wind—taps her forehead when discussing Diamond:

" . . . the cabbies call him God's baby," she whispered. "He's not right in the head you know. A tile loose."

Diamond is not well; he is sent to live for awhile with his aunt at the seaside. Here he has a serious illness but recovers. The family's fortunes take an upward turn when his father's previous employer (Mr. Coleman) regains his wealth, re-employs Diamond's father, and they all move to the country, where Diamond serves as a page to Mrs. Coleman, meets the narrator of the story, and dies.

MacDonald the realist can be seen in his vignettes of the Victorian London slums and of the working class. Nanny is cold, starved (of both food and love), and forced to work for an evil old slattern who gives her only crusts in return. Diamond's family has hardly enough sustenance to keep body together when the father is out of work and little enough when he is working. Through Diamond's acquaintances, we see, in contrast, the pleasant lives of the rich. MacDonald observes; he does not preach social reform, but his views are clear, nonetheless: birth has nothing to do with character or with one's real place in life. North Wind tells Diamond: "Every man ought to be a gentleman and your father is one," and Nanny "might have had a lady and a gentleman for a father and mother." Mr. Coleman and Mr. Raymond, who befriend Diamond and Nanny, are treated gently, but for the rich in general, MacDonald had little use.

MacDonald the visionary is seen in his portrayal of North Wind as she "sweeps" out London, blows through a cathedral, rages over the ocean, turns herself into a wolf to frighten a drunken nurse, or as she becomes small enough to spin the sails of a toy windmill and to help a bumblebee out of a tulip. North Wind usually comes to Diamond at night when he is in bed, and it is easy for the reader to believe that all his journeys while nestled in her hair are but a dream. Occasionally, though, the world of dreams and the world of reality commingle. North Wind sets Diamond down on a gusty London street to help Nanny; she comes to Diamond in the daytime in a garden and in a toyshop, and Diamond never forgets North Wind even when he is about his ordinary business. These are not jarring elements in the story; the whole book is MacDonald's way of extending the natural imagination through the vivid realization of ordinary things, as in a beautiful dream.

North Wind is somewhat of an enigmatic figure, however. She has her work to do, she tells Diamond, which includes the sinking of a ship (Mr. Coleman's ship) with everyone on board. She does not know from whom she takes her orders. East Wind has told her that they come from a baby, but North Wind does not know whether or not to believe it. The serious reader of MacDonald believes it, however. The pure child is part of the MacDonald mythology; we have met the all-knowing child, who is also "the Old Man of Fire," in *The Golden Key*, and we meet one again in *The Princess and the Goblin*. The narrator of *At the Back of the North Wind* senses a divinity in Diamond:

> The whole ways and look of the child, so full of quiet wisdom, yet so ready to accept the judgment of others in his own dispraise, took hold of my heart, and I felt myself wonderfully drawn towards him. It seemed to me, somehow, as if little Diamond possessed the secret of life, and was himself what he was so ready to think the lowest living thing—an angel of God with something special to say or do.

For MacDonald, the secret of life was death. At the end of the story, we know North Wind's real task—to prepare Diamond for a desirous and joyful death.

Ordinary goodness was not enough for MacDonald. Even a "God's baby" had to be brought to a higher spiritual plane and, finally, to use Tolkien's word, to *evangilium*, "joy beyond the walls of the world, poignant as grief." Oddly enough, Diamond is less perfect in North Wind's company than he is with his family and friends; he can be a bit stubborn, demanding, and questioning. His conversations with North Wind sometimes verge on the metaphysical. Diamond has asked her how she can bear to hear the cries of the people who are drowning when she sinks a ship. She replies that she can bear it because through all the noise she can hear the sound of a far-off song. She adds that it would help Diamond to bear the cries if he could hear it, too:

> "No, it wouldn't," returned Diamond stoutly. For *they* wouldn't hear the music of the far-away song; and if they did, it wouldn't do them any good. You see, you and I are not going to be drowned, and so *we* might enjoy it."

But, of course, he comes to love and trust North Wind completely.

Part of Diamond's preparation for death is a sojourn—when he is ill—in the land "at the back of the North Wind." This land is not Paradise; rather, it appears to be a kind of limbo, a waiting station where not much happens and where the people don't look glad but "as if they were waiting to be gladder someday." Diamond, as we find continually in the latter part of the book, has learned "to look through the look of things."

At the Back of the North Wind can be read on one level as simply a fascinating and rather puzzling story. On a secondary level, it contains MacDonald's most cherished beliefs and is his most profound book, whether for adults or children. At both levels, though, one has to plunge into it and not try to describe what cannot be described, for, as Mac-Donald himself has said, "Nothing is more wearisome."

On a storytelling level, *The Princess and the Goblin* is MacDonald's most successful fantasy. It has a tightly woven, simple, fast-paced plot with familiar figures moving across the landscape—a princess, a fairy godmother, evil goblins, and Curdie, the miner's son, who resembles the kind and shrewd youngest son of the folktale. For these reasons, this story has been popular with children and holds a place in their reading even today. There are no entrances to the world of *The Princess and the Goblin*—no English rivers or rabbit holes or mirrors. From the very first page, we are plunged into a folktale world. It exists on two physical levels: there is the mountainside where Princess Irene lives in her father's castle and where Curdie and his mother and father dwell in their humble but loving home, and there are the underground caverns of the goblins. The physical split also represents one between good and evil.

The goblins hate the upper world. A long time ago, they felt that they were treated unfairly by the king of the country and withdrew from human contact, setting up their own society modeled on that above ground, but one infused with feelings of rage and revenge. The princess, who has been ill and sent to the mountains to receive the benefits of the fresh air, is not allowed to go out after dusk for fear of the goblins. One evening, however, Irene and her nurse linger too long in the open air, and the goblins begin to press upon them. The goblins are dispersed by Curdie, who, as a mine worker, has had a long acquaintanceship with their ways. He has made up a song that they "can't stand":

> "Hush! scush! Scurry!
> There you go in a hurry!
> Gobble! gobble! goblin!
> There you go a wobblin';
> Hobble, hobble, hobblin';
> Cobble! cobble! cobblin';
> Hob-bob-goblin!————Huuuuuh!"

The goblins disappear, and the princess (who is eight years old) is so delighted with Curdie that she wants to give him a kiss, but the nurse objects. Before this episode, Irene, with a child's natural curiosity, explores the upper rooms of the castle, and there she finds an old woman who tells Irene that she is Irene's great-great-grandmother. When Irene awakens in her own bed the next morning, she thinks she has had a dream. On a second visit, though, she comes to believe in her grandmother and accepts the talismans she is given, including a magic thread. Later, Curdie is captured by the goblins and is rescued by Irene, who follows the thread to find him. Irene brings Curdie to her grandmother, but Curdie cannot see the grandmother. Instead of a beautiful room and a beautiful woman, he sees only

> a big bare garrett-room . . . a tub and a heap of musty straw. . . .

The grandmother advises a disappointed and tearful Irene:

> "I did not mean to show myself. Curdie is not yet able to believe
> some things. Seeing is not believing, it is only seeing."

When Curdie learns that the goblins intend to undermine the castle, kidnap the princess, and marry her to their prince, he foils the plot and comes to believe in the great-great-grandmother, who heals him after he becomes wounded. He also gets a kiss from Irene; a true princess never breaks a promise. It is a page-turning story, as easy to follow as grandmother's thread unwinding itself through the labyrinthian caverns.

Like Kingsley, MacDonald was a supporter of Darwin's evolutionary theory; and also like Kingsley, he conceived of it in reverse—in *The Water-Babies,* for example, the Doasyoulikes regress into apes. In the *Princess* books, however, reverse evolution becomes a main theme. No creature, whether human or animal, can stand still, goes the message; we are all in a process of development or degeneration. The goblins, who had once been like other people, are now "not ordinarily ugly but either absolutely hideous or ludicrously grotesque, both in face and form." Their animals, once ordinary farm animals or wild beasts, have taken on the characteristics of their owners.

In *The Princess and Curdie,* there is a whole company of mutant creatures who assist Curdie and who are obviously climbing back up the scale of redemption. Conversely, the evil courtiers and servants in the story are degenerating into beasts. Grandmother has given Curdie the power to recognize the good or the bad in a person by the touch of the hand, and so he can tell the animal within the person or the child within the animal.

The Princess and Curdie also has a very simple plot; but like many sequels, it does not match its predecessor. Without the influence of Irene, and therefore again doubting the existence of her great-great-grandmother, Curdie becomes coarsened. He shoots a pigeon and then, in a fit of remorse and recollection, rushes to the castle. Grandmother heals the pigeon, as she has once healed both Irene and Curdie, and sends him on a mission to Gwyntystorm, the capital of the country where the King and Irene reside. He arrives to find a city full of selfish, grasping people; a king drugged and in the power of his dishonest ministers; lazy, thieving servants; and a helpless Princess Irene. With the power of perceiving evil that he has been given and with the help of the strange animals, Curdie drives the evildoers from the palace just as Christ drove the money-lenders from the temple. He and Irene marry and rule the kingdom with kindness and justice, and use the gold from the mines for everyone's benefit.

Thus far, the plot has as predictable a happy ending as that of *The Princess and the Goblin,* but the surprise comes in the last three paragraphs. Although Irene and Curdie have presumably reached MacDonald's concept of goodness, they are childless. After their deaths, a new king is chosen who is so greedy for gold that the very supports of the city are eroded; meanwhile, the people, lacking a good example, become as sinful as their king:

> One day at noon, when life was at its highest, the whole city fell with a roaring crash. The cries of men and the shrieks of women went up with its dust, and then there was a great silence.
> Where the mighty rock once towered, crowded with homes and crowned with a palace, now rushes and raves a stone-obstructed rapid of the river. All around spreads a wilderness of wild deer, and the very name of Gwyntystorm has ceased from the lips of men.

MacDonald could not hide his feelings even in a children's book. Here he appears to be commenting on the state of industrial England with the type of savagery exhibited by Jonathan Swift in *Gulliver's Travels.* When Curdie first arrives in Gwyntystorm, he finds the inhabitants self-satisfied and prosperous, living off the profits of the gold mines. They are also unfriendly, selfish, greedy, suspicious of strangers, and unjust. They are degenerating into beasts, as Curdie discovers when he has occasion to touch their hands. They are beyond redemption except for one old woman who shelters Curdie. The holocaust in the palace is described with almost a kind of gleeful revenge. The doctor who is poisoning the king has his leg crushed by Lina, the most important of the mutant animals, "like a stick of celery." The other beasts attack the servants:

> . . . the scorpion kept grabbing at their legs with his huge pincers, a three-foot centipede kept screwing up their bodies, nipping as he went . . . they were bespattered with the dirt of their own neglect; they were soused in the stinking water that had boiled greens; they were smeared wtih rancid dripping; their faces were rubbed in maggots; I dare not tell all that was done to them.

In retrospect, *The Princess and Curdie* can be seen as a foreshadowing of the last years of MacDonald's life (he died in 1902). He had come to despair of human nature, the erosion of moral standards in a materialistic society, and the rape of the natural environment. He had also come to question the most important tenet of his religious beliefs—God's redeeming love. He appears to have faltered under the blows that life had dealt him. All his children and many other members of his family were to die before him, most decimated by tuberculosis; his material fortunes, precarious in the best of times, were further eroded, and he came to doubt the value of his own work. For the last five or six years of his life, MacDonald withdrew into silence; Gwyntystorm had crashed about him. The pessimism of *The Princess and Curdie* was certainly out of tune with the children's literature of the time and did not surface again until the harsh realistic novels for the young appeared in the 1960's and later.

Although MacDonald in his later years seemingly lost faith in his own vision, his followers did not. They seized upon his overall concept of fantasy—the creation of another dimension based upon a unified moral purpose that was Christian but not doctrinaire. Even when Christian thought yielded to a more existentialist viewpoint, MacDonald's vision of a universal morality still lingered. Later fantasists also provided their youthful protagonists with guides and mentors who acted in much the same capacity as "the wise woman," North Wind, and Irene's great-great-grandmother. Most of all, they accepted the serious imagination that he brought to bear upon the fabric of his stories. Kingsley's tone is often half-joking, causing one to wonder whether to really believe in the story; and Carroll is more concerned with words than with ideas. However, MacDonald's sincerity commands belief in every sentence, even when he is expressing himself lightly and humorously. From him, too, later writers learned the art of creating a multi-level fantasy—stories with plots that have their own inner consistency and inevitability without the overt intrusion of an exterior purpose, but which, indeed, also have such a purpose. No one, though, has been able to make pure "goodness" as exciting as MacDonald's portrayals of Mossy, Tangle, Diamond, Irene, and Curdie, and few child characters from fantasy have lingered as long in the memory once their stories have been laid aside.

Stories of Magic and Later Victorian Literary Fairy Tales

The seriousness, depth, and tough moral stance that MacDonald brought to fantasy were not duplicated until C.S. Lewis's *Narnia*

Chronicles of the 1950's. The intellectualism of Kingsley and Carroll also disappeared for a considerable time. Heavy didacticism was muted under the prevailing view of childhood: all is gentleness. This quality is epitomized by Mrs. Molesworth's *The Cuckoo-Clock* (1877). Griselda, who turns out to be not as patient as her name would suggest, is sent to live with her two great-aunts, leaving her boisterous family of brothers for a reason that is never explained. To Griselda, the house is large and lonesome and as old-fashioned as her aunts' ideas on the upbringing of a little girl: "Punctuality, for one thing, and faithful discharge of duty," says Aunt Grizzel, and is faithfully echoed by Aunt Tabitha. Griselda must take her lessons with a tutor (who despairs of her lack of ability), and her aunts' idea of recreation is a solitary walk on the terrace. One of their prized possessions is a cuckoo clock that every day, on the hour, announces Griselda's strict timetable. One day, in a fit of rebellion, she hurls a book at the cuckoo, and so the magic starts. The cuckoo takes Griselda to various fairylands—the country of the nodding Mandarins, Butterfly-land, and the other side of the moon—in an effort to teach her patience:

> "Griselda", said the cuckoo, "I told you once that there are a great many things you don't know. Now, I'll tell you something more. There are a great many things you're not *intended* to know."

Despite its admonitory tone, there are memorable images in *The Cuckoo-Clock*—the nodding Mandarins from the aunts' china cabinet, the tiny little carriage in which Griselda travels to fairyland, and the warm cloak of feathers in which she is enfolded. The butterflies provide her clothing for their banquet:

> And how do you think they dressed her? With *themselves*. . . . One set of blue ones clustered round the hem of her little white nightgown, making a thick *"ruche"* as it were: and then there came two or three thinner rows of yellow, and then blue again.

The Cuckoo-Clock is the first of the domestic fantasies (later brought to a high point by Edith Nesbit), a story of nighttime magical adventures set against the details of a humdrum daytime existence. Mrs. Molesworth was at her best in her realistic stories of child and family life, such as *The*

Carved Lions, the setting of which owes much to her own childhood. However, both *The Cuckoo-Clock* and *The Tapestry Room* (1879) were innovations in fantasy in their portrayal of well-cared for but lonely children who are sensitive, as Mrs. Molesworth herself put it, to the suggestion "of the infinity of worlds not realised. . . . "[10] She also had a true grasp of the meaning of fairyland. When Griselda asks the cuckoo to take her there, he replies:

> And as to those who have been there, you may be sure of one thing—they were not *taken* to fairyland—to the real fairyland.

As different as they are from one another, the Victorian fantasies all have some of the qualities of the traditional fairy tales and, indeed, owe their existence to them. Kingsley, Carroll, MacDonald, and Mrs. Molesworth transformed them into full-fledged fantasies by virtue of the qualities and beliefs of their own lives, which formed the foundations for their works. However, most of the imaginative literature of the later period is simply a softer, extended use of some of the better-known conventions of the oral tale, such as that of the childless king and queen who eventually produce an heir or an heiresss with a consequent disruption at the christening, for good or for ill, by the fairy godmother.

In the earlier fantasies, such as Francis Edward Paget's *The Hope of the Katzekopfs* (1844), the moral tone is predominant; it is a Victorian *Pilgrim's Progess* without the latter's majestic language. It is also now a nineteenth-century tract on child-rearing, as the Fairy Abracadabra tries to instruct the foolish king and queen on how to control their son, Eigenwillig, so named because from birth he was "a wilful little brat." (Paget was obviously more Puritanical than Wordsworthian!) It takes a forced trip to fairyland to cure the Prince and to remove the malicious Sprite "Selbst" from his back. Thackeray, of course, poked fun at this type of literary fairy tale in the *The Rose and the Ring,* while Thomas Hood the Younger, in *Petsetilla's Posy* (1870), turned the now-established court fairy tale into a rather wearisome political satire.

The true literary fairy tale was re-established by Andrew Lang with *Prince Prigio* (1889) and *Prince Ricardo* (1893). Underneath the jesting in

10. Margharita Laski, *Mrs. Ewing, Mrs. Molesworth, and Mrs. Hodgson Burnett* (London: Arthur Baker, 1950), 71.

both these tales, one can sense Lang's true love of fairy stories, shown so completely by his retellings of the oral tradition in the "Colored Fairy Tales," which have delighted generations of children.[11] Prince Prigio begins life with two disadvantages: a mischievous fairy godmother has made him "too clever," and he does not believe in magic. This combination is disastrous for him until he falls in love and learns to use other gifts his godmothers have given him at his christening—a cap of darkness, seven-league boots, a flying carpet, and so on. The whole paraphernalia of fairyland is at his disposal. Prince Ricardo is Prince Prigio's son, and because of these gifts, his life is made easy. However, Prince Ricardo uses them without discrimination until he too falls in love and learns better. Lang's contribution to the literary fairy tale includes not only his sparkle and humor, but, more importantly, his childlike view of the fairy tale itself. His country of Pantouflia would have been more easily traversable for a child than Thackeray's Paflagonia and certainly Hood's complicated kingdom of Aphania. Lang has an indisputable place in the literature of faerie, as has been shown by the republication of *Prince Prigio* and *Prince Ricardo* in 1961 and the "Colored" fairy books in the 1970's.

A more homespun quality entered the literary fairy tale with *The Adventures of a Brownie* (1872) by Dinah Marie Mulock (Mrs. Craik) and *The Brownies and Other Tales* (1872) by Mrs. Juliana Horatia Ewing. The "brownies" were traditional, British country fairy-types. They made themselves responsible for the farms or houses in which they lived by carrying out a variety of domestic tasks. In return, they had a right to a bowl of cream or the best milk, and a bannock was set out for them in the evening. They were easily driven away, and if sighted, they would turn to mischief, eventually becoming malicious boggarts. *The Adventures of a Brownie* is a series of short episodes that follow this basic pattern, except that the children of the household dissuade the brownie from harmful tricks when he is driven from his hiding place under a lump of coal. In staying closely to the roots of folklore, Miss Mulock produced a charming, lighthearted, and authentic little work.

Mrs. Ewing is best remembered for her stories of child and family life—*Mrs. Overtheway's Remembrances, Six to Sixteen, Jan of the Windmill,* and many others—all of which were based on her recipe for a good

11. *The Blue Fairy Book*, the first of the "Colored" series, was published in 1889.

children's book: "strict fact and genuine feeling." While this formula made her realistic stories the best of the Victorian age, it did not mix so well with fantasy. It is the domestic details in *The Brownies* that are the most appealing. One can sympathize with the two lively, motherless boys who wish for a brownie to light the fire, hew the wood, and carry out all the endless tasks of a poor household. The existence of a true brownie is described as accurately as that in *The Adventures of a Brownie,* but Mrs. Ewing cannot resist an overt moral—the boys are persuaded by a wise old owl to become "brownies" themselves, and they feel the better for it. *Timothy's Shoes,* another tale in *The Brownies and Other Tales,* is also based on practicality. The sensible fairy godmother gives her godchild— eventually to be the mother of nine boys—"a small pair of strong leather shoes, copper-tipped and heeled." They will not wear out, and "the little feet that are in them cannot easily go astray." At last the shoes descend to Timothy, who, being more willful than his older brothers, does his best to get rid of them. The results of his efforts are frequently more amusing than punitive, as, for example, when he plays truant—the shoes turn up at school in his place. At the story's end, Timothy hopes that he will always "walk as he has been taught."

The morality displayed in Mrs. Ewing's works is of an open, sturdy kind. No doubt, Dinah Maria Mulock intended to be just as open, since she subtitled *The Little Lame Prince and His Travelling Cloak* (1874) "A Parable for Young and Old." Whatever parable there is is soon lost in a story of almost unbearable sadness. Prince Dolor is unfortunate from the moment of his birth; his nurse drops him at his christening, causing him to be lame. His disability is used as an excuse by his uncle to usurp Prince Dolor's throne, and the little lame prince is banished to a lonely tower, with only a servant for an attendant. Prince Dolor is the ideal inwardly perfect Victorian child, a true companion of Lewis Carroll's Alice and George MacDonald's Diamond and Princess Irene. He endures his suffering with patience and fortitude until his fairy godmother gives him a magic traveling cloak and a pair of magic spectacles so that he can go a-voyaging and see the world close at hand. Prince Dolor's goodness finally wins the heart of his dour nurse (a former criminal), who informs his subjects that he is still alive. He is restored to the throne, rules with wisdom and justice, but finally renounces the crown and disappears on his traveling cloak. Miss Mulock tells the reader that there is a deeper meaning to the story than that found in an ordinary fairy tale but that she has "hidden it so carefully that the smaller people, and many larger folk ,will never find it out. . . . " *The Little Lame Prince and His Travelling Cloak* was one of the most popular books of the later Victorian era—children then, as now, loved a good cry—and retained a readership for many years after, being reprinted as late as the 1960's. In its simplicity of style and its ability to evoke emotion of a very direct kind, it has probably only been matched in pathos by Louise de la Ramé's story of a poor little Dutch boy and his dog, as related in *A Dog of Flanders.*

In its form and intent, however mysterious the latter may be, *The Little Lame Prince* lies happily between a literary fairy tale and a fantasy; but by the end of the era, the literary fairy tale had pushed aside its more exacting rival. Fairies were popping out of every English glade or dell, and the human child's journey was one to fairyland rather than to a fully created Other World. The creatures of fairyland were the fays of romance rather than of the folktale; they were derived from Edmund Spenser's *Faerie Queene* and Shakespeare's *A Midsummer Night's Dream* rather than from traditional English tales. They tasted more of Frances Browne than of Dinah Mulock's *The Adventures of a Brownie.*

The culmination of the Victorian concept of faerie was best exemplified by Richard Doyle with his illustrations for William Allingham's verses in *In Fairy Land,* subtitled "A series of pictures from the elf-world." Here is the fairy world at its most enchanting: the elf-queen and elf-king (in many stories named Titania and Oberon) are surrounded by trolls, nixies, pixies and other delicate, gauzy fays; birds, butterflies, and other insects are steeds for fairy royalty; and toadstools and other flora abound. Through Richard Doyle's pictorial representations, it can be seen that the fairies were truly back in England. Again, the Wife of Bath would have been delighted!

The literature itself frequently fell short of its illustrations; not only Doyle, but Arthur Hughes, Walter Crane, Eleanor Boyle, Laurence Housman, and many others succeeded in transforming mediocre writing into memorable visual images. Walter Crane's children in *The Cuckoo-Clock* and *The Tapestry Room,* in their white nightdresses seem already en route to fairyland. Victorian children probably fell avidly upon such journeys to fairyland as Jean Ingelow's *Mopsa the Fairy* (1869), which contains a series of trips to the elfin kingdom; Mark Lemon's *Tinykin's Transformations* (1869), in which a forester's son in turn becomes a fish, a bird, and a deer through the magic of the fairy queen and is finally transformed into a prince; Mary de Morgan's series of tales in *On a Pin-cushion* (1877), which is filled with fire-fairies, water-fairies, and wind-fairies; and Andrew Lang's *Princess Nobody* (1884), which is appropriately subtitled "A Tale of Fairy Land." All of these stories, and many more, are now forgotten.

Such tales had little to do with the Christian ethos so prominent in the works of Kingsley and MacDonald, but this ethos returned to the literary fairy tale with Oscar Wilde's *The Happy Prince and Other Tales* (1888). Wilde saw literary fairy tales as

> . . . studies in prose, put for Romance's sake into a fanciful form;
> meant partly for children, and partly for those who have kept the
> childlike faculties of wonder and joy, and who find in simplicity a
> subtle strangeness.[12]

Some of Wilde's stories are reminiscent of those of Hans Christian Andersen: "The Fisherman and His Soul" echoes Andersen's "The Little Mermaid," and "The Nightingale and the Rose" echoes "The Constant Tin Soldier." "The Birthday of the Infanta" has more than a touch of Andersen's ironic despair. However, in his two most popular stories, "The Happy Prince" and "The Selfish Giant," the theme is the attainment of a higher state of spirituality. The "happy prince" leads an existence of pleasure before he becomes a statue and learns of the poverty and misery in his city. The "selfish giant" drives the children from his garden and has to learn to love so that spring will return to it. In Blakean terms, these stories are "songs of innocence" that lead to "songs of experience" and, through sacrifice, to the final ecstasy that is death. While many of the asides in Wilde's stories are for adults, most of the images are for children: the swallow helping the poor and the aged in *The Happy Prince,* just as Diamond sang to a dying old woman on his last journey with North Wind. What child would not have experienced a pang of guilt at the giant's words in "The Selfish Giant" as he drives the children from the garden:

> "My own garden is my own garden," said the giant; "anyone can
> understand that, and I will allow nobody to play in it but myself."

12. Oscar Wilde, *The Letters of Oscar Wilde,* ed. Rupert Hart-Davis (New York: Harcourt, Brace, and World, 1962), 219.

The Victorian literary fairy tale reached its peak with the tales of Oscar Wilde; but the true British folktale gained added strength with the definitive versions of Joseph Jacobs. His *English Fairy Tales* appeared in 1890, *Celtic Fairy Tales* in 1892, and *More English Fairy Tales* in 1894, and thus broadened the scope of future fantasies.

The Road to Oz: American Fantasy of the Nineteenth Century

The period from 1839 to 1901 in the United States was also one of great change, although a consistent progress was interrupted by the crisis of the Civil War and its aftermath of a recession. Nevertheless, it was a society that had an abundance of energy and inventiveness, a burgeoning population, an expanding industry, and a movement westward as enterprising adventurers and pioneers seized the opportunity either to escape from the fetters of eastern stability and regulation or to make a better life for themselves in the spirit of the Declaration of Independence, which promised "life, liberty, and the pursuit of happiness." The very nature of the society and the spirit of freedom it engendered had its effects upon childhood. By the middle of the nineteenth century, most adults would have agreed that

> . . . children had the right to develop spiritually, socially and mentally by a gradual process. Parents and guardians no longer expected their small charges to leap at one bound from infancy into maturity in order to play the role of "little men and women" without the stabilizing interlude of carefree childhood.[13]

As the English attitude toward childhood is revealed in Carroll's *Alice's Adventures in Wonderland,* so the American view is apparent in a simple little verse published in *Our Young Folks* magazine in 1866:

> In the depths of a cool and breezy wood
> Three little children romping all day,

13. Monica Kiefer, *American Children through Their Books* (Philadelphia: Univ. of Pennsylvania Pr., 1948), 229.

Frolicsome, laughing, and bright and good,
   Happily passing the time away,
And the old woods ring, as the children sing:
   "Give Work to the old folks,—the young must have Play!"[14]

Certainly this attitude was abroad in the children's realistic fiction of the period, which shows a greater insouciance, levity, and humor toward childhood than its English counterparts do. British boys had to go abroad to escape from a structured society and to taste the exuberance of youth (R.M. Ballantyne's *Snowflakes and Sunbeams* [1856], an English boy's adventures with the Hudson's Bay Company, is a typical example), while English girls were confined to home and hearth. American children had more fun, more room for maneuvering in their own country, and more determination to be free. At the end of Mark Twain's *The Adventures of Huckleberry Finn* (1884), for example, Huck says, "I reckon I got to light out for the Territory ahead of the rest, because Aunt Sally she's going to adopt me and civilize me, and I can't stand it. I been there before." American children, as seen through their books at least, were all Huck Finns at heart. Even some of the titles have an iconoclastic ring to them: Thomas Bailey Aldrich's *The Story of a Bad Boy* (1870) and George Wilbur Peck's *Peck's Bad Boy and His Pa* (1883). John Habberton's *Helen's Babies* (1876) is subtitled "With Some Account of Their Ways Innocent, Crafty, Angelic, Impish, Witching and Repulsive." Of course there was also that all-American purveyor of mischief, Twain's Tom Sawyer. When the young are caught in trying circumstances such as those found in Louisa May Alcott's *Little Women* (1868) or in Margaret Sidney's *Five Little Peppers and How They Grew* (1880), these circumstances are seen as regrettable impositions on a happy childhood as well as opportunities for character building.

There were other streams-of-writing as well. The moral tale still plodded on its weary way as it did in England, but unique to the United States was the creation of the American newspaper boy. Horatio Alger's *Ragged Dick* (1868) was the first of a long series of self-help stories in which determined boys won their way to fame and fortune through industry, honesty, and kindness. While English children were still being told to keep their stations in life, American children were assured that

14. *Our Young Folks*, 2 (April 1866): 244.

they could rise "from log cabin to White House." Abraham Lincoln thus was enshrined in boys' fiction.

The United States in the nineteenth century was not a land conducive to fantasy. There was no ambience of the fantastic among writers for adults as there was in England and which tended to sift down into writing for the young. Edgar Allan Poe may have dreamed "dreams no mortal ever dared to dream," but his tales of terror and death would hardly have been considered wellsprings of inspiration for writers for the young. Also, unlike English writers, American retellers of old tales appear to have had no impact on fantasy. They mined British and European material—Nathaniel Hawthorne with *A Wonder Book* (1852) and *Tanglewood Tales* (1853); Thomas Bulfinch with *The Age of Fable* (1855) and *The Age of Chivalry* (1859); and Howard Pyle with *The Merry Adventures of Robin Hood* (1883), his *King Arthur* cycle (1903–07), *Pepper and Salt* (1885), and *The Wonder Clock* (1887). While there was an audience for imported myth, legend, and folktale (the early booklists of the American Library Association attest to this fact), such stories did not take root in American soil. When fantasy did arrive, it was as home-grown and as homespun as the American realistic novel.

The arrival of fantasy did, however, take some time. The first American literary fairy tales have a whiff of the *Arabian Nights* about them. These include Frank Stockton's *Ting A Ling* (1870), later republished as *Ting-A-Ling Tales*. Ting a Ling is a minute fairy (much like Richard Doyle's fairies) who rides his insect chariot to the rescue of veiled princesses and handsome princes with the help of a friendly giant—probably the first friendly giant in children's literature. These tales are more absurd than their English counterparts, revealing a world of cheerful impossibility on the order of a Gilbert and Sullivan opera. Stockton's finest achievement after "The Lady or the Tiger," is *The Griffin and the Minor Canon* (1900). The setting is European—a small village with a medieval cathedral bedecked with stone carvings of griffins. The real griffin is a forerunner of Kenneth Grahame's *The Reluctant Dragon,* but with far more character as he takes on the duties of the canon—teaching school, tending the sick, and, all in all, keeping the villagers in order. *The Casting Away of Mrs. Lecks and Mrs. Aleshine* (1886) is completely American in its setting and characters. It is also the first of the "tall tales," which were to become such a strong part of American children's literature. In this story, two middle-aged women (and the narrator) are shipwrecked in the Pacific Ocean. They paddle their way to a desert island, using oars as if they were brooms, where they find a furnished house. There they set up housekeeping, depositing their rent money each week in a ginger jar, but paying themselves wages for their housework. Stockton here becomes a domestic Baron Munchausen.

Homegrown folklore first appeared with Joel Chandler Harris's *Uncle Remus: His Songs and His Sayings: The Folk-lore of the Old Plantation* (1881). Many of these stories have variants in older cultures, particularly African, but as Harris himself says in his introduction, they form "part of the domestic history of every Southern family" and were intended "to give vivid hints of the poetic imagination of the Negro." However, it was to be a long time before blacks and the black experience figured to any great extent in American fantasy.

Palmer Cox's *The Brownies* (1887) and its sequels did not have roots in traditional folklore as did Dinah Mulock's *The Brownies*. These American brownies are really lighthearted, mischievous American children in disguise. They mean no harm as they try to study and mess up the schoolroom or harness horses to go for a ride but have no time to unharness them before dawn comes. Cox portrays them, in pictures and in verse, as spirited little elves rather than as the down-to-earth English brownies who had household responsibilities. These tales delighted generations of American children, as can be seen in Eleanor Estes's *Rufus M*, where the first book that Rufus wants to borrow from the library is a "brownie" book.

Throughout Albert Bigelow Paine's *The Arkansaw Bear* (1898) rings the sound of the fiddle and the words to "The Arkansaw Traveller":

Oh, 'twas down in the woods of Arkansaw,
And the night was cloudy and the wind was raw,
And he didn't have a bed and he didn't have a bite,
And if he hadn't fiddled, he'd a' travelled all night.

The folksy tone continues as all the events, in calypso-like fashion, are sung to "The Arkansaw Traveller." Bosephus, a runaway orphan, and Horatio (known as "Ratio" to his friends), a talking, fiddling bear (with a unrequited taste for human flesh), are still two of the most endearing heroes in American children's literature. They are a Don Quixote and a Sancho Panza, tilting at windmills as they travel from Arkansaw to

Louisiana and back again. In spite of the use of the conventional terms of the day—"darky" and "nigger"—this is as much an anti-racist book as is Mark Twain's *Huckleberry Finn*. Also, Horatio Alger's philosophy wins at the end as Bosephus leaves the idyllic life of the "bear colony" and opts for education and a consequent advancement in life. Arkansaw is in no way seen as a land touched by enchantment. It is shown simply and clearly as it must have been in 1898, with its people, flora, and fauna carefully described and imbued with a spirit of adventure, independence, and freedom. Despite how lightly *The Arkansaw Bear* is touched by the fantastic, it is still the first full-fledged fantasy in American children's literature and proved that American soil and American ways could be an inspiration for stories other than the realistic. Paine staked out the territory.

L. Frank Baum deliberately set out to break the European tradition of fairy tale and fantasy. However, his *American Fairy Tales; Stories of Astonishing Adventures of American Boys and Girls with the Fairies of Their Native Land* (1901), written after *The Wizard of Oz* (1900), was not well received. Evidently, American children still wanted a taste of what they had been used to in English imports and what they had received in Baum's *The Wizard of Oz*, although he did his best to convince them otherwise. In his introduction to the first edition, Baum praises Grimm and Andersen for having "brought more happiness to childish hearts than all other human creations." However, he then goes on to say:

> Yet the old-time fairy-tale, having served for generations, may now be classed as "historical" in the children's library; for the time has come for a series of newer "wonder tales" in which the stereotyped genie, dwarf and fairy are eliminated, together with all the horrible and blood-curdling incidents devised by their authors to point a fearsome moral to each tale.

He did not succeed entirely, of course. There are morals all over the place in the *Oz* books and also violence, if one cares to look closely; but nothing is truly fearsome, not even the Wizard himself. Adults have confessed that, as children, they were frightened by *The Wizard of Oz*, but one suspects that the scariness came from the portrayal of the Wicked Witch of the West in the 1939 movie rather than from the book. However, Baum did eschew the struggle between good and evil that is so basic to the folktale and that formed so great a part of English fantasy of the same period, and he was not concerned with the moral development of his characters. The protagonists in the *Oz* books stem from a stoic philosophy—they mean well, and they do the best they can in any circumstance. The Scarecrow loses his sawdust, the Tin Woodman falls apart, the Sawhorse loses a leg, but they are all put back together again with little effort and even less ingenuity.

It is Baum's originality that must be saluted. *The Wizard of Oz* is not only the first Other World fantasy in American children's literature; it is the first fully created imaginative world in the whole of children's literature, all the more remarkable because in his own country there were few signposts to point Baum along "the yellow brick road." Charles Kingsley made use of a natural underwater setting in *The Water-Babies,* George MacDonald of a familiar folktale world in *The Princess and the Goblin,* and Carroll's *Alice* books are premised on artifices; but as Dorothy says at the end of *The Wizard of Oz,* when asked where she has come from, "From the Land of Oz." Oz was a place. It is true that the full cosmology of Oz did not develop until the later books (and is fully explained in Raylyn Moore's *Wonderful Wizard, Marvellous Land*),[15] but there was sufficient detail in the first book to make one believe in Oz.

Water-babies and goblins, and rabbit holes and looking-glasses were not for Baum. It is a natural—though unusual—event, a Kansas cyclone, that whirls Dorothy away from the gray fields, gray Uncle Henry, and gaunt, gray Aunt Em, to the bright blues, reds, yellows, and greens of the Land of Oz. The plot is a very basic one—the quest story. Dorothy, of course, wants to go home again. In her search, she is joined by the Scarecrow, who wants brains; the Cowardly Lion, who wants courage; and the Tin Woodman, who wants a heart. Dorothy has to perform a task to achieve her wish (which she accomplishes accidentally), and the others have had what they desire all along; but the Wizard, by means of stage tricks, gives these characters the assurance they need in their own abilities.

The Wizard of Oz began a publishing phenomenon. There has been nothing in children's literature to match the commercial success of Baum's Oz books and their spin-offs (fourteen of them) and twenty-seven by other writers published up until 1963.

15. Raylyn Moore, *Wonderful Wizard, Marvellous Land* (Bowling Green, Ohio: Bowling Green Univ. Popular Pr., 1974).

After the second Oz book, *The Marvellous Land of Oz* (1904), the series steadily deteriorated, especially those stories written by Ruth Plumly Thompson, a fact that in no way bothered Baum's adoring and faithful child audience nor the innumerable adult fans of today who are gathered into various *Oz* clubs and who assiduously seek out and produce "Baumiana." To this latter group in particular, the Baum books are not to be criticized in any literary sense; they have become a cult.

In many ways, it is easy to sink into the *Oz* books. The well-loved and familiar figures occur over and over again, and the style makes no more demands on the reader than does a simple school text, although the stories are frequently far less grammatical. Inconsistencies also abound. Many inconsistencies are those of mere reportage, resulting from pressure: Baum wrote one book a year to please his insistent audience. But their greatest flaw derives from the fact that the books lack a coherent or logical philosophy of life such as that evident in the works of Charles Kingsley, George MacDonald, and Lewis Carroll, and later in such key fantasies as C.S. Lewis's *Narnia Chronicles* and Susan Cooper's *The Dark Is Rising* quintet. Baum presents Oz as an American utopia; yet in *Dorothy and the Wizard in Oz* (1908), there is surely more than a hint of un-American snobbery in the statement that the Princess Ozma of Oz welcomed Dorothy, "for girls of her own age with whom it was proper for the princess to associate were very few." In the same book, the trial of the kitten, Eureka, could hardly be considered just. This scene is more reminiscent of the absurd trial of the Knave of Hearts in *Alice's Adventures in Wonderland*—"Sentence first, verdict afterwards."

Nonetheless, many of the *Oz* characters are memorable and very American, such as the Sawhorse, the Patchwork Girl, and the talking phonograph that plays both classical and ragtime music, to the disturbance of everyone who hears it. Then there is Dorothy herself, as presented in *The Wizard of Oz*—the ultimate in American childhood of the late nineteenth century. She is used to a harsh life induced by the droughts of Kansas. She has had a childhood where she may be seen but not heard. However, she is also a child of the Western frontier and meets all difficulties with courage and aplomb. Her goodness, kindness, and generosity win her friends who help her on the way to Oz; but it is frequently Dorothy herself, with childlike commonsense, who sees solutions when difficulties arise and who (like Alice) advises very politely.

Dorothy meets the Wizard with modest but disarming candor: "'Why should I do this for you?' asked Oz. 'Because you are strong and I am weak, because you are a Great Wizard and I am only a helpless little girl,' she answered." It is distressing, then, in later books to find Dorothy relegated almost to the role of onlooker and her plain but pungent Midwestern speech reduced almost to baby talk—'scaped used for escaped, s'pose for suppose, 'bout for about, and so on.

The road to Oz will probably be repaved with the appearance of the 1985 movie Return to Oz, based on the second and third books in the series—The Marvellous Land of Oz (1904) and Ozma of Oz (1906)—but if children go to any book after The Marvellous Land of Oz, they will find, as James Thurber pointed out, "the whimsical rather than the fantastic"[16] and a host of cardboard characters rather than the Scarecrow, the Cowardly Lion, and the Tin Woodman.

For its time, however, The Wizard of Oz was a tour-de-force. It was a book that stemmed directly from a society, without the aid of literary antecedents. It was a new fairy tale for a new world. It was freshly conceived, inventive (especially in the animation of the inanimate), exuberant, open, and direct. Many of the images it projected were reinforced in later books, especially that of unusual assortments of people and creatures all living peacefully together.

It is rather mystifying to note that the Oz books did not engender other fantasies. It was to be almost a quarter of a century before the appearance of another major work. Perhaps the very numbers and popularity of the Oz books discouraged rather than encouraged other writers; or, considering historical implications, it may be that the people of "the land of the free and the home of the brave" did not need fantasy. Deep in the American psyche of the period was still the conviction (inherited from Puritan times) that an Earthly Paradise created by ordinary, everyday people was the true goal of life. The land of Oz with its many resemblances to American culture did indeed strike a responsive chord; but beneath the surface, the fantasy, and the dream was America itself. The "yellow brick road" was a highway of prosperity, peace, and togetherness for everyone, not just for creatures of fantasy.

16. James Thurber, "The Wizard of Chittenango," The New Republic 81 (12 Dec. 1934): 141.

The Victorian Achievement

In any complete edition of *Grimm's Fairy Tales,* there appears a short, short story called "The Golden Key." In it, a poor boy is sent out into the forest on a cold winter's day to bring back firewood. After gathering the wood, he becomes so cold that he makes a fire to warm himself:

> He cleared a space, and as he was scraping away the snow, he found a little golden key. "Where there's a key," he said to himself, "there's sure to be a lock." So he dug down into the ground and found an iron box. "There must be precious things in it," he thought. "If only the key fits!" At first he couldn't find a keyhole, but then at last he found one, though it was so small he could hardly see it. He tried the key and it fitted perfectly. He began to turn it—and now we'll have to wait until he turns it all the way and opens the lid. Then we'll know what marvels there were in the box.

Children's literature, too, had to wait for generations for the discovery of a golden key. This was found in the revival of the folk- and fairy tale, and it, in turn, opened the box to the marvels of fantasy. The total achievements of the writers of fantasy and of the literary fairy tale match, though in microcosm, the many achievements of the Victorian Age itself. These writers brought back the fairies; they created nonsense; they broke through the limitations that had been set by reason, opening the doors to other dimensions of time and space, and to dreams and visions. They established a respect for children's intelligence and emotional maturity. They showed that a tale could be exciting yet still show concern for spiritual well-being, for the state of society, for the environment, and for poor, neglected, crippled, lonely, and displaced children. In so doing, these writers produced a cataclysm. They proved that children's literature could be literature in its own right. This shift was not only a courageous and original literary innovation but it marked the greatest change in children's literature since its inception—and after. No change since—and there have been many—has been as important.

Chapter 4

Dream Days:
The Edwardian Age and After

Concepts of Childhood

In Edith Nesbit's *The Enchanted Castle* (1907), we meet a maidservant who, in order to impress her gentleman friend, appropriates and wears a ring that makes her invisible. In her frightened state, she is reassured by the children, who know how the magic works. "Now," said Gerald, "it's all over. Nothing but niceness now, and cakes and things." That comforting remark defines fantasy for about the next twenty-five years. Edwardian writers were children during the Victorian age, and they were determined to expunge from children's literature the last remnants of nursery discipline and the tyranny of nannies, nursemaids, governesses, and parents. Childhood was seen at this time as "the best of all possible worlds," and the separation of childhood from adulthood was well-nigh complete. This shift was a remarkable feat in view of the fact that most of the major writers of the period—Edith Nesbit, Beatrix Potter, Rudyard Kipling, and Kenneth Grahame—had far from idyllic childhoods. Their early unhappiness was not something that they pushed aside in their adult lives, however. In her book of childhood recollections, *Long Ago When I Was Young*, Edith Nesbit states that, "There is nothing here that is not in my most clear and vivid recollection."[1]

1. Edith Nesbit, *Long Ago When I Was Young* (London: Ronald Whiting & Wheaton, 1966), 27.

Rudyard Kipling revealed his harrowing exile from India in his short story "Baa, Baa Black Sheep," and Beatrix Potter in her adult life ultimately rejected the narrow standards of her parents. In their books for the young, whether using children or animals as protagonists, these writers drew a curtain firmly down on the adult world and therefore also on pain and distress.

In the world of childhood they created, however, there is still a moral code, but it is one to which the children themselves subscribe: kindness, helpfulness, politeness, generosity, and family solidarity. Gone is the tough moral fiber of the great Victorian fantasies as well as the iconoclastic nonsense of Edward Lear and Lewis Carroll. The Puritan ethos disappears—hardly ever to return—and along with it any references to religion or struggles to reach higher levels of goodness. Edwardian book-children are rarely even admonished, except by their siblings or by their fantasy parental surrogates, and they always instinctively "do the right thing."

The changes in actual childhood, however, were probably neither as great nor as rapid as the books suggest. Even Gwen Raverat, the daughter of an upper-class family, speaks in her reminiscences of a late Victorian and Edwardian childhood, *Period Piece,* of the bland nursery food and the "discomfort, restraint, and pain" of the clothes the young were forced to wear.[2] There is certainly much talk of uncomfortable clothes in the Nesbit books also, but these are minor inconveniences in an otherwise blissful child world.

The Edwardian Age itself was a kind of pause in English history, a pause between the excesses of the Industrial Revolution and the horrors of World War I. It was a decade of much progressive social legislation, but little of this progressiveness shows in fantasy; nor is there a concern for the lot of the poor, as exhibited in the works of Charles Kingsley, George MacDonald, and Oscar Wilde. However, the Edwardians had a fascination for English tradition and a concern about the destruction of the countryside, which was heralded by urbanization and the appearance of the automobile; these themes appear in Edwardian fantasies along with the playful spirit of childhood. Barbara Tuchman has described the last two years of the decade as a "rich fat afternoon"[3]—and one in which

2. Gwen Raverat, *Period Piece* (London: Faber, 1960), 258.
3. Barbara Tuchman, *The Guns of August* (New York: Macmillan, 1962), 9.

a popular tune heard then would have been "The Teddy Bears' Picnic." Gwen Raverat describes this time as a "Utopia of tea-parties, dinner-parties, boat-races, lawn-tennis, antique shops, picnics, charming young men, delicious food and perfect servants. . . . "[4] Translate these adult pleasures into childlike ones, and we have most of the books of the Edwardian age, especially those by Kenneth Grahame, Rudyard Kipling, and Edith Nesbit.

The Magic of Edith Nesbit

Edith Nesbit's first substantial excursion into magic, *A Book of Dragons* (1900), up-ends the former soft and serious literary fairy tales as the dragons are tamed by resourceful children who take over the duties and responsibilities of adults. In one story, for example, a little boy is called upon to be king. There is little fairy-tale atmosphere; the conversations and references are contemporary with 1900, and there is not a moral to be found in the story. The book was republished in 1972 as *The Complete Book of Dragons* with the addition of a story taken from *Five of Us—and Madeline,* first published in 1925, in which a dragon becomes the first airplane. Oswald Bastable, Nesbit's most perceptive young character in her stories of child and family life, would have called it a "jolly" book.

In *Nine Unlikely Tales for Children* (1901), Nesbit's view of childhood is seen more clearly, as well as her special brand of magic. A cross nursemaid is turned into an Automatic Nagging Machine, and the children are allowed food generally forbidden to them—a combination of the gourmet and the infantile, such as lobster, toffee, and ginger-beer. Stiff and starchy clothes are shed for sealskin, which "could not be spoiled with sand or water or jam, or bread and milk, or any of the things with which you mess up the nice new clothes your kind relatives buy for you." The last sentence is an example of Nesbit's constant reproof to adults who misuse their authority over children.

With the exception of *The Magic City* (1910), the Nesbit books—such as *Five Children and It* (1902), *The Phoenix and the Carpet* (1904), *The Story of the Amulet* (1906), and *The Enchanted Castle* (1907)—are stories

4. Raverat, 16.

of magic rather than fantasies, and Edith Nesbit is the greatest magician in the whole of children's literature. In essence, she laid down the rules for the use of magic. First of all, there has to be a talisman that sparks the adventures. The talisman can be as fabulous as the Psammead of *Five Children and It* or as common an artifact as the ring in *The Enchanted Castle.* Once the magic begins, it must work consistently; there can be no departure from its rigid rules. There are frequent caveats and prohibitions, as in the folktales. Eldred and Elfrida, for example, in the historical fantasy *The House of Arden* (1908), cannot find the door into the past unless they have not quarreled for three days—a most difficult feat for two lively children to accomplish. It also is generally accepted that adults are *not* to be drawn into the magic. Some exceptions include, on the one hand, good-natured cooks and housemaids who will swallow a swiftly concocted explanation or, on the other hand, a learned professor or the Board of Directors of the Phoenix Fire Insurance Company who will put the events all down to a dream.

Parents, however, are totally excluded from the children's adventures. In *The Phoenix and the Carpet,* Anthea, who has a sensitive conscience, feels she should explain to her mother why the cook is missing (the children have left her happily ensconced as queen of a cannibal island), but to no avail:

> "Darling one," said mother, "you know I love to hear the things you make up—but I am most awfully busy."
> "But it's true," said Anthea desperately.
> "You shouldn't say that, my sweet," said mother, gently. And then Anthea knew it was hopeless.

Overall, it is belief that counts in Nesbit's magic. Nothing can happen unless the children respond to its imperious call. In *The Enchanted Castle,* the children debate whether or not the castle is an enchanted one:

> "Wireless is rather like magic when you come to think of it," said Gerald.
> "Oh, *that* sort!" Jimmy's contempt was deep.
> "Perhaps there's given up being magic because people didn't believe in it any more," said Kathleen.

"Well, don't let's spoil the show with any silly old not believing," said Gerald with decision. "I'm going to believe in magic as hard as I can. This is an enchanted garden, and that's an enchanted castle, and I'm jolly well going to explore."

In other words, the more one believes, the easier belief becomes. As the children moved farther into the garden, "the feeling of magic got thicker and thicker."

Nesbit's chief claim to remembrance lies in her creation of the Psammead (in *Five Children and It* and in *The Story of the Amulet*), the mythological Phoenix (in *The Phoenix and the Carpet*), and, to a lesser extent, the Mouldiwarp (in *The House of Arden* and in *Harding's Luck*, 1909). The Psammead, with its eyes like a snail, its bat's ears, its spider-like body and a monkey's hands and feet, is a creature from Megatherium times who hates the damp and loves dry, warm sand. He is, indeed, a sand-fairy. The Phoenix is best described by Jane in *The Phoenix and the Carpet*: "You are the most beautiful person we've ever seen." The Mouldiwarp leads a more ordinary life than either the Psammead or the Phoenix. Although he is the badge of the House of Arden come alive, he is still just a mole; the magic in him appears to lie in his white coloring. Nesbit's sure touch of magic had faltered, however, by the time *The House of Arden* was conceived, and the Mouldiwarp did not achieve the memorable personality of his two predecessors. Nonetheless, all the creatures know their worth; and although they are at the children's beck and call, they manage to persuade the children and the reader of the opposite.

To a considerable extent, these creatures also substitute for absent fathers and busy mothers. They provide information and advice, and lay down the rules for conduct as well as magical procedures:

> "I shouldn't advise that," said the Phoenix very earnestly.
> "Why not?"
> "Well, for one thing, it isn't true."

and

> "Now you're talking," said Robert.
> "Of course I am," retorted the Psammead tartly, "so there's no need for you to."

The children accept all rebukes with equanimity, and they never argue back. They show their mettle and resourcefulness during the course of their magical adventures.

Nesbit's greatest strength lies in her ability to mingle the ordinary and familiar with the fantastic. When the children get their wishes from the Psammead in *Five Children and It,* they are not whirled away to enchanted lands but must cope with the wishes in their own time and place, where the golden guineas they have received are not current exchange and where the servants refuse to let the children into the house since, being "as beautiful as the day," they are not recognizable. In *The Phoenix and the Carpet,* journeys into the past are linked to an acquisition of artifacts for mother's bazaar. The children are the epitome of Edwardian middle-class values. They are intelligent, well educated (Anthea learns "Algebra and Latin, German, English and Euclid"), well read (they also know how to use reference books), considerate, and polite. They are also ordinary children in their carelessness:

> It was breakfast-time, and mother's letter, telling them how they were all going for Christmas to their aunt's at Lyndhurst and how father and mother would meet them there, having been read by every one, lay on the table, drinking hot bacon-fat with one corner and eating marmalade with the other.

Nesbit is most successful with the short story format and the episodic novel. Both *Five Children and It* and *The Phoenix and the Carpet* are based on a series of separate adventures linked only by the magic of the Pasammead and the Phoenix, without whose powers the adventures cannot even begin. *The Story of the Amulet* is her most continuous purposeful narrative as the children quest for their heart's desires—the return of their parents and their baby brother, and the joining together of the halves of the amulet to help their friend the absent-minded professor. It is also the book that comes closest to successful fantasy. The amulet has a presence that borders on the awesome:

> Then out of that vast darkness and silence came a light and a voice. The light was too faint to see anything by, and the voice was too small for you to hear what it said. But the light and the voice grew. And the light was the light that no man may look on and live,

and the voice was the sweetest and most terrible voice in the world. The children cast down their eyes and so did everyone.

There are many humorous moments in the story, but they are merely decorations to its overall serious thrust. The Egyptian mythology that ultimately subsumes the ordinary events of child and family life, which are so much a part of the first two books, gives the aura of an Other World that is both powerful and believable.

In spite of its episodic chapters, *The Story of the Amulet* is, as its title suggests, a whole story. *The Enchanted Castle,* on the other hand, moves from a humorous, magical adventure story into a burst of pantheistic fantasy as the statues in the garden are reincarnated as the Greek gods themselves, but the sudden change is far from convincing. *The Magic City* (1910) is a totally created building-block world, but as in *The Enchanted Castle,* Nesbit's inventive spirit flags, and the complex magic demands overly concentrated attention. Both books, however, have memorable episodes. In *The Enchanted Castle,* the most memorable episode involves the "Ugly-Wuglies"—creatures made by the children out of broomsticks, umbrellas, coathangers, and paper masks. These creatures come alive through the magic of the ring and provide the only true shiver of horror in any Nesbit book. One of the most original touches of her fertile imagination was to provide the Ugly-Wuglies with consonantless speech. *The Magic City* also has its marvelous moments, especially its beginning. Philip, a lonesome young boy who is harassed by his nurse, builds—as an anodyne for his misery—a beautiful city, first of all from his own toys and then from everything useful, beautiful, and exotic that he can find in a luxurious drawing room. Suddenly, he can enter the magic city, where he finds his step-sister, Lucy, a little girl whom he had previously disdained. Together they have a series of "do-good" adventures while being pursued by a female villain, who turns out to be Philip's nurse. The story is all a bit of a hodgepodge.

Edith Nesbit and her husband, Hubert Bland, were active socialists and founding members of the Fabian Society, and so they moved in the same circles as George Bernard Shaw and H.G. Wells. Little of her reforming zeal appears in her writing, however, but it does break through on occasion. For example, when the nurse in *The Magic City* is unmasked and defeated, she speaks her mind about her condition in the real world:

" . . . You don't understand. You've never been a servant, to see other people get all the fat and you all the bones. What you think it's like to know if you'd just been born in a gentleman's mansion instead of in a model workman's dwelling you'd have been brought up as a young lady and had the openwork silk stockings and the lace on your under-petticoats."

Nonetheless, her words fall on deaf ears and do not mitigate her punishment.

Genteel poverty is well described in *The House of Arden* in the lives of Eldred, Elfrida, and their aunt before they inherit Arden Castle. Similarly, in 1909, Dickie Harding of *Harding's Luck* is poor, orphaned, and lame. When he travels into the past, however, he is metamorphosed into healthy and wealthy Lord Arden. Obviously, Edith Nesbit did not regard a children's book as a vehicle for social reform as did Charles Kingsley in *The Water-Babies*. Only in *The Story of the Amulet*, when the children go into the future, does she allow herself a vision of Utopia. In this story, the children find London unrecognizable. The Thames runs as clear as crystal, there are motor carriages that make no noise, and there is no smoke. And the people? "I know," said Anthea suddenly. "They're not worried; that's what it is." From a little boy named Wells (after the great reformer), they discover that future children like school (they can choose their own subjects for study) and that they have comfortable padded playrooms with no open fireplaces. Robert knows that three thousand children a year in his time are burned to death because of open fires. In a beautiful park, groups of people are gathered, and "Men, as well as women, seem to be in charge of the babies and were playing with them." This chapter, "The Sorry-Present and The Expelled Little Boy," is the first venture into science fiction in children's literature and the strongest statement of Nesbit's socialist ideals. She is typically Edwardian in her dislike of cities; all her children prefer the country and frequently say so.

Nesbit also had an affinity for the past, as is evident in her major characters—the primeval Psammead; the Phoenix, who might have stepped out of a medieval bestiary; and the ancient Mouldiwarp, who speaks with an earthy, old-fashioned Sussex accent. *The Enchanted Castle* ends in a burst of Greek mythology. Her two time fantasies, *The House of Arden* and *Harding's Luck*, take us back into various reigns of English history, notably those of Queen Elizabeth and James I. Although both these latter books have intriguing beginnings and the history is well used as a springboard for adventure, the events become tedious and repetitive, the magic complicated, and everything verges on the sentimental.

Edith Nesbit's books were written solely to give children pleasure (as well as to fill the often empty Nesbit family purse), not to inculcate moral principles or to express her adult views of society. Nor was she concerned about creating Other Worlds or dimensions of them. Her children step eagerly but lightly through the rifts in the curtain of fantasy into other real worlds and are not affected by them. However, her special and consistent use of magic, combined with her observation of the small delights of childhood (mostly derived from her own children) and her strong feeling for family life, gave rise to a Nesbit tradition that has lasted until our own time. Like so many other Edwardian writers who saw their adult works as of greater importance than those they wrote for children, by the time of her death in 1924, Nesbit was saluted in *Punch* magazine only for her children's novels. For an epitaph, C.L. Graves wrote:

> You pass, but only from the ken
>   Of scientists and statisticians,
> To join HANS CHRISTIAN ANDERSEN,
>   The Prince of all the good Magicians.[5]

Perspectives of Childhood in the Works of Rudyard Kipling, W.H. Hudson, and James Barrie

History itself provides almost enough magic for Rudyard Kipling in *Puck of Pook's Hill* (1906) and *Rewards and Fairies* (1910). The fantasy lies only in the appearance of Puck, "the oldest Old Thing in England"; and why shouldn't he appear when the children have "acted out *Midsummer Night's Dream* three times over, *on* Midsummer Eve, *in* the middle of a Ring, and under—right *under* one of my oldest hills in Old England"? The magic continues as Puck parades before Dan and Una, figures from England's past, ranging from the god Weland (turned blacksmith) through the Vikings, the Romans, Harold (the loser at Hastings), King

5. Noel Streatfield, *Magic and the Magician* (London: Ernest Benn, 1958), 156.

John (of the Magna Carta), and a host of others. Although the great names of history are legion, the narrators are most frequently minor figures who give their personal view of events. This is not the history of the history books, but a kind of *tableaux vivant* with the addition of dialogue.

Dan and Una are not participants in the action as are Eldred and Elfrida in Nesbit's *The House of Arden;* they are eager listeners, questioners, and, only occasionally, commentators. At the end of each episode, they are "de-magicked" by means of Oak, Ash, and Thorn; for, as Puck says, if they told at home of what they had seen and heard, human beings would "send for the doctor." In a way, Dan and Una do not need magic. They are children of the Sussex countryside and already "seized" of their own private domain, where not even their great friend old Hobden the hedger (and poacher) would venture without permission. Sussex, which Kipling loved and where all the stories are set, is seen as a land of enchantment in "Puck's Song," which begins *Puck of Pook's Hill* and which ends:

> She is not any common Earth,
>   Water or wood or air,
> But Merlin's Isle of Gramarye,
>   Where you and I will fare.

Although there is talk of getting home to tea and Latin lessons and governesses, Dan and Una are true children of the Edwardian age in their freedom from adults:

> When they had seen their dear parents and their dear preceptress politely off the premises they got a cabbage-leaf full of raspberries from the gardner, and a Wild Tea from Ellen.

Kipling's style in *Puck of Pook's Hill* and in *Rewards and Fairies* has neither the brilliance of his *Just So Stories* (1902) nor the rhythmic cadence of his Mowgli stories in *The Jungle Book* (1894) and in *The Second Jungle Book* (1895), but it is effective nonetheless. It changes from the natural conversation of the children to the colloquial speech of some of the narrators to heightened language when deep-felt emotions and strained loyalties are revealed. No one, until Rosemary Sutcliff in her

novels of early Britain, has written so passionately about history as
Rudyard Kipling.

W.H. Hudson's *A Little Boy Lost* (1905) owes almost everything to his
childhood in Argentina. It is the book of a naturalist combined with the
mysticism of Blake, from whom he tells us that he took his title and
"something too of the semi-wild spirit of the child hero. . . . "[6] All of
Hudson's writing can be summed up in Blake's lines from *Auguries of
Innocence:*

> To see a World in a Grain of Sand,
>   And a Heaven in a Wild Flower,
> Hold Infinity in the palm of your hand,
>   And eternity in an hour.

In its imagery and feeling of something beautiful but intangible that escapes the conscious mind, *A Little Boy Lost* resembles George Mac-
Donald's *The Golden Key* more than any other book in children's literature. But it is, in essence, unique.

Martin, the little boy of the story, has an immediate affinity with the
unnamed pampas land to which his parents have moved after his father
abandons an ordinary carpenter's life in England. At age seven, and even
more in tune with the natural world than ever before, Martin does not
understand things mechanical and accidentally kills a spoonbill with his
father's gun. A drought comes, mirages occur—again, which Martin
does not understand—he follows their enticements as once mortals pursued the will-o-the-wisps, and he is lost. Figures emerge from the
mirage—a dying prince who has the features of a spoonbill and a queen
and her entourage, who give Martin gifts: "he shall be a wanderer all his
days on the face of the earth," "let the sea do him no harm," and "let all
men love him." Martin's adventures from then on are a combination of
fantasy and reality, dream and awakening. Into them are woven legends
of the country. One day, however, he glimpses the sea, and not all the
love and enticements of the lovely "Lady of the Hills" who has adopted
him can keep Martin from it. However, when he achieves his goal, he
finds the sea uncontrollable—not subject to him as were the birds and

6. W.H. Hudson, *A Little Boy Lost* (New York: Knopf, 1918), PS.

beasts of the pampas—and he lies naked, hungry, cold, and wretched on a sea-worn raft until he is rescued by a passing ship.

In his innocence and naiveté, Martin is like Diamond in George MacDonald's *At the Back of the North Wind*. Like Diamond, too, he hears a song of "Wonderful Death and Wonderful Life," but it is beyond his understanding. Diamond's experience is religious and mystical, leading him to a joyful acceptance of death. Martin's is of the natural world—a journey into the mysteries of nature and pantheism that ends with the knowledge that the ultimate ideal cannot be reached.

Whereas W.H. Hudson created a half-fantasy world out of the flora and fauna of Argentina, Sir James Barrie created a complete fantasy island out of his own boyhood, his love of boys' books, his companionship with boys, and the Edwardian perspective of childhood. All of these influences combined to make *Peter Pan* one of the most successful children's books of all times. It influenced both the spirit and content of fantasy for several generations. The genesis of *Peter Pan*—from a first appearance in Barrie's adult book *The Little White Bird* (1902) to its performance as a stage play in 1904 through the publication of the novelette *Peter Pan in Kensington Gardens* (1906) and then to a full-fledged novel, *Peter and Wendy* (1911), that is frequently republished as *Peter Pan and Wendy* or *Peter Pan*—has been well documented in Harry M. Geduld's book *Sir James Barrie*.[7]

The first sentences of *Peter and Wendy* give the kernel of the story: "All children, except one, grow up. They soon know that they will grow up. . . . Wendy knew it after she was two years old. Two is the beginning of the end." Peter escapes the fate of adulthood because he runs away the day he is born:

> "It was because I heard father and mother," he explained in a low voice, "talking about what I was to be when I became a man. . . . I don't want ever to be a man," he said with passion. "I want always to be a little boy and to have fun. So I ran away to Kensington Gardens and lived a long time among the fairies."

Peter has to "pay the Piper" for his defection, however; he is neither mortal nor fairy. As the raven points out to him in *Peter Pan in Kensington Gardens,* he is "a Betwixt-and-Between."

7. Harry M. Geduld, *Sir James Barrie* (New York: Twayne, 1971).

The half-fairy Peter holds sway over Never-land. It is a tropical island (Barrie loved islands) with white sand, a blue lagoon, and a forest. It is peopled with Indians, pirates, mermaids, bears, wolves, tigers—and a crocodile. Food is ready-to-hand—"roasted breadfruit, yams, coconuts, baked pig, mammee-apples, tappa rolls and bananas, washed down with calabashes of poe-poe." But best of all, there are adventures every day. Never-land is the eternal land of make-believe, made of the stuff of dreams, old tales, and adventure stories. Here children can have all the fun and none of the responsibilities of the grown-ups; they can fight without being hurt, kill and see their foes rise again. They can wage war with pirates and Indians and fierce animals—and then do it all over again. They can even face death with impunity. When Peter is left alone on a rock in the sea with the tide rising, a drum beats within him that says, "To die will be an awfully big adventure." Never-lands are in all children's minds, Barrie tells us. "We too have been there; we can still hear the sound of the surf, though we shall land no more."

Peter lures the Darling children—Wendy, John and Michael—to Never-land chiefly by appealing to the oldest wish of all, that of being able to fly. What Peter really wants, though, is a mother for his "Lost Boys" on the island, and like the winged Greek god Hermes, he uses every wile at his command. Off the children fly to Peter's address, "second to the right and straight on till morning." When they reach the island, they hail it "not as something long dreamt of and seen at last but as a familiar friend to whom they were returning home for the holidays," for below them lie all their imaginings, just as Peter has said. They have flown by means of Peter's fairy powers—he has sprinkled fairy dust on them—but now there is no more magic. The island is a place of wish fulfillment, but it also comes astonishingly close to their home routine. "Do you want an adventure now," [Peter] said casually to John, "or would you like to have your tea first?" Wendy, in the house underground, prepares the meals, darns the socks, sets the bedtime hours, and generally keeps the boys in order as they wrangle in a familial way. She is, of course, the mother; Peter is the father; and Michael, much to his chagrin, has to sleep in a cradle like a baby. The island is so real a make-believe world that the children still make-believe. Meals are frequently make-believe; and when Wendy is stunned by an arrow, Slightly (one of the lost boys) makes believe he is a doctor. Peter is the greatest make-believer of them all; he can even pretend not to have adventures!

Because of his attachment to his mother, Barrie himself has been called "the boy who wouldn't grow up." However, *Peter Pan* shows him as much a realist as any other fine fantasist. It is filled with references to the selfishness and egotism of Peter and the other children, although, like real children, they are not aware of any flaws in their nature. Wendy, John, and Michael give not a thought to their parents as they fly out the window, and they are superbly confident of hugs and kisses when they return. At the thought of losing Wendy, the Lost Boys threaten to keep her a prisoner; but Peter, who has been described by some critics as the personification of selfishness, lets Wendy go. He does so out of pride, of course, but he does let her go—and the Lost Boys as well—and arranges for her journey home (she cannot fly without his magic power). Peter is far more than a one-dimensional character; he was, after all, created to entertain Barrie's favorite boy in real life—Peter Lewelyn Davies. The human side of Peter has a complete personality. It is his fairy side that easily becomes a stereotype: he is forgetful and mischievous, the two most traditional qualities of fairies. He is ignorant of things that Wendy takes for granted because he is uneducated. He has lived too long among the fairies.

Of course, there is no doubt about Peter's cockiness. Indeed, the verb most often used to express his manner of speech and attitude is "crowed." He cannot resist taunting Captain Hook, the pirate, and it is almost his undoing. The fairy Tinkerbell, although she loves Peter, is the only one to see through him. "You silly ass," is her usual comment.

The book is filled with Barrie's open jibes against adults and the middle class. For instance, underneath his bumbling exterior, Mr. Darling is a loving father, but "he had to be exactly like his neighbours" and he worries about what they would think of his having a dog as a nurse for his children. (Barrie injects fantasy into the real world, just as he injects realism into the fantasy one.) Mrs. Darling, although Barrie approves of her more than Mr. Darling, "loved to have everything just so." The make-believe family life on the island is modeled on that of the Darling family, and Barrie reveals this fact with gentle humor. However, it is with Captain Hook that he has the most fun—at the expense of the English public school system, which Barrie describes as being built on "good form" learned on "the playing fields of Eton." Peter Pan has natural "good form"; he never takes unfair advantage of an enemy (neither do the Indians)—and the best form of all is to have "good form" without knowing it. Hook hates Peter for this quality, for he knows he can never achieve it. Having played with the idea thus far, Barrie has still another ace up his sleeve. As the fight between the boys and the pirates comes to a close, Hook

> had one last triumph, which I think we need not grudge him. As he stood on the bulwark looking over his shoulder at Peter gliding through the air, he invited him with a gesture to use his foot. It made Peter kick instead of stab.
> At last Hook got the boon for which he craved.
> "Bad form," he cried jeeringly, and went content to the crocodile.

The title *Peter and Wendy* is a more apt one than *Peter Pan,* for the book really belongs to Wendy; she is the only real person in it. The boys are colorless, for the most part, especially John and Michael. The pirates and Indians are book characters transferred to another book; and Peter Pan embodies many of our beliefs in the freshness and wonder of childhood. When Captain Hook asks him who he is: " 'I'm youth, I'm joy,' Peter answered at a venture, 'I'm a little bird that has broked out of the egg.' " This statement, Barrie adds, is "nonsense," but "good form." In contrast, Wendy is a whole girl, just as she later becomes a whole woman. She delights in her domestic tasks (she is, after all, an Edwardian girl), but they do not crush her spirit. She knows her worth. When she is tied to the mast on the pirate ship, Smee (her favorite pirate) whispers to her:

> "I'll save you if you promise to be my mother." But not even for Smee would she make such a promise. "I would almost rather have no children at all," she said disdainfully.

Most significantly of all, Wendy is able to grow up, a process that, Barrie is clearly trying to show, does not require the abandonment of imagination. While becoming the perfect mother, Wendy retains and values the dreams of childhood. Both her daughter, Jane, and Jane's daughter, Margaret, fly off with Peter. This revivification of such dreams in succeeding generations signals Wendy's embrace of them not only as a child, but also as an adult. *Peter Pan and Wendy* extols the joy of imagining at any age—it is not merely a fantasy about growing up—or not growing up.

Woodland Magic: The Golden Age of Animal Fantasy

It was probably inevitable that the use of animals in folklore, parable, and fantasy (such as in Charles Kingsley's *The Water-Babies,* Lewis Carroll's *Alice's Adventures in Wonderland,* and George MacDonald's *The Princess and Curdie*) should give rise to a new genre—animal fantasy. It is equally not surprising that this usage should originate from the late Victorian and Edwardian eras. Writers such as Richard Jefferies, Beatrix Potter, Kenneth Grahame, and Walter de le Mare drank deeply of the wellsprings of Victorian fantasy, but they added to its heady drafts an idealization of the animal world (akin to the prevailing idealization of the child's world) and a nostalgia for the countrysides of their childhood, which were threatened by mechanization—a threat that in literary form comes to its fruition in Toad's fascination with change and the automobile in Kenneth Grahame's *The Wind in the Willows* (1908).

Although Richard Jefferies's *Wood Magic* (1881) is subtitled "A Fable," the word *fable* is not used in the Aesopian sense, but rather to indicate the imaginative quality of the story. Little "Sir Bevis" (his name refers to the old English hero of romance, Sir Bevis of Hampton) is a child of seven who roams his father's estate in Wiltshire, seemingly totally free from parental restraint. Sir Bevis can communicate with the birds and the animals as well as with the inanimate forces of nature—the trees, the streams, and the wind. Bevis is not naturally good, although in his communication with nature he has a Wordsworthian touch. He is, at times, capricious, egotistical, and even cruel. He steals the swallow's eggs, and flings a knife at the swallow and a spade at the robin. However, he is "deared" and "darlinged" throughout the book by the denizens of the wood. It is a long book—two volumes in its original publication— and its most dramatic and lengthiest incident, the battle of the birds, has little to do with the beauty of nature or with Sir Bevis's education. The birds are used here in a kind of Orwellian parable of dictatorship and rebellion as in *Animal Farm;* and in this respect, *Wood Magic* is aptly subtitled. The birds retain their natural characteristics, but they are also personified as military commanders, strategists, and soldiers of the line. After this "fable," Jefferies returns to the mystical powers of nature and the concept of time. The wind tells Bevis: "If you want to know all about the sun, and the stars, and everything, make haste and come to me, and I will tell you, dear. . . . drink me . . . and drink still more of me. . . . " The concept of time, which has become the preoccupation of many modern fantasists, is first elucidated by Jefferies, as the wind explains:

> "There never was a yesterday . . . and there never will be a tomorrow. It is all one long to-day. When the man in the hill was you were too, and he still is now you are here; but of these things you will know when you are older, that is if you will only continue to drink me."

Wood Magic is perhaps more a book about childhood than it is a children's book, and in its diverse purposes it is seriously flawed. Nevertheless, it is still light years away from Mrs. Trimmer's *The History of the Robins* and Mrs. Gatty's *Parables from Nature,* and it is the first genuine animal fantasy in children's literature.

In reference to a child's play, and education through nature and the animal world, Rudyard Kipling's India is not all that far removed from Richard Jefferies's Wiltshire. In an early scene in *The Jungle Book*— "Mowgli's Brothers"—Mowgli plays with pebbles as the wolves decide his fate. He romps with Baloo the bear and Bagheera the panther and idles within the coils of the serpent Kaa in a scene as sensuous as that of Sir Bevis and the wind. All the animals become Mowgli's teachers: Baloo imposes the kindly and necessary discipline of the housemaster of an English public school, Bagheera supplies the sophistication of an Oscar Wilde, and Kaa, the traditional wisdom of the serpent, while the wolves are the epitome of family loyalty. Together they teach Mowgli (named "Little Frog" by Mother Wolf) the Law of the Jungle, of which the most important rule is: "But kill not for pleasure of killing and *seven times never kill Man!*" In spite of being a child, Mowgli is the Lord of the Jungle (certainly a forerunner of Edgar Rice Burroughs's *Tarzen of the Apes,* 1914), and so great is his human power that the animals can look him in between the eyes only for half a minute. Mowgli learns his lessons well, but it is his human intelligence that allows him to outwit the Banaderlog (the monkeys), drive Shere Khan (the tiger) to his death, and save the whole jungle from the slaughter of the Red Dogs.

Kipling's chief art in the Mowgli stories, which form the bulk of *The Jungle Books,* lies in his convincing mingling of the animal world with that of humans. The animals are anthropomorphized just enough to give them strong and distinctive personalities; so while their speech and thoughts reflect certain types of human beings, their feelings and habits are always those of their own species. It is the superiority of mankind, however, that is Kipling's main concern. In his first contact with his own kind, Mowgli shows himself as the true "noble savage." All his intelligence, compassion, and disdain for those who break "the Law of the Jungle" are brought into play when he rescues the native man and woman who "adopted" him from the superstitious villagers who are going to burn them alive. That Kipling intended such reality to be the strongest force in *The Jungle Books*—as it was in *Puck of Pook's Hill*—can be seen in the first story he wrote about Mowgli, although he is not so named in it. He appears as a young man in "In the Rukh," from *Many Inventions* (1893), who is inducted into the Indian Forest Service because of his uncanny knowledge of the jungle and his affinity with the animals. His employers accept that he has been raised by wolves because of the marks on his knees and elbows, and this is the only aspect of the tale where there is even a hint of the fantastic.

In their mythic sense of the beginning of things, *The Just So Stories*— "How the Camel Got Its Hump," the elephant its trunk, the leopard its spots, the rhinoceros its skin, (excluding "The Cat that Walked by Himself" and "The Butterfly that Stamped")—are pure fantasy. The "once upon a time" opening is given new zest by the sing-song phrase, "In the high and far-off times, O Best Beloved." They are the funniest and most playful stories in children's literature and certainly also the most stylistic. They are so perfect in their construction and language that they demand to be told or read aloud:

> Still ran Dingo—Yellow Dog Dingo—always hungry, grinning like a rat-trap, never getting nearer, never getting farther—ran after Kangaroo.
> He had to!
> Still ran Kangaroo—Old Man Kangaroo. He ran through the ti-trees; he ran through the mulga. . . .
> He had to!

The words Kipling uses have either a childish twist—"he was filled with 'satiable curtiosity" and "he was most 'scrutiatingly idle"—or they have a magnificent adult ring to them—"more than oriental splendour" and "two piggy eyes and few manners." Wordplay is abundant. In "How the Leopard Got Its Spots," the Ethiopian says to the Leopard: "'You take Baviaan's advice too. He told you to go into spots.' . . . 'So I did' [said the Leopard]. 'I went into this spot with you, and a lot of good it has done me.'" This kind of verbal wit is for children, but the whole underlying joke of the "how" stories is for adults. Here Kipling is playing with the Darwinian theory of evolution by adaptation, and if children do not understand this banter (and they probably do not), it is Kipling's way of uniting a child and an adult audience for his stories, the most successful way for perpetuating one's work.

Like *The Jungle Books,* the world Kipling describes in *The Just So Stories* is a natural one, somewhat touched with a romantic vision; but it all exists, chiefly recollected from Kipling's life in India and his journeyings in Africa. His geography and natural history are impeccable and clearly divorced from his playful exaggerations. The "great grey-green greasy Limpopo River, all set about with fever trees" in "The Elephant's Child" is real. So is the African veldt with its "forest full of tree trunks all 'sclusively speckled and sprotted and spottled, dotted and splashed and slashed and hatched and cross-hatched with shadows" in "How the Leopard Got Its Spots"; and "the starfish and the garfish, and the crab and the dab, and the plaice and the daice, and the skate and his mate, and the mackereel and the pickereel and the really truly twirly-whirly eel" in "How the Whale Got Its Throat" swim in the same waters as the whale. They all are very visual stories. It is perhaps to be regretted that Kipling occasionally chose to drop the first syllable of a long and rather difficult word that a child might have difficulty pronouncing, but the words are in tune with the whole jocular spirit of the stories and are more satisfying to the ear than L. Frank Baum's truncation of simple words in some of the *Oz* books. Both in their word-magic and their link with myth, *The Just So Stories* convince because we believe that things happened "just so."

In the works of Beatrix Potter (which span thirty years), we come to that great anomaly of animal fantasy—wild creatures often dressed in clothes and often housed in (nearly) human quarters yet with their animal natures retained to the utmost degree. The clothes are always appropriate to both the animal and the occasion. For example, Mrs. Tiggy-winkle, the hedgehog, wears a cap that shows her quills; Mr. Tod, the villainous fox, is in the attire of an Edwardian country gentleman; and Tom Kitten has grown so plump that when he is put into his best and most uncomfortable clothes, the buttons pop off.

Like Lewis Carroll, Beatrix Potter had a host of child friends with whom she corresponded assiduously. She had an instinctive knowledge of what would please them, and this included her drawings from real life, around which she gradually spun her simple stories. Her field and farm animals are the result of years of study of them on her family's annual migrations to the north of England. Some were even kept as pets in her London home. Her interiors, especially kitchens (how she loved them!), were drawn and furnished from personal observation of and participation in country life. The doll's house in *The Tale of Two Bad Mice* (1904) was built by her publisher, who provided photographs of it and searched London for appropriate doll's house food. Potter's skill in drawing in miniature was developed over years of copying flora and fauna from books of natural history and specimens in London museums. Her artwork cannot be divorced from her texts; both are meticulous creations.

Beatrix Potter's art dictated her writing. It is accurate, visual, and as fresh as crisp lettuce. She hardly uses an adverb; adjectives are only for the precise description of sensory experience, to match an illustration, or to describe an atmosphere that cannot be shown in a picture. The coat the tailor is making in *The Tailor of Gloucester* (1902) is of "cherry-coloured corded silk," and when Lucie enters Mrs. Tiggy-winkle's kitchen, "There was a nice hot singey smell; and at the table with an iron in her hand stood a very stout short person. . . . "

With the exception of *The Tailor of Gloucester,* none of Potter's books has fantasy at its core. There is, of course, the "speech" of the animal characters and there are the incidental actions that are so often visual puns: the mice in *Two Bad Mice* act as naughty, destructive children, and the squirrels in *The Tale of Squirrel Nutkin* (1903) use their tails as sails. It is these slight, humanizing touches that move the animals on to a human level so that we care deeply about what happens to them.

Regarding animal fantasy, however, Beatrix Potter is the greatest realist of the Edwardian age and possibly of all time. All the animals are shown in their natural surroundings, which are as accurately portrayed as her interiors; and in spite of being "dressed animals," they are more frequently shown in their own fur, feathers, and skin. She was too clear-eyed and clear-headed an observer of animal life to ignore its predatory aspects, and from these stem most of her plot lines. Peter Rabbit's father has been consumed in Mrs. McGregor's pie dish, the rabbits are afraid of Mr. Tod, the trout is food for Mr. Jeremy Fisher, Johnny Town-Mouse has to hide from the cat, and Simpkin the cat yearns after the mice in the tailor of Gloucester's kitchen. In *The Tale of Ginger and Pickles* (1909), Ginger, the yellow tomcat, and Pickles, the terrier, keep a shop for the animals. Ginger usually requests Pickles to serve the mice, "because he said it made his mouth water":

> "I have the same feeling about rats," replied Pickles, "but it would never do to eat our own customers; they would leave us and go to Tabitha Twitchit's."
> "On the contrary, they would go nowhere," replied Ginger gloomily.

Although her stories were often first conceived as picture-letters to the many children to whom she wrote, they were honed and polished over and over again, as is attested to in Leslie Linder's *A History of the Writings of Beatrix Potter*.[8] Potter does not shy away from difficult words: "It is said that the effect of eating too much lettuce is soporific" (from *The Tale of Peter Rabbit*, 1902), or "My Uncle Bouncer has displayed a lamentable want of discretion for his years," said Peter reflectively, "but there are two hopeful circumstances" (from *The Tale of Mr. Tod*, 1912). Of course, there is also a liberal sprinkling of period words: *clear-starcher, roly-poly pudding, goffered,* all of which produce a feeling of understanding within their pictorial context even if they are not now (or perhaps even then) current or "popular" words. It is easy to believe that when Potter felt that her style needed disciplining, she re-read the King James Bible. Believable pictures and simple, believable stories, told directly to the children she knew, gave pleasure not only to their original recipients but later to millions of children in the nursery-age group. Beatrix Potter provided the very young with their own classics.

8. Leslie Linger, *A History of the Writings of Beatrix Potter* (London: Frederick Warne & Co.), 1971.

She also had a sound business sense: "She wanted little books for little hands to hold"; and they had to be inexpensive: "All my little friends happen to be shilling people," she wrote to her publisher.

In a somewhat tongue-in-cheek essay, Graham Greene wrote a critique of Beatrix Potter's works as if he were dealing with one of the great names in literature.[9] However, in the midst of the fun, his admiration for her shines through. In its totality, Beatrix Potter's craft has a very wide range, both graphically and emotionally. Each book is a little drama, modeled on the structure of a folktale—a brief introduction, a building up of suspense, and a happy ending: Peter Rabbit escapes Mr. MrGregor, Tom Kitten is not made into "a kitten dumpling roly-poly pudding" (in *The Roly-Poly Pudding,* 1908), and Jemima Puddle-Duck survives the attentions of Mr. Fox to enjoy maternity (in *The Tale of Jemima Puddle-Duck,* 1908). If there is a moral to any of these tales, it is only that small animals have to be very careful and very clever if they want to live.

Kenneth Grahame's riverbank world is far more idealized than Beatrix Potter's barnyards, gardens, and hedges, or Rudyard Kipling's Indian jungle; and his animals are almost completely humanized. The Thames is a river flowing out of Eden, and Rat, Mole, and Badger are its rightful inhabitants; they are princes of their kind, and *The Wind in the Willows* lives on because of them, along with that disturber of the peace, Mr. Toad.

Who can forget Mole throwing down his paintbrush and exclaiming, "'Bother!' and 'O blow!' and also 'Hang spring-cleaning!'"; or Rat, who believes that "there is *nothing*—absolutely nothing—half so much worth doing as simply messing about in boats"; or Badger, who has learned how to wait and be patient? And who has not wanted to drive a motorcar like Mr. Toad? All of these animals first appeared as characters in bedtime stories that Grahame told his only son, Alistair, who elected "moles and giraffes and water rats" as subjects.[10] (Happily for the English countryside, Grahame discarded the giraffes.) Toad also made an early appearance in this nightly riverside saga. These storytelling sessions perhaps account for the episodic structure of the book (most chapters are complete in themselves), but there are underlying links to them.

9. Graham Greene, "Beatrix Potter," in *Collected Essays* (London: The Bodley Head, 1969), 232–40.

10. Peter Green, *Beyond the Wild Wood: The World of Kenneth Grahame* (Exeter, England: Webb & Bower, 1982), 137.

The first link is the very real presence of the River, which Mole finds on his first day of liberation from his underground home:

> He sat on the bank, while the river still chattered on to him, a babbling processing of the best stories in the world, sent from the heart of the earth to be told at last to the insatiable sea.

Here he meets the Water Rat, who introduces him to the joys—and perils—of sculling, and provides a picnic lunch of cold chicken and

> coldtonguecoldhamcoldbeefpickeldgherkins—
> saladfrenchrollscressandwidgespottedmeat
> gingerbeerlemonadesodawater—

Like Edith Nesbit and Beatrix Potter, Grahame knew the appeal of food to children.

Beyond the River is the Wild Wood where the river-bankers do not go very much, as Rat tells Mole. It is inhibited by

> "Weasels—and stoats—and foxes—and so on. They're all right in a way—I'm very good friends with them—pass the time of day when we meet, and all that—but they break out sometimes, there's no denying it, and then—well you can't really trust them, and that's the fact."

Through Rat, Mole meets the other friendly animals, Otter, Badger, the field mice—and wealthy Mr. Toad. Toad provides the counterpoint to the stable life of Rat and Badger. When we meet him, he has already "taken up" sailing, punting, and house-boating. Caravaning is his next fad, and then—he falls in love with the motorcar! His arrest for speeding, his imprisonment, and his escape while disguised as a washerwoman are among the few truly comic episodes in fantasy. Toad's incarceration has given the weasels and stoats the opportunity to seize his manor, but under the generalship of Badger, the threesome—Rat, Mole, and Toad—recapture the castle in a scene of humorous "derring-do." With a touch of irony, Grahame entitled this chapter "The Return of Ulysses." In the classical tradition of great comedy, all the disorder returns to order; even Toad promises to behave, but we rather hope that he will not. By this time, we, the readers, have forgotten that our heroic friends are animals. Grahame strives, at times even valiantly, to remind us of their animality:

> No animal, according to the rules of animal-etiquette, is ever expected to do anything strenuous, or heroic, or even moderately active during the off-season of winter.

However, the effort does not work, and more importantly, it does not matter that it does not work.

Rat and Mole and Toad and Badger may have been created for a child's pleasure, but *The Wind in the Willows* is also a multi-layered book, the most complex of all Edwardian fantasies. Its true genesis lies in the two semi-autobiographical accounts of Grahame's childhood that first brought the author to public attention and to his views of Edwardian society. *The Golden Age* (1895) and *Dream Days* (1898) are a series of vignettes describing incidents in the lives of Kenneth Grahame and his brothers and sister when they lived with their grandmother in Berkshire, close to the Thames. Except for a slight intrusion of governesses, mandatory church-going and visiting, the children were free of adult supervision to such an extent that it is difficult to remember that Grahame was a Victorian child rather than an Edwardian one. The glow around the children's lives was golden and dreamy, yet they themselves were sensitive and keen observers of adults (the Olympians, as they called them), whom the children saw as wasting their power and freedom:

> Indeed, it was one of the most hopeless features in their character (when we troubled ourselves to waste a thought on them: which wasn't often) that, having absolute licence to indulge in the pleasures of life, they could get no good of it. They might dabble in the pond all day, hunt the chickens, climb trees in the most uncompromising Sunday clothes; . . . yet they never did any one of these things.[11]

When adults did intrude on the children's lives, their dictas were like the bursting of a bubble, the destruction of the play of the imagination. In the chapter of *Dream Days* called "Its Walls Were of Jasper," the youth-

11. Kenneth Grahame, *The Golden Age and Dream Days* (London: The Bodley Head, 1962), 19.

ful narrator describes his fascination with a picture in the dining room, which showed a medieval scene of a walled town. Try as he might, the young observer cannot imagine what lies beyond the wall. He feels constantly balked. One day, while taken on a visit to a wealthy household, he escapes the adult chatter and finds his way to the library, where to his surprise and joy he finds a book (in a foreign language) filled with glowing colored pictures of his walled city and what is inside it. He is just about to savor the greatest joy of his dream picture—to embark on a ship to sail to a happy island—when the book is "ravished from his grasp" by its irate owner. It is not an incident that any child would ever forget, much less Kenneth Grahame, who, we assume, is the unnamed boy in the book.

The Golden Age, Dream Days, and The Wind in the Willows are not linked through animal lore; animals are hardly mentioned in the first two books. However, these books all have a feeling of a private separate world. Just as the children live apart from the grown-ups, so the animals keep to themselves. As Rat tells Mole:

> "Beyond the Wild Wood comes the Wide World, . . . And that's
> something that doesn't matter, either to you or me. I've never been
> there, and I'm never going, nor you, either, if you've got any sense
> at all. Don't ever refer to it again, please."

The young narrator of The Golden Age and Dream Days has moments of intense happiness, even ecstasy, and such moments are relived again in The Wind in the Willows as Mole returns to his home and when Rat and Mole hear the music of Pan in the chapter "The Piper at the Gates of Dawn."

It is a tribute to Grahame's art that The Wind in the Willows is both a timeless book for children and an evocation of the Edwardian Age for adults. Into it he poured all his love for unspoiled nature and his fear and dislike of changes that were already afoot in England. This attitude would suggest a use of a high degree of symbolism, but Grahame opts instead for a simple personification of various animals. Toad, of course, with his passion for cars is the heralder of a force that was already destroying the green and peaceful countryside. Love of the open road can be felt in much of the literature of the time, such as Jeffrey Farnol's The Broad Highway, which was a best-seller in 1910. The car as a menace is shown not only in *The Wind in the Willows* but also in Marie Corelli's adult fantasy *The Devil's Motor,* in which Satan appears over the earth amid "the stench and muffled roar of a huge Car" to call mankind to Hell: "Come, tie your pigmy chariots to the sun," says the Father of Lies, "and so be drawn into its flaming vortex of perdition. . . . "[12] Rat and Mole and Badger—especially Badger—are the threatened country gentry, and although they win the battle with the Wild Wooders, who are so crass that they keep coal in the bathtub in Toad Hall, we know, with hindsight, that they will not win the war. Social change is in the air.

The Wind in the Willows may be a eulogy for a life that was already past, and certainly Grahame was as much a confessional writer as Charles Kingsley or George MacDonald, but neither his nostalgia for a lost childhood nor his satirical view of many aspects of Edwardian life can dispel the feeling of being "surprised by joy" as one enters the world of the Riverbank.

Walter de la Mare's *The Three Mullah Mulgars* (1910), later reprinted as *The Three Royal Monkeys,* is a completely internal book. It owes nothing to literary trends or social concepts. It simply exists in its own time and space. Thumb, Thimble, and Nod are the three royal monkeys, who have been taught by their father Seelem, brother to Assasimmon, Prince of the Valleys of Tishnar, to "walk upright, never to taste blood, and never, unless in danger or despair, to climb trees or to grow a tail." Their father leaves them to find his way back to Tishnar, and their mother dies. Before she dies, she gives Thumb and Thimble each a White Man's jacket with curved metal hooks, and to Nod, the little coat of mountain-sheep's wool, with its nine ivory buttons. To Nod, however, she also gives a Wonderstone, for "he is a Nizza-Neela, and has magic in him." The mother's last words are to urge her children to follow their father, words that the Mulgars forget until months later when Nod causes their hut to burn down. Then they remember and determine to set off into the forest to seek their uncle in Tishnar and their royal heritage; and so they

> combed themselves, and stood up to their trouble, and thought stubbornly, as far as their monkey-wits would let them, only of the future (which is easier to manage than the past).

12. Jefferson Hunter, *Edwardian Fiction* (Cambridge, Mass.: Harvard Univ. Pr. 1982), 46.

With these words, de la Mare's approach to animal fantasy is revealed. Thumb, Thimble, and Nod behave, react, think, and speak as we become convinced that monkeys should. They have a touch of the extraordinary that derives from their royal blood, but basically they are primitives in a primitive world. When Nod is captured by the sailor Andy Battle, who tries to teach Nod English, we are surprised both at the closeness of the human and the animal world and at the gap between them. Nod is the poetic child of the human race. Whereas monkeys are treated with scorn by Kipling in *The Jungle Books* and as friendly assistants in Hugh Lofting's later *The Story of Doctor Dolittle* (1920), de la Mare's Mulgars have their own dignity and integrity. When Nod capers before Andy Battle, for example, he does so deliberately to amuse him and to further his own unselfish ends.

The Three Mullah Mulgars is a traditional quest story—the three monkeys adventure through forest and swamp, and over river and mountain to reach their goal. The hero is Nod, the little monkey in the sheepskin coat with its nine ivory buttons, who clutches his Wonderstone. Like the youngest son in the fairy tale, he is never motivated by greed or selfishness, and his heart is as big as his tiny body. It is Nod who outwits Immanala. Immanala means "unstoried, nameless, unknown, darkness, secrecy. All these the word means . . . So, too, is the dark journey to death or the Third Sleep." This mysticism aside, Nod's tricking of Immanala is as dramatic an incident as Mowgli's triumph over Shere Kan the Tiger or the Red Dogs in *The Jungle Books*, but it is far more intensely emotional. The Wonderstone, although a talisman, has few magic properties; instead, it is a reflection of Nod's own sweet nature. He is even charmed out of it by the Water Maiden, whose sad little song Nod cannot resist when she asks him to lend the Wonderstone to her. It has the perfection of a song in a Shakespearian play:

> Bubble, Bubble,
>   Swim to see
> Oh, how beautiful
>   I be.

> Fishes, Fishes,
>   Finned and fine,
> What's your gold
>   Compared with mine.

Why, then, has
    Wise Tishnar made
One so lovely,
    One so sad?

Lone am I,
    And can but make
A little song,
    For singing's sake.

The Mulgars reach Tishnar, and there the story ends. It is the journey that is important for Tishnar can mean many things. But mostly it "means that which cannot be thought about in words, or told, or expressed."

The Three Mullah Mulgars is set apart from all other children's fantasies in its use of an invented language. By comparison, Tolkien uses a linguistic pattern in his *The Lord of the Rings* to convince us of the reality of his Middle-earth. Because it is used in three volumes, with constant repetition, his language is no barrier even to the most casual reader. Similarly, Anthony Burgess's futuristic slang in *A Clockwork Orange* can be read as easily as plain English. On the other hand, the monkeys in *The Three Mullah Mulgars* have a wonderful language of their own, but one that cannot be decoded. It is filled with proper names such as Arakkaboa, Oomgarnuggas, Immanala, and Noomanossi, which have a feeling of perfection to them in their application. De la Mare also plays with words as does Kipling in the *Just So Stories*—elephants are "elephantos." There are also syllabic, onomatopoeic songs:

Talaheeti sul magloon
Olgar, ulgar Nanga-noon;
Ah-mi, sulani!

This is the language of the Mullah Mulgars; the ordinary forest Mulgars have an even more primitive speech. Such uses of language all evoke a feeling of a poetic, primitive world. It is as if children were playing with words or inventing new ones to satisfy some emotional need for which their ordinary vocabulary is deficient.

Passages of a great and simple beauty can be found in de la Mare's work and also many with a rush of action, as when Nod outwits the

Gunga-Mulgar (Gorilla). There is no doubt, however, that the language, compressed as it is into one book (although a lengthy one), will daunt modern children, who seem to prefer the idioms of their own times. This preference means the loss of one of the most evocative, open-ended books in children's literature and one of the most delicate treatments of animals.

The *Magic Pudding* (1918) by the Australian writer Norman Lindsay certainly shows the diversity of animal fantasy—although it perhaps should simply be described as a comedy, and a rare one at that—in children's literature. This book has dressed talking animals: Bunyip Bluegum (a koala bear), Sam Sawnoff (a penguin), and two villains, a Possum and a Wombat. Bunnyip Bluegum, Sam Sawnoff, and Bill Barnacle, the sailor, are traveling throughout Australia, in picaresque fashion, with a magic pudding named Albert, who can walk and talk. He is a "cut-an'-come-again Puddin'"; "the more you eats the more you gets." By virtue of his outspokenness and irascibility, Albert really belongs in the company of Edith Nesbit's Psammead:

> "I am delighted to make your acquaintance, Albert," said Bunyip.
> "No soft soap from total strangers," said the Puddin' rudely.

The "three musketeers" are followed by Puddin'-thieves, who provide most of the hilarity and who finally get their comeuppance. The language moves from the deliberately pompous:

> Bunyip Blueglum reproved this despondency. "Come, come, this is no time for giving way to despair. Let us, rather, by the fortitude of our bearing prove ourselves superior to this misfortune and, with the energy of justly enraged men, pursue these malefactors, who have so richly deserved our vengeance. . . . "

to Australian slang:

> "Well, all I can say is that if yer don't take yer dial outer the road I'll bloomin' well take an' bounce a gibber off yer crust." . . .

The *Magic Pudding* is not well known outside of Australia, where, quite rightly, it is considered a classic. Especially when considered in the midst of the "sweetness and light" of many English fantasies of the time, this story is a treasure indeed.

In comparison with the nuances of Walter de la Mare's *The Three Mullah Mulgars*, Hugh Lofting's *Doctor Dolittle* books appear as simplicity itself. The books began in reality as Lofting observed the treatment of animals while he was a soldier in the trenches during World War I. "If we made the animals take the same chances we did ourselves, why did we not give them similar attention when wounded?"[13] The idea of an animal doctor was worked out in the letters he wrote home to his two children, but there is no mention of the war in *The Story of Doctor Dolittle* (1920). The book begins with that magical phrase, "once upon a time" and proceeds to tell of a respected medical doctor who prefers animals to people.

> Besides the gold-fish in the pond at the bottom of his garden, he had rabbits in the pantry, white mice in his piano, a squirrel in the linen closet and a hedgehog in the cellar. . . . But his favourite pets were Dab-Dab the duck, Jip the dog, Gub-Gub the baby pig, Polynesia the parrot, and the owl Too-Too.

Soon there are so many animals, including a crocodile, that the "Best People" will no longer come to Doctor Dolittle; and his sister-housekeeper, upset at both the animals and the lack of money, flounces off to get married. It is then that the Cat's Meat-Man suggests that Doctor Dolittle become an animal doctor and Polynesia, that he learn animal language. Soon the doctor can communicate with all animals, birds, fish, and eventually plants.

In this idea lies the originality and the credibility of *The Story of Doctor Dolittle* as an animal fantasy. Just as one learns the language of one's adopted country in order to be able to maneuver in it, so too does Doctor Dolittle move easily among the animals with his newfound knowledge. He can now tend them more skillfully and practically (the farm horse, for instance, can tell Doctor Dolittle that he needs glasses), and he can respond to their needs for a better life.

Beginning with the second book, *The Voyages of Doctor Dolittle* (1923)—there were 13 books in all—Doctor Dolittle has a young assis-

13. Humphrey Carpenter and Mari Prichard, eds. *The Oxford Companion to Children's Literature* (Oxford Univ. Pr. 1984), 324.

tant, Tommy Stubbins, who also becomes his biographer and recounts the Doctor's achievements and successes with the detail and admiration that James Boswell accorded to Dr. Johnson. These achievements are considerable. He not only tends his own now extensive menagerie at his home in Puddleby-on-the-Marsh in England, but he also cures the monkeys in Africa (in *The Story of Doctor Dolittle*) and the insects on the moon (in *Doctor Dolittle in the Moon*, 1928). As the *deus ex machina* of the animal world, Doctor Dolittle oversees all the animals' plans for a better life, although the animals do make suggestions. According to the various books, the animals band into societies, set down rules and regulations for living together, learn to read and write, form an orchestra, go caravaning, grow food, worry about a lack of funds, have adventures, and solve mysteries. Fantasy here ceases to count, as it is all such a familiar world. There is more of a touch of the fantastic when the Doctor and Tommy Stubbins—and usually Polynesia, Chee-Chee, Dab-Dab, and Gub-Gub—go a-voyaging. In Africa, they meet the Pushmi-Pullyu, who has a head at each end of his body; the monkeys form a bridge with their tails so that the Doctor and his friends can cross a gorge; and a giant moth takes them to the moon, which is far from being a dead planet.

The books shine with the doctor's benevolence and simple good humor. His appearance is extraordinarily well shown in Lofting's own illustrations, where Doctor Dolittle moves through the pages with his ever-present top hat like a benign W.C. Fields. Beyond his goodness and unflappability in any circumstance, Doctor Dolittle has little personality; yet he has won for himself a place in the pantheon of children's literature. Like Frank Baum with the Oz books, it is the totality of Lofting's inventive powers that is impressive, although both writers found an immediate audience with their first books because of their storytelling abilities. The writer and critic Edward Blishen best explained the appeal of the Doctor Dolittle books (and the Oz books) when he observed that "in their rambling amplitude, their very unevenness, they are like life itself, and the children can live in them, in a most generous sense."[14]

The *Story of Doctor Dolittle* has been described as a children's "classic." Hugh Walpole, in the preface to a 1962 edition, compared it to *Alice's Adventures in Wonderland* and put it in a higher category than

14. John Rowe Townsend, *Written for Children* (Harmondsworth, England: Kestral Bks., 1965), 167.

The Wind in the Willows. His comments are over-praise. While it is true that any classic has a basic simplicity of theme and plot, as in music, it is the variations on a theme, the orchestration, and the "fillers" that lift a piece out of the ordinary. The Doctor Dolittle books lack the images and the multi-level structure that are the marks of true fantasy and that the reader can accept at their most basic or return to time and again for richer interpretations.

The Doctor Dolittle books have been criticized in modern times for racism[15] and with some justification. The good Doctor paid the animal, bird, insect, and plant worlds the highest compliment of all in wanting to communicate with them on their terms, but it was not an idea that he transferred to the blacks whom he succored in Africa. In this case, he is certainly the "great white father" helping the ignorant. Interestingly, the book's patronizing tone generally comes from the animals. In *The Story of Doctor Dolittle,* for instance, Dab-Dab comments on Prince Bumpo, who wants to be white and whose face becomes so through the Doctor's medical mixtures: "He looked better the way he was, I thought. But he'd never be anything but ugly, no matter what colour he was made." Doctor Dolittle, who feels uneasy about the trick that has been played upon the African Prince, even though it was the only means of escape from the King's prison, remarks that "he had a good heart" and that " 'handsome is as handsome does.' " The Doctor Dolittle stories are very much books of their time. Hugh Lofting wrote them when the British Empire was at its height and "the white man's burden" was taken for granted. He was also a long resident of the United States and traveled in Africa on his engineering jobs and was probably unconsciously parroting the social mores of the day toward blacks. In any case, revisionist principles cannot be applied to literature, and the Doctor Dolittle books will have to be appreciated for their look at the animal world rather than the human.

In a related area of animal fantasy, toys are used as characters because they are very real to children as an imaginative outlet for children's fantasies. The earliest toy animal fantasy was Margery Williams Bianco's *The Velveteen Rabbit* (1922), who is loved into being "Real" by the little boy who owns him. When the toy rabbit is finally discarded, he is turned

15. Donnarae MacCann and Gloria Woodward, eds. *The Black American in Books for Children* (Metuchen, N.J.: Scarecrow, 1972), 78–88.

into a real rabbit by the nursery fairy who takes care of all playthings that the children have "REALLY" loved. With William Nicholson's charming, full-page, color drawings, it becomes a picture-storybook for younger readers and is one of the few such books, even in our own time, that has genuine depth and emotion. The little rabbit's question is a profound one: "What is REAL?" he asks one day. It is a question that philosophers have wrestled with, but here in this little book is answer enough on a child's terms. Not only are you real when you are loved, but when you are real you do not mind being hurt; and once you are real you cannot be ugly, "except to people who don't understand."

As real as the Velveteen Rabbit became, he was soon overshadowed by that toy bear of "very little brain," A.A. Milne's *Winnie-the-Pooh* (1926). By the 1920's, teddy bears were firmly established in the lives and hearts of young children, being given their name from President Theodore (Teddy) Roosevelt's refusal to kill a small brown bear while on a hunting trip. Pooh himself first appears in Milne's book of verses for children *When We Were Very Young* (1924) as "Teddy Bear." The last verse reads:

> A bear, however hard he tries,
> Grows tubby without exercise.
> Our Teddy Bear is short and fat,
> Which is not to be wondered at.
> But do you think it worries him
> To know that he is far from slim?
> No, just the other way about—
> He's *proud* of being short and stout.

From this verse it can be seen that Winnie-the-Pooh did indeed deserve a book to himself, and Milne found his inspiration in his son's nursery.

Pooh was Christopher Milne's oldest companion, later to be joined by Piglet and Eeyore the donkey. Rabbit and Owl were A.A. Milne's inventions, and Kanga (the kangaroo) and Tigger (the little tiger) were presents to Christopher from his parents, "not just for the delight they might give to their new owner, but also for their literary possibilities."[16] Pooh, Piglet, and Eeyore were "real" to Christopher before his father

16. Christopher Milne, *The Enchanted Places* (Penguin Books, 1976), 90–91.

put them into stories for him, which somewhat explains their sturdy and lovable qualities. They had also taken on the expressions and shapes that resulted from much love and use before Ernest Shepard came to the nursery to draw them from real life, as it were. The combination of Milne and Shepard was as felicitous as that of Kenneth Grahame and Shepard in *The Wind in the Willows,* but both *Winnie-the-Pooh* and *The House at Pooh Corner* (1928) show a simpler expression in art and story than does Grahame's minor Edwardian classic. Whether it is the dot of the eye that gives Pooh Bear his expression or Piglet's ears flying in the wind or the numerous "hums" of Pooh, both books are perfect expressions of a young child's play with toy animals.

The Pooh stories are made up of a series of small situations, each complete in itself. Pooh gets stuck in Rabbit's window because he has eaten too much honey, and while he is waiting to get thin, he asks Rabbit to read to him "a sustaining book such as would comfort a wedged bear in great tightness." There is an "expoition" to find a pole, even if it is not the North Pole; Pooh also invents a game called "Pooh-sticks," and Tigger finds out what he likes to eat. Each chapter is perfect for bedtime reading, which is the way millions of children have heard them.

Milne's craftsmanship lies in his ability to make the animals come alive as *toys,* not as animals. Pooh and Tigger have neither teeth nor claws, and Piglet does not need to fear that he is being slated for breakfast. Certain characteristics adopted from the characters' nursery appearances are merely emphasized. There is Pooh's paunch, for instance, Tigger's bounciness, Kanga's maternalism for her baby, and Eeyore's pessimism. Most of the time, the characters are revealed through action or conversation—not through description. "I might have known," said Eeyore. "After all, one can't complain. I have my friends. Somebody spoke to me only yesterday." Although we laugh at them, Milne's characters are never figures of ridicule; nor are they used for higher levels of meaning. Indeed, Milne makes sure that his child readers, in the person of Christopher Robin, are always just enough ahead of the animals to give children a great deal of satisfaction and pride. Readers know that Pooh and Piglet are following their own tracks in the snow and that Pooh and Rabbit have taken sticks from Eeyore's own house to build him a new one. In this sense, *Winnie-the-Pooh* and *The House at Pooh Corner* are very clever books, indeed.

In his own child's childhood, Milne found his own special genius. His first fantasy, *Once On a Time* (1917), is in the gentle tradition of William Thackeray's *The Rose and the Ring. A Gallery of Children* (1925) is an anthology of insipid fantasies that is valuable now only for its illustrations by H. Willebeck le Mair. Christopher Milne was a protected, adored child, and it is in a protected world in an Arcadian forest that he lives with his toy animals who, in turn, adore him. His father did not surround him with Wordsworthian clouds of glory; he did not write of the depths of a child's sadness or its heights of wonder. The miniature world Milne created is as safe as the nursery; Heffalumps and Woozles are hunted but never seen. His prose does not have the evocative power of Kenneth Grahame's or the innate magic of Walter de la Mare's, but he could effectively express the small delights of childhood and also its childish egotism. Here he has no equal.

Perhaps Milne's greatest triumph was that he knew when to stop. *The House at Pooh Corner,* unlike most sequels, is as peerless as its prototype; but children grow up and nursery toys are put away or given away, and so boys and bears must part:

> But wherever they go, and whatever happens to them on the way, in that enchanted place on the top of the Forest, a little boy and his Bear will always be playing.

For that, we should be grateful.

. . . and After

The Edwardian Age ended officially with the death of Edward VII in 1910, but its influence on children's literature lingered for another two decades, as can be seen in the works of Hugh Lofting and A.A. Milne. It was, all in all, an era of outright sentimentality in children's literature, as it also was in much of adult literature. Romantic and escape writers such as Marie Corelli, Jeffrey Farnol with *The Broad Highway,* Robert Hichens with *The Garden of Allah,* and Elinor Glyn with *Three Weeks* were on the best-sellers' list. "Sentimentality," wrote A.A. Milne, "is an appeal to the emotions not warranted by the facts."[17] The fact about us human

17. A.A. Milne, *Autobiography* (New York: Dutton, 1939), 287.

beings is that we all have faults or at least eccentricities, and it is a fact that the best fantasists did not overlook in the portrayal of their child and surrogate animal characters. These writers did, however, suggest that the world and everyone in it was "all right":

> "Tigger is all right *really*," said Piglet lazily.
> "Of course he is," said Christopher Robin.
> "Everybody is *really*," said Pooh. "That's what I think," said Pooh. "But I don't suppose I'm right," he said.
> "Of course you are," said Christopher Robin.

If such writers were eventually proved wrong—within their worlds almost "bounded in a nutshell"—they nonetheless revealed the best aspects of human nature: love, kindness, friendship, helpfulness, and the beauties of nature.

The success of these writers, whether in human or animal terms, is perhaps best judged against the fantasies that were overly sentimental. Mary Stewart's *The Way to Wonderland* (1917) is typical of the period in its presentation of sweet little children who, without effort, find their way into a stereotyped fairyland. The Thornton Burgess animal fantasies, as exemplified by *Old Mother West Wind* (1910), are an anthropomorphized mishmash of Beatrix Potter and Kenneth Grahame's *The Wind in the Willows,* with flatly described animals such as Peter Rabbit, Reddy Fox, Johnny Chuck, and fairy-like minions of the West Wind. Burgess's works are a perfect example of the "pathetic fallacy."

This trend, hardly ever to be repeated, is also obvious in the popular so-called realistic stories of the period: Alice Hegan Rice's *Mrs. Wiggs of the Cabbage Patch* (1901), Gene Stratton Porter's *Freckles* (1904) and *A Girl of the Limberlost* (1910), Eleanor H. Porter's *Pollyanna* (1913), Nellie McClung's *Sowing Seeds in Danny* (1908), and L.M. Montgomery's *Anne of Green Gables* (1908) and its sequels. These are American and Canadian publications (the latter two being Canadian), but British children's novels, such as Frances Hodgson Burnett's *A Little Princess* (1905) and S.R. Crockett's *Sir Toady Lion* (1897) "(this being his own first effort at the name of his favourite hero Richard Coeur-de-Lion)," contained equally romanticized views that all was well with the world when the young were in control.

The fine fantasies of the Edwardian Age—and after—escape the charge of sentimentality, although sometimes just barely. They escape it chiefly by the quality of their writing. All of their authors—Barrie, Kipling, Hudson, Grahame, de la Mare, and Milne—were craftsmen and had practiced their art for years before bringing their talents to a full blossoming in their writing for children. Edith Nesbit and Hugh Lofting were not great stylists, but both were adept storytellers and both had an ear for dialogue. Almost paradoxically, their characters become real in the midst of impossibilities, while in the realistic fiction of the period, the events are real but the protagonists are "too good to be true." An exception in this latter respect is Frances Hodgson Burnett's *The Secret Garden* (1910), where both Colin and Mary have faults in their natures that they must strive to overcome—a piece of naturalism in an otherwise sentimental plot that probably accounts for the book's continued popularity. Actually, in its emphasis on character building, *The Secret Garden* has the feel of a Victorian book rather than an Edwardian one.

Although there also were war adventure stories concerning young people in both England and the United States, World War I had no effect on fantasy neither during the war nor afterward, unless one counts the fact that *The Story of Doctor Dolittle* grew out of Hugh Lofting's wartime experiences. Fantasy may have been a means of escape for those who wrote before, during, and after those terrible war years. A.A. Milne has said that in writing *Once on a Time* "it made the war seem very far away. . . . "[18] This feeling has never been expressed as longingly as in H.G. Well's adult novel of the war, *Mr. Britling Sees It Through*. In writing home from the trenches, Mr. Britling's son asks for books:

> So send me some books, books of dreams, books about China and the willow-pattern plate and the golden age and fairyland. And send them soon and address them very carefully.[19]

His father might well have sent him the children's books of his own time.

One such book could have been *The Treasure of the Isle of Mist* by W.W. Tarn. Although first published in 1919, it was written in the win-

18. Thomas Burnett Swann, *A.A. Milne* (New York: Twayne, 1971), 66.
19. H.G. Wells, *Mr. Britling Sees It Through* (New York: Macmillan, 1916), 335.

ter of 1913 to 1914 to amuse Tarn's daughter, who was ill.[20] Fiona is an ideal child, living a lonely but happy life with her scholar-father, the Student. The conversations between Fiona and the Student have the same philosophical tone as those between the two philosophers in James Stephens's adult fantasy *The Crock of Gold* (1913), but everything is expressed in much more childlike terms. Both books, too, have the same undefinable aura of half-hinted truths.

In its plot, Tarn's book is direct enough. Fiona is given the gift of "the Search" for the treasure of the Isle of Mist by an old peddler, and along with it a bracelet. Through the bracelet's power she can understand the language of all creatures on the island. Her young friend the Urchin wants the actual treasure, and so does his uncle, Jeconiah Johnson, who is the first villain in fantasy to inhabit the real world and who sets the pace of the story. Both are abducted by the fairies and brought to trial, Jeconiah for "being a worthless character" and the Urchin because he has killed a shore-lark with a stone. Fiona, who has found her way to fairyland with the help of her bracelet and of the animals, gives up her own wish to save the Urchin, and the Urchin gives up his wish to save his uncle. Jeconiah is hypnotized into being good (for a while) and as a punishment has to tell a fairy tale to the Urchin. However, it is the Isle of Skye itself that is the principal character. No fairyland can match it. Fiona delights in the island, even during the stormy season. "No one can really love this island who only knows it in summer," she shouts above the wind. At the story's end, Fiona receives a gift from the Fairy King. The gift is in keeping with the whole spirit of the book: Fiona receives the spirit of the island, which will stay with her wherever she may go. In its serenity, its fairy-tale atmosphere—both real and imagined—its feeling of security in child-adult relations, and its humanity and wisdom, *The Treasure of the Isle of Mist* provides a fitting conclusion to this era.

20. W.W. Tarn, *The Treasure of the Isle of Mist* (London: Oxford Univ. Pr., 1959), Preface.

Chapter 5

A Box of Delights:
Fantasy of the 1920's and 1930's

In comparison with the memorable fantasies of the Victorian and Edwardian eras, those of the 1920's and 1930's appear to be rather bland. Certainly the writers stood aloof from any social considerations. No aspect of "the Gay Twenties" or the Great Depression of the Thirties or the rising clouds of World War II was allowed to impinge on fantasy. Writers for children did not see themselves as an F. Scott Fitzgerald or an Ernest Hemingway. Many of them, whether in England or the United States, opted for the short story, either the literary fairy tale, the nonsense tale, retellings of the oral tradition, or the linked story with each chapter complete in itself, a formula made popular by Edith Nesbit with *Five Children and It* and Rudyard Kipling with the Mowgli stories and *Puck of Pook's Hill*. It is possible that in England the greatest influence derived from *Joy Street,* a popular children's annual published from 1923 to 1938, which drew to its pages most of the prominent writers of the time, including Walter de la Mare, Laurence Housman, Eleanor Farjeon, and A.A. Milne. In their own separately published works, these writers continued the form that was imposed by a periodical. Thus, there are few fully sustained fantasies like George MacDonald's *The Princess and the Goblin* or L. Frank Baum's *The Wizard of Oz*.

The exigencies of World War I, of course, explain the sharp drop in the production of children's books in all genres in the Twenties, and the wish to forget the war's devastation may well account for the overall

115

mood of gentleness—a trend found in all the children's books of these two decades. The issues of *Joy Street* itself are marked by a soft poetic imagination as if its writers (and illustrators such as Edmund Dulac and Arthur Rackham) were answering Hugh Britling's call for stories of a golden age remote from reality.

Short Story Writers

Laurence Housman and Eleanor Farjeon are the exemplars of the period, although each spans several decades in their writings: Housman with *The Field of Clover* (1898), *Moonshine and Clover* (1922), *A Doorway in Fairyland* (1922), and *What O'Clock Tales* (1932), and Farjeon with *Martin Pippin in the Apple Orchard* (1921), *Martin Pippin in the Daisy-Field* (1937), and *The Little Bookroom* (1955). Laurence Housman's tales are elegant and mannered, often containing charming variations on traditional tales, but almost soporific in their total effect. A wandering minstrel is the storyteller in Eleanor Farjeon's "Martin Pippin" stories, who thus gives a feeling of the oral tradition to this author's often charmingly inventive tales. While the stories have some sturdiness to them, Martin Pippin's listeners—young maidens and little girls—are the personification of naiveté and innocence, almost cloyingly sweet. All these collections should be sipped at intervals rather than swallowed whole, for only then is the flavor of each story evident. However, all the collections contain individual stories that a storyteller would not want to be without—Housman's "The Rat-catcher's Daughter" from *A Doorway in Fairyland* and Farjeon's "Elsie Piddock Skips in Her Sleep" from *Martin Pippin in the Daisy-Field*.

While Farjeon, Housman, and others of the period put on even rosier-colored spectacles than the Edwardians when writing for children, the same charge cannot be brought against Walter de la Mare. Of all writers for children, he most defies classification. He was neither a revolutionary nor a traditionalist; he did not start a school of writing, nor did he follow the modes of time. His short story collections, such as *Broomsticks and Other Tales* (1925), are as timeless as his poems.[1] His retellings of old

1. Walter de la Mare's short stories have been reprinted many times in various collections with stories being dropped or added. Two such collections are *The Magic Jacket* (1943) and *Collected Stories for Children* (1977).

tales in *Told Again* (1927) and *Animal Stories* (1939) always have a touch that enriches the originals. His extended Aesop's fable "The Hare and the Hedgehog" is the most humorous and tellable version extant.

De la Mare's writings for adults are filled with references to children and comments on childhood. "Children," he said,

> . . . do not gape at their own innocence, or marvel at imaginations as natural to them as spectacles on an elderly nose, or sit cherubically smiling at themselves amid their trailing clouds of glory. They dwell and flourish in their own natures, preternaturally practical and crafty pygmies in the world of dull tyrannical tyrants into which it has pleased God to call them.[2]

Some of his original stories are based in folklore: "Dick and the Beanstalk" is a title that speaks for itself; "The Lovely Myfanwy" is the princess in the tower; "The Dutch Cheese" concerns malevolent and thwarted fairies; and "The Lord Fish" begins with the "Lazy Jack" theme. The youthful protagonists in these stories are indeed "pygmies" as they face the tyranny of giants, possessive fathers and brothers, and fairies and magicians. If the protagonists win by means of some craftiness, they are also motivated by love and selflessness, and they rarely have magic to help them. De la Mare treads very delicately with magic; indeed, it might be said that he is hardly interested in it. In "The Magic Jacket," for example, the old admiral believes that a jacket he was impelled to purchase as a boy changed his life and gave him his heart's desire. Now he wishes to offer it to a neglected young chalk-pavement artist, but dubiously:

> . . . In the long run we have to trust what we have in us that's constant and natural, so to speak. . . .

The magic jacket may have helped, but at story's end, the boy's natural talent is discovered and he goes off to his future without relying on magic. In "Alice's Godmother," little Alice, by holding on to her childlike sense of reality, rejects her great-great-great-great-great-great-great-great grandmother's gift of near immortality. Most fine fantasists,

2. Walter de la Mare, *Pleasures and Speculations* (Freeport, New York: Books for Libraries Press, 1969), 18.

both before and after de la Mare, have endowed their young characters with just such inner strength, which extends far beyond talismans or supernatural powers.

De la Mare was the first to write so-called "ghost" stories for children. "Alice's Godmother," "Miss Jemima," "Lucy," and "The Scarecrow" are marked by atmosphere and mood, delicate relationships, and ambivalent shades of meaning. It is ultimately up to the reader to resolve the inconclusiveness of the endings: Is the author really describing the Other World of the occult, or is it the sensitive imagination of the characters themselves that is at the core of the story? However one decides, the suspense of waiting for something indefinite to happen is a knife-edge experience and one not hitherto offered to children in their own literature. Similarly, in "The Riddle," seven orphaned children who have been given a home by their grandmother disappear one by one into an old chest that they have been forbidden to touch. However, were the children ever really in the house? Or did the old lady imagine them? The story ends thusly:

> But in her mind was a tangled skein of memories—laughter and tears, and children long ago become old-fashioned, and the advent of friends and last farewells. And gossiping fitfully, inarticulately, with herself, the old lady went down again to her window-seat.

De la Mare's longest and most moving story is "The Old Lion," which was first published in *Joy Street* and later reprinted as *Mr. Bumps and His Monkey* (1942). Mr. Bumps is a sailor, and his ship is called "The Old Lion." On a voyage to West Africa, he buys a monkey (at quite a high price, he feels); and he and Jaspar, as he calls the monkey, become great friends. On the long, monotonous voyage home, Mr. Bumps teaches Jaspar the ways of the humans and even simple speech. In England, however, Jaspar is stolen by the owner of a pet shop and so comes into the care of a showman who trains him for the stage. As with Mr. Bumps, Jaspar is treated with the greatest kindness and respect, even to having his own bank account. In his performance, Jaspar is billed as "The Master Mimic of Man." However, his true nature remains intact:

> All the time he was really and truly himself, and only himself— thinking his own thoughts, gazing out of his bright, darting, round,

dark-deepened, and now almost amber-coloured eyes over the
glare of the footlights at the people beyond. . . .

Jaspar and Mr. Bumps eventually are reunited, and the sailor, sensing
Jaspar's unhappiness and loneliness for his own kind, takes him back to
Africa. But will he be accepted? We never know. The whole aura of sadness in the story suggests not, but for de la Mare to explain completely
would be to destroy the story's suspense. One could even ask: Is the story
really fantasy?

Many of de la Mare's stories are set in old, mysterious houses such as
that described in the Introduction to his anthology of poetry Come
Hither:

> . . . It seemed to be a house which might at any moment vanish
> before your eyes, showing itself to be but the outer shell or hiding
> place of an abode still more enchanting.[3]

In contrast, the interiors of de la Mare's houses are described with the
realism of a Vermeer. So is the English countryside, although it evokes a
past time. The countryside de la Mare depicts is the open area of the
Southern Counties with fields in growth, gentle woods, winds soft and
caressing, and churchyards not so safe under the moonlight.

The child-alone, bolstered only by imagination and sensitivity, is the
common thread in de la Mare's stories. When his children have company, it is usually that of an elderly or eccentric adult. His children seem
too ethereal and fragile to climb trees or even to play with dolls; yet, for
all their seeming fragility, they face and overcome spiritual dangers. One
senses that like Simon, in de la Mare's own half-autobiographical story
that precedes Come Hither, the children "set off on a journey that has not
yet come to an end."[4]

In his writings both about childhood and for children, de la Mare was
consistent in his viewpoint. Not so Richard Hughes, whose adult novel A
High Wind in Jamaica relates—in a most chilling manner—the evil inherent in children, that can surface when children are wrenched away
from knowing and loving parental supervision. Hughes was a forerunner

3. Walter de la Mare, comp., Come Hither (London: Constable, 1962), xvii.
4. de la Mare, xxxi.

of William Golding, whose better-known novel *The Lord of the Flies* also deflates the myth of the innate goodness of children. In his books of short stories *The Spider's Palace* (1931) and *Don't Blame Me* (1940), Hughes proved himself a master of nonsense. Most of the stories have an unexpected twist, as when the bicycle turns into a crocodile at the end of "Don't Blame Me." Others are dependent upon incongruous images and punning, such as a whale who has swallowed a little girl buying a bed for her in one of London's most famous department stores in "Living in W'ales." In keeping with other writers of his time, Hughes obviously felt that the dark and complex sides of life were not suitable fare for the young themselves.

The short story form also had an appeal for writers in the United States. Irish folklore and legend came into prominence with retellings by Padraic Colum in *The King of Ireland's Son* (1916), a series of tales woven into one narrative, and in *The Island of the Mighty* (1924), stories from the Welsh Mabinogion. The Irish tales drew forth Colum's storytelling talents (he was born in Ireland) to a greater degree than did his retellings of the Greek and Norse myths in *The Adventures of Odysseus* (1918) and in *The Children of Odin* (1920). Ella Young, also an emigrant to the United States from Ireland, introduced the tales of the Gubbaun Saor in *The Wonder Smith and His Son* (1927), and the Irish hero, Finn McCool, in *The Tangle-Coated Horse* (1929). All of these collections contained universal tales of the childhood of the world. Elizabeth Coatsworth in *The Cat Who Went to Heaven* (1930) retold a Chinese legend of the Buddha, Kate Seredy in *The White Stag* (1937) softened a legend of Attila the Hun, and Katherine Gibson in *Cinders* (1939) played with the Cinderella story.

Imported legends did not appeal to the American poet Carl Sandburg, however. He created his own in three books of short stories—*Rootabaga Stories* (1922), *Rootabaga Pigeons* (1923), and *Potato Face* (1930)—and his Rootabaga Country has now passed into American mythology. It is reached by taking a ticket "to ride where the railroad tracks run off into the sky and never come back." You know when you get there because "the railroad tracks change from straight to zigzag, the pigs have bibs on, and it is the fathers and mothers who fix it." Its capital is the "Village of Liver and Onions," although the "Village of Cream Puffs" is a very nice place too. Rootabaga Country represents a geographic reality—the American Middle West. It has a railroad, a post office, ragpickers, policemen, ball games, corn, corn fairies, and popcorn. Its inhabitants are the Potato Face Blind Man, Jason Squiff, a little girl called Wing Tip the Spick, the Gray Man on Horseback, and many others who move in and out of the stories. All of these characters do things a little differently: Henry Hagglyhoagly plays the guitar with his mittens on, two skyscrapers decide to have a child, and the Rag Doll and the Broom Handle have a grand procession when they get married. For want of a better word, Sandburg's stories can be described as nonsense, but it is of a homelier sort than that of Edward Lear, Lewis Carroll, or even Richard Hughes, composed, as it were, of gingham and calico rather than tightly woven of parody and satire.

His word-magic, which is as American in speech and diction as is the Rootabaga Country itself, comes from his constant use of alliteration— Blixie Bimber, Bozo the Button Buster—and onomatopoeia:

> The train ran on and on. It came to the place where the railroad tracks run off into the blue sky. And it ran on and on chick chick-a-chick chick-a-chick chick-a-chick.

and euphony:

> When the dishes are washed at night time and the cool of the evening has come in summer or the lamps and fires are lit for the night in winter, then the fathers and mothers in the Rootabaga Country sometimes tell the young people the story of the White Horse Girl and the Blue Wind Boy.

Sandburg's was the most original voice in American children's literature in two decades.

Stories of Magic

The first full-length fantasy of the 1920's, after Hugh Lofting's *The Story of Doctor Dolittle,* was John Masefield's *The Midnight Folk* (1927). Masefield, poet laureate of England, had the sea in his blood, and he extolled it in such poems as "Cargoes" and "Sea-fever." There is more than a whiff of the sea about *The Midnight Folk.* There is a treasure lost at sea, a ship that sails out of a picture and is captained by a Water-Rat, and a dive beneath the sea with mermaids. However, Masefield's concept of fantasy goes beyond the image of the sea as a source of inspiration. He loads his tale with most of the accoutrements of magic: witches on broomsticks, magicians, talking animals, and toys that come alive. Somehow it all works. The sequel, *The Box of Delights* (1935), has much the same ambience but now seems almost a forerunner of Ian Fleming's James Bond stories, as the villain kidnaps the entire clergy of Tatchester Cathedral (and at Christmas time) and has at his command a car that turns into an airplane—or an airplane that turns into a car.

Kay Harker, the young hero of both books, represents the typical child of the period—far removed from Walter de la Mare's "child-alone." In *The Midnight Folk* he should be unhappy (and most modern writers would make him so), yet he isn't. Kay is an orphan, but obviously a wealthy one. He has a guardian whom he detests and a governess who is a witch; she is so bad (or prescient) that she has even discarded Kay's old and beloved toys. Nevertheless, Kay is the perfect English boy of his time—self-contained, polite, beloved by *good* animals and maidservants, and even able to cope with going-to-bed fears in a huge darkened room. Most of all, he is trustworthy. In *The Midnight Folk,* a treasure is recovered with the help of animals and toys, and Kay returns it to its rightful owners and thereby clears his grandfather's name. Equally, in *The Box of Delights,* he is entrusted with a treasure that he is not even tempted to keep for himself. *The Box of Delights* has a more original cast of characters than *The Midnight Folk.* It is enlivened by the appearance of Maria, the first feisty girl character in children's literature. When she is kidnapped, the reader feels sorry for the kidnappers. There is also a cameo appearance by Herne the Hunter, a figure of British romance and legend who was to spark the imagination of several fantasists of the 1970's. The events in *The Midnight Folk* are played out in the real world, chiefly on Kay's manorial estate, while *The Box of Delights,* surprisingly, turns out to be a dream sequence—Kay has fallen asleep on his trip home from school for Christmas. Both books are best described as fantasy-adventure stories.

So too is John Buchan's *The Magic Walking Stick* (1932). However, this book points up the fact that even a one-dimensional fantasy-adventure story needs some enrichment. In many ways, Buchan's young hero, Bill, is a cousin to Kay Harker; he is well-adjusted, polite and certainly happy. We are told that he likes history and the pageantry of history, and perhaps it is this sensitivity that propels him to buy a walking stick from an old man for a farthing. Bill discovers that with three twirls of the stick's knob, he can be transported to any place he desires. His main achievement is to defeat a usurper to the throne of a small Balkan country in scenes that are but a pale reflection of Buchan's adult spy story *The Thirty-Nine Steps*. *The Magic Walking Stick* also lacks John Masefield's commitment to fantasy; his rich, descriptive style and his convincing details.

For most of the 1930's, the fantasy scene belonged to English writers. In 1934, Pamela Travers's *Mary Poppins* sprang out of England as sparkling as one of the rockets in which she so often appeared and disappeared. *Mary Poppins* was followed by *Mary Poppins Comes Back* (1935), *Mary Poppins Opens the Door* (1944), *Mary Poppins in the Park* (1952), and *Mary Poppins in Cherry Tree Lane* (1982). In part of her nature, Mary Poppins is the very model of a Victorian English nanny. She is a stickler for propriety (she undresses under a tent-like nightgown), is always right, and always has the last word—or words, which are always directed at her charges and usually consist of "Spit spot into bed." She is also as conceited as Edith Nesbit's Phoenix, continually admiring herself in her navy-blue coat trimmed with silver buttons, her straw hat (often with new trimmings), white gloves, and parrot-headed umbrella. As Jane Banks whispers, she looks "rather like a wooden Dutch doll," and she has certainly all the habits of cleanliness and order associated with the Dutch housewife.

But Mary Poppins is also magic. She arrives at the Banks's residence blowing in on the East Wind, slides *up* the bannister, and unpacks a carpetbag that, like the miraculous pitcher of Greek mythology, is never empty. She also is badly needed. The household is in constant disarray; Mrs. Banks cannot cope with domestic crises; and Mr. Banks (like Mr. Darling in Barrie's *Peter Pan*) becomes petulant when the clockwork of his daily life is disturbed. The family is served by a cook, a parlor-maid, a boot-boy, and a nanny (when one can be found)—certainly a considerable staff for a financially hard-pressed family of the 1930's. The role of these ancillary characters is to increase the humorous, domestic chaos that Mary Poppins restores to order.

The children—Jane and Michael (and to a lesser extent, the twins)—need Mary Poppins most of all. They are very young—one guesses Jane and Michael to be between seven and nine years of age—and they are the most ordinary children in the whole range of fantasy. Being confined to the nursery, they have none of the restlessness, curiosity, and independence of Edith Nesbit's creations. "Everybody's got a fairyland of their own," says Mary Poppins, but she has to "open the door" for her charges. The children are led into a world that chiefly stays real but is turned upside down. They go out for tea and have it in the air (in "Laughing Gas"); they go to have a bowl mended, and everything is upended—even the buildings (in "Topsy-Turvy"); and they go to find a piano-tuner and spin on musical boxes (in "Mr. Twigley's Wishes"). Jane and Michael know that there are "not enough words in the Dictionary to explain the things that happened to Mary Poppins," and they love her with all their prosaic little hearts. The children enjoy their return to the routine and discipline of the nursery; they have been given delicious freedom for a while, but not license to explore on their own. Mary Poppins thus comes to represent adventure within well-defined limits.

Herein lies much of the wide success of the *Mary Poppins* series—an easy, guided entry into magical adventures in an otherwise commonplace world, a brief sojourn into the bizarre, and a quick return to safety and security with each episode (although not of equal memorability) being satisfyingly complete. However, Mary Poppins is mythic as well as magic—her appearance from and to the sky leave little doubt of the author's intentions in this regard. Like Peter Pan, she may simply be "Betwixt and Between," a child who has never grown up. In "The New One," the Starling tells the newborn baby, Annabel, that she will forget where she came from. Everyone does:

> "Every silly human except"—he nodded his head at Mary Poppins—"her! She's Different, she's the Oddity, she's the Misfit—"

In "The Evening Out," however, Mary Poppins is hailed by the Planets and the Constellations and is kissed by the Sun, which puts her among the Immortals. The long short story *Mary Poppins in Cherry Tree Lane* ends in a cosmic dance, a linking of humans and heavenly luminaries that "would go on turning forever." These portrayals all seem like the pantheism of the Edwardian age, but printed at the bottom of the last page of *Mary Poppins Opens the Door* are the words, "Gloria in Excelcis Deo."

Pamela Travers may keep the adult reader guessing, but for children in general, as for Jane and Michael:

> And the thing they wished was that all their lives they might remember Mary Poppins. Where and How and When and Why— had nothing to do with them.

While Mary Poppins controls the adventures, much as do the great-grandmother in George MacDonald's *The Princess and the Goblin* or the old Irishwoman in Charles Kingsley's *The Water-Babies,* Peter Grant in Hilda Lewis's *The Ship That Flew* (1939) is a true Nesbit child—he invites magic. In the window of an antique shop, he sees a tiny Norse ship, not longer than six inches. It has "tiny round shields, smaller than threepenny bits, that hung over the side" and "a boar's head carved in gilt." He desires it profoundly, and the old man in the shop with a patch over one eye sells it to him for all the money he has in the world, and a little bit over. It is, of course, a magic ship, and in it Peter and his brothers and sisters go a-voyaging, chiefly into the past. They return to Aesir, the home of the Norse gods, and discover that their ship is Skidbladnir, Frey's ship, given to him by Odin as a wedding gift but stolen from him. Peter promises to return the ship when he no longer wants it—a promise that brings a guffaw from Frey, for who would want to give up a magic ship? Like A.A. Milne in *The House at Pooh Corner,* Hilda Lewis knows how to bring a story to an end. The children are growing up; their adventures seem but stories told to them by Peter, and he, still believing that it all really happened, returns the ship to Odin, who is also the old man of the antique shop. Peter is given, in return, his heart's desire—he becomes a famous writer.

The Ship That Flew is completely in the Nesbit tradition; some scenes are almost duplicates of hers, as when the children use magic to visit and comfort their ailing mother. However, the story has its own touches of individuality, especially in the appearance of Matilda, a little girl from Norman England who finds the children's life of the 1930's too bland and easy for her liking. Most importantly, Hilda Lewis follows Nesbit's rules of magic—belief, consistency, and restraint. When these are broken, the result is simply a mishmash of uncoordinated events, as can be seen in two stories by Patricia Lynch, *The Turf-Cutter's Donkey* (1934) and *The Turf-Cutter's Donkey Goes Visiting* (1935).

Animal Fantasy

The animal fantasies of the Edwardian era, however different from one another, all had multi-layered meanings. Walter Brooks succeeded by working only on one level. On an upperstate New York farm live Freddy the pig, Charles the rooster, Hank the horse, Mrs. Wiggins the cow, and a host of other animals who re-enact the human comedy on a childlike level. The farm is owned by Mr. Bean, but it is the animals who make it prosper, and they know their worth. In the first book, *To and Again* (1927), later republished as *Freddy Goes to Florida,* the animals, disapproving of Mr. Bean's treatment of them, decide to winter in Florida. During their trek, they overcome many difficulties, all of which are described with hilarity and with a linking thread of a run-in with robbers who are outwitted somewhat in the style of the folktale "The Musicians of Bremen." As the change in the book's title suggests, it is Freddy the pig who comes to the fore in the series (26 books were published between 1927 and 1958); thus, the books are correctly and affectionately referred to as the "Freddy books."

Freddy plays many roles, ranging from pilot and poet to politician and everything in between; yet it is evidence of Brooks's skill that he could avoid turning Freddy into a super-pig. Freddy is modest, helpful, and self-effacing. He is always willing to learn and does his best for the good of everyone. In *Wiggins for President* (1939), it is Mrs. Wiggins, the gentle cow, who becomes president of the First Animal Republic, not Freddy. Brooks can even ironically but gently make fun of Freddy. As is pointed out in *Freddy and the Perilous Adventure* (1942), pigs don't wear clothes, but Freddy likes to wear the right expression for the right occasion:

> When he went down to the First Animal Bank, of which he was president, he wore the "serious-pig-with-grave-responsibilities-on-his-shoulders" expression. When he was doing detective work, he wore the "keen-eyed-pig-who-misses-nothing" expression. . . . This morning he hesitated between the "intrepid-pig-who-scoffs-

at-peril" and "the-pig-who-is-about-to-go-up-in-a-balloon-and-thinks-nothing-of-it." They were a good deal alike, so he combined the two and wore them both.

There is often a touch of A.A. Milne in the "Freddy" books.

Most of these works have been out of print for twenty years, but Freddy is now enjoying a renaissance, due partly to the formation of a "Friends of Freddy" Club," not quite yet on the scale of that formed by fans of the *Oz* books, but gaining momentum. As a result, four Freddy books have been republished.[5]

The "Freddy" books were very popular in their time, and it is easy to see why. They have a warmth and simplicity that is typical of American writing for children at its best. The animals are not parodies of human beings—as are sometimes those of *The Wind in the Willows* (especially Toad)—but they exhibit the qualities that we would like to think we humans instinctively possess. As described by Michael Cart in his introduction to the reprinted series, these qualities include; "the joys—and responsibilities—of friendship, of sharing and caring, of loyalty and constancy, of kindness, compassion, and forgiveness, and above all—of *helping.*" But, as he goes on to say,

> Don't think for a minute that this means the books are preachy or moralistic or dull. On the contrary, they are exciting and unfailingly *funny!* . . .

They are, indeed, in the classic humorous mold; the stories begin with order, move to disorder, and revert to order. Walter Brooks was a fine storyteller, and with his collection of "baddies" as well as "goodies" he makes the disorder full of suspense. In our own time—when fantasists tend to concentrate on older protagonists and use plot lines filled with harsh problems, almost to the exclusion of the sunnier aspects of life—the "Freddy" books shine with the joy of being alive. Now, as well as then, these books are also genuine little novels for young children.

The credibility of Walter Brooks's animal fantasy can be seen more clearly by contrasting it with Richard H. Hatch's *The Curious Lobster*

5. *Freddy the Politician, Freddy and the Perilous Adventure, Freddy Goes Camping,* and *Freddy the Pilot* all were reissued in 1986.

(1937). Like the Bean farm or Florida or the North Pole in the "Freddy" books, the setting is real enough—the waters and shores of a New England state—and one suspects that the author intended to be playful. However, the tone is labored, and Hatch's natural history is deliberately made misleading, a most serious sin in animal fantasy. As shown in the works of Beatrix Potter and Rudyard Kipling, the animals may talk; they may even wear clothes; but the forces of nature must not be tampered with. In *The Curious Lobster*, however, tides are for the convenience of the sculpin; "Water has no salt in it unless you put it in. Somebody has put salt in the Ocean. Probably the same person who planted all the trees in the woods"; and owls go out at night because they are so wise that they cannot associate with other birds. The animals also are not treated consistently. Mr. Lobster is seen at home in his sea environment (although the length of time he spends on land without protection is suspect); but Badger can ape the life-style of many animals, and Bear is "civilized"— he lives in a house and fries his food. As J.R.R. Tolkien remarked about another fantasy failure, "disbelief had not so much to be suspended as hung, drawn, and quarterd."[6]

In *Ben and Me* (1939), Robert Lawson shows the perfection that can be achieved through working in "small" rather than "large." In a matter-of-fact way, he gives us a view of Benjamin Franklin as seen by his mouse companion, Amos. Unlike Tommy Stebbins, the biographer of Doctor Dolittle, who extolled his patron upon every possible occasion, Amos has some reservations about his subject:

> Ben was undeniably a splendid fellow, a great man, a patriot and all that; but he *was* undeniably stupid at times, and had it not been for me—well here's the true story, and you can judge for yourself.

It is really Amos who invents the Franklin stove, writes (with the help of his friends) the Declaration of Independence, and saves Ben from totally falling for the ladies of Paris who call him "Cher Papa"—much to Amos's distaste. Very cleverly, though, Lawson does not make Amos infallible either. He scoffs at the invention of the lightning rod, and when he revises *Poor Richard's Almanack*, he tampers with the tide schedules, to

6. Tolkien, *Tree and Leaf*, 46.

the dismay of the fishermen. The bare bones of both mouse life and history make a delightful vignette while showing another permutation and combination of animal fantasy.

Doll Fantasy

Dolls are among the earliest toys ever made, and they make an early appearance in children's literature, both English and American. Dolls were generally used to point out a moral of some sort for little girls.[7] By the Victorian Age, however, toys that reigned at the center of infants' lives were even seen as the companions of infants' dreams. The older and more battered the toys were, the greater they were loved. In Charles Kingsley's *The Water-Babies*, Mrs. Doasyouwouldbedoneby sings of "The Prettiest Doll in the World" who was lost on the heath and so suffered the exigencies of the weather and some destruction by animals—her arm was trodden off by a cow. To the doll's owner, however:

> . . . for old sakes' sake, she is still, dears,
> The prettiest doll in the world.

It is more difficult for a writer to interject fantasy into a doll story than into an animal story, for dolls are limited in their movements. As Rumer Godden was to point in *The Dolls' House* (1947): "Dolls cannot choose; they can only be chosen; they cannot 'do'; they can only be done by." However, they can talk; and in early doll stories, such as Rachel Field's *Hitty* (1929), they also learn to read and write, being very proper dolls indeed.

Richard Horne's *Memoirs of a London Doll* (1846) is the first story in which dolls are given speech and intelligence. Maria Poppet does not have extraordinary adventures, but she does have little mistresses from various walks of life; and she offers her observations (pungent and moralistic) on the life-styles of the rich and the poor. What we learn chiefly about, however, are London amusements that would have entertained English children of the time: Twelfth Night celebrations, a

---

7. An example here is *The New Doll, or, Grand-mama's Gift* (London: R. Ackerman, 1826) in which a doll is used to promote virtue in a "wild" child.

Christmas pantomime, going to the opera, watching a Punch and Judy show, and listening to the organ-grinder.

Rachel Field's *Hitty* is as "genuine early American" as Maria Poppet is English. Hitty is a six and one-half inch tall doll made out of a piece of mountain ash from Ireland. Mountain ash has power over evil, and Hitty's survival over a hundred years may, at least partly, be attributable to the magic property of her wood. Although she has periods when she lays shut up in boxes or under the cushion of a sofa—"going to camphor," as she calls it—she has many extraordinary adventures. She goes to sea on a whaling ship and is abandoned when the ship catches fire; she becomes a "heathen idol" on a coral island, travels in India, survives the Civil War, becomes a doll of fashion, is held in the hand of the famous Charles Dickens, and inspires a poem by Mr. John Greenleaf Whittier. She also has a succession of little girl "mamas," whose differences in character and stations in life add interest to Hitty's autobiography, which covers the first one-hundred years of her life. What intrigues Hitty most are the changes in transportation; she travels by cart, train, automobile, and, finally, airplane. Like Maria Poppet, she speaks and writes in a rather prim and formal style as befits a doll born in the early nineteenth century, and like Maria, too, she is a social commentator.

A far more imaginative approach to dolls is shown by Anne Parrish in *Floating Island* (1930). Here the dolls can move about at night in the toy shop, and we neither know nor care how they move. Rachel Field explains that Hitty is a single-jointed doll, so certain movements are either difficult or impossible for her. Maria Poppet is a double-jointed doll, so she can even dance. However, when the dolls in *Floating Island* are cast away on a tropical island where they have to "make do" like Robinson Crusoe, all such explanations are superfluous. The dolls are alive— miniature people in a frightening jungle where the leg of a tiger looks like the trunk of a tree. Here the doll family—Mr. and Mrs. Doll and their children, William, Annabel, and baby—survive frightening adventures that are nonetheless humorous for the reader. The author has knowledge of tropical natural history, but this information is kept to footnotes (often very entertaining ones). Mr. Doll confuses snippets of lore picked up from reading books in the toy shop, but Mrs. Doll does not aspire to erudition: "And I want to keep my head empty," Mrs. Doll replied, "I don't know what I should do if I got something in it." Mr. and

Mrs. Doll are unlike Hitty and Maria Poppet (who were very clothes-conscious) in their lack of concern about their attire. When their clothes are ruined by the seawater, they wear leaves and flowers, and bell-shaped petals for sun-helmets. The one thing the dolls cannot do is eat. They do have doll's house food that has been saved along with the doll's house itself, but Finney and Lobby and Chicky and Pudding are part of the family. There is a touch of *Peter Pan* to the story because even on a fantasy island there is make-believe: the dolls eat "air sandwiches flavoured with ham." However, it all must end: dolls need children to love them. Therefore, reluctantly, they build a signal fire, and a passing ship sends a lifeboat to the island, where the sailors find only a doll's house and some dolls. However, we readers know that the story really happened, because the black cook, Dinah, has elected to stay on the island and be served by the monkeys.

Past-Time Fantasy

None of Alison Uttley's earlier works for children, neither her slight and sentimental picture books of *Little Gray Rabbit* (beginning in 1929) nor her book of indifferent short stories *Mustard, Pepper, and Salt* (1938), give the least forewarning of her time fantasy *A Traveller in Time* (1939). However, its roots can be found in Uttley's account of her own childhood, *A Country Child*, which she wrote in 1931. *A Traveller in Time* is compounded of her youth in Derbyshire, dreams and imagination, and a piece of authentic history—the Babington plot to rescue Mary, Queen of Scots, from Wingfield Manor.

Uttley's Penelope Taberner is one of the early ultra-sensitive protagonists in fantasy; she is almost a Walter de la Mare child. When she first comes to the old, old manor house of Thackers from London to stay with her great-aunt and uncle, she is recovering from an illness. The farm with its history-haunted atmosphere and the house itself with its still-used household goods of times past increase her perception that she is where she belongs. Doors open to her, the landscape shifts, and Penelope comes and goes between the present and the past. Her own nature is the bridge between the two worlds, and of the two, it is gradually the present that seems the most unreal to her. Although in its style and in its delicate concept, the story is a far superior work to Nesbit's historical fantasies *Harding's Luck* and *The House of Arden,* the same rules hold. It is time in the real world that stands still; the presence of the time traveler must be accounted for in the Other World; and, most important of all, history cannot be tampered with. Penelope's foreknowledge of events cannot change the historical facts of the failure of Anthony Babington's plot and his ultimate execution and the story thereby gains an extra dimension of almost unbearable sadness and an insight into the human condition that goes far beyond the events of history. *A Traveller in Time* may all be a dream—it may even be a wish-fulfillment dream—but in showing the bricks upon which Penelope dreams, Alison Uttley has created a model time-travel fantasy.

Epic Fantasy

There are no bridges into J.R.R. Tolkien's *The Hobbit*—no talisman, no dreams, no perceptions of other realities. From the very first line of the very first page, we are in a hobbit hole under the Hill "in the quiet of the world, when there was less noise and more green. . . . " It is a perfectly created subworld, akin to that of George MacDonald's *The Princess and the Goblin* and *The Princess and Curdie,* but more richly and substantially described and much more original in its main character. One might have expected Tolkien, a writer and lecturer on Beowulf and Sir Gawain, to write a quest story about a dragon. Smaug, who knows every glittering piece of his dragon-hoard, has stepped from the pages of the Anglo-Saxon epic *Beowulf,* and the hero, Bilbo Baggins, shows the commitment of an Arthurian knight as his journey reaches its climax. However, to conceive of a little race of people called "hobbits" was the mark of creative genius. What is a hobbit? Tolkien knows hobbits well, and he shares his information with the reader:

> I suppose hobbits need some description nowadays, since they have become rare and shy of the Big People, as they call us. They are (or were) a little people, about half our height, and smaller than the bearded dwarves. Hobbits have no beards. There is little or no magic about them, except the ordinary everyday sort which helps them to disappear quietly and quickly when large stupid folk like you and me come blundering along, making a noise like elephants which they can hear a mile off. They are inclined to be fat

in the stomach; they dress in bright colours (chiefly green and yellow); wear no shoes, because their feet grow natural leathery soles and thick warm brown hair like the stuff on their heads (which is curly); have long clever brown fingers, good-natured faces, and laugh deep fruity laughs (especially after dinner, which they have twice a day when they can get it).

The story concerns one particular hobbit, Bilbo Baggins of Bag End, who is as peaceful and respectable a citizen of Hobbiton as can be found. There is just enough spark of adventure left in him (especially when his courage is impugned) to succumb to the wizard Gandalf's prodding and to join thirteen dwarves to help them recover their gold from Smaug. Their journey through well-defined landscapes (Mirkwood, Rivendell, and the Misty Mountains) is filled with exciting and dangerous adventures, but not without traces of humor. The incidents themselves appear not to be linked, but they serve two purposes: they eventually sort out the friends and enemies who take part in the last battle, and, more importantly, they are building blocks to the development of Bilbo's character. Not only do we see him become like Kipling's sailor in "How the Whale Got Its Throat"—a hobbit "of infinite resource and sagacity"—but he achieves the nobility of a true quest hero. Like the protagonists in the Christian fantasies of the Victorian Age, this quality is not achieved without the turmoil of an inward struggle. The moral dimensions of the story are both considerable and complex.

Bilbo, in his role of burglar to the dwarves, not only steals into Smaug's chamber but pockets for himself the Arkenstone—a jewel that Smaug values above all others and that legally belongs to Thorin, the king of the dwarves. Bilbo assuages his conscience by assuring himself that the jewel is only his percentage of what he has been promised for his services. Later, he gives the Arkenstone to Thorin's enemies in an effort to compensate them for Smaug's destructive actions and so to prevent war. On his deathbed, Thorin recognizes Bilbo's gesture:

"Since I leave now all gold and silver, and go where it is of little worth, I wish to part in friendship from you. . . . If more of us valued food and cheer and song above hoarded gold, it would be a merrier world."

The subtitle, "There and Back Again," is the key to *The Hobbit*. Bilbo does not simply go on a journey and return home. He is also changed internally:

> Gandalf looked at him. "My dear Bilbo!" he said. "Something is the matter with you! You are not the hobbit that you were."

The Hobbit, as Tolkien's biographers tell us, began as a "winter read" for his own children.[8] It is now often seen as only a prelude to greater efforts by Tolkien: to his major three-volume fantasy *The Lord of the Rings* (1954–55) or to his theories on fantasy that were so admirably expressed in his lecture "On Fairy-Stories" given in 1939 and later published in *Tree and Leaf.*[9] So limited a view of *The Hobbit* does not do it justice, however. As a children's book, it has its own very firm place in children's literature. It is a wonderfully exciting and satisfying story on an adventure level, while readers can choose for themselves whatever application of the story they desire. Among the stories of simple magic that surrounded the book in its own time, *The Hobbit* shines as a beacon of true fantasy, a total subcreation that convinces totally.

With *The Hobbit,* Tolkien also brought to new heights George MacDonald's concept of fantasy (a debt that Tolkien acknowledged)[10] and gave a much-needed impetus to epic fantasy, an impetus that had been lost in the whimsy of most of the writers of fantasy between MacDonald and Tolkien. Like MacDonald in *The Princess* books, Tolkien made use of the material of folklore, myth, and legend in a world of his own creation, giving his story a deeper level of meaning beyond its fast-moving plot and memorable characters.

Religious conviction, as deep in Tolkien as in MacDonald, permeates the work. Although *The Hobbit* is played out in a pagan world, it operates under a familiar code of Christian values. Bilbo is faced with a challenge to his conscience as well as to his courage and resolution: he must change either for better or for worse. Like MacDonald's *Curdie and Diamond,* he cannot stand still in a spiritual sense. As Tolkien built on MacDonald, so

8. Humphrey Carpenter, *J.R.R. Tolkien* (London: Allen & Unwin, 1977), 177 passim.

9. Tolkien, *Tree and Leaf* (London: Unwin Bks., 1964), 11–70.

10. J.R.R. Tolkien, *Letters of J.R.R. Tolkien,* eds. Humphrey Carpenter and Christopher Tolkien (London: Allen & Unwin, 1981), 31.

later writers adopted the Tolkien method: protagonists must go "there and back again," returning with a new look at their old world, and at themselves.

If this interpretation seems too much to attribute to one book, it may be well to remember that influences can sometimes be greater than immediate events seem to suggest. Bilbo and Gandalf look back at the adventure at its end:

> "Then the prophecies of the old songs have turned out to be true, after a fashion!" said Bilbo.
> "Of course!" said Gandalf. "And why should not they prove true? Surely you don't disbelieve the prophecies, because you had a hand in bringing them about yourself? You don't really suppose, do you, that all your adventures and escapes were managed by mere luck, just for your sole benefit? You are a very fine person, Mr. Baggins, and I am very fond of you; but you are only quite a little fellow in a wide world after all!"

The even more popular *Lord of the Rings* (which children could also enjoy) recreates the same theme in more heroic proportions. It also influenced later writers of fantasy for both children and adults, but it added nothing to the seminal structure of *The Hobbit,* which took twentieth-century fantasy onto a high moral plane.

The works of the 1920's and the 1930's lack a strong focus; they are much like dipping into a fish pond at an old-fashioned fair. One expects only a trifle or a trinket that gives pleasure for a fleeting moment, but then, unexpectedly, there is the surprise of pulling up a treasure—a story by Walter de la Mare or Walter Brooks or Carl Sandburg—or even a hobbit.

Chapter 6

Playing in the Shadows of War:

Fantasy of the 1940's

The children in John Masefield's *The Midnight Folk,* John Buchan's *The Magic Walking-Stick,* and Pamela Travers's *Mary Poppins* are typical fantasy protagonists of the 1920's and 1930's. Things happen *to* them, not *because* of them; the characters are chiefly respondents to adventure rather than initiators of it. They are not even asked to have faith in magic; magic seemingly operates on its own. Rather than leading children's literature as in Victorian and Edwardian times, fantasy remained rather static during these years, particularly in its portrayal of childhood.

It was a realistic story of children at serious play—Arthur Ransome's *Swallows and Amazons* (1930)—that can now be seen as promulgating a new doctrine of childhood. Ransome formulated his ideas as early as 1906 in an essay on books and children. His biographer, Hugh Brogan, paraphrased these ideas:

> The essence of the child, he held, is its imagination, the way in which, left to itself and not withered by obtuse or manipulative adults, "it adopts any material at hand, and weaves for itself a web of imaginative life," building the world again into a splendid pageantry: and all without ever (or hardly ever) blurring its sense of the actual.[1]

1. Hugh Brogan, *The Life of Arthur Ransome* (London: Jonathan Cape, 1984), 313–14.

Swallows and Amazons (and his succeeding books) illustrates Ransome's philosophy. When the Walker children ask their father for permission to go sailing and camping on thier own, he telegraphs a reply that is now famous in children's literature: "BETTER DROWNED THAN DUFFERS: IF NOT DUFFERS WON'T DROWN." John Walker's comment shows the author's faith in adults as well as in children: "Daddy knows we aren't duffers," he says. Children in the Ransome books (and in many other stories of child and family life after Ransome)[2] are given a good deal of freedom from parental supervision. They are sensible and responsible, and they engage in activities that call for the develpment of self-reliance, generosity, friendship, and the expansion of knowledge—all qualities deemed vital for maturity. Although few adults are in the forefront of the children's pleasures, the adults are supportive, understanding, and appreciative of the young—and parents in particular are always there, if only in the background. There thus is no unbreachable wall between childhood and adulthood. These life stages are instead in a tandem relationship, and if the young do not actually yearn to be grown up, they nonetheless have no resentment against the adult world. Ransome children are also imaginative, and they "weave for themselves a web of imaginative life" that is based in reality. They play not only at being pirates and castaways; they take on the grown-up roles of prospectors, surveyors, explorers, and detectives. Moreover, the children can turn the most mundane events into adventures; indeed, they make up fantasy adventures (such as those of *Missee Lee* and *Peter Duck*) and put themselves into them. These kinds of children are also apparent in Hilda Lewis's *The Ship That Flew* and became strong factors in the fantasies of the 1940's and 1950's.

Enchanted Realism

The five young Treguddicks in Elizabeth Goudge's *Smoky House* (1940) are lively and independent; and except for the oldest, Jessamine—who sees herself as their substitute mother—the Treguddicks

2. Some such titles are, for example, Eleanor Estes's *The Moffatts* (1940), Eve Garnett's *The Family from One-End Street* (1937), and Elizabeth Enright's *The Saturdays* (1941).

have a great deal of freedom in handling their own affairs while participating, when they can manage it, in those of the adults as well. The Victorian village of Faraway in the county of Devon in which the Treguddicks live has a natural magic of its own—like Kipling's Sussex—and the children are in tune with its magic. For instance, they sense the presence of the fairies, the "Good People":

> "They don't live in our world," explained Tristram wisely. "I suppose we can only be absolutely certain about the things that *do* live in our world. Yet if one didn't believe in other worlds this one would be very dull, wouldn't it?"

A kind of happy dullness is swept aside when a mysterious traveling fiddler arrives in the village and betrays the local smugglers to the soldiers. With the help of the "Good People" and the animals, the children outwit the law and save their adult friends.

The Treguddicks and Maria Merryweather in Elizabeth Goudge's second book, *The Little White Horse* (1942), are very real and normal young people; it is the animals who have heightened powers. In *Smoky House,* the animals are the first to sense danger, inspire the children to action, play a key part in the events, and have a superior attitude toward the human race. This attitude is frequently expressed by the dog, Spot:

> We animals must keep up the standards of the world. We don't want to fall to the human level.

It is a viewpoint that was much later to rise to misanthropic heights in Richard Adams's beast tale *Watership Down* (1972). In 1940, with Europe already enmeshed in the ravages of war and with an invasion of England expected, Spot's comments had validity; however, in the context of the book, it is the Napoleonic Wars that illustrate man's inhumanity to man. Other moral judgments are not as clear-cut as Goudge's disclaimers of war.

The young squire, who is also the magistrate, equates smuggling with free trade and also keeps up his Robin Hood activities of robbing the rich to give to the poor. In *The Little White Horse,* the good are not all good nor the bad all bad; Maria must oppose her otherwise kindly uncle, who is using others in his scheme for revenge. Both books are outrightly romantic and even sentimental—in *Smoky House,* Jessamine receives four babies from her Guardian Angel; and in *The Little White Horse,* Maria marries her boyhood sweetheart and lives happily ever after except for undefined yearnings for "the little white horse" (a unicorn). Both stories, too, are early examples of enchanted realism; with only a few strokes of the pen to expunge the aura of magic, they would be romantic adventure stories. However, it is the touch of the fantastic, as well as the Devonshire countryside, that makes these stories memorable—especially the image of the little white horse "with flowing mane and tail, head raised, poised, halted in mid-flight in the moonlight."

Influences of World War II

While the production of children's books naturally dropped during the years of World War II, the few fantasies that were published in England had common themes—oppression and tyranny and the need to fight against these conditions in whatever form they appeared. Writers wove these themes into their plots, more or less distancing themselves from the actualities of conflict. Eric Linklater's *The Wind on the Moon* (1944) is one of the more specific expressions of these themes. It is almost three books in one, but the story is linked through its child characters, Dinah and Dorinda, who become experts at putting things right. When they are through being naughty, they release the Falcon and the golden Puma from the Zoo, give a stubborn judge a lesson in democracy, and set off for Bombardy to rescue their father—who has been imprisoned by the tyrant Count Hulagu Bloot (a thinly veiled Hitler). With the help of the Puma and the Falcon (with whom the children can converse), their dancing master, and two engineers who think that Queen Victoria is still on the throne of England, Dinah and Dorinda effect a rescue. In spite of its lack of cohesion, *The Wind on the Moon* has many humorous moments, especially in the first half of the story; and Dinah and Dorinda are spunky, ingenious, and well-organized heroines.

Linklater's second book, *The Pirates in the Deep Green Sea* (1949), is also based on a power struggle. The drowned sailors who hold the world together at the bottom of the sea by guarding the knots of latitude and longitude are challenged by pirates; a great underwater battle ensues. It is a more fully developed fantasy than *The Wind on the Moon,* but it is too long and overly plotted, and the two young male protagonists lack character. Whatever show there is is stolen in a few scenes by Cully, the singing octopus.

The war was evidently very much on Vaughan Wilkins's mind when he wrote *After Bath or (if you prefer) The Remarkable Case of the Flying Hat* (1945). It is a fantasy farce (the king's son and daughter search for his magic moustache), but the book is also filled with battle scenes and with most of the paraphernalia of war, which varies from cutlasses to bombs and from nineteenth-century sailors to parachutists. It is a far less satisfying book than Wilkins's high adventure story *The City of Frozen Fire* and is only important now as showing World War II as an influence on the fantasy of the period.

The forest, the stream, and the mountain in Beverley Nichols's trilogy *The Tree That Sat Down* (1945), *The Stream That Stood Still* (1948), and *The Mountain of Magic* (1950) are enchanted places; but within these settings, the young protagonists have to fight for their very lives. In the first book, wickedness and tyranny appear in the person of Sam, the first youthful villain in children's fantasy. He and his grandfather destroy the peace of the forest and the amity among the animals by setting up a rival animal shop to that of Judy and her grandmother. Sam not only attracts customers away from Judy's shop by using modern techniques of advertising, but he cheats Mrs. Rabbit, makes a fool out of Miss Squirrel, and enslaves Bruno the Bear. Judy's goodness in the face of commercial disaster is appalling to him. He hires a witch, Miss Smith, to assist him in his nefarious deeds, and together they plot to kill Judy.

Nichols was a noted and outspoken pacifist, and he uses *The Tree That Sat Down* to express his views on war. Mr. Justice Owl is the spokesman as he explains that he fights only when attacked; but, he says:

> . . . what would you think of me if I were to take a rock and fly off with it to a farmyard and drop it in the middle of a basket of eggs? That is what the Humans call "bombing." They all do it, and they think it is wonderful, and they give medals to the Humans who break the most eggs. . . .

Nichols also indulges in jibes against advertising and the gullibility of those who are swayed by it, but here he treads both lightly and humorously. In the two sequels, Sam and Miss Smith pursue their murderous designs against Judy's children. Although these two stories are more consistent in their construction than *The Tree That Sat Down,* they somehow lack the charm of this first book, flawed as it is. Nichols indulges in pathetic fallacy (a super-being called "the Clerk of the Weather" causes a storm), a stagy trial (during which Miss Smith is shown for what she is), and a final transformation scene straight out of "The Frog Prince" (this unexpected Prince Charming is a tortoise, restored to his human self through the power of Judy's love). The mixture is greater than its separate parts.

There are always a few books that are difficult to define as intended for children or adults. Some writers, such as Lewis Carroll with the *Alice* books and Kenneth Grahame with *The Wind in the Willows,* escaped such a difficulty by writing for children but also including levels of meaning sufficient to attract an adult audience as well. T.H. White, in the first book of his tetralogy, *The Once and Future King,* which was published as *The Sword in the Stone* (1938), was seemingly puzzled by his own work:

> It seems impossible to determine whether it is for grown-ups or for children. It is more or less a kind of wish-fulfilment of the things I should like to have happened to me when I was a boy.[3]

Certainly in this first book, White's interpretation of the Arthurian legend (an imaginative re-creation of Malory's imaginative fifteenth century) is accessible to children. Here we meet the young Arthur—"the Wart," as he is called—being trained by Merlyn for kingship. (Merlyn knows what is going to happen because he is living backward in time.) In an effort to offset the ritual knightly fights that Arthur sees all around him, Merlyn transforms the boy into various creatures—animals, birds, a fish, and an insect. Arthur is to learn from these experiences that Might is not Right, a concept that he struggles for unsuccessfully during his kingship. The narrative moves between cartoon-like, slapstick comedy (scenes for which Walt Disney paid movie rights) and philosophical and satirical asides on the follies of the human species. If White had doubts about his audience, he had none at all about his overall theme. In the

3. Sylvia Townsend Warner, *T.H. White* (London: Jonathan Cape, 1967), 98.

third book, *The Ill-Made Knight* (1941), Arthur tells Merlyn that he wants to use Might to do Right. The magician is furious:

> "Very interesting," he said in a trembling voice. "Very interesting. There was just such a man when I was young—an Austrian who invented a new way of life and convinced himself that he was the chap to make it work. He tried to impose his reformation by the sword and plunged the civilized world into misery and chaos. . . . "

Might is never Right, goes the book's message; and Arthur's world ends in chaos too, as we see in the totality of *The Once and Future King,* which was not published until 1958. *The Sword in the Stone* has the largest component of fantasy with its transformation scenes and Merlyn's other humorous and magical tricks; the fantasy decreases in rapid proportion, however, as the series advances.

Just as Malory provided White with the inspiration for his Arthurian retellings, so another English classic—Jonathan Swift's *Gulliver's Travels*—gave White a model for *Mistress Masham's Repose* (1946). On the first page, we meet Maria, who is ten years of age:

> She had dark hair in two pigtails, and brown eyes the color of Marmite, but more shiny. She wore spectacles for the time being, though she would not have to wear them always, and her nature was a loving one. She was one of those tough and friendly people who do things first and think about them afterward.

She is an orphan and an heiress, living in a mansion "about four times longer than Buckingham Palace" and in the charge of a governess whom she detests and who is in league with the local Vicar (Maria's guardian) to defraud Maria of her fortune. Few heroines in children's literature are more persecuted and more helpless. One day, managing to escape supervision, Maria rows to an island on her estate and discovers a race of little people—the adults no more than six inches tall. They are the descendants of Swift's Lilliputians, and Maria is delighted with them. Her size quickly gives her a sense of power, and she begins to act like a Brobdingnagian amongst them and even like a Yahoo. She interferes with the island people's ordered life, ruining their fishing boat with her clumsy fingers and introducing them to modern technology with disastrous results. Maria finally learns—with the help of her one friend, the absent-minded professor—that "Might is not Right." When "the People," as they call themselves, are discovered by the governess and the Vicar—who want to exploit them—Maria does her best to protect "the People." Her best, however, is not good enough; and it is the Lilliputians who come to the rescue of Maria and the Professor. The story ends in true melodramatic style, with the villains unmasked and arrested, and Maria's fortune restored and used to protect "the People" forever.

As a kind of sequel to "A Voyage to Lilliput" in *Gulliver's Travels*, *Mistress Masham's Repose* is an intriguing children's book. Its miniature society is perfectly conceived, and Maria's attempts to dominate it have both humor and pathos. Her inner journey from being an unthinking and possessive child to one with a sense of responsibility toward others is shown without sentimentality. However, it is also a rather heavy-handed satire—a vehicle for T.H. White's adversely critical views on everything ranging from England's colonization policies to its laws, police, and religion. Like its prototype, this book can be read as an adventure story, with the Lilliputians providing the only fantasy element; but the polemics—and the link with *Gulliver's Travels*—take up a good deal of space in a lengthy book. Its frequent asides and often esoteric references call for a literary and historical background that have made the story a constant source of delight to a small circle of adult readers. Not even the title is intriguing to children;[4] it refers to an eighteenth-century type of "folly" that the Lilliputians use as their main living quarters. For those children who can take out of a book just what they want, or who have learned to skip the dull parts in their reading, *Mistress Masham's Repose* would be a most rewarding experience; but if White designed this book specifically for children, it is a magnificent failure.

Doll Stories

In comparison with the anti-war polemics of such writers as Beverley Nichols and T.H. White, Rumer Godden's *The Dolls' House* (1947) seems at first to be light-years away from any concept of tyranny. It is a

4. White himself considered other titles, such as *Lilliput in Exile, Lie Low,* and *As Yahoos Like It.*

dramatic novel in miniature, with conflicts, jealousies, and even murder carried out within the tiny compass of a doll's house. It is also a story of delicate relationships, both doll and human, but with a touch of steel beneath a rather fragile appearance. It is a conventional doll story in the tradition of Richard Horne's *Memoirs of a London Doll* and Rachel Field's *Hitty* only in regard to what dolls can do in a fantasy: they can wish, and they can talk among themselves. However, they cannot move on their own, and much of the action in the story is the result of where the children place the dolls in relation to one another.

Emily and Charlotte are the doll-owners, Emily being assertive, stubborn, and outspoken, and Charlotte quiet and sensitive. It is Emily who introduces Marchpane, a valuable antique doll, into the home of the Plantagenet doll family. Marchpane, as Charlotte points out, smells strongly of a nasty cleaning fluid, and she has a nature to match it: She reeks of evil. In comparison, Sam and Miss Smith in Beverley Nichols's *The Tree That Sat Down* and the governess and the Vicar in T.H. White's *Mistress Masham's Repose* are merely stock characters from a melodrama. Marchpane is real, and the force of her cold, dominating personality influences even Emily. Emily makes Marchpane the mistress of the household and the other dolls her servants. However, Marchpane's lust for power knows no bounds, and she is finally responsible for a simple-minded celluloid doll (Mrs. Plantagenet) being burned to death as the doll rescues her son from a candle flame. Things are righted, as best they can be, when Emily agrees with Charlotte that Marchpane should be sent to a museum. Right triumphs over Might.

Much is made in *The Dolls' House* (as in other Godden stories, such as *Mouse House,* 1957) of the order, security, and beauty of a beloved home and its furnishings. Much, too, is made of the solidarity of the family and its constancy, unselfishness, and sacrifice. In the uncertainty and anxiety of the post-war world of the 1940's, Rumer Godden re-affirmed the worth of these virtues.

The Dolls' House begins in a simple narrative manner, but Godden soon reveals herself as a stylist. She uses conversation extensively but economically, along with a slight use of interior monologue, to carry the plot. Her technique did not surface again until after 1960. Here Tottie, a tiny farthing doll and the most important character in the book, explains to the other dolls that they must keep wishing for furniture to be put into their house:

"Are you still wishing, Tottie?" asked Mr. Plantagenet anxiously.

"Yes," said Tottie firmly.

"You—see what I mean, don't you?" said Mr. Plantagenet.

"You must wish about the curtains," said Tottie. "You must wish about the couch and chairs. You must wish about the beds."

"Curtains, chairs, beds," said Mr. Plantaganet. He wished he could shut his eyes in order to wish harder but, of course, he could not because they were not made to shut.

"Over and over again," said Tottie. "You must never leave off wishing."

"Beds, chairs, couch, curtains; beds, chairs, couch, curtains; beds, chairs . . . "

"My cot. My own little cot," wished Apple.

"My bird-broom-feather," Birdie still did not know which to think of first.

"Beds, couch, curtains, chairs . . . "

Frequently the dolls reveal *their* thoughts, adding a counterpoint to those of the children:

"Look at her clothes," said Emily.

"My clothes," said Marchpane in a complacent voice.

"They take off and on. Look at the tiny buttons and the lace edgings."

"The lace edgings," said Marchpane still more complacently.

"And her hair! We can really brush it and comb it."

"It is real hair," said Marchpane.

"And her eyes. Look. They open and shut. None of the others' can open and shut."

"Mine open and shut. They are the best blue glass," said Marchpane.

Rumer Godden's delicately precise style and mastery of dialogue were unique in the fantasy of the period, and few writers since have matched her. Equally, no writer since has used dolls as simply and sensitively to probe the emotions of children. In a doll story of the same period, *Miss Hickory* (1946), the American writer, Caroline Sherwin Bailey, merely uses Miss Hickory, a doll made of apple-wood and hickory, to show determination and survival skills during a New Hampshire winter.

In Godden's *Home Is the Sailor* (1964), the lives of the dolls and the children are again intertwined. This book is stylistically similar to *The Dolls' House;* but in its basic plot of a boy doll returned to his family, the story cannot compare to the tension caused by Marchpane. The greater length of the later book tends to operate against it: coincidences become strained, the moral is too obvious, and the story descends into sentimentality. Rumer Godden is at her best as a writer in cameo. Her short short stories, such as *Impunity Jane* (1954), *Mouse House* (1957), and particularly *The Mousewife* (1951), a moving story of friendship between a mouse and a dove, show novelistic skill within a microcosm.

Epic Fantasy

The Tolkien influence can be seen in both William Croft Dickinson's *Borrobil* (1944) and in Denys Watkins-Pitchford's *The Little Grey Men* (1949), but neither writer had a deep understanding of fantasy. In Watkins-Pitchford's novel, Borrobil is a dwarf whom Jane and Donald meet when Jane accidentally dances in the Nine-Stone Ring on Beltane Eve (a Celtic spring festival); and with Borrobil, the children enter a past world. Almost every traditional accoutrement of fantasy is packed into the story, including a fire-breathing dragon, a fairy queen, a giant, a talisman, a lost kingdom, a prince and a princess, and a final battle with the outcome known almost as soon as the story begins. It is a plot gone wild and points up Tolkien's thesis that it takes an "elvish craft" to produce a fine fantasy.

The Little Grey Men is about gnomes (somewhat hobbit-like in their appearance), three of whom go off on a quest to find their brother and who are helped by the birds and animals of wood and stream. The riverbank scenes are reminiscent of Kenneth Grahame's *The Wind in the Willows,* as is the brief appearance of the god Pan. However, in this story, Pan is not Grahame's god of ecstasy, as pictured in his chapter "The Piper at the Gates of Dawn." Here Pan gives the dwarves a poisoned plant, which one of them puts into Giant Grum's sandwiches and which, as is later implied in the story, causes his death. This is a misuse of magic, especially on the part of the so-called "good" people in the story.

A rather terrible scene is worsened by the fact that Grum is not really a giant; he is the keeper of a riverside estate. Another flaw in the book is that the dwarves do not recognize Grum as such, especially when they can identify both a boy and a fisherman for what they are. While fantasy is a highly eclectic literary form, a writer must produce at least one note of originality or, at a minimum, obey the reasonable rules of fantasy. Watkins-Pitchford does neither.

Light Fantasy and Animal Fantasy

American fantasies of the 1940's are chiefly marked by lightness and humor; but with such writers as James Thurber in *The White Deer* (1945), E.B. White in *Stuart Little* (1945), and William Pene du Bois in *The Twenty-One Balloons* (1948) and in *Peter Graves* (1950), the comedy has an underlying seriousness.

Thurber's *The White Deer* is basically a fairy tale. The setting moves from an enchanted forest (where white deer, when held at bay by hunters, turn into beautiful princesses) to court scenes (which at first appear to be merely a spoof on fairy tales on the order of Thackeray's *The Rose and the Ring* or of A.A. Milne's *Once on a Time*) to a quest by the king's three sons (in which, of course, the youngest wins). However, while the story can be read on this simple level, somehow Thurber does not believe in his own fairy tale. This lack of conviction—combined with an overdose of satire, parody, and parable in a vehicle that is too brief and too fragile to sustain it—makes *The White Deer* less than successful as a book for children. The story mocks the despot, the technician, the bureaucrat, and the specialist, while also posing questions about reality—the Royal Astronomer, for example, covers the end of his telescope with a rose-colored lens. Thurber is on the side of the poets, such as the king's youngest son—who can see through disguises and thus more clearly into what is real. Thurber's previous short story, *The Great Quillow* (1944), is a more childlike expression of this idea, as the little toymaker Quillow, an artist who loves the children, defeats the marauding giant Hunder (a thinly veiled Hitler) by distorting Hunder's sense of reality. *The Great Quillow* is a simple parable of its time.

In the opening paragraph of *Stuart Little*, E.B. White calls for the greatest suspension of disbelief of any fantasy preceding or following it.

The idea of a mouse born as a child of an ordinary American family so offended even such an avant-garde critic of children's books as Anne Carroll Moore of the New York Public Library that she tried to prevent the book's publication.[5] Many other adults have found this kind of link between the human and animal world to be distasteful and unacceptable as a fantasy device, particularly from a writer whose essays are so sunnily sane. Still and all, children, with their ready acceptance of animals, were not and are not daunted by the story's incongruity as an entry into animal fantasy; and in great measure they are right. Stuart's family readily accept him, love him, and make provision for his needs, such as sleeping quarters and clothes (infant wear is unnecessary). As a member of the family, not even the household cat dares pounce on him. Indeed, Stuart does not raise eyebrows in any adult whom he meets. His adventures, both domestic and in the outside world, are scaled to his size. He is snapped up in a blind, rescues his mother's ring from the bathroom drain, and races a toy sailboat in Central Park. He also falls in love with a sparrow and at the end of the story is headed north to find her in the true spirit of the quest hero. There are minor inconsistencies in some of Stuart's actions: he cannot pay his fare on a streetcar because a dime is too heavy for him to carry, and yet he can pay for the gasoline for his toy car. However, the greatest inconsistency lies in White's portrayal of Stuart. Is he a child surrogate, a Lilliput in Brobdingnag, or an unconventional person in a conventional society? Certainly what he is least of all, in spite of his appearance, is a mouse. Whatever White had in mind, he lacked in *Stuart Little* the sure touch for animal fantasy that made his *Charlotte's Web* (1952) a modern classic.

Robert Lawson's *Rabbit Hill* (1944) is a more conventional animal fantasy than *Stuart Little*. It is played out in the countryside, the animals keep most of their natural characteristics and the moral is direct and simple: there is enough food for everybody if everyone shares—both animals and humans. In style and concept, *Rabbit Hill* is considerably above the works of Thornton Burgess and was deservedly popular for many years. Its humor, however, lacks the neatness and slyness of Lawson's earlier *Ben and Me,* and its language is mundane. One wishes that Georgie, the young rabbit, had taken lessons in songwriting from Winnie-the-Pooh.

5. Dorothy L. Guth, ed., *Letters of E.B. White* (New York: Harper, 1978), 266–67.

William Pene du Bois keeps a firm hold on reality in *The Twenty-One Balloons,* especially regarding the pleasures and skills of ballooning—a field of great public interest in the late Victorian period in which the story is set and a passion with du Bois himself. As he says in the first few pages, "Half of this story is true and the other half might very well have happened." The ballooning and the great volcanic eruption on the Island of Krakatoa in 1883 are true, but so is the portrayal of Professor William Waterman Sherman, who is quite rightly tired of teaching arithmetic to children for forty years and so takes off in a balloon—a vehicle in which one might never get to school. He lands accidentally on Krakatoa, where he finds a hidden society of Americans who have brought cooking and loafing to the highest possible art. The inhabitants manage this achievement because they have learned how to control the world's diamond market (the island is perched on the world's largest diamond mine) and because of their inventiveness: they manufacture household aids such as revolving self-cleaning bedsheets and retractable tables.

A prescient look at American "know-how" is also evident in *Peter Graves.* In this story, a young boy joins with a "mad inventor" named Houghton F. Furlong to try to make a fortune out of "Furloy," a substance that conquers gravity. The substance is finally to be patented for air travel safety and will work very well:

> "—unless" Peter coughed, then shouted, "unless some *idiot* starts mass-producing the *ball that bounces higher than the height from which you drop it.*"
> "What would that mean?" breathlessly asked Houghton F. Furlong and Llewellyn P. Boopfaddle.
> "The End!"

Du Bois's final exclamation is a clear, sharp—and unexpected—warning of the dangers of uncontrolled technology.

Most fantasies have some moments of charm even if they do not have the power, as Tolkien suggested, to cause "a catch of the breath, a beat and lifting of the heart."[6] In Julia Sauer's *Fog Magic* (1943), it is the fog itself—with its sometimes sharp, sometimes delicate reshaping of the real world—that one remembers. Otherwise, it is a quiet little story of a

6. Tolkien, *Tree and Leaf,* 68.

young girl who goes through the Nova Scotian fog to a village of a hundred years ago. The pace is faster in *My Father's Dragon* (1948), in which Ruth Gannett tells, in dead-pan style, of her father, who packed his knapsack and went off to Wild Island to rescue a baby dragon. It is a rare book in fantasy in that it is a picture-storybook tall tale for younger readers, perfectly conceived within its limited perimeter. It does not deserve to be forgotten.

Every period has its light and charming fantasies that stand outside the mainstream. In general, however, those of the 1940's have a sense of children at play, but with play used as a metaphor for experiencing life. In this aspect of their works, writers such as Rumer Godden, Eric Linklater, Beverley Nichols, Elizabeth Goudge, and T.H. White are on a very safe psychological ground. Play is seen not as a trivial, time-filling activity. As Huizinga points out in *Homo Ludens*, "play cannot be denied."[7] Through play, children rehearse, in a safe environment, for the unsafe things to come in adult life. If, in books, children of the decade are not shown as actually being aware of what is going on in the outside world, there can still be seen a kind of half-step toward an understanding of themselves and of the larger issues that surround them. Chiefly, there is a scenario of mini-war. Tyranny is fought and defeated. Might goes down before courage and cunning, goodness and generosity. Rumer Godden's *The Dolls' House* is the most telling example of a power struggle, as the evil Marchpane affects a whole family. Marchpane is a doll, and dolls are playthings, but the oppressive atmosphere in the dolls' house leaves its impression on the children, who only vaguely suspect its source, but ultimately they act upon their instinctive childlike feelings of fairness and justice.

The writers of this decade present their ideas quite plainly and endow their young heroes and heroines with a kind of stylized innocence. With the exception of *The Dolls' House*, none of these books are major fantasies. However, they are halfway houses to those stories of the 1960's and 1970's where time and distance from real battles resulted in a highly mythic and symbolic approach to the struggle between good and evil.

7. Johann Huizinga, *Homo Ludens: A Study of the Play Element in Culture* (Boston: Beacon, 1955), 21.

Chapter 7

There and Back Again:
Fantasy of the 1950's

The decade of the 1950's is almost as remarkable a period in the
development of fantasy as the Victorian Age. From it stem most of
the fantasies that are now designated as "modern" classics: C.S. Lewis's
Narnia Chronicles, Mary Norton's *The Borrowers* (and its sequels), Lucy
Boston's *Green Knowe* series, Philippa Pearce's *Tom's Midnight Garden,*
and E.B. White's *Charlotte's Web.* These writers were not great origi-
nators, as were Charles Kingsley, Lewis Carroll, and George MacDonald;
but each made a unique contribution to fantasy—together they brought
it into the modern age.

Epic Fantasy

C.S. Lewis is certainly the most traditional of the group. It is almost as
if he put into practice all of J.R.R. Tolkien's theories of fantasy as propounded in his essay "On Fairy-Stories."[1] Lewis's Narnia is a Secondary
World running parallel to our own and peopled with kings and queens,
princes and princesses, talking beasts, fauns, centaurs, dwarves, giants,
and other fabulous creatures. The "matter" of fantasy crammed into
Narnia would be overpowering were it not spread over seven books.

1. Tolkien, op. cit.

These books are, in order of publication date, *The Lion, The Witch, and The Wardrobe* (1950), *Prince Caspian* (1951), *The Voyage of the Dawn Treader* (1952), *The Silver Chair* (1953), *The Horse and His Boy* (1954), *The Magician's Nephew* (1955), and *The Last Battle* (1956). When Lewis wrote the first book, he had not yet conceived of a whole history of Narnia, and so in its chronology the order should be *The Magician's Nephew, The Lion, The Witch, and the Wardrobe, The Horse and His Boy, Prince Caspian,* and the rest as published. Each story, however, is complete in itself.

The *Narnia Chronicles* commanded a wide readership in their day, and they still do. They are extensions of a literary world with which children are familiar—that of the fairy tale. The series' characters—both human and non-human—its code of ethics, and its swift action make an entry to Narnia easy indeed, even for those readers not particularly enamored of fantasy. Narnia is not a vague land, however, such as "east of the sun and west of the moon" or "in a dark forest"; it has a history—a chronology—and its inhabitants have a genealogy. Narnia also has a specific geography: by following directions, one can find Cair Paravel, Ettingsmoor, the Lone Isles, and the adjoining kingdoms of Calormen and Archenland. Lewis knew that happy countries have no history, and so we enter Narnia only at times of crisis. Whether the various plots revolve around rescues or quests, there is always a sense of urgency and immediacy to each visit. But underlying all these stories, and always expressed in straightforward terms, is Lewis's Christian morality.

The *Narnia Chronicles* have a huge cast of characters, but not one is extraneous and many are memorable, such as Reepicheep the valiant, cocky mouse; Puddleglum, the Marshwiggle; Mr. Tumnus, the faun; and Bree, the talking horse. While all the books are imbued with Lewis's religious apologetics, he managed to keep this philosophical aspect of the stories on a childlike and realistic level. The children have no magic powers. They are the norm in the fantastic events (as Alice is as she moves through Lewis Carroll's Wonderland), and their ready acceptance of their roles—even when Peter and Susan and Edmund and Lucy become Kings and Queens and so take on the roles of adults—helps to convince us of the plausibility of the events. The children are far from being only cardboard fantasy characters; each has a well-defined personality (especially Lucy, who is the one most receptive to spiritual mystery and love), and they react to situations and ideas according to their natures. When they first hear the name of Aslan:

> Edmund felt a sensation of mysterious horror. Peter felt suddenly
> brave and adventurous. Susan felt as if some delicious smell or
> some delightful strain of music had just floated by her. And Lucy
> got the feeling you have when you wake up in the morning and
> realize that it is the beginning of the holidays or the beginning
> of summer.

Lewis is also a traditionalist in the way he presents Narnia. In spite of its exotic denizens, such as the White Witch who gives Narnia "always winter but never Christmas," he convinces us of Narnia's reality by the introduction of the commonplace. In scene after scene, there is an enjoyment of homely meals, hot baths, and peace and contentment before a roaring fireplace. As in the Secondary Worlds of MacDonald's *Princess* books, Barrie's *Peter and Wendy*, and Tolkien's *The Hobbit*, adventures in Narnia are interludes between the daring of leaving home and the comfort of returning to it.

The Narnia books are also kept alive by C.S. Lewis's biographers and critics. As with Charles Kingsley, George MacDonald, Lewis Carroll, and J.R.R. Tolkien, Lewis's children's books cannot be divorced from his writing for adults, and so his Narnia books, too, have found a place in the Halls of Academe. However, Lewis does not lend himself to varied interpretations. No author has left a clearer statement of his intentions in combining theology and fantasy. In discussing the Narnia books, Lewis said:

> Why did one find it so hard to feel as one was told one ought to feel
> about God or about the sufferings of Christ? . . . But supposing that
> by casting all these things into an imaginary world, stripping them
> of their stained-glass and Sunday School associations, one could
> make them for the first time appear in their real potency? Could
> one not thus steal past those watchful dragons? I thought one
> could.[2]

2. C.S. Lewis, "Sometimes Fairy Stories May Say Best What's to Be Said," *New York Times Book Review* (18 Nov. 1956): 3.

The books' theological basis is evident in everything from the biblical echoes in the doubting Thomas episode in *The Horse and His Boy*—in which Aslan insists that the skeptic horse, Bree, touch him to assure himself of Aslan's existence—to the major stories of the Crucifixion and Resurrection in *The Lion, The Witch, and The Wardrobe* to that of the Creation in *The Magician's Nephew* and ending with the Day of Judgment in *The Last Battle.*

However, unlike Kingsley's didacticism in *The Water-Babies*, Lewis's theological thread is a literary asset. On it hangs plot, characterization, and inward coherence apart from external events. They are indeed books that grew, to use a Tolkien phrase, "out of the leaf mould of the mind." Lewis's almost seamless combination of personal belief and the imagery of fantasy is seen at its greatest in the portrayal of Aslan—the Christ-figure whose presence, whether seen or felt, is at the crux of each of the books. Lewis's conception of a majestic golden lion who rewards and punishes but who is frequently seen as a playful, magnified kitten is a perfect expression of the Narnia books themselves. They are serious, but never solemn; moral, but not didactic. Just as Lewis himself was "surprised by joy" when he discovered God (as he tells us in his autobiography)[3] the reader of the *Narnia Chronicles* is frequently "surprised by joy" at the festivities and merrymaking, and at a land where all beings in various shapes and forms—ranging from cabbies to kings, from rabbits to giants—can dance and sing together.

Perhaps only Tolkien with Middle-earth, in *The Lord of the Rings*, has created a universe as believable as the epic fairy-tale world of Narnia. This believability is best expressed by the usually dour Puddleglum in *The Silver Chair* when the witch tries to convince the children that Aslan does not exist and that the witch's dark, underground world is the only *real* one:

> " . . . Suppose we *have* only dreamed, or made up, all those things—trees and grass and sun and moon and stars and Aslan himself. . . . We're just babies making up games, if you're right. But four babies playing a game can make a play-world which licks your real world hollow.

3. C.S. Lewis, *Surprised by Joy* (London: G. Bles, 1955).

. . . I'm on Aslan's side even if there isn't any Aslan to lead it. I'm going to live as like a Narnian as I can even if there isn't any Narnia. . . . "

Most of our modern epic fantasists have been to Narnia.

In keeping with his affinity for the fairy tale, Lewis chiefly used the simple and intimate style of the oral storyteller. *The Horse and His Boy* begins:

> This is the story of an adventure that happened in Narnia and Calormen and the lands between, in the Golden Age when Peter was High King in Narnia and his brother and his two sisters were Kings and Queens under him.

His childhood love for the books of Edith Nesbit sometimes trapped Lewis into English schoolboy slang, but he mostly adopted the simple, flowing, evocative language of George MacDonald (whom he also admired). Like MacDonald and most other writers before him, Lewis also used the technique of the authorial intervention, such as:

> If one could run without getting tired, I don't think one would often want to do anything else.

or

> People who have not been in Narnia sometimes think that a thing cannot be good and terrible at the same time.

Such asides were a tradition in children's literature, generally introduced to reinforce a moral, as in Charles Kingsley's *The Water-Babies* or George MacDonald's *Princess* books, but never used as blatantly as in early and Victorian stories of child and family life. Like Tolkien's interjections in *The Hobbit* (which he came to regret), Lewis's are used sparingly. However, Lewis was the last major writer to use such authority; even his contemporaries deemed it condescending to children, and its use disappeared—almost abruptly.

Miniature Worlds

In working on the large canvas of epic fantasy, Lewis's grand design sometimes faltered in its execution. Inconsistencies and stylistic flaws are noticeable, and the religious dragons that he wanted to "slip by" sometimes disturb by their overpowering presence. By contrast, in the world of *The Borrowers* (1952), Mary Norton creates perfection in miniature. Her first two books, *The Magic Bedknob* (1945) and *Bonfires and Broomsticks* (1946), were very much in the Nesbit tradition as a traveling bed takes two contemporary children on a series of adventures—those in the second book having a more serious purpose than the first. Little in these stories, however, foreshadowed the complete harmony of concept, characterization, and style that was to make *The Borrowers* so memorable and that was to be sustained, moreover, through four more books dealing with the same family—all set in the Edwardian period: *The Borrowers Afield* (1955) *The Borrowers Afloat* (1959), *The Borrowers Aloft* (1961) and *The Borrowers Avenged* (1982).

"The borrowers" are "little people about six inches high but otherwise as nearly human as makes no difference." Their supposition is that big people ("human beans") exist to support *them*, and so they have no hesitation in taking (they call it "borrowing") from people what they need to live—a morsel of cheese, leftover toast, three tea leaves, pins, needles, empty match-boxes, candle stumps, chiefly the detritus of humanity. Their greatest fear is that they may be seen. "The borrowers" are no different in size, ability, and ingenuity from Jonathan Swift's Lilliputians or T.H. White's characters in *Mistress Masham's Repose;* as in both of these books, minuteness is the only element of the fantastic in *The Borrowers*. Here the similarity ends, except that *The Borrowers Aloft* revolves around the exploitation of the weak and the helpless by the strong and the powerful, as does White's book.

In essence, the Lilliputians are indistinguishable from one another, and—as members of a well-defined society—they have the support and consolation that a community offers. The Clock family of *The Borrowers*—Pod (the father), Homily (the mother), and Arrietty (the twelve-year-old daughter)—are individuals, and we follow their personal fortunes with breathless interest. Moreover, they are a dying breed, fighting a rearguard action for their very existence. Swift's Lilliput, of course, provides a framework for satire and White's, for a considerable amount of polemic. *The Borrowers,* as Mary Norton explains in her preface to *The Complete Adventures of the Borrowers,*[4] grew out of her experiences as a near-sighted child when she saw nature in small rather than in large and from her imaginative play concerning little people. If Mary Norton propounds a message at all, it is simply a lesson in living.

Any survival story has echoes of Daniel Defoe's Robinson Crusoe, but "the borrowers" outdo Robinson with their ingenuity. The lone boy borrower, Spiller, has to scavenge in a world made for giants, subject to attack at any time from a field animal who could crush him in its paws. Pod is a cobbler-craftsman, and all of his makeshifts actually work in real life, including his escape balloon in *The Borrowers Aloft.* Pod and Homily are also well-defined, if static, personalities. Pod is cautious and responsible, with every move planned in advance. Homily is the traditional housewife and somewhat acquisitive, but she is a force to be reckoned with. The domestic exchanges between husband and wife are enlivened by considerable wit.

But the books belong to Arrietty. When we first meet her—and barring her size—she might be any girl protagonist in an Edwardian story of child and family life; she is living a routine and sheltered life in a cocoon. However, an unfulfilled longing is stirring in her: she yearns for a life above the floorboards. Her mother sees the advantage of Arrietty's going a-borrowing along with Pod. On her first trip

> Panting a little, Arrietty gazed about her. She saw great chair legs rearing up into sunlight; she saw the shadowed undersides of their seats spread above her like canopies; she saw the nails and the strapping and odd tags of silk and string; she saw the terraced cliffs of the stairs, mounting up into the distance, up and up . . . she saw carved table legs and a cavern under the chest. And all the time, in the stillness, the clock spoke—measuring out the seconds, spreading its layers of calm.
>
> And then, turning, Arrietty looked at the garden.

Arrietty is seen by the boy who lives in the house, and from him she learns that it is the borrowers who are few and that there are "thousands and millions and trillions of great, big, enormous people." It is her first

4. This edition does not include *The Borrowers Avenged.*

traumatic experience. Nonetheless, it is her reaching out to the world, her growth, adaptability, and imagination that, in the end, will save the few of her people who are left. Age must give way to youth.

To begin *The Borrowers,* Mary Norton uses the device of a story within a story. Did the Mrs. May who first told the story simply make it up? Or are "the borrowers" real characters in the tale? This narrative ambiguity gives readers the freedom to work within their own imaginations, tabling their skepticism for the duration of the compelling adventures.

Most of the dramatic tension in *The Borrowers* series comes simply from size; Mary Norton has been able to ring every possible change on the dangers of being little. Carol Kendall in *The Gammage Cup* (1959) uses her freshly created miniature world to convey a strong social message. Her "Land Between the Mountains" is inhabited by the Minnipins, or "Small Ones," who have set up a simple agricultural society. Generations ago the Minnipins had come from somewhere else, fleeing for their lives from "the Mushrooms or the Hairless Ones" and had accidentally found haven in a now inaccessible valley. The story has tones of science fiction in reverse. The Minnipins have forgotten the uses of the artifacts their ancestors brought with them, and their veneration of these artifacts keeps their society a static one. A landscape painting with a tree in it is now regarded as a family tree, while a genealogical chart is a painting. Scraps of paper with such words printed on it as *Co., Ltd., Bros., Wm.,* and *Geo.* have become the names of the ruling class, called "The Periods." Now the village is a peaceful, ordered, almost feudal place where all the Minnipins wear sober green or brown cloaks, paint their small doors green, and frown upon any divergence from the norm. When the Mushrooms return, it is the four free spirits of the village (outlawed for insubordination), who rouse the village to arms and defeat the invaders with the use of knightly armor that has been discovered in a treasure chamber and swords that have a magical quality in the presence of evil. At the story's end, the villagers understand that they have been misinterpreting their ancestry and that there is room for individuality. The epic conclusion certainly sweeps out what little consideration of size there has been, leaving *The Gammage Cup* as an interesting and innovative fantasy but without the empathy aroused for the small characters in both Norton's *The Borrowers* and T.H. White's *Mistress Masham's Repose.*

Enchanted Realism

Age and youth, past and present meld in an almost seamless pattern in Lucy Boston's *Green Knowe* sequence: *The Children of Green Knowe* (1952), *The Chimneys of Green Knowe*[5] (1958), *The River at Green Knowe* (1959), *A Stranger at Green Knowe* (1961), *An Enemy at Green Knowe* (1964), and *The Stones of Green Knowe* (1976).

The link between the old and the young is made very clear in *The Chimneys of Green Knowe*. In this story, Tolly is indignant when a schoolfellow expresses sympathy for Tolly for having to spend the holidays with his great-grandmother. Tolly loves to be with her:

> His great-grandmother, Mrs. Oldknow, was waiting for him at the door. They hugged each other, and she was little and soft and shaped like a partridge. She was very pleased to see him again and he to see her. She understood what nobody else did. When he was with her, he forgot at once about being a schoolboy. He and she were just two people.

The house where Tolly, and later Ping and other children, are so happy is a real house, Mrs. Boston's own. It was built in Norman times and seems to have a power all its own. Lucy Boston says in her autobiography:

> It was not that I was living in an escapist dream. The house was *there*. It was dominating. It was, and I hope still is, haunted and it-self a haunter. It has a power felt by almost everybody who comes here.[6]

In *The Children of Green Knowe,* the house captivates Tolly immediately:

> The entrance hall was a strange place. As they stepped in, a similar door opened at the far end of the house and another man and boy entered there. Then Toseland saw that it was only them-selves in a big mirror. The walls round him were partly rough stone and partly plaster, but hung all over with mirrors and pictures and china. There were three big old mirrors all reflecting each other so

5. Published in the United States as *The Treasure of Green Knowe.*
6. Lucy Boston, *Memory in a House* (London: The Bodley Head, 1973), 32–33.

that at first Toseland was puzzled to find what was real, and which door one could go through straight, the way one wanted to, not sideways somewhere else. He almost wondered which was really himself.

Just as Mrs. Oldknow is at one with her house, so is she at one with "the Others"—children from the past who still make their presence felt in the house, but whom she can no longer see. Age has not dimmed Mrs. Oldknow's faculties; it is the power of the house itself that passes to the young. Thus, it is seven-year-old Tolly who bridges time and who hears, then sees, and then talks to Toby and Alexander and Linnet—all of whom died on the same day in the Great Plague of 1666. Tolly finds some of the children's possessions in the house, ones included in a picture of the children that dominates the main room of the house. These possessions are not used as talismans to mark the children's appearance; rather, the children come when Tolly desires companionship or when he learns more and more about them from his great-grandmother or from Boggis, the gardener. The same pattern is used in *The Chimneys of Green Knowe,* in which Tolly's companions are Susan, a blind child of the eighteenth century, and Jacob, her black pageboy and friend.

Tolly is a type of fantasy protagonist with whom we are now familiar—sensitive, curious, loving, and imaginative. However, he is also a displaced person, as are other Green Knowe children. Tolly's father and new stepmother are in Burma; Ping's father has disappeared (in *The River at Green Knowe, A Stranger at Green Knowe,* and *An Enemy at Green Knowe*); Oskar's parents are dead (in *The River at Green Knowe*); and Hanno, the great ape, has been taken from his home in Africa (in *A Stranger at Green Knowe*). The house and its garden and grounds offer hospitality to everyone, as well as a place in which to grow. The garden leads to the river, as much a symbol of the continuity of time as Green Knowe itself. Along its banks, in *The River at Green Knowe,* Oskar, Ida, and Ping see a midnight celebration by horned dancers before the stones of the house were erected and meet a modern giant, a leftover from prehistoric times. This is Lucy Boston's least successful book, chiefly because of the strain the giant episode places on one's credulity and because two eccentric women are substituted for Mrs. Oldknow's empathetic presence.

Sometimes evil enters Green Knowe. As the author says in *An Enemy at Green Knowe:*

Surely Now and Not-now is the most teasing of all mysteries, and if you let in a nine-hundred-year dose of time, you let in almost anything.

An ancient and cursed yew-tree, clipped into the shape of a man named Green Noah, brings Tolly to the edge of terror in the otherwise gentle story *The Children of Green Knowe*. The total theme of *An Enemy at Green Knowe* is the struggle between good and evil, brought about by a witch—Melanie D. Powers (her ancient name is Melusine Demogorgona Phospher)—who invades the house in search of a seventeenth-century manuscript that was once owned by a wicked necromancer. In comparison with Beverley Nichols's witch in *The Tree That Sat Down*, Melanie is evil incarnate. She is also crass and vulgar, both in her intrusion into the lives of Tolly and Ping and Mrs. Oldknow, and in her use of magic. This aspect of her nature gives the book a very modern touch indeed in showing the vulnerability of those who wish to be private when assailed by the outside world. Eventually, Ping and Tolly defeat Melanie, not only through study and ingenuity, but through schoolboy-type taunts and jeers. The story is not subtle enough to be entirely successful, however.

A Stranger at Green Knowe is not really a fantasy, but it is touched by enchanted realism. It is a story of the friendship that exists for a short period between Ping and Hanno, the giant ape who has escaped from the zoo and taken refuge in the woods of Green Knowe. The events are highly improbable, but the relationship between the boy and the animal—both displaced people—is charged with almost unbearable emotion. It is Lucy Boston's finest piece of writing, and the book's opening paragraphs are among the most memorable in children's literature:

> To look for the hero of the story, you must venture into the haunted gloom. Even at noon it is dark like a heavily curtained room, and at night like a closed oven. From among the roots of the trees, ropes of creeper loop up, weighing the leaf-ceiling down and tying trees together, sometimes knitting square miles into an unbroken tangle.

Here the brooding jungle of central Africa seems a place of enchantment.

The Stones of Green Knowe tells of the building of the house in A.D. 1120 and of how it captures the imagination of the son of the Manor,

Roger d'Aulneaux. Through Roger's passionate longing to know what the house will be like in the future, past and future meld, and he meets the other children of Green Knowe—both in their time and in his. As with so much of enchanted realism, the continuum of time is at the heart of the Green Knowe sequence. This continuum is perhaps most delicately perceived in *The Children of Green Knowe* when, close to Christmas, Tolly and his great-grandmother hear a lullaby being sung:

> It was queer to hear the baby's sleepy whimper only in the next room, now, and so long ago. "Come, we"ll sing it too," said Mrs. Oldknow, going to the spinet. She played, but it was Tolly who sang alone, while, four hundred years ago, a baby went to sleep.

The enigma of time is also at the heart of Philippa Pearce's *Tom's Midnight Garden* (1958). Tom Long, the young protagonist, wrestles with its secrets more than do Lucy Boston's Green Knowe children and it yields them up to his probings. Images of time hover in the air: the old grandfather clock strikes thirteen; on its pendulum is a quotation, "Time No Longer"; there is a sundial in the garden; and, finally, Tom notices that the child that he plays with in the garden is changing, growing up, while he is not. It is part of the book's perfection that abstract ideas of time are clothed in a concrete and childlike form. When Tom's Uncle Alan tries to explain time to him scientifically, Tom is bewildered. Only the mention of Rip Van Winkle (who slept for twenty years) seems to enlighten his own experience.

Tom is upset when he is exiled from his home because his brother, Peter, has the measles. Both boys had looked forward to their summer holidays and to building a treehouse in their garden. In itself, it was in no way an exciting garden, but it would have been colored by the boys' imaginative play. In his aunt's and uncle's dull, gardenless flat, Tom is bored and restless; and from a lack of exercise and too much rich food, he spends many a sleepless night. One night he hears the old grandfather clock in the hall downstairs strike thirteen:

> He was uneasy in the knowledge that this happening made some difference to him: he could feel that in his bones. The stillness had become an expectant one; the house seemed to hold its breath: the

darkness pressed up to him, pressing him with a question: Come on, Tom, the clock has struck thirteen—what are you going to do about it?

Tom answers the call to adventure, and he discovers a late Victorian house in place of the converted flats; a large, beautiful garden in place of the dusty paved yard; and a spirited but lonely girl, Hatty.

Hatty is also a displaced person, an orphan living on the charity of a less-than-generous aunt and often an unwelcome fourth in the activities of her older male cousins. Tom's midnight visits to the garden and Hatty become the center of his life, even an obsession; he does not even want to go home when his brother has recovered. Tom's games and explorations with Hatty can be seen as a celebration of the vital energy and excitement of childhood; at first these aspects of childhood are held in check by the garden walls, and both children are content with their confinement. Soon, however, Hatty breaks through the boundaries. Extremely cold weather freezes over the river, and Hatty and Tom skate down to Ely and then climb to the top of its cathedral tower. It is on this first, wonderful journey that Tom notices a change in Hatty:

> Tom thought of time: how he had been sure of mastering it, and of exchanging his own Time for an Eternity of Hatty's and so of living pleasurably in the garden for ever. The garden was still there, but meanwhile Hatty's Time had stolen a march on him, and had turned Hatty herself into a grown-up woman.

The garden disappears, and Tom's grief is extreme as he discovers that time is a thief. He is comforted, however, when he also discovers that old Mrs. Batholomew who lives in the top flat is also his child friend, Hatty. They had come together across the boundaries of time because both

> ... had longed for someone to play with and for somewhere to play; and that great longing, beating about unhappily in the big house, must have made its entry into Mrs. Batholomew's dreaming mind and had brought back to her the little Hatty of long ago.

There is a special victory for Tom in the story, but the victory is not over time. Instead, it lies in the depth of Tom's love for Hatty as a child and now for her as an old woman:

> Afterwards, Aunt Gwen tried to describe to her husband that second parting between them. "He ran up to her, and they hugged each other as if they had known each other for years and years, instead of only having met this morning. There was something else, too, Alan, though I know you'll say it sounds even more absurd. . . . Of course, Mrs. Batholomew's such a shrunken little old woman, she's hardly bigger than Tom, anyway: but, you know, he put his arms right round her and he hugged her good-bye as if she were a little girl."

The range and delicacy of Philippa Pearce's emotional grasp as shown in this book is unmatched in children's literature, and her stylistic craftsmanship is impeccable. But she never forgets that she is writing for children: Tom's search to uncover the mystery of the garden and his ghost-life therefore has the pace of a detective story.

The 1950's also saw the emergence of Canada's first serious writer of fantasy, Catherine Anthony Clark. Her first book, *The Golden Pine Cone,* was published in 1950. She followed this with *The Sun Horse* (1951), *The One-Winged Dragon* (1955),*The Silver Man* (1958), *The Diamond Feather* (1962), and *The Hunter and the Medicine Man* (1966).

Clark's books are set in the mountainous land of British Columbia. Those who know the province well take delight in pinpointing some of the places she describes. Clark's great strength is in her settings and in her ability to people the snowy peaks, the forests, and the lonely paths by the lakes with a peculiarly Canadian kind of spirit-folk—the Rock Puck, the Ice Folk, the Head Canada Goose, the Lake Snake, and prospectors who live on the borderline between the real world and the world of fantasy.

On the periphery of her plots are the symbols of some of the ancient myths and legends of the Indian tribes of British Columbia. There is the Raven, the Thunderbird, the Magic Woman, and the Killer Whale. Although these symbols are not central to the plot, they succeed in creating atmosphere. Alongside them are numerous witches, sprites, and enchanted animals. More symbolic are the Indian chiefs and princesses—shining personages who rule the spirit lands with justice.

The children in these books are at one with their setting. They are not, like Alice in Wonderland, aliens in a card game or in a looking-glass world. They are not wrenched, as are the children in C.S. Lewis's *The Lion, The Witch, and The Wardrobe*, from English school holiday life to a wholly unrecognizable land. Clark's children drink sparingly from the magic potion. They are exposed to events that seem only somewhat larger than life and to a land that remains familiar to them.

Like many fantasists, Clark's strength lies not so much in the allure of the strange as in the homely charm of the realistic. The children are seen as frequently in their domestic surroundings as in the midst of their self-initiated quests. When Jenni in *The One-Winged Dragon* drops an egg on the floor, her reaction is quick and simple:

> So Ruggles, the bushy, white, foxy dog was called in and made to lick the egg off the linoleum.

The same kind of no-nonsense is applied to morality. Clark is a moralist through and through. In every one of her stories, the underlying theme is the search for happiness and the way in which children can find it for themselves and for adults. However, the purpose, though explicit, is accomplished through the plots themselves and not through extraneous incidents. There is no overt preaching such as that found in Beverley Nichols's *The Tree That Sat Down* or T.H. White's *Mistress Masham's Repose* or in Carol Kendall's *The Gammage Cup*. Although Clark has not matched writers such as Lucy Boston or Philippa Pearce in matters of style, she is very much a part of her decade in her treatment of children. Their basic good sense and intelligence carries children through their adventures, and they return from these experiences with a greater understanding of themselves and their world.

Animal Fantasy

The works of C.S. Lewis, Mary Norton, Lucy Boston, and Philippa Pearce put British writers in the forefront of postwar fantasy just as such writers were in Victorian and Edwardian times; but there was one great exception—E.B. White with *Charlotte's Web* (1952). As evidenced by his essays, short stories, and articles for the *New Yorker* magazine, White had the great gift of inspiring affection in the reader. *Charlotte's Web* has liveliness and tenderness, humor and pathos, and, above all, a backbone of reality that all the greatest fantasies possess. If one could emulate Charlotte the spider in web-spinning and succinct writing, the phrase "SOME BOOK" would be most appropriate.

Unlike other writers of animal fantasy, such as Kenneth Grahame in *The Wind in the Willows*, White did not use animals as personifications of humans, nor did he write for children on one level and for adults on another. Charlotte, Wilbur, the hero pig, Templeton the rat, and the goose who says everything twice are essentially what they are—barnyard animals. The author himself has left us his view of this classic in a letter to the producer of the movie:

> . . . I do hope, though, that you are not planning to turn "Charlotte's Web" into a moral tale. It is not that at all. It is, I think, an *appreciative* story, and there is quite a difference. It celebrates life, the seasons, the goodness of the barn, the beauty of the world, the glory of everything. But it is essentially amoral, because animals are essentially amoral, and I respect them, and I think this respect is implicit in the tale. . . . I discovered that there was no need to tamper in any way with the habits and characteristics of spiders, pigs, geese and rats. No "motivation" is needed if you remain true to the spirit of fantasy. . . . [7]

White's "spirit of fantasy" has the earthiness of his barnyard characters, but it is enough to turn a New England farm into a place of magic. The story begins with the small girl, Fern, who wished to save her pet pig from the usual fate awaiting the porcine breed. Her longing is communicated to the animals. Charlotte makes Wilbur, the pig, a local celebrity by spinning slogans about him into her web:

> It is not often that someone comes along who is a true friend and a good writer. Charlotte was both.

For a single-level fantasy, *Charlotte's Web* has extraordinary depth. It is a story of friendship and loyalty, an insight into the naturalness and in-

---

7. E.B. White, *Letters of E.B. White*, comp. and ed. Dorothy Lobrano Guth (New York: Harper, 1976), 613.

evitability of death and the continuity of life as Wilbur befriends Charlotte's children when she dies giving birth to them. It is also a story of growing up, as we see Fern putting aside her involvement with the animals for the glittering excitements of the County Fair. But most of all, it is a celebration of nature. On the Sunday after Charlotte has written "SOME PIG" in her web, Dr. Dorian, the minister, has this to say to his congregation:

> "Oh, no, I don't understand it. But for that matter I don't un-
> derstand how a spider learned to spin a web in the first place. But
> nobody pointed out that the web itself is a miracle."

White's only comment is: "Charlotte was in a class by herself."

Of Charlotte, E.B. White has said, "perhaps she is magnifying herself by her devotion to another, but essentially she is just a trapper."[8] Louis, the trumpeter swan (named after Louis Armstrong), in White's *The Trumpet of the Swan* (1970), is less natural. With the artifacts of humans around his neck (his trumpet, his slate, and his moneybag), he belongs more in the company of the mouse in *Stuart Little* than of Templeton in *Charlotte's Web* who starts as a rat and stays as a rat. *The Trumpet of the Swan* has the same absurdity as *Stuart Little*, and in both books the absurdity must be accepted with a straight face. Louis is born mute, which means that he cannot woo a mate, especially the one he desires with all his heart. His father steals a trumpet for him, which he learns to play but also feels obliged to pay for. Louis goes to school to learn to read and write, and the first-graders "liked the look of the new pupil." After he becomes famous, Louis performs in nightclubs and rides in taxis, and upon checking in for the night at the Ritz Carlton Hotel in Boston, he orders up a watercress sandwich. Finally, he wins his love by playing her one of his own compositions. The story contains many such humorous and even moving episodes, but they are not coordinated to make a whole; the premise of the story—a trumpet-playing swan—is inventive but not magical, and White the stylist almost disappears. The chief human element in the story is the boy, Sam, who is quiet, serious, and responsible. He moves in and out of the story; but it is kinship with nature (the woods, lakes, animals, and birds of northern Ontario) that im-

8. E.B. White, *Letters*, 613.

bues the book with love. The actual love story, that between Louis and his mate, lacks the pathos of that between Stuart Little and the sparrow, however.

Many of the minor fantasies of the 1950's have an endearing quality to them, but none more so than the Miss Bianca series by the English author Margery Sharp. Miss Bianca is a white mouse who lives in the Embassy as the pet of the Ambassador's son. Little is known about her except that

> ... she lives in a Porcelain Pagoda; that she fed exclusively on cream cheese from a silver bonbon dish; that she wore a silver chain around her neck, and on Sundays a gold one. She was also said to be extremely beautiful, but affected to the last degree.

We meet Miss Bianca first in *The Rescuers* (1959), where her true nature is revealed.[9] Although used to luxury, she is brave, modest, and resourceful. She is persuaded by the Prisoner's Aid Society (mice have traditionally been the friends of prisoners) to lead a rescue party to the Black Castle in order to rescue a young poet from this impregnable fortress. Miss Bianca is a poet herself, and she has means of transportation via the diplomatic pouch. Her two companions, the adoring (of Miss Bianca) and self-effacing Bernard and the diamond-in-the-rough Norwegian mouse Nils, are as well delineated as Miss Bianca herself, and they accomplish their missions by use of their mouse-like skills and qualities. It is all a miniature world presented with the control of Mary Norton's *The Borrowers* but with touches of acceptable exaggeration and doses of humor in the tall-tale style.

Miss Bianca has not achieved the long-lasting popularity of Paddington, the honey-bear from South America, first created by Michael Bond in *A Bear Called Paddington* (1958). Other books in the series, such as *More About Paddington* (1959), were published in rapid succession.

After stowing away on a ship to England, the independent little bear arrives at Paddington Station in London, is adopted by the Brown family, and (appropriately) is given the name of Paddington. He has much of the

9. The series is continued with *Miss Bianca* (1962), *Miss Bianca in the Salt Mines* (1966), *Miss Bianca in the Orient* (1970), *Miss Bianca in the Antarctic* (1971), and *Miss Bianca and the Bridesmaid* (1972).

lovableness of A.A. Milne's Winnie-the-Pooh as well as Pooh's ability for getting into awkward situations. Like Milne, Bond made no attempt to keep an animal's natural characteristics, beyond constant references to paws rather than feet. There is also more than a touch of Milne's cleverness in the scenes leading up to the disasters. These events can be easily anticipated by child readers and thus bolster their egos. However, Bond has none of Milne's magic with words, his is an almost sparse style that is easily open even to reluctant readers.

The *Paddington* series, as examples of light fantasy, are very much in tune with their time in their portrayal of Paddington as a surrogate child (the Brown's real children are colorless). He is allowed freedom (and pocket money) to explore and experiment without supervision. He is curious, thoughtful, and alway polite. Most importantly, he has a loving family (even the cook spoils him) who stand up for him against any threat of disapproval from others. (Of course, they realize that life would be dull without him.) Paddington's mishaps would become boring if they were applied to children; but because he is an animal who looks somewhat human (like H.A. Rey's Curious George), the mishaps always have an element of the ludicrous. Paddington gained further fame and memorableness when he appeared on the market as a stuffed toy. He can now be seen everywhere, dressed in his broad-brimmed hat, duffle jacket, and Wellington boots.

Stories of Magic

Although Barbara Sleigh's *Carbonel* (1955) is a talking cat, the story cannot be described as an animal fantasy; there is too much human interaction in the story to make it such a fantasy and the cat can speak only through the medium of a witch's broom. The plot slightly echoes Joseph Jacob's English folktale "The King O' the Cats" as two children help to restore Carbonel to his rightful royal place. The book's chief charm lies in its portrayal of a poor, single-parent family and of an uncomplaining little girl who finds companionship with an equally nice wealthy boy. In Nesbit-like fashion, the family's situation is improved at the end of the story. The sequel, *Carbonel and Calidor* (1978), is about Carbonel's son.

Edith Nesbit is the total inspiration behind the works of the American writer Edward Eager, but he gives her type of magic a novel twist. In

Half Magic (1954), the children find a magic charm that gives them only half their wish. When, for example, one of them wishes to be on a desert island, the children find themselves in a desert but not on an island. In *Seven-Day Magic* (1962), the children find themselves as characters in a book in which the story unfolds with their adventures. In both stories, the children must learn the rules of the magic "and tame it and make the most of it." Both books have a softer and less rigorous quality than do those of Nesbit; nevertheless, they are still fun to read, especially because the children themselves are such voracious readers.

Fantasy Based on Folklore

K.M. Briggs's *Hobberdy Dick* (1955) is replete with folklore as befits the author of the celebrated *Dictionary of British Folk-Tales* and of *The Fairies in Tradition and Literature*. "Hobberdy Dick" is a household hobgoblin (like that found in Dinah Mulock's *The Adventures of a Brownie*), and he has watched over Widford Manor in the Cotswolds for two hundred years. However, Hobberdy Dick is not happy when the Puritan branch of the family takes over from the Royalist branch after the Civil War: The Widdisons forbid all Christmas and Easter festivities and, indeed, celebrations of any sort. Hobberdy Dick's tricks are many and successful. He comes to care for the eldest son, Joel, however, who loves the manor house and its land, and he is fiercely protective of Anne, the penniless cousin whom Joel loves and the true heiress to the manor. Because of them, Hobberdy Dick rouses his friends—the other hobs and ghosts—to save the child, Martha Widdison, when she is captured and entranced by the witches.

Briggs's *Kate Crackernuts* (1963) is a powerful interpretation of Joseph Jacob's English folktale of the same name but transported from a king's palace to an impoverished Scottish castle and a witch-infested countryside during the seventeenth century. From the simple tale of *Hobberdy Dick* to the more complex *Kate Crackernuts,* Briggs's works are exemplars of the use of traditional material transferred to novelistic form. She is no mere reteller; rather her scholarly knowledge, scholarly insights and her ability as a storyteller allow her to probe more deeply the themes and images of the oral tradition.

Simplicity combined with depth of feeling is one of the chief hallmarks of the fantasy novels of the 1950's. These writers did not, like Edwardians such as Kenneth Grahame with *The Wind in the Willows*, J.M. Barrie with *Peter and Wendy*, and later even A.A. Milne with *Winnie-the-Pooh*, write with one eye on children but the other on the adult world. Nor did they, like the Victorians, indulge in the metaphysics of George MacDonald as in *At the Back of the North Wind*, in the polemics of Charles Kingsley as in *The Water-Babies*, or in the (even then and certainly now) esoteric allusions that make Lewis Carroll's *Alice* somewhat forbidding to the modern child reader. Even C.S. Lewis's many-faceted *Narnia Chronicles* are all of a piece and are told without irony, satire, parody, or even a double meaning. Certainly, writers such as Lucy Boston, Philippa Pearce, Mary Norton, and E.B. White proved that great fantasies could be written by appealing directly to children and by not circumnavigating them in order to gain the applause of the adult world. These are all child-centered books, and childhood is seen as a very natural state—one that mostly needs time for its development into maturity. Their writers sensed that children had an inward life of their own, one that was worth probing, but only so far as a delicate lifting of the veil for the elucidation of the children themselves.

The storybook children of the 1950's frequently have problems. Those in Lucy Boston's *Green Knowe* series are without parents (except for Roger in *The Stones of Green Knowe*); those in C.S. Lewis's *The Lion, The Witch, and The Wardrobe* have been sent to the country because of the expected bombing of London; Arrietty in Mary Norton's *The Borrowers* has to face physical dangers almost every day; and the school child in Barbara Sleigh's *Carbonel* is far from privileged. But they do not brood on their difficulties; they are accepting and uncomplaining, but they are also resourceful, cheerful, and have never heard of an identity crisis. Yet they do change. Except perhaps for Edmund and Eustace in C.S. Lewis's *Narnia Chronicles*, who are brought to repentance for their naughty deeds, the protagonists do not have a change of heart. They do not need one. Their hearts are very much in the right place even as their stories begin. (The Chinese boy, Ping, in Lucy Boston's *Green Knowe*, for example, is very much his own person and remains so.) It is the children's own sensitive natures that are uncovered; they see more deeply into themselves, and they develop a greater empathy with others and with the natural world. They also learn more about the adult world when they are ready to taste of it, whether of its delights or of its shortcomings. Generally, their trust in the adult world is not misplaced. Thus, while they are drawn into the unreal and the unusual for a while, they return to their normal life with heightened emotions and a new perceptive vision of it. We feel that they will become very fine adults indeed.

Most of the writers of the fifties (with the exception of C.S. Lewis), are satisfied with the real world, whether that of contemporary life, such as in Lucy Boston's *The Children of Green Knowe* and Philippa Pearce's *Tom's Midnight Garden*, put into Edwardian times as in Mary Norton's *The Borrowers*, or set in a recent past as in Edward Eager's *Half Magic*. All these worlds are peaceful and settled milieus.

Moreover, all of these backgrounds suit the general tone of the 1950's very well indeed. The war to end war had receded into the background, and conflicts such as the Korean War did not touch a large proportion of lives. Economic stability was also the order of the day; and although the atomic bomb was a reality, there was as yet no feeling of one's standing on the brink of disaster. As brilliantly and nostalgically described in John Updike's short story, "When Everyone Was Pregnant,"[10] the emphasis was on the family and family life. The children's books of the period all have this sense of security and hope.

Perhaps it was the serenity of the decade that released the imaginations of such writers as Lucy Boston, Philippa Pearce, E.B. White, and Mary Norton and impelled them to explore such ideas as the continuity of time, the links between old age and childhood, the cycle of the seasons, and the ongoing plight of the small and the weak against the large and the powerful. However, the greatest triumph of these writers lay in their ability to present such concepts in a clear, lucid style and with memorable images. Who can forget Mr. Tumnus, the faun, carrying an umbrella in the snow when he first meets Lucy in *The Lion, The Witch, and The Wardrobe*, or the demon tree, Green Noah, as it moves stealthily toward Tolly in *The Children of Green Knowe?* These writers' creations have been rewarded by a wide range of readership that has extended into the 1980's.

---

10. John Updike, "When Everyone Was Pregnant," in *Museums & Women* (New York: Vintage Books, 1981).

Chapter 8

Extensions of Reality:
Fantasy of the 1960's

The 1960's brought dramatic changes to children's literature, chiefly in the area of realistic fiction. Indeed, it was the decade when the term "realism" was first applied to a novel for the young. In earlier times, one usually spoke of "stories of child and family life," meaning domestic dramas or insights into the everyday doings of children at home, school, or on vacation, such as Edith Nesbit's *The Treasure Seekers* or Edward Taylor's *The All-of-a-Kind Family*. The new realism concentrated on social problems (frequently harsh ones) that affected the young directly and that immediately caused psychological and even traumatic disturbances in their lives. The books themselves soon came to be described as "problem" novels and matched to an uncanny degree Walter de la Mare's definition of realism:

> What is called realism is usually a record of life at a low pitch and ebb viewed in the sunless light of day—so often a drab waste of grey and white, and an east wind blowing.[1]

1. Walter de la Mare, *Pleasures and Speculations* (Freeport, New York: Books for Libraries Press, 1969), 20.

Changing Concepts of Childhood

This new literature emanated from the United States, the country in which the social turmoil of the sixties was most evident. The culture that sparked it was youth-oriented. It was the decade when the young discovered that there was power in numbers (they sprang from the largest baby-boom in American history),[2] disputed the wisdom of their elders, defied established authority, and discovered the word "relevance."

It was natural that the youth revolution (ranging from teenagers to those aged thirty) should reflect upon children, even if one accepts only the simple theory that the youngest child in the family gets more freedom than the oldest in similar circumstances. However, many children, too, had their own share of responsibilities and problems. With the increasing numbers of one-parent families and mothers who worked outside the home from either necessity or for personal fulfillment, the traditional family structure was shattered. It was inevitable that under any such circumstances children's lives would be affected, although not necessarily to their detriment. Certainly, however, the seeds were planted for anxiety complexes, for the carrying of more than the usual responsibilities, and for the development of more insights into the workings of the adult world than occurred in previous decades. Certainly, too, all these events led to an erosion of childhood. Children's rights became a battle cry; children were to be liberated from the restrictions of childhood. Subterfuges and evasions in dealing with children were out; honesty and openness were in. To support these views, useful ammunition was found in the fields of physiology and psychology. It was plausibly claimed that children matured earlier, in a physical sense, than they once did. Freud's theories on the early sexuality of children became an argument for greater frankness, and modern child psychology revealed that children, too, had fears and anxieties, suppressions and repressions, as did their elders.

Reflecting and contributing to this disorienting change was the influence of television. The shared content of the screen drew children into the adult world, even if much of that world was an illusion. "It's life's illusions I recall. I really don't know life at all," went a popular song of the period.

2. Landon Y. Jones, *Great Expectations: America and the Baby Boom Generation* (New York: Ballantine, 1980), 1.

The most obvious manifestation of these changes was that long-standing convictions about what children *were* and thus how to treat them faltered and failed. Children were no longer considered special or different, or even delicately balanced in their passage between childhood and adulthood; they were considered adult to an extent not known since the Middle Ages. However, there was a difference, as there was (and is) a difference between the passive viewing induced by television and the active communication that existed between the medieval storytellers and their audiences—who not only frequently participated in the stories through requests and song and dance, but who listened in order that they themselves might remember and pass on the tales to others. Most significantly, although children were now considered more adult, they were, paradoxically, now alienated from adult society, unlike their position in the Middle Ages. Moreover, the state of growing up, called adolescence, peaked in the 1960's and threw up an additional barrier between childhood and adulthood. If children had no special wish to grow up, they ardently desired to be adolescents. During this decade, the new freedom was seen at its most exciting. Adolescents had been steadily assuming more and more of the attributes, perquisites, and powers of their elders. Like adults, teenagers now had money, cars, and jobs, together with drugs, liquor, and sex and their attendant problems.

The New Realism

This changing view of childhood was validated by the literature of realism itself. Not since Puritan days had the literature so clearly followed the mores of a society. Hundreds of books were written about divorce and its effects upon the young: parents deserted children in life, and they did so also in fiction. Drug addiction, alcoholism (parental or youthful), sex, sexuality, and child abuse were among dozens of other related topics that were deemed appropriate for a story background. Overriding all these concerns, however, was a concentration on a sense of malaise, which was generally translated into a search for identity.

While the contents of the new realism were thus adult, and sophisticatedly so, the style was most often puerile, flatly conversational, and geared to the expectations of the television-age child. The style was also curiously didactic—a return to the Puritan ethos—but, of course, with socialization as its basis rather than religion. Influences from current American adult novels, notably the concept of existentialism and the promulgation of the anti-hero, were also obvious. Like their adult counterparts, the young protagonists of the problem novel for children swung through to an understanding of themselves and with a determination to "go it alone."

Epic Fantasy

At first it appeared that fantasy stood aloof from these changes, hewing to traditional settings, characters, and values. In the early 1960's, Lloyd Alexander was in the forefront of American fantasy, achieving with his Prydain series,[3] and related books such as *Coll and His White Pig* (1965), a popularity close to that of Frank Baum with the Oz books. Prydain is an Other World, loosely modeled on some of the tales from the Welsh Mabinogion as well as on its characters and society—its princes and war leaders and its hierarchy—all imbued with a feeling of enchantment. Most specifically, Alexander borrows the black cauldron, which brings a living death to those who are plunged into it, and such place names as Caer Dathyl. However, he himself had considerable imaginative powers. He constructed a believable, medieval world, one with a restrained use of magic that is completely plausible to its inhabitants and so to us who are experiencing it with them. Alexander also had considerable descriptive powers, which are almost lyrical when he writes of the high fortress of Caer Dathyl on the eve of its destruction or of the secret Edenic valley of Medwyn. In contrast, his portrayal of Hen Wen—the oracular pig who, when gladly deprived of her seeress qualities, gives birth to piglets—has an earthy humor.

There are some flaws in the series, most evident in its beginning tone, which suggests comedy rather than high and serious events. Taran, the Assistant Pig-Keeper, whose very title suggests a tongue-in-cheek adventure story rather than epic fantasy, is first seen as a superficial youth who prefers to turn ploughshares into swords rather than tend to his mundane duties and who has already exhibited the qualities of "The Sorcerer's Ap-

---

3. *The Book of Three* (1964), *The Black Cauldron* (1965), *The Castle of Lyr* (1966), *Taran Wanderer* (1967), and *The High King* (1968).

prentice" by trying to dabble in forbidden magic. The lesser characters are defined by a repetition of characteristics or phrases (much like Homeric tags)—the bard Fflewddur Fflam, with a string of his harp forever breaking when he contorts the truth; or the half-man, half-animal, Gurgi, with his constant moaning about his poor tender head and his desire for "crunchings and munchings" or his fear of "slashings and gashings" and "beatings and cheatings." The cameo comedies—the portrayal of the King of the Fair Folk, who is as much lacking in dignity as the Wizard of Oz, and the dwarf Foli, who resembles Walt Disney's dwarf Grumpy—are less appealing and believable than their originals. Nonetheless, the repetition and the consistency of such details make for a strong link among the five books of the series and for an immediate recognition of the characters. These are no small assets.

The tone of the series changes, however. This shift does not come with a shock as does the last book of T.H. White's *The Once and Future King*. In the latter, gone are the puns, the slapstick comedy, and the deliberate anachronisms of *The Sword in the Stone* and *The Witch in the Woods,* and we see Arthur at last in the full dignity and tragedy of his kingly office. By contrast, the Prydain series changes gradually, almost imperceptibly, and so more satisfactorily. In the midst of increasingly grave events, the humor becomes bittersweet and the ending is in the true spirit of epic fantasy—Taran's acceptance of the responsibilities of kingship.

It is in its main theme—Taran's search for identity and his maturation—that the Prydain series breaks with earlier fantasies. While the impetus for the adventures of Tolkien's Bilbo Baggins and C.S. Lewis's Narnia children sprang from outside themselves, Taran has serious personal problems. He is, first of all, a foundling, chafing at his humble position (a contrast to the boy Arthur in T.H. White's *The Sword in the Stone,* who was quite happy in his humble lot as Sir Kay's half-brother); and, most importantly, he feels that he must be of noble blood and thus dreams of attaining glory through warlike deeds. When he has his first chance at adventure, Taran assumes responsibility over-quickly, and only circumstances save his leadership from disaster.

In *The Black Cauldron,* Taran learns to see part of his own character in that of the bitter, twisted one of the youth Ellidyr (who takes pride in his princely birth); and he sacrifices a precious gift for the common good. However, it is in *Taran Wanderer* that Taran undergoes the full rites of passage from adolescence to adulthood. In contemporary realistic fiction, such a process is also a major theme; and the end result—that of growing up or of coming to terms with oneself or one's problems—is generally accomplished quickly by writers such as Barbara Wersba, Isabelle Holland, and hundreds of others by creating for their protagonists some violent or even traumatic event in their lives. Taran's initiation is longer. It takes a whole year of apprenticeship with the artisans of the Free Commots and a whole book in which Taran learns both to come to terms with his position in life (he now believes that he is lowly born) and to learn that the skills of the craftsman are more valuable to a society than the battleskills that he has already mastered. Both the slower pace of *Taran Wanderer* and Taran's acquaintanceship with another segment of society (the people of the Free Commots who welcome him have more than a suggestion about them of American pioneer independence) make credible the subsequent events and choices in Taran's life.

When the battle against evil is finally won, Taran rejects the gift of immortality in an idyllic land with all his friends around him—his mentor-mage Dalben, and the Sons of Don, who now have to leave Prydain to human resources—and chooses to remain human and a builder-prince. Taran will rebuild the land that was almost destroyed by the Dark Lord of Annuvin. Although he has won his right to rule through the power given to him by the magic sword, Dyrnwyn, he thinks that it is better to be simply a man.

In Taran, Alexander has created an acceptable and believable cross between a modern and a traditional fantasy hero, but his frequent companion (and later his beloved), the Princess Eilonwy, is all too frequently seen as a pert, self-assured American teenager wandering through a medieval landscape. At the beginning of the story, her teasing of the Assistant Pig-Keeper quickly becomes tiresome, and her flippant remarks (perhaps an attempt to bring a modern tone to the series) is an intrusion into Alexander's otherwise simple but effective language. Somehow, Alexander seems to lose interest in Eilonwy. Like Taran, she is older in the last book, *The High King,* and almost colorless, not even seeming important when she renounces the last vestiges of her enchanted heritage in order to remain with Taran.

With Taran and Eilonwy, we see the arrival of the older fantasy protagonists. In the 1960's, these protagonists are rarely children, as in the past; and if they are, they are special children with special gifts.

Teenagers now made an impact on literature as they did in society in general. They also linked hands with the protagonists in the realistic novels, who had to be older so that they might cope with the heavy burdens that their creators laid upon them.

In Ursula Le Guin's *Earthsea* trilogy,[4] a longer life span is allotted to the hero, Ged, than was to Taran in Alexander's stories. We follow Ged from child to youth to man and then to the height of his powers as an Arch-mage. These three stages are well-defined, but *A Wizard of Earthsea* is the most childlike of the series as well as the most tightly plotted and exciting.

Earthsea is a very different land from Prydain and not solely because it has been conceived as an archipelago rather than as a corner of a mountainous Celtic country. Unlike Prydain, it has no fairy folk and no magic sword or cauldron or half-immortals such as the Sons of Don. It does have dragons, but these are not the fire-breathing, princess-eating ones of legend. Earthsea dragons have a deep knowledge of the Old Speech and the old ways, and they use wiles and blandishments rather than brute force to maintain their power. Nonetheless, Earthsea is premised on magic. Its well-being (rather than its control) is in the hands of the wizards of the island of Roke, who are chosen for their early-recognizable, innate powers and who weave the spells that keep the hundreds of islands and their people in balance. Magic is seen as a normal way of life, not as an intrusion into it that must end, as in the Prydain series, where evil is overcome and where only human resources can contravene it in the future. However, the magic must never be manipulative, as it is in so much of fantasy—working through a sword of might, a ring of invisibility, or some extrasensory power that give the good an advantage over the evil. As the Master Hand of Roke tells the apprentice wizard Ged in *A Wizard of Earthsea*:

> "You must not change one thing, one pebble, one grain of sand, until you know what good and evil will follow on the act. The world is in balance, in Equilibrium. A wizard's power of Changing and of Summoning can shake the balance of the world. It is dangerous, that power. It is most perilous. It must follow knowledge and serve need."

4. *A Wizard of Earthsea* (1968), *The Tombs of Atuan* (1971), and *The Farthest Shore* (1974).

It is this balance that Ged upsets as an impatient, overconfident adolescent who needs no instruction from his teachers (he has already been taught some spells by his aunt). His first "show-off" exhibition of sorcery (as opposed to simple spells) is easily rectified by his master, Ogion, but his second has serious consequences. In a duel of power with a fellow apprentice, Ged calls forth a shadow of death and so causes "a ripping open of the fabric of the world." Ged almost dies from this encounter, and when he recovers, he finds that he cannot undo what he has done but that he has to finish what he has begun. Thus begin Ged's rites of passage to an understanding of the true use of sorcery as he is first pursued by and then, in turn, pursues the malevolent shadow "towards the very centre of that balance, towards the place where light and darkness meet." The ensuing conflict is not resolved by magic but by mutual recognition when both Ged and his shadow speak the word "Ged":

> Ged reached out his hands, dropping his staff, and took hold of his shadow, of the black self that reached out to him. Light and darkness met, and joined, and were one.

The power inherent in knowing a person's true name is a common theme in folklore. The dwarf Rumplestiltskin, for example, must yield to the queen when she learns (not guesses) his name. This motif is a recurring one in the *Earthsea* trilogy. To be unnamed is to be false, destructive, and evil. Such Nameless Ones are the gods that Arha serves in the second book of the trilogy, *The Tombs of Atuan*. Her own name, Tenar, is taken away from her at the age of five when she is chosen as the reborn princess of the Tombs of Atuan and she is re-named Arha. After a loveless childhood, she enters the maze-like passages of the Undertomb to protect its treasures, to perform the dark rites of religion—and to live in perpetual darkness. Light is eventually brought to Tenar by Ged, now a mature mage, who has entered this Underworld in search of the half of the ring of Errerth-Akbe that when joined to the half he has already been given will bind together the islands of Earthsea under one great, peaceful ruler. Even with the appearance of Ged, however, this is Tenar's book. Her quest for identity is even more moving than that of Ged because she is so alone. She has only evil at her side, in contrast to his apprenticeship to wise and kindly mages. Even alone, Tenar begins to disengage herself from her training, feeling an abhorrence for her priestly duties and coming to a realization that the Nameless Ones are not as they appear to be. In the end, she trusts Ged as he tells her of the joy and freedom of the outside world, and he confides his true name to her as she becomes Tenar again rather than Arha. Together they flee the tombs to Earthsea, where a new life will begin for her.

In *The Farthest Shore*, Ged is seen at the height of his powers and engaged in a struggle that again almost destroys him, but it is not one of his making. Earthsea is going awry because it is being drained of its magic, and so its balance is upset. Crops fail, trade ceases, and the population sinks into apathy. The epigraph that is at the heart of the trilogy no longer holds true:

> Only in silence the word,
> only in dark the light,
> only in dying life;
> bright the hawk's flight
> on the empty sky.

All this natural, moving, and joyous existence has been destroyed by an evil wizard, Cob, who has found a way to keep the door open between life and death and in so doing has become not only a non-person but also one who has to drain the living to sustain his power. Ged must restore the balance by closing the door between the two lands and thus liberating Cob from a negative life into the positive one of death. Ged is accompanied on his journey by the young prince, Arren, who is to become the foretold ruler of Earthsea. Arren is in many ways a young Ged, impatient, critical of Ged because he does not use his mage's powers in every difficult circumstance, and not understanding that one must save one's strength for the important things in life. Arren does not really hear when Ged tells him early in the story

> We must look to the deep springs, I think. We have enjoyed the
> sunlight too long . . . accomplishing small things, fishing in the
> shallows. Tonight we must question the depths.

Ged's words, "question the depths," are appropriate for the *Earthsea* trilogy in general and *The Farthest Shore* in particular, for the latter novel is the most complex in its symbolism and in its major theme—that of death. The plots of these stories do not move in broad sweeps leading to a definitive conclusion as do the Prydain series; instead, they are composed of multitudinous, interlocking episodes that defy summary unless plot is one's main concern.[5] This does not mean that the stories are badly plotted; rather, they are intricately woven together. So are their themes, which make an impressive, even formidable, list: good and evil, light and dark, life and death, balance and imbalance, youth and age, wisdom and ignorance, sex and its repression (specifically in *The Tombs of Atuan*), the loss of identity, the burdens of responsibility, and the loss of enchantment. These themes are generally worked out through images (indeed image piles upon image) that, together with Le Guin as a wordsmith, make the trilogy the most intellectual and quotable of modern fantasies written for the young: "to light a candle is to cast a shadow" or "Deep are the spings of being, deeper than life, than death."

The *Earthsea* trilogy has commanded a wide readership among adults and is critically examined by readers of science fiction as well as of fantasy who seek interpretations of Le Guin's rich symbolism and a link with Oriental philosophy and religion, especially Zen and Taoism. However, humor is an aspect of both life and artistry (as Shakespeare knew well when he wrote the "porter scene" in *Macbeth*), and one eventually wishes for some surcease from the life-and-death events, perhaps even for a touch of Lloyd Alexander.

With their older protagonists who search for identity and an integration of self, Alexander and Le Guin can be seen as harbingers of change, even although their works are filled with the conventional "matter" of fantasy. A more obvious change is apparent in Sheila Moon's *Knee-Deep in Thunder* (1967). It is seriously flawed, being overly long, overly ambitious, and overcrowded with characters who are frequently inconsistently portrayed. Nonetheless, it is an interesting example of the therapeutic aspects of modern realism applied to epic fantasy. Maris is a young teenager (aged thirteen) who is unhappy, particularly with her parents. An early paragraph reads like a problem novel:

> But the wretched morning scene paraded back and forth,
> Mother's tension, Dad's awkwardness, my own frustration as I
> slammed the kitchen door on the perennial bickering about
> money. It would be nice if we could have just a little more money,

5. The plots are well described in Pat Pflieger's *A Reference Guide to Modern Fantasy for Children* (Westport, Conn.: Greenwood, 1984).

so Mother wouldn't have to work and Dad wouldn't have to look so small and distressed when shopping times came round. Like today.

Moon is the first writer of fantasy for chilren to use the first-person narrative, which is the usual technique employed in the problem novel, and she shows the difficulties incurred when an adult writer pretends to be a child. Writers of realistic fiction frequently tried to overcome this problem by descending to what they deemed was the banal, everyday conversation of the young, sprinkled with slang and expletives. Moon goes to the other extreme by attributing to a thirteen-year-old concepts and phrases that are hardly appropriate to her age and to what we know of her in the real world. For instance, in commenting to herself on the strange insects that are to accompany her in her quest, Maris describes them as "ill-assorted" and notes that "each one seemed to have been mysteriously drawn from his usual life to struggle towards an unknown goal. . . . " The goal they struggle toward is exceptionally burdensome and dangerous, with mayhem and death along the way; and like the existentialist protagonists of the realistic novels, they must, for a long time, discover the nature of their quest for themselves. Maris, who has mused on the emptiness and narrowness of her former life ("How limited my days had been!"), learns that she has the courage "to choose to go on the path chosen" for her, and she experiences a "wordless" love for her companions far beyond anything she has ever experienced.

The story ends in a burst of mythology, with the mysterious "Them" who are behind the events becoming the "Holy Ones" of Navajo mythology. This turning to Indian mythology is a refreshing change from the use (almost overuse) of Celtic and Arthurian material as a basis for fantasy, but Moon's American Indian figures of legend, such as Arache for Spider Woman, would not be recognizable to a casual reader, particularly a child, nor are they naturally woven into the plot as were Catherine Anthony Clark's Indian chiefs and princesses in her stories of British Columbia.

Prydain and Earthsea are fully created Secondary Worlds, the last to be envisioned for almost two decades. British writers, such as Alan Garner and William Mayne, in spite of their heritage (Carroll's Wonderland, Barrie's Never-land, Milne's Enchanted Place, Lewis's Narnia, or Tolkien's Middle-earth) used the Primary World as their scenario, with the supernatural breaking in from the past or co-existing with the present. Their works are freighted with myth and legend to a far greater extent than those of American fantasists.

Alan Garner's *The Weirdstone of Brisingamen* (1960) derives from the original Brisingamen, a fiery necklace belonging to the Norse goddess, Freya, but it is set in modern England. Alderley Edge in Cheshire is within two miles of an old farmhouse, with every path and hill named, as in a map of the district. Still, there is magic in the area, as it is the gateway to Fundindelve where King Arthur's knights lie sleeping, each beside a milk-white steed and guarded by Cadellin—a Merlin-like figure. The magic was sealed by Firefrost, a jewel of the Brisingamen, but the jewel is now missing, and so evil forces can prevent the knights from ever awakening in England's time of need. Joining Cadellin in the struggle are two children, Susan and Colin, on a visit to their mother's old nurse. Susan wears a bracelet that contains the missing stone, a bracelet that had been handed on to her mother by the nurse and then to Susan.

Garner's second book, *The Moon of Gomrath* (1963), is similar in plot and has some of the same characters—Cadellin, Susan, and Colin. Together these stories contain a gallery of creatures drawn from Welsh, English, and Norse mythology—elves, dwarves, svarts, the morthbrood, the Morrigan, and a formless creature called the Brollachan. Also, *The Moon of Gomrath* ends with the wild ride of Herne the Hunter and his followers, here called by their Scandinavian name—The Einheriar. The books are crowded with these characters in a Tolkienesque manner, but they are portrayed without Tolkien's "elvish craft." The children are courageous, helpful, but colorless, a throw-back to John Masefield's Kay Harker. Nonetheless, the stories have a page-turning quality and are far better than average fantasy-adventure stories.

Garner's concept of the difference between High Magic and Old Magic was one that later fantasists were to use with even more effectiveness. High Magic is for the good. Old Magic is primitive and amoral and dangerous to rouse, for no one knows which side it will take. This concept of magic also rouses Garner to his best writing. When Colin searches for the Mothan, a magic flower that might release Susan from the Brollachan's spell, he has to follow the Old Magic track that is visible only under a full moon. His race against its power is the finest passage in *The Moon of Gomrath:*

... then he burst from the wood, and there was the old straight
track, dipping and flowing over the rounded fields and rising, a
silver thread like a distant mountain stream, up the face of the hills
to the peak of Shining Tor, and behind it the broad disc of the
moon, white as an elvan shield.

However, while the fast-paced events in both books tend to over-
shadow all other considerations, one can feel Garner's belief in the
natural commingling of the world of myth and the world of reality.
Already much has been lost. The withdrawal of the fairy folk began, as
Cadellin tells Susan, in the "Age of Reason"; and now the last remnants
of these folk may disappear, for the elves (the lios-alfar) are dying from
the "smoke-sickness" caused by modern, industrialized England. Here
Garner is the heir of Blake and Kingsley. In the almost primitive air of
Alderly, with its country people—such as Bess and Gowther Mossick,
whose family has dwelt on the same farm for three hundred years—elves
and dwarves and their ilk also seem its rightful inhabitants. Their presence is necessary for the well-being of the modern world.

In *Elidor* (1965), Garner tries, and on the whole successfully, to
parallel two devastated worlds—the dying one of Elidor, and the bombed
(in World War II) city of Manchester, now undergoing redevelopment
but not of a type to satisfy the eye or the spirit. Old buildings are being
bulldozed to put up even uglier ones.

The Watsons—David, Nicholas, Helen, and Roland, who is the
youngest—are the children of a lower middle-class family. They have
just moved to Manchester, and in exploring their new environment,
Roland is drawn to a particular street where the children find an abandoned church. Through the music of a lame fiddler, they are pulled into
Elidor—the older children first, and then Roland. Here Roland meets
Malebron, the lame king of the land, and finds that it is his task to release
his brothers and his sisters from an enchantment (as in the old stories,
the eldest siblings have failed), to find three lost treasures, and to make
the unicorn, Findhorn, sing. Thus will the prophecy be fulfilled and Elidor restored to its former glory. Roland is at first rebellious. "I don't
care," he says to Malebron. "It's nothing to do with me." Then he
realizes, however, that he has no choice in the matter. With a newly
found power of being able to make images into reality, and—again like

the youngest son in the fairy tales—with the strength to obey instructions, Roland rescues his brothers and sisters and finds the treasures: a spear, a sword, a stone, and a grail—all things of shining beauty. However, Malebron's enemies are pursuing the children, and they escape into the real world and into their own time, carrying the treasures— which have now become an old railing, two splintered lathes, a heavy stone, and an old, cracked cup.

The children hide the treasures, but they cause havoc in the Watson household: electrical appliances, such as a shaver and a beater, are set humming without being plugged in; a comb crackles; and, worst of all, the television set will not work. For some fleeting moments, Garner shows himself as a social satirist in the parents' sense of deprivation when denied the soothing comfort of TV:

> Mrs. Watson took the evening paper, and made a point of reading it. Every minute or so she would turn the pages fretfully, as if they were responsible for the television breakdown.

The children have to bury the treasures in the earth to prevent a continuous electrical overload. A year passes, and, except for Roland, Elidor fades from their minds. Then the boundary between the two worlds is breached by two of Malebron's enemies in search of the treasures and in pursuit of Findhorn. There is a violent chase, ending at the church. Findhorn is wounded unto death, and in his final agony, he gives tongue to notes "of beauty and terror." Through the windows of the church, Elidor springs into life, and the children throw the treasures through the window, where, for a moment, the treasures hang in their true shapes; then "the children were left alone with the broken window of a slum."

Garner tells us something about Elidor's past and about the reason for its present crisis, but he gives us no details about its landscape or people, as Le Guin does for Earthsea. Woven in evocatively, however, is a vision of Elidor's past glory:

> Findias . . . Falias . . . Murias . . . Gorias. The Hazel of Fordrium . . . the Forest of Mondrum . . . the Hill of Usna. Men who walked like sunlight. Cloth of gold. Elidor,—Elidor.

The real world is delineated with swift, sure strokes:

Beyond the alley they came to a warren of grimy streets, where old women stood in the doorways, wearing sacks for aprons, and men in carpet slippers sat on the steps. Dogs nosed among crumpled paper in the gutter; a rusty bicycle wheel lay on the cobbles. A group of boys at the corner talked to a girl whose hair was rolled in brightly coloured plastic curlers.

In this environment, and coming as they do from a home that is devoid of any beauty or sensitivity (although it is safe and secure), the children need the concept of Elidor to give their lives something beyond the humdrum and the economic lockstep that their parents' lives suggest. Garner does this by weaving into his Other World various strands of folklore and legend. Roland is the Childe Roland of the folktale who goes to the Dark Tower to rescue his sister, Burd Ellen, from an enchantment. A white plastic football is translated into the golden ball of the Welsh fairy tale "Elidore," and echoes of the "Grail" legend come in the person of Malebron (Merlin) and the golden cup.

The two older brothers are colorless, cardboard characters who remain untouched by their experiences. Helen, who has cradled the dying unicorn in her lap (only a virgin can capture a unicorn), has the possibility of holding her experiences in her memory. However, it is Roland— who has fought the pressures of his parents, his brothers, and his own doubts and who has entered the Mound of Vandwy, combatted the warriors of Elidor, and persuaded Findhorn to sing—whose life is enriched by a belief in a world beyond his own.

All epic fantasies (as well as those touched with an epic quality), as has been noted earlier, are played out over broad landscapes; they are also all set in a moral climate that can vary as much as the settings. That of Charles Kingsley's *The Water-Babies* is specifically Christian (and Anglican). George MacDonald's *Princess* books have an aura of Christianity, embodying his belief that God does indeed have a pattern for behavior—one that is best understood by the imagination rather than by reason. In the Edwardian animal epics, such as Kenneth Grahame's *The Wind in the Willows* and Walter de la Mare's *The Three Mullah Mulgars,* there is more than a hint of pantheism in the ecstatic appearance of the god Pan in Grahame's work and in the visionary goal—the Valleys of Tishnar—in that of de la Mare. Both epics, however, are based on Christian ethics of a universal order, particularly the ethic of "the Golden

Rule." Coaxing children into Christianity (although not necessarily into Catholicism) was certainly C.S. Lewis's intent in the *Narnia Chronicles*.

The last book of Lloyd Alexander's Prydain series provides the greatest understanding of the series' moral philosophy. Prydain is to be united under one ruler, Taran, who has been trained for this position and who will be the font of wisdom and justice in all matters. However, he must follow his own conscience. As the three sisters of the Marshes of Morva (who are less deterministic than the three fates of Greek mythology) tell him, they may weave the pattern of events into their tapestries, but the pattern itself is chosen by the individual. In essence, Taran will be a Holy Roman Emperor but without religious significance. It is interesting that so many twentieth-century fantasists—J.R.R. Tolkien in *The Hobbit* and *The Lord of the Rings*, C.S. Lewis in the *Narnia Chronicles*, and Lloyd Alexander, among others—have modeled their Secondary Worlds on feudalism, a system that was to a large extent held together by religious beliefs.

Ursula Le Guin's *Earthsea* trilogy breaks the dominance of the concept of feudalism in epic fantasy. Earthsea is a pre-feudal, almost primitive group of islands that are bound together by faith in magic rather than in supernatural beings such as Aslan in the *Narnia Chronicles* or the half-immortal Sons of Don in the Prydain series. Indeed, the second book of the trilogy, *The Tombs of Atuan,* can almost be seen as antireligious, since the priestly caste are exposed as charlatans and are destroyed by the very edifice they constructed to keep the rites in darkness. But the magic of Earthsea is at its most superficial when it is based only on memorized spells and incantations. To become a mage is to study rigorously and systematically (magic is as much a discipline as is philosophy or science), and to use one's powers wisely and responsibly. The development of character is as important as the acquisition of skills. At the story's end, it is Ged's courage and integrity that defeat evil, not his magical powers. The morality of the *Earthsea* trilogy is one of austerity; Ged's success brings him no personal reward.

Science Fiction Fantasy

The ethics observable in all epic fantasy, whether in the past or in the present, whether overtly or obliquely religious, are based on common ground. Children are innately good but need guidance and experience (a chance to learn from their own mistakes) to reach either a higher level of goodness or an acceptance of responsibility for the welfare of others. Such noble goals are also part of Madeleine L'Engle's interplanetary stories about the struggle between good and evil in *A Wrinkle in Time* (1962) and *The Wind in the Door* (1978). However, she added a new dimension—a vague, ecstatic religious quality—that is rarely found outside of books of religious experience and one that has not re-entered fantasy for children.

A Wrinkle in Time begins with a firm basis in reality. Meg Murray is age thirteen (she and her friend Calvin are among the early teenage protagonists) and is unhappy with herself and her appearance—she has mouse-colored hair, braces on her teeth, is doing badly at school, and does not know the meaning of the word "patience." She longs to be like her beautiful, calm, auburn-haired scientist mother. However, there is a shadow on the otherwise happy Murray household—which also includes a five-year-old genius, Charles Wallace, and twin boys who are nicely normal and who play no part in the story—because the father, a scientific advisor to the President of the United States, has not been heard from for over a year. This fact has been noted by the neighbors in the small village where the Murrays live and has been given the usual social interpretation for disappearing husbands. Fantasy arrives with the appearance of three transubstantial beings from outer space—Mrs. Whatsit, Mrs. Which, and Mrs. Who. These beings are differentiated by specific attributes that are constantly repeated: Mrs. Which always speaks in an exaggerated stutter, Mrs. Who quotes adages from foreign languages (but always giving the translation), and Mrs. Whatsit is a bundle of awkwardness in the type of clothes she adopts when she materializes. These women bear obvious resemblances to Kingsley's Mrs. Bedonebyasyoudid and Mrs. Doasyouwouldbedoneby in *The Water-Babies;* and like them, L'Engle's beings represent the moral conscience of the universe, as well as being the arbiters of personal behavior.

They transport Meg, Charles Wallace, and Calvin O'Keefe (a neighbor boy who becomes fond of Meg) to another planet by "tesseracting," which shortens distances by way of a pleat or "a wrinkle in time." From this planet, the children see the Dark Shadow that is hovering around Earth and are told that they are to go to the planet of Camazotz to rescue Mr. Murray, who is being held by the same force of evil that surrounds the Earth. Camazotz is a world held in thrall by IT—a pulsating, quivering, nauseating brain. Mr. Murray, Calvin, and Meg escape from IT through Mr. Murray's power to tesseract (he is not very skillful at it, but he has been working on the theory with a group of government scientists), while Charles Wallace is left behind because he has succumbed to the power of evil. Meg has to return alone to the planet and face IT. This feat she accomplishes through the power of the love she has for her little brother.

In *A Wrinkle in Time* in particular, science and scientific concepts hover in the air. Einstein's mathematical formula is quoted (Meg's forte is mathematics); there are numerous references to Mrs. Murray's lab experiments; and at the end of the book, Mr. Murray warns his colleagues about the danger of using a scientific experiment (such as tesseracting) when they do not fully understand it. "We're children playing with dynamite," he says, a remark that, taken together with "the Dark Thing" hanging over Earth, may be seen as a warning about the uses of nuclear power. In *The Wind in the Door,* scientific concepts are confined to the use of the word "mitochondria," which are parts of a human cell that are too small to be seen even with a micro-electron microscope. By the end of the series (in *A Swiftly Tilting Planet,* 1978), we learn that both Mr. and Mrs. Murray are Nobel-Prize winners in science.

However, the fantasy in all the books soon takes precedence over both science and reality. The idea of "tesseracting," of course, places the book in the realm of fantasy rather than in that of science fiction, as do the trio of Mrs. Whatsit, Mrs. Which, and Mrs. Who. When the children are carried into the upper atmosphere, they obtain their oxygen from bell-shaped flowers; and in *The Wind in the Door,* the farandola that upset Charles Wallace's mitochondrion and thus bring him close to death is a fantasy device, as is his journey back into time through the power of a unicorn in *A Swiftly Tilting Planet.* However, L'Engle also uses many of the conventions of science fiction. "Kything" is a word for mental telepathy; the tentacled beasts of Ixchel have a loving nature, but in their appearance they come straight out of early science fiction pulp magazines; and the planet of Camazotz is an Orwellian vision. The journey that Meg, her friends, and their teachers make into Charles Wallace's cells echoes the science fiction story and movie *Fantastic Voyage,* but L'Engle's characters are questing for spiritual unity rather than for a purely medical cure. Atomic disaster is also a major theme in science fiction, and in *A Swiftly Tilting Planet,* a dictator in a small South American country threatens nuclear war. However, this latter book is, for the most part, a past-time fantasy in which Charles Wallace (now aged fifteen) travels back into time, on the back of a unicorn, in order to change the genealogy of the dictator so that he calls for peace rather than war. The family histories, Welsh in origin, are as complicated and difficult to remember as are those of a Russian novel.

Much of the tone in the first two works is highly reminiscent of that of the Moral Tale of the eighteenth and early nineteenth centuries. Meg is chided by Mrs. Whatsit, Mrs. Which, and Mrs. Who and has to be shown that she alone can save Charles Wallace; he, in effect, is punished for overreaching his special powers. However, a sterner note is evident in *The Wind in the Door,* as Meg and the Cherubim, Proginoskes, are given definite tasks to accomplish that will affect their own natures as well as the fate of Charles Wallace and the world. Moreover, Charles Wallace, who is only six years old, is so teased and so physically abused by his schoolmates, because he has told the class about his scientific interests, on his first day of school that he becomes seriously ill. However, both his mother and the galactic Teacher, Blajeny, insist that Charles Wallace has "to learn to adapt" while remaining himself—surely a heavy burden for a six-year-old. Moreover, considering the realism of the family life that is portrayed, one cannot help wondering why two intelligent parents plus two healthy older brothers cannot somehow, and in a small town, save a child from a daily beating by his peers.

In their mystical sense, *A Wrinkle in Time* and *The Wind in the Door* have an affinity with Charles Williams' adult religious fantasies, such as *Descent into Hell* or *War in Heaven,* in that L'Engle's fantastic element is used as a springboard to reveal a vision of the ordered dance of the universe in praise of the Creator. Also, as in Williams, a major theme is "co-inherence" (to use Williams' word), whereby each person is more truly him- or herself when sacrificing for another. Also, it is the ordinary people who are called upon to be the saviours, rather than the extraordinary ones—it is Meg who saves her young genius brother, Charles Wallace. In *A Wrinkle in Time,* the religious element is provided chiefly by Mrs. Whatsit's chanting Psalm 149 and by Mrs. Who's reciting Corinthians. In *The Wind in the Door,* Meg, in a euphoric state, becomes at one with the universe by naming almost everything in it.

Both books are highly eclectic even for fantasy, which is, in general, an eclectic literature. They are uneven in style, rising, in their fantastic scenes, to portentousness. All in all, they have been best described by John Rowe Townsend as being "in the small, frustrating but fascinating category of good bad books."[6]

The English writer, Peter Dickinson, combines technology and legend in *The Weathermonger* (1968), the first published book in his "Changes" trilogy,[7] but the last in the series in the order of events and the only one that can be described as fantasy rather than science fiction.

In *The Weathermonger,* the time is the present, but England has reverted to a pre-industrial era. The Change has been brought about by King Arthur's mentor, Merlin, who has been roused from his long sleep by a second-rate chemist and subjected to regular doses of morphine. In his stupor, Merlin re-creates England as he once knew it and in so doing instills in the populace an antipathy to machines and a superstitious horror of and punishment of (like the witches of old) anyone caught tinkering with the scattered debris of the industrial society. Merlin is the chief weathermonger, but each village has its own—a person who has power over the local weather and uses this power for the benefit of the community. Such a one is sixteen-year-old Geoffrey, who, as the story opens, is caught tinkering with his uncle's motorboat and is deliberately left to drown along with his eleven-year-old sister. Geoffrey summons his powers of weathermongering (much like those of Roland, who thinks his way into the Mount of Vanwy in Alan Garner's *Elidor*), and he and his sister escape to France. They are, however, asked to return (indeed commanded) to England to seek the cause of the weather over England, since Geoffrey and his sister are unaffected by the Change. Temporary guides and transportation in the form of a Rolls Royce (a Silver Ghost that is very lovingly described) are provided for them. The two children finally trace the source of the trouble to Wales and find Merlin. With a great deal of ingenuity and beginning Latin, they make him understand what has happened, and Merlin returns England to normal.

The plot is fast-paced, with hunts and chases and cliff-hanging situations and a simple comparison between an industrial and pre-industrial society. In the trilogy as a whole, there is some nostalgia for

6. John Rowe Townsend, *A Sense of Story* (New York: Lippincott, 1971), 126.
7. In order of events: *Heartsease* (1969), *The Devil's Children* (1970), and *The Weathermonger* (1968).

clean air and a pre-pesticide era, but Dickinson is definitely on the side of progress, seeing the present as more rational and less cruel and superstitious than the past. *Heartsease* and *The Devil's Children* have more fully developed characters than *The Weathermonger* but have nothing of the supernatural beyond England's reversion to a machineless age, and thus strain credulity less than does the intrusion of Merlin. After all, Merlin's re-creation of England supposedly in his own image is certainly not that of Malory's *La Morte d'Arthure*, which is peopled with knights rather than commoners.

Fantasy Based on Myth and Legend

William Mayne's portrayal of King Arthur in *Earthfasts* (1966) is not that found in Malory either, but it is based on the legend that has grown up around King Arthur—he lies sleeping with his knights until England needs him again. Before *Earthfasts*, Mayne had been noted for his broad range of stories depicting some unusual incident in the hitherto even flow of a child's life (such as in *A Swarm in May* or in *A Grass Rope*), his insights into childhood, and his ability to express those insights. Above all, Mayne is a stylist. His love affair with words is most obvious in his dialogues—those among children and those between children and adults (his grown-ups are never merely cardboard characters). Mayne's child characters do not have a star quality. They do not leap to mind as do Louisa May Alcott's Jo, Mark Twain's Tom Sawyer, Lewis Carroll's Alice, or Mary Norton's Arrietty. However, Mayne's children have an acute consciousness of their own small world; they become involved in a problem relating to it rather than in high adventures; they can also articulate what is happening, often in oblique and delicate language and just as often with childlike jokes and puns. Although they are children of the 1950's and 1960's, Mayne's child characters have never been near a television set; therefore, their minds are constantly active and probing. There also runs through all of his books, as a contrapuntal theme to the actual events, a sense of the continuity of time and the effects of the past upon the present.

While *Earthfasts* retains most of the Mayne stylistic touches, it bursts out of his hitherto controlled and narrow boundaries of realistic child life to show a world of the present in which giants play ball, boars run wild in the streets, a boggart joins a farmer's household, and King Arthur (unlike his portrayal in most fantasies) lets loose his anger at being disturbed. These events all occur because time has been put out of joint.

Mayne's hold on reality is shown chiefly through his delineation of place, his amalgam of science and myth, and in his two protagonists, who are (to date at least) his most memorable. The market town of Garebridge has, like so many of its English counterparts, a past steeped in tradition and history. Just outside of the town is a ring of standing stones dating from Neolithic times; and in the town itself is a castle under which King Arthur and his knights are said to be sleeping. Garebridge also has a fine modern high school, a sprinkling of professional people, kindly policemen, and sturdy, unflappable countrymen. Into his wild fantasy, Mayne also adds a story of friendship, an interest in science, and, most particularly, a view of intelligence put to work. David Wix and Keith Heseltine are well-educated, curious, articulate, and sensitive teenagers; however, at story's end, it is the more practical-minded Keith who is able to solve the mystery of the timeslip and rescue David, who has been trapped in it.

The story begins when Keith and David, investigating a strange noise in a mound of earth, meet Nellie Jack John, an eighteenth-century drummer boy stepping into the twentieth century and carrying a candle that he has appropriated from King Arthur's sleeping place. Nellie Jack John thinks that he has been exploring for only a few hours in his own time and refuses to believe what Keith and David tell him about the present. It is here that Mayne sets the tone for a warmly human story. Keith at first takes the scientific view of Nellie Jack John, speculating on his reaction to his strange surroundings. The ensuing conversation between the two boys is Mayne at his conversational best. David has pointed out that Nellie Jack John is not a "rat":

> "You've said that," said Keith.
> "I know," said David. "It's the most important thing after saying he *is* human. He isn't a rat, so there's no excuse for observing him. . . . So stop being a scientist, and start being a person yourself, and let's try to help him."
> "I agree with you, really," said Keith. "Only it's easy to see the other way. That's all. It's the quickest thought."

"It's a hire-purchase thought," said David. "You think of it and buy it and pay for it all the rest of your life."

The candle that the drummer boy has brought with him from the passage puts time out of joint and causes the strange happenings in the town. Its cold, white, unextinguishable flame fascinates David, who tries numerous experiments with it. He finally succumbs to its power and is swallowed up by a crack in the sky. The coroner's verdict is that David has been vaporized by lightning. Months pass, but Keith, who has been injured by the same power that caused David to disappear, cannot forget his friend. He, too, probes the secret of the candle and, without being entrapped by it, realizes that King Arthur wants him to return the candle. This he does at great danger to himself. David is rescued, as is Nellie Jack John, who has returned to the passage to try to find his way back to his own time. Things in the town and the countryside return to normal— but not all together. There are strangely bred piglets on the farms, Nellie Jack John is taken in by a country couple (a strange boy is regarded with the same equanimity as a boggart), and David himself is not regarded as a seven-day wonder.

Mayne is determined to make us believe that the events really happened. Unlike Philippa Pearce's *Tom's Midnight Garden* or Lucy Boston's *The Children of Green Knowe,* we are not allowed to believe in either a dream or an overly sensitive imagination. The message is that there is more on this earth than objective reality.

Earthfasts breaks several of the heretofore rigid rules of fantasy—one, that time should stop in the real world (here it is stopped in the supernatural one); and two, that there should be a rational explanation for an event in the real world (one is not vaporized by lightning), and to a lesser extent, that the supernatural events should be confined to the participants in it and not affect a whole population at various points, such as in church, in a pub, in the marketplace, and on a farm and hillside. Nonetheless, it can be assumed that Mayne does all this with deliberation. The title *Earthfasts* gives a clue to his purpose. "Earthfast" has various meanings: "earth bound" and "fixed in the ground"; "a stone appearing on the surface, but stuck fast in the earth"; and "one lacking in a spiritual quality or outlook." Mayne wants his scientifically-minded boys to think subjectively about time as well as objectively; time past is still alive through primitive legends. If Mayne breaks the rules, he does so brilliantly and compellingly. He is never more cogent than when he is in between opposing views: science versus religion. When the boys think that the drummer boy might be dead

> Keith knelt down, because he was not firm on his feet. When he was down he felt he might be praying, but he did not know how to pray. "Prayer is telepathy," he thought, "and the human brain shows no evidence of being able to transmit any sort of signal, therefore telepathy does not exist, therefore prayer does not exist, therefore, therefore, therefore there is no receiver, no God. But I believe in God, they tell me. Oh God, don't let him be dead. Don't let David find him dead. Don't let me see him if he's dead."

Keith's prayer is revealing (particularly in the 1960's) of the abandonment of the conventional, formal religions for a belief in the truths of science. However, science seemingly cannot help in times of stress; a void has to be filled. As the World War II saying went: "There are no atheists in the fox-holes." However, in *Earthfasts* the supernatural takes the place of religion.

In Garner's *The Owl Service* (1967), mythic forces break through into the real world with a violence hitherto unknown in fantasy. In the *Weirdstone of Brisingamen,* the chases and hunts and spells are in the convention of the folktale, so feelings of familiarity and safety are in operation. In *Elidor,* the violent ending is meshed with the glorious resurrection of the Other World, and even the unicorn's death can be taken as symbolic: the unicorn may rise again, like the Phoenix from the ashes. In *The Owl Service,* however, a concentrated violence that has built up for centuries within a Welsh valley attacks three modern young people— emotionally and psychologically—thus exacerbating their worst tendencies. The battle is for the mind.

The myth here is specific rather than allusive as in so many fantasies. The Welsh legend tells of Blodeuwedd, who is fashioned out of flowers to make a wife for a magician's son. She betrays her husband, brings death to her lover, and, as a punishment, is turned into an owl. In seeking to escape from her imprisonment as a hunting bird and to be again made of flowers, Blodeuwedd continually brings disaster to others.[8] In the pres-

---

8. For the complete story see *The Mabinogion,* trans. Lady Charlotte Guest (London: Dent, 1906), 61–80.

ent, her destructive force falls on a young English girl, Alison, who has inherited a house in the valley and is staying there with her mother, stepfather, and stepbrother, Roger. When an old dinner service is found in the attic and Alison, under an almost hypnotic compulsion, traces the design on it and makes paper owls rather than flowers, Blodeuwedd is on the hunt again, and her presence is felt in the whole valley, as if a storage house of power were ready to explode.

Even without a mythic intervention, the temperaments of the cast of characters are set for a confrontation. There is tension between English and Welsh, upper class and lower class, and there are adolescent problems, such as falling in love for the first time. Gwyn, the Welsh boy (who is the most fully described character), is bitter at his mother's rejection of his education and of his ambitions, is harassed by Roger, and is already caught up in the myth through his unwed parents. Gwyn is also hopelessly in love with Alison. Alison is a passive creature who takes her code of conduct from her snobbish, narrow-minded mother, just as Roger does from his snobbish, materialistic father. Roger, too, is in love with Alison. The mythic pattern is finally broken, but, surprisingly, not by Gwyn but by the superficial Roger, who persuades Alison to believe that owls should be flowers. There is tension in the ending but little or no evidence that any of the young people will be changed by their experiences, except that Gwyn may be left with an additional sense of failure.

Garner's style gives an especially modern touch to *The Owl Service,* as plot and characterization are revealed through conversation rather than through narrative. The exchanges among the young trio and among the young and the adults are frequently marked by clichés, slang, and crudities, but the narrative and descriptive passages have a rhythmic power:

> He saw mountains wherever he looked: nothing but mountains away and away and away, their tops hidden sometimes, but mountains with mountains behind them in desolation for ever. There was nowhere in the world to go.
> "Alison—"
> He stood and the wind was cold through him. He looked again, but there was nothing, and the sky dropped lower, hiding the barren distances, crowding the hills with ghosts, then lifting, and he looked again. Nothing.

The book was exceptionally well received upon its publication, winning both the Carnegie Medal and the *Guardian* award; the story was subsequently made into a successful television play. *The Owl Service* has also been adversely criticized, with some justice.[9] It is, however, in the forefront, along with Mayne's *Earthfasts,* of what might best be described as the "fantasy of reality," certainly a contradiction in terms but descriptive of the increasing number of stories in which the fantasy elements are overshadowed by realities or in which the realistic element is so strong that the fantasy requires a large swallowing of disbelief.

Rosemary Harris pulls the Ark story somewhat out of joint in her *The Moon in the Cloud* (1968), but with some humor. The tale of Noah's Ark is the Bible story that has most captured children's imaginations. Even modern toy shops stock a Noah's Ark alongside their most advanced robots. The biblical details in Harris's version have an irreverent tone, and some certainly are erroneous—as when Noah's son, Ham, is crushed by an elephant before he enters the Ark. Nonetheless, his character is not out of place; according to Harris, Ham is a nasty and selfish person; and in the Bible, it is Ham who tells his brothers of seeing Noah in his drunken nakedness. *The Moon in the Cloud* uses a clever mixture of Old Testament times, ancient Egyptology, and animal fantasy. In this last area, we are close to the fantasy of the beast tale, with the animals commenting on human nature, but only to their master Reuben, the animal tamer. The animals assist Reuben with both sagacious advice and deeds rather than with magic, much like "Puss in Boots."

While the story of the Ark, which begins and ends *The Moon in the Cloud,* has certainly some childlike appeal, the reader eventually becomes conscious of the fact that Harris has nothing to communicate. This lack of depth may well result from the fact that all the human characters are rather superficially drawn adults. Its two sequels, *The Shadow on the Sun* (1970) and *The Bright and Morning Star* (1972), are equally entertaining and are best described as well-researched but deliberately fantastic Egyptology.

Penelope Farmer has retold several Greek myths for children: *The*

9. See David Reese, "Alan Garner," in *The Marble in the Water* (Boston: The Horn Book, 1980), 60–65, and Eleanor Cameron, "The Owl Service: A Study," in *Children's Literature: Criticism and Response,* ed. Mary Lou White (Columbus, Ohio: Merrill, 1976), 191–201.

Serpent's Teeth, The Story of Cadmus, Daedalus and Icarus, and *The Story of Persephone.* While they are not particularly distinguished retellings, they do indicate her interest in myth; therefore, the reader is not surprised to find mythic symbols and images at the core of Farmer's fantasies. Her *The Summer Birds* (1962) is based on one of the oldest dreams of humankind, that of being able to fly. The children of a small English village are taught to fly by a mysterious boy (also with the power of invisibility before adults) during their summer holidays. They do not learn to fly immediately by thinking "wonderful thoughts" that "lift you up in the air" as did Wendy and John and Michael as encouraged by Peter Pan. In Farmer's story, flying is a matter of leg and arm exercises and innate ability, and some of the children are more skillful at it than others. Neither do they fly to a country of their dreams such as Barrie's Neverland, but remain in their own village and its surroundings. The consequent necessity of avoiding parental discovery brings both humor and naturalness to the story, as do the characters and interactions of the children. Farmer is adept at providing just enough personal characteristics and family background to make the children individuals. They quarrel, squabble, and make plans, and the boys finally challenge the leadership of their strange mentor in an aerial battle, which he wins.

The heady joys of flying continue:

> The time that followed the battle was the children's glorious summer. The days were golden, corn-cut days, blue days, days that began grayly in mist and grew slowly to color as the morning strengthened. Autumn things ripened, hips and haws, blackberries sweet and sour, and chestnut burrs from the trees that guarded the schoolyard.
>
> . . . Mad children they were, bird children, for this year the best nuts did not stay on the topmost branches, safe from the stones thrown to knock them down. The children, flying, brought them to earth triumphant over the tallness of the trees.

However, underneath all the fun is the feeling that everything must end. The holidays will soon be over. The mysterious boy grows ever more withdrawn and birdlike: "His limbs were more stretched and angled, his nose longer. His cockleshell was plain." He also devours insects with greater avidity than ever. Charlotte, who was the boy's first pupil and is therefore most closely drawn to him, senses that something is wrong. Then he tells the children the reason for the strange summer:

> He was a bird, he said, of a bird kind dying out, extinct almost in memory but for a museum skeleton. He alone existed, the last bird of his race. The summer had been given to him by the mighty bird-lord, the fiery Phoenix, as a last chance to restore his kind. "Renew yourself," the lord had said. "Renew yourself as I renew myself, by fire. Fly to the furnace of the human world, find fellows for yourself, take them to your island, and your race will go on. Of any kind or form they may be. Your form and kind they will become. Go, the summer is yours. Use it well.

Now the children are presented with a choice: they can be immortal birds or remain human and never fly again. Charlotte persuades the children to stay as they are, with the exception of one older girl who has nothing to hold her to her present life. Thus, at the story's end, we are back with Barrie's *Peter and Wendy* but with a harsher choice involved. Wendy has known from the age of two that someday she will grow up; therefore, her decision to do so is natural and inevitable. Barrie mixed the everyday world with fairyland and brought us to the borderline of laughter, where we suddenly found ourselves close to tears at the thought of the loss of childhood dreams. Farmer encloses her fantasy within the real world; yet although her mixture is courageous and innovative, it lacks purpose and thus memorableness.

Emma, of *Emma in Winter* (1966), is a character from *The Summer Birds* (Charlotte's lively and willful younger sister), as is fat Bobby Fumpkins, who is jeered at by the other children for his clumsiness in flying and called "Jemima Puddleduck." As the title suggests, the season is winter, and an unusually snowy one for the village. Winter's pleasures (such as sledding) are soon dissipated by its length and bitter cold; its pristine whiteness, trampled to dirty gray. Emma is lonesome in the huge house with her aloof great-grandfather and careless housekeeper and longs for Charlotte, who is away at boarding school. Emma is also restive in the village school, fretful, and even resentful of the attention paid to her by Bobby Fumpkins, who longs to have her as a friend. In the daytime, Emma and Bobby's school activities force a closer companionship upon them, but at nighttime they are even more closely united through their shared dreams of flying, which become increasingly nightmarish as the two children are impelled backward in time to the beginning of the world. Here they find no Garden of Eden (which Emma had hoped for) but a bleak sea and a rocky shore. Now Emma and Bobby are faced with distorted visions of themselves as they are in the real world and of their teacher, whom they have caricatured in the schoolroom. They escape these horrors when Bobby urges Emma to think of herself in the real world, much as Roger persuaded Alison to think of flowers rather than owls in Alan Garner's *The Owl Service*. There is more than a hint of therapy in the adventure, since we feel that Bobby will become more self-confident and so refrain from overeating and that Emma will be more generous and less superior to others. Nonetheless, it is a harsh lesson for two children who, if they are not faultless, are basically very sound children with far less than ideal home environments.

Farmer's *The Magic Stone* (1964) is chiefly a piece of social realism that contrasts the lives and families of two young teenaged girls. Alice comes from a working-class environment and is destined to become a store clerk; Caroline, who comes from the middle class, will go on to higher education. For one brief summer, Alice and Caroline are friends, drawn together through a magic talisman—a stone with an insert of blue steel that can be pulled out only when the girls do it together. Then their natural senses become heightened, as do their understanding and appreciation of one another. At the end of the story, they use the stone's power (it is beginning to wane) to quell the animosity between their brothers.

Like many other British writers of her decade, Penelope Farmer tries to move her readers into new realms of perception through a fantasy experience. Her simpler conventions, such as a dream sequence in *Emma in Winter*, work to more effect than does her allusive mythology—the renewable Phoenix in *The Summer Birds* or a piece of King Arthur's sword in *The Magic Stone*, neither of which are well integrated into their plots. Farmer's social realism of class distinctions, which is so much a part of British realistic fiction for the young in the same period, is the major theme of *The Magic Stone*, but it is presented blandly in comparison with that found in Alan Garner's *The Owl Service*. In *The Summer Birds* and *Emma in Winter*, such distinctions add an unfortunate note of caricature—the village children are endowed with such names as Fumpkins, Scobb, or Scragg, while Charlotte and Emma, who live in genteel poverty, are given the prestigious last name of Makepeace.

Animal Fantasy

Just as Kenneth Grahame's *The Wind in the Willows* can be read as a parable of Edwardian England, so Russell Hoban's *The Mouse and His Child* (1967) can be taken as a fable of our own times. Like Grahame, Hoban has an eye on both the adult and the child world. At its story level, *The Mouse and His Child* has the simplicity and gentle tutelage of Hoban's picture books about Frances, the child badger; but it also has drama, adventure, and pathos.

Two clockwork toys, a father and child mouse, are linked together face to face; once a year they are wound up and dance for a family of children under the Christmas tree. When they are broken, the toys are tossed out into a junkyard, where they are found by a tramp who roughly repairs them and sets them on their way. "Be tramps," he says to them. Their moment of freedom is brief, for they are captured by rats under a Mafia-type leader, Manny, and forced to work as slaves. The toys escape into the surrounding countryside with the help of a fortune-telling frog, but they find themselves in a world as cruel and as dangerous as the rats' dump-heap. "War," mutters the father. "The dustbin, the dump, murder, robbery and war." Through it all, however, the toys pursue their quest—to be free and independent, that is, to be self-winding. The child has an additional dream. He wants a home and a family, and he perseveres in his dream even in the face of his father's discouragement. His idea of a home is the doll's house he remembers from his days in the toy shop; for a sister, the windup seal; and for a mother, the clockwork elephant who once sang him a lullaby:

> Hush, hush, little plush,
> Mama's near you through the night.
> Hush, hush, little plush,
> Everything will be all right.

In the end, everything *is* all right. The mouse and his child succeed against all odds, chiefly by virtue of their integrity, naiveté, and the child's faith. Like all quest heroes, they gather friends about them who help them in their territorial battle for the doll's house, a battle on the order of that for Toad Hall in *The Wind in the Willows*. Manny Rat, who with his usual ingenuity has found a way to make the toys self-winding, is reformed (he likes to have the child call him "Uncle"), and they all live happily ever after.

On its secondary level, *The Mouse and His Child* is a satire—in the Swiftian and Orwellian tradition—on American society; and in this respect, it is the most socially oriented of all the American fantasies of the modern era. At the heart of the story is Hoban's view of a civilization he condemns as materialistic, conformist, and as one built on obsolescence. Here the chief image is that of the toys themselves being trapped in a mechanical dance, discarded when broken, and always at the mercy of those who can manipulate their machinery. The dump over which Manny Rat holds sway is a "rat race," built on the castoffs of humans, and exhibiting the worst aspects of human society as the rats vie for Manny's favors and try to climb the social ladder. The birds, insects, and small animals whom the mouse and his child meet on their journey are (as in most animal fantasies) anthropomorphized types of humans: the charlatan Frog soothsayer; Muskrat, the pure scientist who cares nothing about the impact of his experiments; the journalist Bluejay, whose squawking is a parody of newspaper headlines; and the crows in the "Caws of Art Experimental Theatre Group," who produce abstruse modern plays while the audience wants pulp. Both the horrors and the uselessness of war are shown in a bloody battle among the shrews. Over it all is the brooding symbolism of the can of Bonzo Dog Food, with its picture of a black-and-white spotted dog carrying a can of dog food—a picture that is endlessly repeated. In one of the most heartrending scenes in the book, when the mice lie abandoned for months at the bottom of a pond, C. Serpentina, the author of avant-garde plays such as "Beyond the Last Visible Dog," refuses to help them:

> "Each of us, sunk in the mud however deep must rise on the propulsion of his own thought. Each of us must journey through the dogs, beyond the dots, and to the truth, alone."

However, just as the mouse's child has persevered in everything else, he perseveres in this existential concept until he discovers that beyond nothingness is himself. Knowing the "Why," he then, with the help of a dragonfly chrysalis, figures out the "How's" and the "What's"—and so the mice escape.

The major flaw of the book is that not all of its separate parts are necessary to the unfolding of the plot, and many are simply diversionary—a scattering of soapboxes for Hoban's social dissatisfactions. It is interesting—and rather sad—that in spite of his natural aversion to war Hoban should use a battle as a denouement to his odyssey. However, the use of this device may simply be an indication of how strong literary conventions can be. Nevertheless, the author ends on a note of hope; his dystopia turns into a utopia even if it is only to be a small and secluded haven apart from the rest of the world and even if only a few individuals can reach it through courage and indomitability and a sense of their own worth. As with their reading of *Gulliver's Travels*, children will take out of Hoban's story what they will, but whatever harvest they reap will be worthwhile.

With its very first sentence, Maurice Sendak's *Higglety-Pigglety Pop* (1967) appears to be a commentary on the youthful malaise of the 1960's. Jennie, a Sealyham terrier, announces:

> I am discontented. I want something I do not have. There must
> be more to life than having everything.

Indeed, she does seem to have everything necessary for canine comfort— a kind master, two pillows to sleep on, two windows to look out of, and all the food she wants. Nonetheless, she packs her bag and leaves home on a classic quest for meaning, eventually seeking out life experience in answer to an advertisement for a leading lady in the World Mother Goose Theatre. Critics such as Selma Lanes have linked the symbolic images in the story and its allusions—in words and drawings—to Sendak's own childhood.[10] In fact, the elegiac tone in Jennie's symbolic death and rebirth is related to the deaths of Sendak's mother and of his longtime companion dog, Jennie, at about the same time. Sendak's love of music, especially opera, are also evident in this tragi-comedy libretto.

However, the story is also a marvelous piece of nonsense, a spoof on the old rhyme

> Higglety-Pigglety Pop!
> The dog has eaten the mop!
> The pig's in a hurry;

10. Selma Lanes, *The Art of Maurice Sendak* (New York: Abrams, 1980).

The cat's in a flurry;
Higglety-Pigglety Pop!

This rhyme was composed by Samuel Griswold Goodridge, who swamped children's literature in the United States in the early part of the nineteenth century with moralistic informational books that were often incorrect and racist. Here his idea was to ridicule the Mother Goose rhymes, little realizing that this rhyme would be the only piece of his writing to survive outside of historical collections of children's books.

Like other fantasists of the period, such as Ursula Le Guin, Sendak revitalizes the traditional patterns of folk literature and makes use of psychological archetypes. His Jennie is a folklore trickster figure; his mysterious Lion, a death figure; and his ineffable Baby, who transforms herself into the Moon and Mother Goose, a kind of goddess guide to a mystery religion of death and rebirth. Even the final tableau of the characters acting out scenes from the Goodrich rhyme for the World Mother Goose Theatre is evocative of a Punch and Judy show or a St. George and the Dragon Mummer's play. Sendak's story is more multi-leveled and sophisticated than any other fantasy.

The dense complexity of Sendak's mythic allusions would seem to require a lengthy novelistic treatment. His genius, however, is compressed into a buoyant picture-storybook, and it is at this level that children will enjoy it. The fun is always there. At the end, Jennie has achieved her ambition to be a successful actress (and she has made it on her own), and she is able to satisfy her ravenous appetite by swallowing a salami mop everyday—"twice on Saturdays."

By contrast, there is nothing sophisticated about George Selden's The Cricket in Times Square (1960) or its sequel Tucker's Countryside (1969). Together, they touch upon the theme of the old folktale "The Town Mouse and the Country Mouse," and on Beatrix Potter's Johnny Townmouse, in their contrast between city and country living; but in their lightheartedness, the novels sit best among Margery Sharp's mouse stories of Miss Bianca, although without the miniature and tongue-in-cheek perfection of Sharp's stories. In The Cricket in Times Square, Chester Cricket arrives in New York City via a picnic sandwich and makes friends with two subway dwellers—Tucker, a streetwise scavenger mouse, and Harry the Cat, a Damon Runyon figure of sagacity and indolence. Tucker and Harry discover and promote Chester's ability to reproduce any music that he hears on the radio; as a result, New York commuters are treated to marvelous concerts, and the livelihood of a newsagent Italian family is preserved. Once back in his own countryside, Chester calls upon his city friends for help in saving his meadow, which is about to be bulldozed to make way for apartments. Tucker and Harry's problems with the bucolic life are presented both realistically and humorously. As Tucker says:

> "Subways I can sleep through! Commuters I can sleep through. But that brook just goes on . . . and on . . . and on!"

The theme of conservation, supported by placard-carrying children who want their playground saved, is certainly a link with the concerns of the 1960's; and while it is not a heavy theme, it is enough to make *Tucker's Countryside* a less charming book than *A Cricket in Times Square*.

Selden's animals have a solidity to them in that their behavior is close to what one expects from crickets, rats, or cats. Their innate abilities are only slightly and charmingly extended. By contrast, Randall Jarrell's little bat in *The Bat-Poet* (1964) takes the reader into a new dimension of experience. First of all, the little bat goes against his own kind by staying awake in the daytime. His world is, in effect, turned upside-down, and the reader shares in his new look at ordinary things, such as sunlight and shadows. In his joy, the little bat tries to express himself in poetry, only to discover that he must have an appreciative audience. The mockingbird is interested only in poetic techniques, the owl is not even aware of the significance of a poem in his honor, and only the chipmunk gives the bat a kind of common-man response to his poem on the predatory owl and asks: "Why do I like it if it makes me shiver?" At the end of his brief experiment in both daylight and poesy, the little bat makes up a poem about his own kind:

> A bat is born
> Naked and blind and pale
> His mother makes a pocket of her tail
> And catches him . . .

The bat then goes to join the other bats in their hibernation but says sleepily to himself: "I wish I'd said we sleep all winter. That would have

been a good thing to have in." As an artist, he is not satisfied with
his performance.

Like all fine writers of animal fantasy, Jarrell observed the habits of
the creatures he wrote about, but *The Bat-Poet* is no more a story about
bats than Walter de la Mare's *The Three Mullah Mulgars* is a study of monkeys. Just as de la Mare's work is chiefly a quest for the ideal, so Jarrell's
has much to do with a poet's search for expression; with feeling over
technique; with art over life. When the mockingbird imitates others, the
little bat asks: "Which one's the mocking bird? Which one's the
world?"

A sense of belonging, even when one is different from others, links
The Bat-Poet to Jarrell's *The Animal Family* (1965). The title of the latter
book also suggests a link between all creatures on land or sea, since the
family is composed of a hunter, a mermaid, a lynx, a bear, and, finally, a
young male child. The hunter is somewhat typical of his species, living à
la Robinson Crusoe, but the mermaid is exceptional. She in no way
resembles Hans Christian Andersen's "Little Mermaid," who suffered to
achieve a soul and thereby win the Prince. Jarrell's mermaid makes the
transition to land and human speech quite easily, although her walk and
her housework suffer because of her tail. The animals, too, are quickly
tamed. With the boy, who is brought home by the lynx, the family is
complete. They have always been together, and the mermaid and the
hunter tell the boy, "We've had you always."

In a reversal of the bat-poet who seeks the day, David of *Fly by Night*
(1969) has his experiences in the dark. It is at night that David sees most
clearly and finds reassurance. Like the little bat, and like the hunter, the
boy, and the animals in *Animal Family,* David finds his mother. In his
dream, the owl invites him to become one of her offspring: "She opened
her wings, they nestled to her breast." Then she tells a bedtime story. In
the morning, David sees that the loving eyes of the dream-owl are those
of his mother. All three books are linked by a mother-image—the bat
makes a poem of his birth, the mermaid is a loving foster mother, and
David understands the love his mother has for him.

These stories are also linked by their openings, all of which invite the
reader into a fairy tale. *The Bat-Poet* begins: "Once upon a time there
was a bat"; *The Animal Family,* "Once upon a time, long, long ago"; and
Fly by Night, as if one were on a journey to Never-land: "If you turn right
at the last stoplight on New Garden Road"; and their endings imply

that "they all lived happily ever afterwards." Like the works of Walter de la Mare, those of Jarrell have an aura of timelessness. They do not belong to trends or patterns but appear to spring only from a poetic imagination.

Light Fantasy

Epic fantasy of the decade is filled with seriousness, momentous events, and protagonists on the verge of adulthood. It was chiefly the writers of light fantasy who kept the adventurous and resilient spirit of childhood. The English novelist Joan Aiken is particularly child-oriented. Her young heroines and heroes are about eleven or twelve years of age. In her quartet about Dido Twite,[11] Aiken plays with history (much as Rosemary Harris played with the Ark story) and invents a historical period that never happened—the reign of James III of England. However, she fills these books and others, such as *The Wolves of Willoughby Chase* (1963), with much of the seamy side of the nineteenth century—the pitiful state of orphan children, the poor but genteel spinsters, and the autocratic power of the wealthy and of those in charge of children. We live with whalers, take a ride on a nineteenth-century train, and learn how both children and adults were dressed in their various occupations and stations in life. Aiken's locations are also real—the streets of London (including St. Paul's Cathedral), the waters and shores of Nantucket, the Sussex countryside. Her humor is not tongue-in-cheek, as is that of Rosemary Harris; instead, it is raucous and outrageous, often to the point of slapstick comedy.

Her children, whether the high-spirited and the responsible Simon of *The Wolves of Willoughby Chase* or the intrepid Cockney Dido Twite, have to cope with the vicissitudes of life without help from adults for most of the time, and they have to put the world to rights when villains are conspiring to set it awry. The events may be hilarious, but through them all, the pains and achievements of the children are taken seriously. There are no supernatural elements in these books, and no natural laws are broken. There are, however, plenty of exaggerations, such as the villainous

11. *Black Hearts in Battersea* (1964), *Nightbirds on Nantucket* (1966), *The Cuckoo Tree* (1971), and *The Stolen Lake* (1981).

Hanoverians in *Nightbirds on Nantucket* who are planning to discharge a cannonball across the Atlantic to destroy James III, and (in the same book) the pink whale who falls in love with the whaling captain who has pursued her with all the intensity of Captain Ahab seeking out Moby Dick.

Despite the lightheartedness in Aiken's fantasies, they appeal also to adults who can appreciate Aiken's spoofs on Victorian melodrama (in *The Wolves of Willoughby Chase*) and the larger-than-life quality of Charles Dickens's novels. Although her use of literary antecedents and her historical perspectives (as hilarious as these are) give most of Aiken's writing a mythic quality, this latter aspect is most evident in *The Whispering Mountains* (1969). The hero's journey through the subterranean mountain passages of Wales in search of the Golden Harp of Teirtu has a link to Welsh legend and to the heroic quest of traditional epic fantasy in spite of the journey's overall burlesque.

That light humor can have simplicity, charm, fun, and some depth is also shown by Helen Cresswell's *The Piemakers* (1967). The setting is real enough—that of Danby Dale on the border of Yorkshire and Derbyshire—but its time is reminiscent of that of a folktale with its sturdy peasants and exaggerated comedy. The Piemaker family (with the help of the whole village) outwits its rivals and bakes the largest pie ever made—and to perfection. The plot is sufficient to make a good story, but it is further sustained by its portrayal of a grave little girl, rightly named Gravella, who loves her family and her surroundings but who yearns to be more than a piemaker. The reader knows that she will.

Cresswell's *The Night-Watchmen* (1969) is as much a piece of minor perfection as *The Piemakers*, but it has a more direct fantasy component. Illness has released Henry from school; and in his lonesome wanderings around his town, he meets Josh and Caleb. At first, Henry takes them for ordinary hobos and becomes entranced with their efficient living arrangements, Josh's writing, and Caleb's cooking. Then he discovers that they are more than vagrants; Josh and Caleb are the watchmen for a mysterious place called There (ordinary people are from Here), and they must stop a large group of men with green eyes who can see like a cat in the dark and who want to find There and use it for their own purposes. Josh and Caleb's means of escape is always a powerful steam train that they whistle up in times of danger. Henry longs with all his heart to see the train. Eventually, he not only sees it, but he has a short ride on it after he becomes instrumental in preventing the Green-eyes from reaching the train. Now the adventure is over. Henry has lost a piece of the train-shaped cake that Caleb had baked for him:

> In the end there was really only one thing of which he could be quite certain. That whenever he heard a train hooting in the night, whenever he saw a tunnel or a hole in the road, he would think of Josh and Caleb, and remember that once, at any rate, they had been as real to him as the fingers of his own hand.

Henry is a true child of enchanted realism. For a brief moment, his ordinary experience is delicately altered, yet his whole life will be enriched by it.

There is little delicacy about Roald Dahl's *James and the Giant Peach* (1961) and even less about that perennial favorite with children *Charlie and the Chocolate Factory* (1964). Nor is there any depth of feeling. However, Dahl pretends to neither, since he is an avowed entertainer of children. Not for him are the struggles between good and evil, insights into the complexities of time, child-adult relationships, or magical adventures or discoveries that heighten reality. He does, however, make use of well-established literary forms.

James and the Giant Peach is an amalgam of the tall tale, the cautionary tale, the folktale, and animal fantasy. In this story, however, the caution is for adults: do not be cruel to children. James's parents are disposed of neatly, on the first page, by being eaten by a rhinoceros (although they appear to have done nothing to deserve it) as fast as Albert was eaten by the lion in Marriott Edgar's famous monologue "Albert and the Lion." The two cruel aunts meet a just retribution (considering that they had starved James) by being squashed to death by a giant peach. The peach itself is of the order of Jack's beanstalk, the seed for it being given to James by a mysterious old man. Once inside the peach, James finds a strange but friendly assortment of giant insects, and they are carried across the ocean by a flock of birds and live happily in Central Park.

James and the Giant Peach contains much humor and provides some visually memorable moments through its illustrations by Nancy Burkert, but *Charlie and the Chocolate Factory,* as its title suggests, is mostly goo. Not that food cannot provide a companionable backdrop to children's fantasy. C.S. Lewis's *Narnia Chronicles* are filled with scenes of eating and drinking. As Lewis said, "I myself like eating and drinking. I put in what I would have liked to read when I was a child and what I still like reading now that I am in my fifties."[12] Lewis's food scenes (like those in Kenneth Grahame's *The Wind in the Willows*) are allied with hospitality, companionship, the comforts of home, and relaxation when the struggles in the outside world are over. By contrast, Dahl's whole book is really an orgy, even when the greedy children are being punished for their excesses. The verses detailing how the punishment fits the crime are also excessively long, lacking the crisp, clean justice found in Heinrich Hoffman's *Struwwelpeter* or Hilaire Belloc's *Cautionary Tales for Children*. The nicest character in the book is Grandpa Joe (Charlie himself is a nonentity), who is rejuvenated by the adventure and whose affection for and understanding of Charlie shine through the otherwise superficial story.

Walter de la Mare's poem about "Poor tired Tim! It's sad for him./He lags the whole bright morning through,/Ever so tired of nothing to do;" could be the inspiration for Norton Juster's *The Phantom Tollbooth* (1961) about "a boy named Milo who didn't know what to do with himself—not just sometimes, but always." De la Mare leaves Tim tired, but Juster reforms Milo. Milo is presented with a magic tollbooth and his own little car, and off he goes to find himself a quest hero. He must restore Rhyme and Reason to the important city of Dictionopolis. This task is accomplished by Milo and his Oz-like companions—a dog with a clock in his body called Tock (it is his brother who ticks) and the Humblebee. On the way, Milo learns the use of language—punning (a witch is a which), synonyms, antonyms, aphorisms, and clichés. It is all good fun for perhaps the first one-third of the story, but then it becomes rather wearisome.

The possibilities for fantasists to ring endless changes on an old theme can be seen in Pauline Clarke's *The Twelve and the Genii* (1962,) [13] which has much of the appeal of T.H. White's Lilliputians in *Mistress Masham's Repose* as well as a somewhat similar literary antecedent. The "Twelve" of the title are wooden soldiers, once owned by Bramwell Bronte.[14] He

12. C.S. Lewis, "On Three Ways of Writing for Children," in *On Stories,* ed. Walter Hooper (New York: HBJ, 1982), 31.

13. Published in the United States as *The Return of the Twelves.*

14. Christine Alexander, *The Early Writings of Charlotte Bronte* (Oxford: Basil Blackwell, 1983), 1.

and his sisters (Charlotte and Emily) not only played with the soldiers but gave each one a history, an adventurous life, and, most importantly, individuality. The Genii are thus the soldiers' creators—the Bronte children.

In modern times, the soldiers are found by an eight-year-old boy named Max Morley, who has come to live in an old house near Haworth, the Bronte parsonage. He also discovers that the soldiers are alive and freeze into toys only when they are threatened. Unlike T.H. White's Maria, Max has an immediate and sensitive understanding of the little people, and so he, too, is accepted as a Genii. His mature handling of the situation is made plausible—especially when he is put under pressure to sell the famous toys—by the brief glimpses we get of his parents, who treat Max with respect and back his determination to keep the toys.

The Twelves, sensing their danger from the threatened sale and the resulting publicity, take matters into their own hands and undertake an escape to Haworth. They are, however, subtly directed by Max, who has developed the power of anticipating their maneuvers. At the end of the story, he is also helped by his brother, his younger sister, and the curator of Haworth. The adventures are perfectly conceived, and all the characters—even the minor ones, such as the newspaper reporter—are deftly and believably drawn.

In *Charlotte Sometimes* (1969), Penelope Farmer brings past-time fantasy closer to the present. Her Charlotte of the title is the Charlotte of *The Summer Birds* and is still a most appealing young character. At a boarding school in 1950, Charlotte goes to bed on her first night and awakens in 1918 in the same school but with a different name. Now she is Clare and with a younger sister named Emily rather than Emma; meanwhile, the real Clare takes on the identity of Charlotte. The shift in time is caused by the beds in which each girl sleeps, which are the same in each historical period but different from any other beds in the room. Beyond this aspect of magic, the story is a fairly simple one of a glimpse into social history (which is not so long ago), a contrast between the schools (which are not very different), and the difficulties (practical rather than strange or dangerous) that Charlotte in particular meets in daily living. Further tension is caused by Charlotte's struggle to keep, and so in a sense to find, her identity and by the possibility that each girl may be locked in the other's time. We are not allowed to believe that the whole experience has been a dream. When Charlotte finally returns to

1950, it is to learn that Clare had died in the post-war flu epidemic of 1919; and Emily, now a mother, sends Charlotte some games and toys that Charlotte (as Clare) and Emily played with in 1918.

By the end of the 1960's, Walter de la Mare's "East Wind" was blowing steadily through realistic fiction published for the young, particularly in the United States. This emphasis in fiction almost swept away the concept of a happy or ideal childhood and even that of childhood itself. It also eroded the storytelling quality of children's fiction; few books had a plot going beyond the personal problems of the protagonists. In these aspects, some fantasists held firmly to the past. Joan Aiken, Helen Cresswell, Pauline Clarke, and Alan Garner (in his first three works)— with their innately good and resourceful children—showed originality within well-established patterns and exciting plots. In general, fantasy remained strongly plotted, but most writers of the decade turned away from child protagonists, seemingly finding the release of their imaginations in the portrayal of adolescents and in moving them through rites of passage from youthful egotism to maturity. In these latter respects fantasy made a strong link with realistic fiction.

A major development was the increased use of myth, legend, and folklore; the majority of writers introduced some mythic content to their works. This use of myth is often observable in light fantasy and in animal fantasy, as well as in epic fantasy. With the exceptions of Prydain and Earthsea, myth was not confined to Other Worlds but became a potent part of the real world. Many writers, including Mayne, Garner, and Farmer saw myth as central to real life, just as our ancestors did, and agreed with Joan Aiken that

> . . . myth overlaps fantasy, and in some way is needed by everyone—not simply as a moral exhortation or parable, any more than the purpose of religion is simply to make people behave better, but because myth is the basic material of a rich inner life, and because a rich inner life does seem to be essential for human equilibrium.[15]

Despite strong injections of the oral tradition, these writers strengthened the realistic components of their works to an extent not known

15. Joan Aiken, "Between Family and Fantasy," *The Quarterly Journal of the Library of Congress* 29 (Oct. 1972): 318.

before, while ignoring Coleridge's plea for "a semblance of truth . . . for shadows of the imagination." Such writers as William Mayne with *Earthfasts,* Alan Garner with *Elidor* and Madeleine L'Engle with *A Wrinkle in Time,* while calling up "shadows of the imagination," gave them a real presence in the real world. Frequently, they compelled belief through the power of their writing. All in all, however, in chiefly rejecting a Secondary World and, to a great extent, a Secondary Belief, these writers changed the face of fantasy.

Chapter 9

Games of Dark:
Fantasy of the 1970's

I n comparison with the literature of realism, works of fantasy declined in the 1960's but took a dramatic upswing in the 1970's. Many major writers of the previous decade, such as Joan Aiken with *The Cuckoo Tree* and Ursula Le Guin with *The Tombs of Atuan* and *The Farthest Shore,* continued in their characteristic form and style, to the delight of their readers. Others, such as William Mayne with *A Game of Dark* (1971), Alan Garner with *Red Shift* (1973), and Penelope Farmer with *A Castle of Bone* (1972), extended their bailiwicks with additional digging into the psyches of their characters. A host of brilliant new writers also entered the field. These included Robert Westall, Penelope Lively, Anne McCaffrey, Patricia McKillip, Richard Adams, Robert O'Brien, and many others who made great individual contributions to the genre but who, like their progenitors, were very much a part of their time. The ghost story also re-entered children's fiction after a hiatus that began in the days after Walter de la Mare. It was represented in its classic form by Leon Garfield's *The Ghost Downstairs* and in modern dress by Penelope Lively's *The Revenge of Samuel Stokes.*

Epic Fantasy

Despite this star-studded cast, one name, like that of Leigh Hunt's Abou Ben Adhem, leads all the rest in attracting widespread attention and a faithful following that has continued to the present—that of Susan Cooper. Cooper's *The Dark Is Rising Quintet*[1] makes its mark on the period chiefly by reason of its grand design and cosmic scale. It is a swirling series about the never-ending battle between the forces of good and evil: the Light and the Dark. It encompasses a thousand years of the struggle; it sweeps from modern Cornwall to Buckinghamshire and to North Wales and back again, with incursions into Other Worlds. Its cosmology is not that of structured Christianity, as in C.S. Lewis's *Narnia Chronicles,* nor is it completely existential, as in Ursula Le Guin's *Earthsea* trilogy, but somewhere in between.

Cooper's universe is a six-tiered one. At its apex is Love, followed by High then Wild Magic. The fourth level is one of conflict. On this level, the forces of the Light and the Dark battle over the fate of the lowest— the human level. Between this last level and the Light and the Dark is a less easily defined group of "special humans"—with or without magical powers—through whom the High Magic can work.[2] However, nothing can conquer Love:

> "Such loving bonds," Merriman said, "are outside the control even of the High Magic, for they are the strongest thing on all this earth."

The powers of the Light are not always used benevolently; the eyes of justice (as in the folktales and in C.S. Lewis's *The Last Battle*) are indeed in a blindfold. Not only do the wicked get their deserts, but at the beginning of *The Grey King* we understand that the chief eleven-year-old protagonist, Will Stanton, has been deliberately made ill so that he can be in the right place at the right time. As John Rowlands points out to Will in *The Grey King:*

> "But those men who know anything at all about the Light also know there is a fierceness to its power, like the bare sword of the law, or the white burning of the sun. . . . At the very heart, that is. Other things, like humanity and mercy, and charity, that most

1. *Over Sea, Under Stone* (1965), *The Dark Is Rising* (1973), *The Grey King* (1975), *Greenwitch* (1976), and *Silver on the Tree* (1977).

2. I am indebted for this concept to a former student, Kevin Kierans, who presented it in a paper in 1983.

good men hold more precious than all else, they do not come first for the Light. . . . At the centre of the Light there is a cold white flame, just as at the centre of the Dark there is a great black pit bottomless as the Universe."

The Wild Magic is personified chiefly in the Greenwitch (the title of the fourth book) and in Herne the Hunter and in various talismans. These characters and talismans all are neutral in the struggle because innately they are neither good nor bad. However, they lend their aid to those who somehow touch their primitive natures, just as the Greenwitch rewards the compassion shown to her by Jane Drew; or they simply release their powers to those who seize them first, as does the harp, the sword, and the midsummer tree. Their powers are not, as was Arthur's sword in the stone or Taran's sword, reserved only for a rightful owner.

Cooper's mythological basis is chiefly Arthurian, with references to British folklore in general (such as "the hunting of the wren" and Druidic power), but she also draws on primitive and even Caribbean magic, no doubt to indicate that the struggle against evil is universal. King Arthur is one of the key figures, as is Merlin in his modern role as Merriman Lyon (Uncle Merry to the Drew children), Weland the Smith, the Fisher King, and Herne. Other figures have obviously risen in obedience to Cooper's imagination: The Walker, The Rider, and The Lady (however, in this latter figure, many interpretations of her origin and nature could be offered).

In spite of its immersion in the roots of fantasy (that is, myth, legend, and folklore), *The Dark Is Rising* sequence is very much a part of its time. Like many other contemporary writers, Susan Cooper experienced World War II as a child, and its effects remained with her. Modern writers of realistic fiction, such as Penelope Lively with *Going Back* and Nina Bawden with *Carrie's War,* have told of its effects (chiefly that of disruption) on an individual child and have done so movingly and brilliantly. However, in expressing the larger aspects of the struggle between good and evil through fantasy—and so externalizing it rather than internalizing it, as in her own somewhat autobiographical story *Dawn of Fear*—Cooper has produced a longer-lasting work and one that is more accessible to a greater number of readers. She also speaks of the ever-present and ongoing struggle against evil. At the end of the last book, *Silver on the Tree,* Merriman tells the children that now that the battle against the Dark has been won, at least for a while, he and Arthur and the other Old Ones are leaving. Only Will Stanton will remain as a "watchman." The fate of the world is now only in the hands of humans:

> "For Drake is no longer in his hammock, children, nor is Arthur somewhere sleeping, and you may not lie idly expecting the second coming of anybody now, because the world is yours and it is up to you. Now especially since man has the strength to destroy this world, it is the responsibility of man to keep it alive, in all its beauty and marvellous joy."

Three of the children—Simon, Jane, and Barney Drew—have no magical powers. They are much like Susan and Colin in Alan Garner's *The Weirdstone of Brisingamen* and *The Moon of Gomrath*—unbeset by family problems and moving through adventures with spunk and a natural childlike goodness. We meet them first in *Over Sea, Under Stone,* which is a better-than-average fantasy-adventure story with numerous cliff-hanging scenes. Power and genuine drama arrive with the appearance of Will Stanton in *The Dark Is Rising.* He is the seventh son of a seventh son; therefore, by all the laws of folklore he is out of the ordinary. On his eleventh birthday, Will learns that he is the youngest of the Old Ones—beings that are half mortal and half immortal—who are of the Light and in opposition to the Dark. Like T.H. White's young Arthur in *The Once and Future King,* Will serves an apprenticeship for his role by being liberated from his own body into other stages of experience. However, his education is condensed into only moments of time as he reads the *Book of Gramarye* (an old word for learning). Nonetheless, he is a very real boy, who is teased by his loving family for his mature ways and disliked by the Drew children when they first meet him in *Greenwitch* because he seems so aloof. Susan Cooper best describes Will's dual nature in *Silver on the Tree:*

> He sat there, self-possessed as a huntsman, a small stocky figure in blue jeans and sweater on the tall golden horse . . .

Bran, whom we first meet in *The Grey King,* is the son of King Arthur, brought into the twentieth century by his mother Guinevere who feared for his life. Although Bran is of the High Magic, he refuses his father's offer to a life of rest "at the back of the North Wind, among the apple trees," preferring instead to join in the human struggle against evil. Will is the most memorable of the children, chiefly because of the contrast (so well brought out in The Dark Is Rising) that is drawn between the possibility of his leading a normal, happy childhood and the extraordinary burdens that are placed upon him. The Drew children add a note of reality to the astounding adventures by their very ordinariness: their conversation, sibling rivalries, and loyalty to one another in times of distress.

The greatest flaw in Susan Cooper's work is an overuse of "the Matter of Britain." This legendary focus is like being presented with a medieval twelve-course meal when one is on a diet. Cooper certainly knows her Arthurian, Celtic, and British legends in general, but not all have a direct relationship to the plot. Recognizing references and allusions is one of the joys of reading; but for symbols to work their emotive magic, the readers must be aware, if only in a vague way, of what those symbols represent. In earlier fantasies, George MacDonald's grandmother and C.S. Lewis's Aslan are not only recognizable to a child in the real world but carry basic mythic resonances. Moreover, both images are integral to these authors' plots and are reinforced by repetition throughout the stories. On the other hand, Cooper's references and allusions are all too often gratuitous and overpowering, probably sending only students of literature on a hunt for their sources.

Cooper's style is also uneven, sometimes falling between pretentiousness and banality. Its overall lushness combined with its panoply of mythical borrowings recalls the warning of the Greek poet George Seferis: "We've decorated our art so much that its features have been eaten away by gold."[3]

Although Cooper's writing can occasionally be adversely criticized, it is also memorably dotted with cinematic techniques that give her otherwise conventional view of fantasy a very modern touch. Super-imposition is used as effectively in The Dark Is Rising as in a film when the towering figure of the Black Rider is superimposed on that of a small island in the River Thames and when, later, the same island crumbles and merges into the golden image of a magnificent Viking long-ship. Toward the end of Silver on the Tree, the children's immediate sur-

3. George Seferis, "An Old Man on the River Bank," in Collected Poems (Princeton, New Jersey: Princeton Univ. Pr., 1967), 285.

roundings meld into the place where in the past six important primitive signs (iron, bronze, stone, fire, water, and oak) had first been buried. Allied with this technique is the use of panning. In *Silver on the Tree*, the flight of a seagull moves into a nineteenth-century shipyard scene. The ear is not neglected either. While music is not used as a special motif, it always portends a shift in time and space.

On the whole, the virtues of *The Dark Is Rising* quintet far outweigh its faults. Susan Cooper never forgets that the novelist's prime function is to entertain, and she tells a story more compellingly than most of her contemporaries who are considered better craftsmen. Each book generates more enthusiasm for the next; and each provides a counterpoint to, not a repetition of, her major theme—the link between myth and reality. It has been said, "fantasy . . . came into being only with the destruction of syncretic thought, wherein the real and the imaginary, the rational and the spiritual are inseparable."[4] More than any other modern fantasist, Cooper has re-established the syncretic thought of old. She accomplishes this, as did C.S. Lewis with the *Narnia Chronicles*, by making the fantasy component the strongest element of her story (she is no subscriber to the realistic school of fantasy) and also through her landscapes, all of which already have built-in mythic associations.

Most of all, Cooper recognizes the fact that epic fantasy teeters on the edge of things. Beyond all else, it exists on the knife-edge of terror. In *The Dark Is Rising*, this terror is palpable. Already the appearance of the rooks has heralded something strange in Will Stanton's life, and that night

> . . . in a dreadful, furious moment, horror seized him like a nightmare made real; there came a wrenching crash, with the howling of the wind suddenly much louder and closer and a great blast of cold; and the feeling came hurtling against him with such force of dread that it flung him cowering away.

In *Silver on the Tree*, Will and Bran are pursued by a skeleton horse—the Mari Llwyd—in a scene that even a master of special effects would find hard to duplicate on film.

4. Julius Kagarlitski, "Realism and Fantasy," in *Science Fiction: The Other Side of Realism*, ed. Thomas D. Clareson (Bowling Green, Ohio: Bowling Green Univ. Popular Pr., 1971), 29.

Just as Susan Cooper is conventional in her approach to epic fantasy, she is also conventional in her endings: the story is over; the magic has gone. However, the effects of the magic remain. The heightened perceptions of their own world that the children have gained will stay with them all their lives; and *children* is the operative word in Susan Cooper's works. In a decade in which writers of fantasy increasingly turned to the personal problems of the adolescent, she stands as a groundplan for epic fantasy, with its sweeping use of myth and its child protagonists who join in an unselfish, universal struggle rather than in a search for their own identity.

An interesting contrast to Cooper's epic is that of Joy Chant's *Red Moon and Black Mountain* (1970). This novel is one of the few modern attempts at creating a full Secondary World. The land of Vanderei has all the conventions of modern myth-making: hierarchies, cultures, histories, and a young teenager who is called in from the Primary World as the expected hero in order to save a land from a destruction caused by evil. In many ways, however, its background does not entirely convince. The portrayal of the Khentori—the horse people—with their magnificent herds, their tribal life, and their primitive magic rouses echoes in the subconscious, but the forces of High Magic—the Star People—are shadowy, and so are the lands and the people they appear to rule.

Chant reveals, however, a deeper and more passionate combination of good, evil, and amorality in one novel than does Cooper in her quintet. Oliver is older than Will Stanton—he is moving from adolescence to adulthood—and he has no Uncle Merriman to come to his rescue in moments of crisis. He defeats the physical enemy in hand-to-hand combat and yet feels his victory sour in his mouth. Then, in a scene out of Milton's *Paradise Lost,* Oliver sees the real evil—"the great enemy; He Whose Name is Taken Away, that Prince of Heaven whom he had always called Lucifer, Star of the Morning." However, after the battle between the good and the evil, the earth goddess, Vir'Vachel, must be propitiated:

> Yet it was not for the slain she mourned; but for the injured earth itself . . . as she moved she sank ankle-deep into the earth, and behind her green welled from the hollows her feet had pressed, welled up and overflowed and spread. Wherever she passed the ground woke to life, and grass grew and flourished.

As the new chief of the Khentori, it is Oliver who must offer himself as a victim to Vir'Vachel's anger so that the tribe may live in peace. In thus plunging into the unknown, Oliver is returned to his own world, as are his brother and sister. Although the real world in no way impinges on the events, the story is powerfully complete and satisfying within its perimeters. The emotion engendered by Oliver's responsibility and sacrifice conquers the looser and vaguer parts of the plot.

Epic fantasy of the decade was also enriched by entrants from Australia and Canada, two countries that had hitherto not been conducive to this genre. While British writers have always been able to find their material ready-to-hand, as it were, in Australia, Patricia Wrightson had to go in search of indigenous folklore. She has written that she "dug them out of the works of anthropologists and early field workers and of laymen who had lived in sympathetic friendship with Aboriginal Australians. . . . "[5] But however much she acknowledges her debt to this older tradition, Wrightson uses it in a refreshingly creative way. *The Nargun and the Stars* (1974), which showed her complete conversion to local folklore, is far more powerful and memorable than her earlier fantasies, such as *Down to Earth* (1965) and *An Older Kind of Magic* (1972). The former falls into the category of science fiction rather than fantasy (it concerns a child visitor from another planet), and *An Older Kind of Magic* veers toward science-fiction fantasy with its combination of the effects of a comet on the human inhabitants of Sydney and its supernatural players in the events—the Potkoorok, the Bitarr, and the Nyols. These Australian spirit-folk do not seem at home, even in Sydney's Botanical Gardens, but they find a natural habitat in Wongadilla, the setting of *The Nargun and the Stars*—a countryside of ridges, spurs, pools, rocks, timberland, and herding grounds. Against this background, too, Wrightson makes convincing the most unusual spirit force in fantasy—the Nargun. The Nargun is a huge rock, forged out of fire at the beginning of the world, barely sentient, with indentations that only remotely resemble human features and limbs, but it is filled with a power that it obeys blindly and instinctively. In its anger and fear, the Nargun raises its snoutless face to the stars and shrieks *Ng-a-a*.

After a hundred years of a slow, rocking journey, the Nargun arrives

5. Patricia Wrightson, "Ever Since My Accident: Aboriginal Folklore and Australian Fantasy," *The Horn-Book Magazine* 56 (Dec. 1980): 612.

in Wongadilla, just as a young boy named Simon comes to live with his aunt and uncle after the death of his parents. That Aunt Edie and Uncle Charlie are drawn into the battle to get rid of the Nargun is believable because they, like Simon, knew the frog-like, trickster Potkoorok as children. The ensuing struggle between the Nargun and the forces of the district—both human and supernatural—is not one between good and evil. It is instead one of territorial imperative:

> "Good?" said the Potkoorok. "What is good? It is the Nargun. It came from a long way south. It should go back."

The Nargun is not defeated, but it is contained by the forces of technology namely, a tractor and a bulldozer. We know, however, that time is on the Nargun's side.

The Nargun may be a local variant on legends of walking stones such as those found in William Mayne's *Earthfasts* and Penelope Lively's *The Whispering Knights,* but it has an even more primal feeling about it than do its English counterparts.

The Nargun and the Stars verges on the epic—chiefly because of the battle fought to contain the Nargun—but Wrightson's "Wirrun" trilogy[6] is a fully fledged one. She almost turns Australia into Another World as she peoples it with spirits and primeval beings from indigenous folklore. The trilogy differs from other epics, such as Tolkien's *The Lord of the Rings* or Susan Cooper's *The Dark Is Rising* quintet, in that each book concerns a separate quest. It is also premised on an imbalance in nature (caused by amoral spirit forces) rather than on a black-and-white struggle between good and evil. The three books are, however, linked through the hero (like the structure of Beowulf), who is called upon to restore his country to the exigencies of nature's physical laws.

All in all, the trilogy is a celebration of Aboriginal culture, the land, and brotherhood. Wirrun is a young man of the People:

> The People are dark-skinned, with heavy brows and watching eyes, and they belong to the land; it flows into them through their feet. The time when they took the land from another people is so long

---

6. *The Ice Is Coming* (1977), *The Dark Bright Water* (1979), and *Journey Behind the Wind* (1981).

224 GAMES OF DARK

ago that they can forget it and claim the land as theirs; but really it
is the land that claims them.

In *The Ice Is Coming,* Wirrun is on a holiday from his job in a service station when he discovers ice on his water-bag in October and, for a moment upon awakening from his sleeping-bag, sees the world upside
down. Later, back in his small boarding house room, Wirrun reads of
strange appearances of ice in the middle of the hottest of the Australian
seasons and feels impelled to investigate. He discovers that the struggle is
between two elemental forces—the Ninya, creatures of rocky caverns
who wish to break out and return the land to the Ice Age, and the Eldest
Nargun, who, as a creature of fire, is the only one who can defeat their
purpose. Wirrun and his friends are able to enlist the spirits of the land
in a race to help the Nargun, spirits that have a kind of admiration
for humankind:

> This, they knew, was the curious thing that men were made for: to
> care. Spirits might care sometimes when something could be done.
> If they were the right kind they might help when help was needed.
> They might be and know and remember and do; but men cared
> even when they could not do.

Although the "Wirrun" trilogy is filled with elements of the supernatural, it is the human spirit that Wrightson salutes.

In the two sequels, Wirrun has to be co-opted by his people, for he
does not enjoy the appellation of "The Hero" that they have accorded to
him. In *The Dark Bright Water,* the land is being drained of its moisture,
and Wirrun is inwardly forced to follow the strains of a song that
haunts him:

> Are you not coming?
> sings the bright water:
> are you not coming?

His own life is dramatically changed when he finally meets and marries
the ondine (the water-spirit) who has called him to her. In *Journey Behind
the Wind,* Wirrun finally faces the Wulguru—a creature of death—and,
as in so many fantasies, by believing in himself, Wirrun breaks free.

In comparison with most modern children's books, fantasies or not, the pace of the telling seems rather slow. There is no use of cinematic techniques of quick change. However, whether Wirrun's journeys are by airplane, automobile, the wind, or on foot, there begins to come that sense of accompaniment that one feels in the journeys of the Companions in Tolkien's *The Lord of the Rings*. There is a feeling of real time.

Patricia Wrightson's achievements in her trilogy are considerable. She has, first of all, made a young man (not a teenager or a surrogate child) a compelling hero in a cycle for children. Of course, children have been attracted to books with adult heroes or heroines ranging from *Gulliver's Travels* to *Jane Eyre* to much of science fiction. However, Wirrun is one of the few adult characters who have been deliberately and successfully created for children. Wrightson has also, and perhaps most importantly, unlocked a door to a culture that has hitherto (one can assume) been unfamiliar to a great many people and has given its even more unfamiliar folklore a considerable stature, much as the Brothers Grimm did when they first retold the stories of the peasantry of Germany.

Canada, too, has been a country inhospitable to fantasy. In 1833, one of its early pioneers, Catherine Parr Traill, unburdened herself in a letter to England regarding the lack of fantasy in her adopted country:

> As to ghosts or spirits they appear totally banished from Canada. This is too matter-of-fact a country for such supernaturals to visit. Here there are no historical associations, no legendary tales of those that came before us. Fancy would starve for lack of marvellous food to keep her alive in the backwoods. We have neither fay nor fairy, ghost nor bogle, saytr nor Wood-nymph; our very forests disdain to shelter dryad or hamadryad.[7]

With hindsight, of course, it became known that the lakes, rivers, mountains and forests of Canada were rife with spirits—those of the native peoples. However, as in Australia, it took a long time for the newer settlers to empathize with the beliefs of the older ones; and if the new settlers heard their old tales at all, such as those of the trickster-heroes, Glooscap, and Nanabozho, they did not see the relationship between

7. Catherine Parr Traill, *The Backwoods of Canada* (London: Nattali and Bond, 1839), 153.

them and the heroes of European myth and legend. Indeed, even their own folktales ceased to have meaning under the pressures of hardship; the chopping down of a tree meant firewood and shelter and farmland, not the disturbance of a tree fairy who would then grant the woodcutter three wishes.

Canada's Catherine Anthony Clark[8] made a strong beginning with fantasy in the 1950's, using a local background and spirit creatures who were as natural to the mountains and valleys of British Columbia as Patricia Wrightson's Nyols were to Wongadilla. Nonetheless, it took more than a decade for another major fantasist to make use of the Canadian landscape. Ruth Nichols, like many writers of fantasy who are deeply committed to the genre, has brilliantly expressed her own belief in fantasy. To her, "fantasy is in essence realism . . . an act of relating ideas to the world in which we all must operate."[9] Both *A Walk Out of the World* (1969) and *The Marrow of the World* (1972) begin and end in the real world, and the heroines of these novels quest—through parallel worlds—for a wholeness of spirit.

Judith in *A Walk Out of the World* (and to a lesser degree, her brother, Tobit) feels claustrophobic in the apartment building in which she lives in a large West Coast city. Judith says:

> "I want to run . . . but it's as if we're shut up in a box and can't breathe."

She and her brother walk "out of the world" through a lightly wooded forest and into an ancient kingdom that is poised for battle against a usurping king and awaiting a promised deliverer. Judith is recognized by her silver hair and light coloring as opposed to the dark-haired people of the Lake House, where the action begins. The children gradually take their places as adults in the epic struggle, much as the children in C.S. Lewis's *Narnia Chronicles* ruled as kings and queens in the enchanted land but who were ordinary school children in their own. It is, of course, up to Judith finally to confront the evil Hagerrak, whose main desire is for power. However, the battle of wills between them has far more

8. See p. 164–65 of this text.
9. Ruth Nichols, "Fantasy and Escapism," *Canadian Children's Literature* 4 (1976): 20–27.

plausibility than does the somewhat similar scene in Madeleine L'Engle's
A Wrinkle in Time, because Hagerrak is a type of villain who is quite common in the everyday world.

The *Marrow of the World* has a greater sense of evil. As an adopted child,
Linda has not yet come to terms with her new life. She is haunted by
dim, troublesome dreams—Jung's race memories—that come to fruition in the fantasy world. Unlike Judith, Linda does not go willingly into
Another World. She is summoned into it by her half-sister, Ygerna, who
is not only a witch but one who uses other people for her own selfish and
destructive ends. In obtaining for Ygerna "the marrow of the world," a
substance that will increase her sister's power, Linda must act under
threat and coercion. Therefore, the final struggle is not only the universal one of good versus evil, but also one between the opposing sides of
Linda's own nature. Like Judith, she finally discovers that, although her
search for identity has been fulfilled in the fantasy world, the knowledge
she has acquired is really only applicable to the real. Both girls receive
strong and loving support—Judith from Tobit and Linda from her
cousin, Philip. The boys are in no way passive characters but can instead
be seen as a duality—part of the girls' own natures.

Nichols's landscapes can be identified as Canadian; however, unlike
Patricia Wrightson's, they are slightly unreal, thus giving more of the illusion of a Secondary World than do those of the Australian writer. For
Canadians, Vancouver can certainly be pin-pointed as the city from
which Judith and Tobit wish to escape. However, the forest through
which they walk out of the world is invested in a "pale twilight like the
ghost of some forgotten day," and in their journey they travel from the
Lake House to the Red Forest to the Whispering Plains to the White
City—all places that are evocative of Canada in general rather than
being geographically indentifiable. *The Marrow of the World* is set in the
country around Georgian Bay, but it, too, becomes an imaginary land
with the under-water domain of the Mer-people, the dark kingdom of
the dwarves, and the forest with a traditional "noble woodsman"—a
land that does not exist under our stars. Philip scans the heavens for
familiar constellations:

> And low over the trees shone a great green star, translucent as a
> jewel. Of Jupiter, whose cold brilliance he was used to seeing in the
> autumn sky, he could find no trace.

Ruth Nichols's works can be considered very traditional fantasies indeed. They are romantic in that they praise love, friendship, courage, and compassion; they are optimistic in that good triumphs over evil. At the end there is a walk *into* the world—a journey that is at the heart of fantasy. However, they are also very modern in their portrayal of character. Both Judith and Linda wrestle with themselves as well as with supernatural forces.

Trilogies and series, such as those by Tolkien, Le Guin, Alexander, and Cooper, lend themselves well to epic fantasy. These formats can be used to create convincing details for imaginary worlds and to establish familiarity with a large cast of characters. They can also be an open invitation to monotony, puffed-up prose, and a reliance on the conventions of the subgenre rather than an innovative interpretation of them. The land of Hed, created by American writer Patricia McKillip in her "Hed" trilogy,[10] is a vaguely feudal one with a hereditary Prince Morgan. His quest, which encompasses the three volumes, is equally vague but also complex in its several-pronged purposes. The quest is somewhat, but only somewhat, redeemed by a familiar concept in epic fantasy—the responsibility of a ruler to his lands and to all who inhabit them.

Fantasy Based on Folklore

Fantasy that is imbued with some aspects of the oral tradition often resembles the epic in its "matter," but lacks the epic's grand design and the traditional heroic quest—the hero's (or heroine's) "departure, initiation and return."[11] However, a smaller pattern does not necessarily mean less pleasing or effective works. Moreover, as a group, these less formal works offer a greater variety of themes and characters, as well as a range of mood from the serious to the light.

Patricia McKillip in *The Forgotten Beasts of Eld* (1974) uses folklore material obliquely rather than directly. Her beasts might have stepped out of a medieval bestiary, and they have powers that match their larger-

10. Patricia McKillip, *The Riddle-Master of Hed* (1975), *Heir of Sea and Fire* (1977), and *Harpist in the Wind* (1979).

11. Joseph Campbell, *The Hero with a Thousand Faces* (Princeton, New Jersey: Princeton Univ. Pr., 1973).

than-life appearance. Among them are a golden eagle, a traditional dragon (he likes jewels), and a white boar who can answer every riddle save one. Despite all their unusual abilities, however, the animals are under the control of sixteen-year-old Sybel, who is a sibyl in craft as well as in name and who has the power of summoning, to which both animals and people must respond. She is silver-haired, beautiful, and lonesome, and spends her time trying to magnify her magic so that she may call to herself the fabled bird the Liralen, which is of the symbolic order of Maurice Maeterlinck's "bluebird of happiness." Love comes to Sybel through a baby boy named Tamlorn, who is put into her keeping, and then through Coren, who conducts his romance with Sybel in the tradition of courtly love. Eventually, a struggle for the possession of Tamlorn ensues, in which the boy's father and Coren and his family are on opposing sides. Both need Sybel's help, yet she must choose between them. In this dramatic situation, Sybel's mind is taken over by a magician who is more powerful than she is. Outraged at this form of mental rape (and forgetting that she has used the animals in much the same way), Sybel plots a subtle revenge and uses Coren's love for her to this end. At the end and feeling herself defeated, Sybel releases the animals from her control; and they, in an act of loyalty to her, rout the enemy and then go off to their freedom. Despite all its medieval trappings, which are often overwhelming, and despite all its wild magic, the story works best on a basic human level. Sybel learns the responsibilities of love and the denigration that comes to others when one is in control of them.

As opposed to Patricia McKillip, Mollie Hunter's approach to fantasy is simple and direct. It is also in strong contrast to that used in her own realistic novel *A Sound of Chariots,* with its poetic and philosophic overtones, in depicting a troubled, alienated Scottish child who matures into adolescence and who is sadly and personally affected by the aftermath of World War I in her village. This kind of emotional tension is not part of Hunter's affinity with the supernatural, which frequently takes a humorous turn. In such books as *Thomas and the Warlock* (1967), *The Bodach* (1970),[12] *The Haunted Mountain* (1972), *A Stranger Came Ashore* (1975), *The Wicked One* (1977), and *The Kelpie's Pearls* (1964), Hunter can be seen as one of the most conventional of modern fantasists, clinging to Scottish folklore for plot and inspiration as lichen clings to a rock.

12. Published in the United States as *The Walking Stones.*

In *The Bodach,* Hunter almost seems to be describing her own works:

> But of all the stories the Bodach told, Donald's favourites were always those that spoke of the strange, shadowy beings of the Otherworld—the world of sealmen, kelpies, urisks, and all the other creatures of Highland and legend; . . .

However, she does more than merely re-create a legend, as does Dahlov Ipcar with the ballad of Tamlane in *The Queen of Spells* (1973). Whether the time is old Scotland (as in *Thomas and the Warlock)* or more modern (as in *The Bodach* and in *The Kelpie's Pearls*), Hunter's chief characters are very much flesh and blood, whether they are sensitive and determined young boys or old men and women who live close to the spirit world and who pass on their knowledge to the young.

Her most powerful book, in regard to keeping the reader on the edge of impending disaster, is *A Stranger Came Ashore.* It is well subtitled "A Story of Suspense." Set on one of the Shetland Islands, the book is filled with Scottish superstitions and folklore, primarily that of the great bull seal—the King of the Selkies—who can throw off his skin and appear as a man to entice golden-haired girls to his palace under the sea. Only ten-year-old Robbie, alerted by his dying grandfather, is suspicious of the dark, handsome stranger who arrives at his home on the heels of a shipwreck to court Robbie's beautiful sister. At the end of the Yule holiday ("Up Helly Aa") and in an explosion of celebrations, ancient customs, and wizardry, Finn Learson (son of the sea-god Lear) is defeated and punished. In the remote areas of Scotland where Molly Hunter places her characters, her special brand of magic always works.

So does Penelope Lively's, although in more varied ways. Her earlier books in particular show a controlled knowledge of some aspect of folklore. In *Astercote* (1970), for example, a medieval village that is destroyed in the Great Plague casts a spell over its adjoining modern village. The ancient and the modern also mingle in *The Whispering Knights* (1971) as Morgan Le Fay is conjured up by three children (who make a witch's brew) and interferes in village life, to its detriment. She is finally put back where she belongs by a magic older than herself—a ring of Stonehenge-like obelisks—the "Whispering Knights." In *The Wild*

Hunt of Hagworthy (1971),[13] the vicar, by reviving the ancient village Horn Dance, unwittingly arouses Herne the Hunter and his red-eyed pack of hounds, as well as mob violence against an outsider. Whereas both Susan Cooper (in *The Dark Is Rising*) and Alan Garner (in *The Moon of Gomrath*) used the "Herne the Hunter" legend (not a firmly established one) simply to portray an amoral form of primitive magic, Penelope Lively (as well as William Raynor in *Stag Boy,* 1972) uses it here to show the incredible power of possession (that is, one's being taken over by an outside influence). In *The Driftaway* (1972), a runaway boy travels on an old Roman road (now a modern highway) and meets people from the past who eventually put his own troubles into perspective.

Ghost Stories

While writers of epic fantasy and those who base their tales on folklore and legend almost invariably re-create mythical figures from the past such as Herne the Hunter or Morgan Le Fay, no major writer since Walter de la Mare had written a ghost story for children until Leon Garfield's *Mr. Corbett's Ghost and Other Stories* (1968) and *The Ghost Downstairs* (1972), and Penelope Lively's *The Ghost of Thomas Kempe* (1973) and *The Revenge of Samuel Stokes* (1981) Neither writer has the delicacy of de la Mare whose ghosts are frequently of one's own making. There is no mistaking those of Garfield and Lively—their ghosts are indeed specters of dead people who haunt the living.

Of these two modern writers Garfield is in the more classic mold in his creation of atmosphere and in his settings of the past. In *Mr. Corbett's Ghost* he rings a change on the cliché opening of "It was a dark and stormy night":

> A windy night and the old year dying of an ague. Good riddance! A bad old year, with a mean spring, a poor summer, a bitter autumn—and now this cold, shivering ague. No one was sorry to see it go. Even the clouds, all in black, seemed hurrying to its burial somewhere past Hampstead.

13. Published in the United States as *The Wild Hunt of the Ghost Hounds.*

Benjamin feels that the ague is also in his master's soul as the apothecary sends him out on a long and cold journey to deliver medicine that its buyer could have taken by hand. Benjamin can think only of his family and friends, with whom he expected to spend New Year's Eve, and of his hatred for Mr. Corbett. At the end of his journey, he is given an opportunity for revenge, and thus Mr. Corbett becomes a ghost. However, as the mysterious old man to whom he has carried the medicine has suggested, the ghost becomes too heavy for Benjamin's soul. In New Year's Eve scenes that range from the macabre to revelry, Benjamin's ghost is laid to rest as well as Mr. Corbett's.

Unlike writers of epic fantasy or, indeed, writers of the classic adult ghost story, Garfield is not so one-dimensional in his treatment of good and evil. His protagonists, in such historical novels as *The Drummer Boy*, generally have to make a choice between who is good and who is evil when the distinction is not all that clear. Equally, Garfield's interpretation of the Faust legend in *The Ghost Downstairs* is far more subtle than the original.

In this novelette, Mr. Fast, who is plagued by the two devils of envy and loneliness, signs a contract with the lodger downstairs—seven years of his life in exchange for a million pounds. With his lawyer's acumen, Mr. Fast draws up a contract that he thinks is foolproof; he signs away the first seven years of his life rather than the last. However, the resulting ghost is that of himself as a seven-year-old child. Mr. Fast feels that both the child and the old lodger are evil spirits, but things are not as they seem. Both spirits—in a reversal of the Faust legend—are there to save Mr. Fast's soul. The story is filled with images of Christianity. Not since C.S. Lewis's *Narnia Chronicles* has there been such a meshing together of Christian symbolism, ranging from the bread and wine of the Communion Table to the passenger who falls asleep in the train compartment whispering in a "confused memory of a child's prayer. 'Our souls to keep. . . . '" Unlike Lewis, however, Garfield makes the reader ponder over Mr. Fast's interpretation of his haunting and indeed keeps the reader on a knife-edge of doubt. In its total imagery and Christian ethic, this book has been matched only by Garfield himself in his historical vignette *The Lamplighter's Funeral*, with its picture of a real child who also functions as the Christ child.

Humor dominates the plots of Penelope Lively's *The Ghost of Thomas Kempe* and *The Revenge of Samuel Stokes;* but as in all her works, Lively infects the present with the past, particularly in her Proustian adaptation of the role memory plays in our lives: "A remembrance of things past," whether collective or personal, affects us and how we behave. Thus, however simple Lively's approach to a story appears to be, there is always a deeper significance behind the action.

Although Thomas Kempe is released from a bottle in *The Ghost of Thomas Kempe,* he is not as obliging as Aladdin's Djinn. He is instead a crotchety seventeenth-century apothecary-magician who is determined to make his powers felt in the twentieth century. Ten-year-old James, in whose house Thomas Kempe escapes, becomes Kempe's unwilling sorcerer's apprentice, is blamed for Kempe's mischief, and (with the exception of an understanding carpenter) has to struggle alone against the supernatural in the modern world. The humor gradually—everything happens gradually, even in this short novel—turns to seriousness as Kempe resorts to genuine evil in order to re-establish the position he had been granted in the past. The tension becomes so great that one has to pause and wonder how Lively can resolve such a tight plot. Simplicity is again her keynote—Thomas Kempe is eventually defeated by the rationality of the late twentieth century and retires to his tomb.

Young James is, at first meeting, seemingly little more than an insouciant Tom Sawyer, but he eventually becomes more like the reflective Huckleberry Finn as he delves into the past and discovers a boy of his own age in the nineteenth century who also suffered in the clutches of Thomas Kempe. Both history and memory are seen as layers of time that can be understood even by a young boy.

For all his intrusion into modern life, Thomas Kempe is a fairly traditional ghost, wreaking his mischief through knowledge and skills gained in his own time. On the other hand, Samuel Stokes, in *The Revenge of Samuel Stokes,* is quick to adapt to the late twentieth century. As an eighteenth-century landscape gardener, Stokes is artistically offended at a modern housing development that has been built over his garden masterpiece; therefore, he brings disaster upon disaster to the promotors and inhabitants of the estate. Although treated with tongue-in-cheek, the calamities could have a natural cause. Like all good comedians, Lively builds her jokes around some facts. Samuel Stokes is not finally defeated as was Thomas Kempe, but he has his attention diverted by the ingenuity of eleven-year-old Tim, Tim's friend Jane, and Tim's grandfather, who is noted chiefly for "cooking up a storm"—a mixture of foods and ingredients that adults shy away from. Together they outwit the irate ghost because, as Grandpa points out, they are not "inflexible people"; they do not think "in straight lines." Samuel Stokes does not operate in straight ghostly lines either. As well as using what might be considered normal ghostly interventions—causing cooking smells from a washing machine or creating floods from nonexistent waters—he uses the telephone and makes broadcasts on television. Stokes falls into L.P. Hartley's definition of modern ghosts, of whom Hartley somewhat disapproves—those who are "able to do a great many things that human beings can't do" as well as "many things that human beings can do."[14] However, even L.P. Hartley would salute the panache with which Penelope Lively brings the supernatural into the modern world.

Introverted Fantasy

The noted writer and critic of children's books Penelope Farmer divides fantasy into basically two types—"extrovert" and "introvert." She writes: "Roughly, extrovert[ed] fantasies rely more on surface mechanics or machinery." Introverted fantasy deals with "interior kinds of subjects," psychological problems that concern the individual author and his or her protagonist.[15] There are very few fantasies (in the past or the present) that can be defined as being completely extroverted. All fine fantasists give some insights into the personalities of their characters, and if they do use some of the machinery of magic (such as transformations in the works of C.S. Lewis, spells in those of Ursula Le Guin, or swords in those of Lloyd Alexander and Susan Cooper), not a squeaky wheel can be heard. Moreover, the use of such conventions, especially in epic fantasy, gives these writers' tales a satisfying link with their prototypes.

William Mayne's *A Game of Dark* can certainly be described as introverted fantasy. The main thrust of the plot is the psychological disturbance of the teenage protagonist, Donald Jackson. Donald is an outsider

14. L.P. Hartley, *The Third Ghost Book*, ed. Cynthia Asquith (London: James Barrie, 1955), viii.

15. Penelope Farmer, "Jorinda and Jorindel and Other Stories," in *Writers, Critics, and Children*, ed. Geoff Fox et al. (New York: Agathon Press, 1976), 57, 61.

in his own home. His father is a cripple who is confined to a wheelchair and is succumbing to his illness; his mother is the breadwinner, and she is so wrapped up in her husband that she has only admonitions left for her son and sometimes even calls him by his last name, Jackson. The parents' grief for an older girl—killed in an accident (Donald has never been told the real story)—and their rigid Non-Conformist religious beliefs provide only a cold, alienating home with never a warm meal or companionship to sustain Donald on his return home from school.

In his misery, Donald's mind enters an even grimmer medieval world, one that is dominated by a Worm—the ancient name for both a serpent and a dragon, which is frequently called "the laidly worm" in folktale literature. Mayne makes the Worm's horror concrete by giving a sense of its smell. This physical sensation seeps through the pages of the book as Donald carries his memory of the smell back to his everyday activities:

> In his mouth and nostrils and throat there was a stench, metallic and rotten and piercing, the most foul he had ever known, and that was the worst thing and what made him feel so sick . . . the stench was not only felt by the ordinary senses of taste and smell but sensed by the whole of his skin, and seemed to weigh in every bone.

In Donald's fantasy world, in which his name is Jackson and in which he serves as both page and squire, it is finally up to him to kill the Worm, which he accomplishes, in Mayne's view, ingloriously. He is no St. George striking face to face but instead slays the killer creature from underneath, in the soft part of its anatomy. Mayne's ending is obscure. In a few brief closing sentences, Donald rejects his fantasy, for he now knows how to love his father, who is dying in the next room. It is difficult to see how an act that is considered dishonorable by both the author and the protagonist can heal a truly sick soul.

A Game of Dark is a most powerful and disturbing use of fantasy as therapy. It has even been dubbed "psychofantasy,"[16] and the term is well

---

16. Lois R. Kuznets, "Games of Dark," *The Lion and the Unicorn* 1 (Fall 1977): 17–24.

applied. It is obvious that Mayne had a serious purpose in mind here. As a protagonist, Donald Jackson is quite different from the well-balanced, intellectually curious boys of *Earthfasts* and distant in conception from the sensitive, sensible children of his stories of child and family life. With the exception of the disturbed young men in Alan Garner's *Red Shift* (1973), no other protagonist in fantasy has had such odds stacked against him. In the realistic fantasy of the 1960's, writers did indeed use other times and dimensions to bring their young characters to a greater perception of themselves and their problems, but Mayne goes far beyond this accepted use of the genre. Indeed, his viewpoint might well be taken as a denigration of fantasy itself, since Donald has to reject the medieval world of the slain Worm in order to recover his mental health. Even as a literary device the fantasy fails, since the parallels between the two worlds do not work out coherently. In spite of the novel's brilliant style, there are simply too many unanswered questions. Perhaps, for example, Mayne intended to push the influence of fantasy beyond what most of its practitioners would claim for it.

Introverted fantasy is also the most appropriate term for Penelope Farmer's own work *A Castle of Bone* (1972). It begins, conventionally enough, with a magic cupboard. "Ah," says the experienced reader, "another Narnia." However, there is no eager entry here into an Other World through the back wall of a wardrobe. The cupboard's quality is to change things into some aspect of their previous existence: a wallet turns into a live white pig; a sweater, into raw wool. A chewed and twisted toothpaste tube is returned, however, "instead of a heap of materials, a new tube, shiny, plump and full. It might have come straight from the manufacturers." We soon discover that the cupboard works according to its own timing and its own changing in its own arbitrary way. This is not the predictable Nesbit magic that is controllable once the rules have been established.

Farmer's seemingly casual approach to magic is matched by her vague mythic sense; however, Farmer herself is definite enough about her schema. She writes that she took her central image—certainly an esoteric one—from the Celtic tree alphabets and calendars.[17] The tree

17. Penelope Farmer, "Discovering the Pattern," in *The Thorny Paradise,* ed. Edward Blishen (Harmondsworth, Middlesex: Kestral Bks., 1975), 106.

alphabet is said to be "a genuine relic of Druidism orally transmitted down the centuries" and forms "a calendar of seasonal tree-magic."[18] Certainly, trees figure prominently in the landscape, whether in that of the real world or in that of the fantasy world. However, as a central image, neither the trees nor their magical qualities (according to the alphabet) play a part in the resolution of the plot as the Druidic tree does in the last volume of Susan Cooper's quintet, *Silver on the Tree*.

The plot is as complex as the workings of the cupboard, although it begins simply enough. Hugh, a young teenager, feels impelled to buy the cupboard from an old antique dealer, a kind of *deus ex machina*. When its magic properties are discovered, Hugh, his sister Jean, his friend Penn, and Penn's sister Anna experiment with the cupboard until, in the midst of a quarrel, Penn is shoved into the cupboard by Anna and is turned into himself as a baby. The children's task of looking after a baby without having the knowledge of adults has some humorous moments, but soon the real task of saving Penn has to begin.

There are contrapuntal themes underlying this major crisis. One is the unacknowledged tensions that exist among the quartet. Another theme concerns the cupboard. With the cupboard's advent into his life, Hugh embarks on nightly journeys to a strange land that is dominated by "a castle of bone." Each night he gets closer to the castle, pushing his way through thickets of alders much as the Prince in "Sleeping Beauty" cut his way through the thorns. But are these dreams or not? Hugh finds concrete evidence (such as damp bedslippers in dry weather) that he has been physically abroad at night.

In the final fantasy scene, the three young people, together with the baby, go through the cupboard into the land of the "castle of bone." The children are not changed physically, but they are separated, one supposes, according to the roles they are to play. Upon reaching the castle, Hugh and Jean find Anna there before them holding the baby, Penn, over a bowl of fire, ready to make him immortal. Although Hugh has been built up as the quest hero, it is practical Jean (like Roger in Alan Garner's

18. Robert Graves, *The White Goddess* (London: Faber, 1948), 164.

The Owl Service) who incites Hugh to break the spell and thus save Penn for an ordinary life.

A Castle of Bone is laden with symbolism. Anna, for example, has aspects of Robert Graves's "White Goddess"[19]—the triple deity of birth, life, and death. However, it is the image of Farmer's own devising that appears to be at the heart of the story. Hugh comes to realize (with the help of the old antique dealer) that the castle is himself—Hugh's spirit is trapped in flesh and bone and is subject to mortality.

While the plot is far from clear on its primary level, and multi-faceted on its interpretative one, it has many passages of fine writing in a cinematic style. The story also arouses undefinable feelings. As Alice said of "Jabberwocky" in *Through the Looking Glass:* "It seems to fill my head with ideas—only I don't exactly know what they are!"

Penelope Farmer's *Year King* (1977) concerns even older adolescents than those found in *A Castle of Bone* and almost reaches the level of a full-fledged adult novel in its characterization, sexuality, and length. It is a completely introverted fantasy that is played out in the mind of one identical twin (Lan) who enters the mind and body of his more dominant and successful brother (Lew) at moments of crisis. Lan finally comes to feel that his brother, Lew, is trying to kill him. It is a powerfully written book, and unlike *A Castle of Bone,* is definitely all of a piece. Farmer's love of Celtic mythology is evident only in the names of the twins—Lew and Lan. Lew—the god of the sun—and Lan—the god of water—are linked with the innate natures of their mortal namesakes.

The seeming urge that many modern fantasists have to explore disturbed young people through some element of fantasy is also seen in Alan Garner's *Red Shift.* Unlike his earlier fantasies, in which the supernatural breaks into the present, here the past and the present mingle, co-relate, and finally become as one until, at the end, the six main characters from different time periods speak their lines without specific identification.

Only the two teenagers in the present are apt to make an immediate impression on the modern adolescent. Their parental problems, their tense relationships, and their burgeoning sexuality are fairly easy for modern teens to identify with. The past—an episode in the English Civil War and an imaginative re-creation of what might have happened to the

---

19. Graves gives many interpretations of this concept in his *The White Goddess.*

ragtail of the famous Ninth Legion that disappeared during the Roman occupation of Britain—is basically left to the reader to set in place. The linkage among the periods is achieved chiefly through place (all the major scenes are played out within a small area of Cheshire). There is also a talisman—an axehead that all the characters handle—and a "blue and white flash" that is experienced by all the young males. The flashes range from a portent of madness (the traditional berserk) to an epileptic fit, and in modern times, to the color of the train at which the two modern teenagers meet and part. Another link is forged through the names of the male characters. They are all called Tom or Thomas or Macey—a diminutive of Thomas.

The young women are the active characters in the book, thus giving the story its strong mythic sense, as they are seen as the descendants of Graves's "White Goddess." The women are the earth mothers—symbols of fertility and of instinctive knowledge—and are both demanding and protective. The men embody an almost primal scream of hopelessness and alienation. The vastness and mystery of the universe also play a part in the story, as Orion shines over both the berserk Macey and the modern Tom and is embodied in the book's title, "Red Shift"—an astronomical concept which postulates that the universe is expanding and thus is causing even more mystery, isolation, and confusion. When the modern Jan and Tom pick Orion as their lodestar, they are already battling fate, for Orion was slain by the huntress Artemis.

The style of Red Shift is almost as difficult to penetrate as are its multitudinous concepts. It is terse, elliptical, and carried on almost entirely by conversation, often without any identification of the character who is speaking. The dialogues in the sections dealing with the Civil War appear most in tune with their time; those of the modern period, particularly between Tom and Jan, are frequently highly intellectual or subtly delicate, reminiscent of the conversational nuances in a Henry James novel. The members of the Roman legion speak as one might feel that the American GIs did in Vietnam, and the massacre scene might also recall to an adult reader the terrible event of My Lai. Garner's work contains many brutal and specific scenes of warfare and its consequences, in sharp contrast to Cooper's distancing of World War II through the presentation of abstract evil.

Garner makes nothing easy for his readers. Red Shift is best described as a script for a play, one that production on a stage would clarify through gestures and inflections of speech. All in all, the novel becomes a mental exercise accompanied by a sense of failure if one cannot crack the code on the back endpapers. Readers may well ask if an author should demand so much effort, concentration, and specialized knowledge from them. The answer in this case is that they will be well repaid for their efforts.

Fantasy as Therapy

Introverted fantasies, as seen in such works as *A Game of Dark, A Castle of Bone,* or *Red Shift,* leave questions in the reader's mind and are certainly open to various interpretations. Their psychological overtones assure debate. Other writers of the decade also dealt with the problems of the young, but in a much simpler manner. Their young protagonists, whether caught in family difficulties or in the winter of their own discontent, might have stepped out of the pages of a problem novel. Nonetheless, the fantasy component that the writers introduce—generally a robustly mythic one—allows them equally to explore the major themes that are so dear to the hearts of modern fantasists—the continuity of time and the commingling of the real and the unreal. Since one of the major purposes of fantasy (perhaps its chief purpose) is to cast new light on some aspect of reality so that these perceptions of reality can be adapted to everyday situations, all serious fantasy might well be described as therapeutic. In the past, the masters of two-level fantasies—chiefly Kingsley, MacDonald, and Lewis—were able to disguise many of their messages within a strong plot line that could be read for entertainment alone. In these newer works, however, the plot is the message. There is no room for maneuvering.

Both Robert Westall's *The Wind Eye* (1976) and *The Watch House* (1977) have young teenage protagonists who are the victims of adult selfishness. Beth of *The Wind Eye* is at the eye of the storm in the disputes between her father and stepmother. She also has the chief care of her younger sister, who has suffered a seriously burned hand. Anne of *The Watch House* is an only child who is manipulated by her mother and seemingly deserted by her father. Both books are set on the coast of Northumberland, and the settings themselves provide a motivation for the plots. The legend at the heart of *The Wind Eye* tells of St. Cuthbert, who destroyed the Vikings who were attacking his monastery on Farne Island. *The Watch House* (now a museum with resident ghosts) was, in the past, the center for coastal rescue operations. The past seeps into the present through the empathy, sensitivity, and unhappiness of the girls. In both stories, the past is laid to rest yet has effects upon the present. A young child's hand is cured by St. Cuthbert, a step-mother becomes part of a family, and a strongly rationalistic father is forced to face the irrational. Anne stands up to her mother and goes to live with her father.

Like William Mayne in *Earthfasts,* Westall is determined to convince the reader that complete rationality is not sufficient to prop up the human spirit, and he does so brilliantly with some of the panoply of the Catholic Church. In *The Wind Eye,* for instance, an eighth-century saint plays a major role, while in *The Watch House,* a Catholic priest performs an exorcism on an evil ghost. There is no hint, however, that religion will be a consolation in the future lives of the young. Religion here is used only as a supernatural force, best described in *The Wind Eye* as *Supernature.*

Christianity also plays a strong role in William Mayne's *IT* (1977) and in an equally unspiritual way. "IT" is a displaced, pagan, amoral force that finds a host body in twelve-year-old Alice Dyson. "There was a strange sky for a strange day," begins the story, and the tone matches the state of Alice's mind. Alice is out of sorts with herself and with her family, and she feels that she can never match the achievements of her grandfather, who has been an explorer, a writer, and now a vicar. On this fateful day, she is drawn to a hill called the Eyell, and her hand is seized by a being from the distant past. Alice becomes a medium for IT and can only slightly control its poltergeist mischief. In the cathedral town— with its long history and relics of the past and where crossroads are still called "Crosses"—Alice finally finds a way to return IT to its place. This task involves persuading the organizers of the St. Cuthbert's parade to change its modern route to that used long ago. The circle among the Crosses must be completed, as must be the ring on Alice's finger. Alice is aided in her aims by the bishop, the minister, the organist, and the choir-boys in a final scene that is close to exorcism. At the story's end

> She had made the great circle, and the smaller one had been made
> on her. She could now keep the ring and with it keep everything,

including IT; but IT was what she had to be rid of. But now, at last, she was true master of IT.

So she hesitated, whether to keep power or keep right. Though IT was not right or wrong, she could herself do right or wrong. And she now knew that IT did not mind whether it slept again, or woke into strength with her.

IT is a highly original combination of realism and the supernatural. Mayne's sense of place, the church activities of a cathedral (and its Low Church counterpart), the various town personalities, and the contrast between Alice's middle-class home and the working-class one of her friend, Raddy, are all well-delineated in Mayne's typical elliptical manner. The only flaw in the book comes from the portrayal of Alice herself. It seems inconceivable that a twelve-year-old would be jealous of a grandfather or that normal growing pains would bring such disaster upon her.

Mayne shows a clear intent in *IT:* the borderline between fantasy and reality is very close indeed, as is the link between primitive worship and Christianity. With catharsis thrown in, Alice and her grandfather learn to appreciate one another; we are also assured, by her new willingness to attend a private girl's school, that most of Alice's rough edges will be honed away.

The young also come to terms with themselves and their trying situations in works by two American writers: *A String in the Harp* (1976) by Nancy Bond and *Saturday, the Twelfth of October* (1975) by Norma Fox Mazer. The harp in *A String in the Harp* is that of Taliesin, the sixth-century bard whose *Book of Taliesin* is one of the great Welsh poetic works and whose deeds are celebrated in *The Mabinogion*. Into his country, in modern times, comes an American family (with Welsh antecedents) who are shattered by the accidental death of the mother. The father, Mr. Morgan, is absorbed in his own sorrow and in his temporary teaching job at the University of Aberystwyth. The youngest daughter, Becky, makes a quick adjustment into this life that is very different from what she has known; nonetheless, with childlike perception, she recognizes the need for togetherness. The elder daughter, Jen, who has adjusted to living with her aunt and uncle in New England, comes to Wales for the Christmas holidays and eventually, forgetting her own concerns, stays to help. The most unhappy person is Peter, the middle child, who resents everything—the loss of his mother, his father's aloof attitude, and the foreignness of Wales. In his anger and estrangement from his family, Peter goes for lonely walks and on one of them finds a key. With it he sees strange images from the past and finally realizes that he has Taliesin's harp-tuning key and that he is a spectator of important events in the bard's life. Peter comes under pressure from the local museum curator to give up what he has found; but with the help and support of his family, Peter realizes what he must do—he buries the key in Taliesin's grave, a grave unknown to everyone but Peter. Peter thus becomes reconciled with himself, his family, and his surroundings. Everyone is happy when the family decides to stay in Wales for another year.

A String in the Harp is both a realistic story about a family's coming together after stress and strain, and a fine fantasy. The details of daily living in an alien environment are aptly and selectively chosen. The villagers and farmers of the small town and the academics of Aberystwyth each have their own flavorful characteristics, yet the fantasy is central to the story. Taliesin's key is the key to the music of Wales, and music brings harmony. The key unlocks Peter's grief and anger as he witnesses life in the long ago, which was also filled with tragedy. Throughout both aspects of the story broods the land of Wales itself, where, to the country folks at least, neither the past nor faerie are very far away. The writing is sturdy and straightforward but without the musical cadences of Welsh speech that are so noticeable in Alan Garner's *The Owl Service.*

Mazer's teenaged Zan in *Saturday, the Twelfth of October* is somewhat of a loner, and she feels unhappy and oppressed in the small quarters of an apartment where close living does not mean close relationships with her family. She is even more emotionally wrenched apart when she discovers that her brother has found her diary and has read it to his friends. Rushing from her home, Zan falls, strikes her head on a rock, and awakens in the land of "the People." We never know their location in time and space, but we do find out that the People are close to nature and that everyone shares, talks, and touches. Zan does not have an easy time adjusting to this strange life, but she learns to love "the People," and her rites of passage into their society are her entrance back to her old world and her acceptance of it. Here time has not passed. Zan finds that she has been unconscious only for a day, due to her accident.

On the surface, Zan finally yields to the school psychologist and admits that she has merely had a dream that lasted one day instead of the eleven months of her sojourn with "the People." However, to herself, she says

> "Am I going to be like everyone else? Afraid. Forgetting everything. Oh, please don't let me forget! Please."

Zan finds credence for her experiences in her science class when her teacher tries to explain time as a continuum in Einstein-like terms: "Imagine time as a curving ribbon in space, an infinite curve without beginning or ending." Zan has been part of that curve.

Enchanted Realism

Mazer's concept of time, as well as the dream-like quality of her heroine's experience, also puts *Saturday, the Twelfth of October* into the subgenre of enchanted realism. While Mazer took her example of time from science, Eleanor Cameron, in *The Court of the Stone Children*, found hers in the art world—in Chagall's painting *Time Is a River without Banks*. There are other resemblances between the two stories. Cameron's young protagonist, Nina, is also at odds with herself and eventually finds solace in San Francisco's French Museum, just as Zan found hers with "the People."

Nina has felt displaced ever since leaving her home in the foothills of the Sierra Nevadas; she misses its wide spaces and her after-school job at the local museum. The family's new apartment in the crowded city is small and dingy and airless. Nina feels exasperated with her father's after-illness apathy, an illness that has necessitated the move. Always somewhat of a loner, she has made no friends at her new school; but then she meets an interesting boy who, hearing of her desire to be a museum curator, directs Nina to the place where dreams and a new concept of time will mold her life. In the wide, spacious halls of the museum where rooms seem to meld endlessly into one another and which are furnished with antiques from an old chateau in France, Nina finds herself both drawn to and puzzled by Chagall's famous painting. As the museum Registrar tries to explain:

" . . . If you try to make sense of it by means of logic, you can't, because Chagall is always remembering his childhood and so, probably, his childhood dreams, and the feeling of losing himself in fairy tales. . . . "

Wandering almost daily in rooms where she feels very much at home, Nina meets Dominique, a girl from Napoleonic times whose father was hanged for murder. At first terrified when she realizes that she is talking to a ghost, Nina comes to understand that life can exist in different layers of time. She also finds out that Dominique's father once appeared to her in a dream and told Nina that a young girl in the future would help her to clear his name. This aspect of the story makes a fascinating mystery as the tale of the past unfolds through Dominique's memories, Nina's dreams, research in diaries, and the discovery of a painting. Nina's connection with the museum leads to a summer job (which promises great hope for her future) and to an apartment with a view and many new friends. However, Nina realizes that time has its sadness too—Dominique will never return to be her friend.

Clare, in *The House in Norham Gardens* (1974), is one of Penelope Lively's most sensitively conceived characters. She is also highly intelligent, mature for her age, and in many ways akin to the overburdened protagonists of the contemporary realistic novels; she has too many responsibilities for her age. She is in charge of a large, dilapidated Victorian house and of her two great-aunts who, as former Oxford scholars, have their thoughts on less mundane things than plumbing and butcher bills. In the attic, Clare finds her grandfather's diary and a strange shield that, as an anthropologist and explorer, he took from a New Guinea tribe. Clare feels that the shield should be returned to the tribe. Under this pressure and under her increasing household cares, Clare finds her dreams invaded by the tribesmen, who also appear to be demanding the return of their ancestral totem. However, Lively never leaves her young characters defenseless in an adult world. Therefore, Clare has access to the practical advice of her working-girl boarder, of the cleaning lady, and eventually of a young African student who assists Clare in her researches into the shield.

As in all stories of enchanted realism, this has no spectacular denouement. In a practical sense, with the addition of another boarder (the young student), the financial pressure on Clare is ameliorated. Her emotional pressure is also relieved as she comes to realize that her grandfather was not aware of the totemic value of the shield when he took it away. Now time has passed for the native peoples too, and Clare sees in her dreams that they are more interested in transistor radios than in their heritage. However, if the tribe has lost something, at least Clare has gained in her knowledge of the past, in her sense of the continuity of time, and even in having a more sensitive appreciation of the great-aunts. In a cogent scene at the end of the book, Aunt Susan pays tribute to Clare:

> "It is only those who have never listened who find themselves in trouble eventually."
> "Why?"
> "Because it is extremely dull," said Aunt Susan tartly, "to grow old with nothing inside your head but your own voice. Tedious, to put it mildly."

The two threads of the story are distinguished by typeface. The connecting portions of the diary and Clare's dreams are set in italic, and the style has a dream quality. Events in Clare's everyday life—household crises, shopping, schooling, and day-to-day conversations—are major realistic counterpoints to her internal struggles, to her dreams, and to the slight displacement of the real world; these events are set in regular typeface. However, through escape, recovery, and consolation, Clare, like Cameron's Nina, becomes a whole person.

Fantasy is even more lightly used, if it is used at all, in Lively's *A Stitch in Time* (1976), a gossamer-like story, but one with a strong thread of the past holding it together. In the holiday resort of Lyme Regis, time moves very slowly. Its cliffs are a fossil hunter's paradise, and *Stomechinus bigranularis* represents millions of years of time. However, young Maria, who is vacationing in an old house, is more interested in a child who lived in the house during Victorian times and who never finished her sampler. In a delicate web of events that is bound up with Maria's imagination, Lively brings the story to a conclusion that writers of the gothic tale would have envied. Has or has not the supernatural played a part in the events? Whatever the reader decides, it is clear that Maria herself has changed from a highly introverted child to one who can communicate with other people, and most importantly, with her mother.

Both Natalie Babbitt's *Tuck Everlasting* (1975) and William Mayne's *A Year and a Day* (1976) are set in the not-so-distant past, but one that gives these stories the aura of "once upon a time." They also differ from most modern fantasies in that none of their child characters—both authors are concerned with childhood rather than with adolescence—are unhappy. They are, instead, curious, courageous, self-sufficient, and far from lacking in imagination.

Babbitt's Winnie Foster, an overprotected child, gives up the idea of running away and settles for a forbidden walk in the woods next to her home—a lightly forested area that belongs to her family. Here she comes upon a teenaged boy drinking from a small spring. To Winnie's annoyance, he refuses her the same privilege, although the day is hot, even for August. Suddenly the boy's mother appears, and with the utmost celerity, they kidnap Winnie and speed her away on their horse. She is frightened, but not overly so, since she is constantly reassured about her safety. They arrive at night at a cottage, a jumbled yet homey place that is far different from Winnie's mother's meticulous housekeeping. It is the home of the Tucks—father, mother, Jesse, who is seventeen, and an older brother, Miles. Winnie feels an odd companionship with all of these characters, especially with rotund Father Tuck and handsome Jesse. Soon she learns the reason for the Tucks' obvious distress over her sighting of the spring: a sip from the spring gives immortality—mankind's desire since the Garden of Eden; it is the Fountain of Youth. In a sudden realization of her own mortality, Winnie blurts out, "I don't want to die":

> "No," said Tuck calmly. "Not now. Your time's not now. But dying's part of the wheel, right there next to being born. You can't pick out the pieces you like and leave the rest. Being part of the whole thing, that's the blessing. If I knowed how to climb back on the wheel, I'd do it in a minute. You can't have living without dying. So you can't call it living what we got. We just *are*, we just *be*, like rocks beside the road."

This thoughtful aspect of the story takes a dramatic turn with the appearance of a dyed-in-the-wool villain. He has made his plan to exploit the spring but is accidentally killed by Mrs. Tuck as he tries to abscond with Winnie. Mrs. Tuck is arrested and is about to be hanged, but as well as being immortal, the Tucks cannot be hurt; and so the secret will be let out. Winnie provides both the solution and the heroic act that are needed for Mrs. Tuck's escape. Many years later, Mr. and Mrs. Tuck— on a return visit to the area—find it changed and modernized, and the woods bulldozed. They also find Winnie's grave. She had chosen to remain on the wheel of life.

In such a short book (139 pages of large type), this combination of the slow passage of time and explosive events is little short of genius. As in all fiction, how things are said is as important as what is said. Sentence after sentence lingers in the mind:

> The first week of August hangs at the very top of summer, the top of the live-long year, like the highest seat of a Ferris wheel when it pauses in its turning. The weeks that come before are only a climb from balmy spring, and those that follow a drop to the chill of autumn, but the first week of August is motionless and hot.

The Tucks themselves also linger in the mind with both their sensitivity to their responsibility and their peasant-like stubbornness, in the face of adversity, to make the best of things. *Tuck Everlasting* is one of the simplest yet most profound fantasies in children's literature. In asking—and answering—questions about mortality, it takes its place alongside E.B. White's *Charlotte's Web*.

William Mayne's *A Year and a Day* is much closer to Mayne's small, sensitive stories of child and family life than to his major fantasy *Earthfasts*. At some vague time in the nineteenth century, in a small Cornish village, on Midsummer's Day, something magical is bound to happen. And it does. Sara and Becca find a naked little boy in the woods. Knowing the story of Adam and Eve, Becca searches for fig leaves but has to use what she can find. The little girls take the boy home, teaching him on the way to hold the leaves in front of him. Mayne's astounding gift for humorous, practical conversation has never been shown to greater effect than when Sara and Becca bring the child to their mother, and with complete confidence:

> "Who be that?" she said, because she did not know the boy.
> "He be mine," said Sara, "Ours. He's called Adam."

"Adam, yes," said Becca. "Sara thought of that."

"And this is his apron made of fig-leaves," said Sara.

"Fig-leaves?" said Mother. "Those are bay-leaves. Are you going to bake him like a mackerel?"

"Keep him," said Becca. "Keep him like a finding. He's ours."

And so the boy becomes theirs, in spite of an abortive attempt to place him in a foundling home, a commentary on the times. The boy is taken to church, baptized, and named Adam, and "everything went well, in spite of his attempts to drink most of the holy water." Adam is not an ordinary child. He never sleeps and never learns human speech, but he can imitate any sound he hears and hear what other people cannot, such as a caterpillar crawling across a leaf. The wise woman of the village offers her opinion:

"He'm fairy folk, and they'm not mortal, and mortal means bound to die; but I say he will not be among us longer than a few weeks more, a year and a day to midsummer last. A year and a day they stay, these pisgy children abide among us, and then back to their own folk, and blessings on those that kept them."

Her prophecy comes true; but then a new male baby is born to Mother, one that replaces a baby boy who had died some time ago. Again the family go to church:

This was another christening, and it was like the boy's again, but this time it was real and the other one an earlier remembrance.

In the last two words of the quote, Mayne gives us a delicate hint as to the boy fairy's purpose—a remembrance of things past, a glimpse of joys to come, and an understanding of the inevitable cycle of birth and death. However, *A Year and a Day* is above all a marvelous story of childhood—a fictional childhood that has almost disappeared. Sara and Becca have time to be children. Surrounded as they are by strong but feisty parents, kind but eccentric adults, and living close to nature, the girls can absorb and build upon simple events.

Past-Time Fantasy

The use of a supernatural entry into the past attracted only a few British writers of the decade, among them K.M. Peyton with *A Pattern of Roses* (1972) and Jill Paton Walsh with *A Chance Child* (1978). For both writers, the concept of time-travel marked their first excursion into fantasy, but they used its possibilities very differently. Peyton's young teenager (Tim) of the 1970's finds that he can enter the mind, feelings, and finally even the body of a boy from 1910 through some drawings he has found in his converted bedroom in an old country town cottage to which Tim and his parents have just moved. These drawings are signed with Tim's initials, and they draw him back into time and into a mystery. Through his empathy with his artist friend of the past, Tim is able to take charge of his own life. These events all form an intricately woven pattern—as the title suggests. Peyton's sense of social history, however, (as effectively shown in her well-known *Flambards* series) ultimately leaves the greatest impression. The modern reader learns with some shock of the wretched lot of the laboring poor ten years into the twentieth century. The story's strong fantasy component thus dwindles under the realism of a misery that can no longer be rectified.

Such feelings of helplessness, compassion, and anger are intensified a hundredfold in Walsh's *A Chance Child*. Here, abuse of children occurs not only in the past but also in the present, an abuse so terrible that it sends Creep ("their Mum always called him that creep") back to the nineteenth century when thousands of children were slaves in mines, factories, blacksmiths' shops, and on farms. Nonetheless, Creep decides to stay in the past, finding friendship and finally love.

Creep's entry into the past (the device is simply that of the continuum of time, as shown in his journey down a river) introduces only a slight element of fantasy, as does his gradual change from a ghost child in the past to a real one. For the rest, the book is a piece of meticulously researched history into the lives of the "chance" children of more than a hundred years ago. In an appealing literary device, the author herself can be seen in the person of Christopher, Creep's half-brother in the the real world. Just as Walsh researched the British Parliamentary Papers to gain evidence of the plight of nineteenth-century working children, so Christopher consults the same sources to assure himself of his brother's survival and happiness. All in all, Walsh's excursion into the past is a far cry from Edith Nesbit's romantic view of history as seen in *Harding's Luck. A*

Chance Child resembles the viewpoint of such modern writers of historical fiction as Hester Burton who are not concerned with the great sweeps
of history, such as wars and shifts of power, but rather with the effects of
social life upon the young who try to survive in an environment that is
hostile to them.

Robert Westall's *The Devil on the Road* (1978) reflects his interest in a
particular aspect of British history—the witch hunts carried out by
Matthew Hopkins during the Cromwellian era. The events impinge upon
the present seemingly only by chance. John Webster, a university student, sets off for a holiday on his motorcycle (which he affectionately
calls "the Cub"), leaving his destination to "Lady Chance." He finds
himself plunged into a time-switch through the power of a cat whom he
comes to love as much as the Cub. In a whirling series of events, he is
drawn back and forth between 1977 and 1677, taking on in the past the
name of a white witch and appearing as the devil himself as John roars on
his motorcycle through the Puritan soldiers and witch-hunters. In the
present, John's life is equally disrupted by the behavior of the Sussex
country folk and by the witch whose life he saves and then brings into the
present. He is both attracted to her sexually and repelled by her.

As in Westall's earlier books, the past and time lie at the heart of the
fantasy; time is even replayed as the witch tries to find, in other periods,
a young man who will be true to her. It will not be John Webster,
however. In spite of Westall's skill in re-creating a cruel and dramatic
period in English history and his equal skill in creating eccentric characters, the book's purpose is not clear. The part played in one's life by
Chance is no doubt purposely left open-ended, but neither is there a clue
as to the effects of the fantastic events on the character of John Webster
as he rides off to reality on his motorcycle. The story is told in the first
person, with an excessive use of slang; the seventeenth century occasions
the uses of more sonorous and lyrical (as well as bawdy) prose. In the age
of its protagonist and in its sexuality, *The Devil on the Road* is a companion volume to Penelope Farmer's *Year King* and Alan Garner's *Red
Shift*.

Science Fiction Fantasy

Although Anne McCaffrey's *Dragonsong* (1976) is set in the future
and on the planet Pern, which has been colonized by people from earth,

the total impression given is one of time past. The feudal structure of Pern's society is made plausible through meticulous but unobtrusive detail. Food has to be gathered, clothes washed, glows (lamps) replenished, and the elderly cared for. As in the reality of feudal life, the teaching of the young is done orally by rote, mnemonics, and music. *Music* is the key word in both *Dragonsong* and its sequel, *Dragonsinger* (1977). The Harpers, led by a Masterharper, are, like the bards and minstrels of old, more than just entertainers. They are also record-keepers and educators, and are close to high places. In Pern, the Harpers have an additional role—that of trying to bring a stagnating society to accept new ideas. In a highly conservative Hold, such as that in which fifteen-year-old Menolly lives, her authoritarian father believes that a girl cannot be a Harper. However, Menolly has very special musical talents and has been trained in all forms of the musical arts of the period by a former Masterharper. When her teacher dies, at the beginning of the trilogy, Menolly is allowed to teach the children, but she is not allowed to play or sing her own "twiddles," as she calls them. She unconsciously breaks her father's injunction (it is rather like telling a bird not to fly) and is subjected to cruel and unnatural punishment. Under this pressure, Menolly runs away.

However, there is another side to Pern besides the Holds and the Harpers. The planet is subject to Threadfall—spores that fall from another planet—and they burn and destroy anyone and anything in their path. Pern's only defenders are the dragonmen and dragonwomen, who ride and cherish magnificent, intelligent dragons and between whom there is a very special empathy. The dragons have been "impressed"—that is, at their hatching from eggs, the riders and the dragonets choose one another in a somewhat mystical ceremony. The dragons and their riders can also "go between"—teleport through space and time.

Through her escape, Menolly becomes a part of these larger aspects of Pern. She finds a cave of fire-lizards (small cousins to dragons) whose potentialities are just being recognized, and she "impresses" them through help, feeding and music—all of which leads to telepathic communication with them. Caught in Threadfall, Menolly is rescued by a Dragonrider and taken to the Weyr, where the dragons are hatched. Here she is made lovingly welcome as a person in distress, then she is especially cherished for her powers with the fire-lizards. Finally, Menolly is discovered as the musical apprentice that the Masterharper has been searching for. It is a most dramatic story, plainly and simply told.

In *Dragonsinger,* Menolly is installed in the Harpers' Hall. She advances her craft but also astonishes everyone by her virtuosity. She is also so good, so modest, and yet so spirited (at least on one occasion) that she comes close to being tiresome. In the third volume of the trilogy, *Dragondrums* (1979), a young boy who has been a minor character in *Dragonsong* takes over the lead as a drumming political messenger for the Masterharper of Pern. It is, perhaps, unfortunate that the various strands of the society of Pern are not really unraveled without McCaffrey's five books written for an adult audience, all of which also have "dragon" in their titles. As with Tolkien's *The Lord of the Rings,* neither the style nor the concepts are beyond the ability of child readers, if they can put up with the length and details of these stories. However, despite the great sweep of the series (both for children and adults), Pern never becomes as real and well-defined as Tolkien's Middle-earth.

Extrasensory perception and telepathy (as well as telekinesis) are also at the center of Virginia Hamilton's *Justice* trilogy: *Justice and Her Brothers* (1978), *Dustland* (1980), and *The Gathering* (1981). Hamilton sees these qualities as representing

> . . . a majestic change in the human race. We find that Justice and her identical twin brothers (Thomas and Levi) . . . have unleashed new gene information, which provides them with psychic powers allowing them to extend themselves into an extraordinary future where things are not as they seem.[20]

Hamilton works within the conventions of science fiction by acknowledging an obligation to give some explanation of such changes, but she deals with them only briefly and only in the first book of the trilogy:

> Their alteration must have been an accident. The difference in one chromosome was enough to alter a few inherited characteristics. Into existence could come sensory and physical changes, the release of genetic information far beyond the ordinary.

In the first volume, these changes in the children erupt in a power struggle among them. At first, the struggle engages Thomas over the

20. Virginia Hamilton, "Ah, Sweet Memory," *The Horn Book Magazine* 57 (Dec. 1981): 639–40.

weaker, but nicer Levi; but then eleven-year-old Justice is trained by a neighbor medium, much as Carlos Casteneda was brought to his full potentiality by Don Juan and so becomes the most important member of the trio.

Despite its dependency on a vision of a new breed of humans, *Justice and Her Brothers* (with its believable family and childhood games) succeeds best as a story of child life in the southern United States. Although Justice and her brothers are supernatural children, they are still children, and the book ends:

> They were on their bikes. Thomas in the lead. Instantly, they raced in a flurry of shining, spinning wheels and glinting metal. . . . They had nothing more on their minds than beating the heat across town. Fresh cold drinks of water. Of getting home. Kids.

This firm hold on reality disappears in the two sequels. Virginia Hamilton herself best explains her own works:

> The fictions depend for effect on the weirdness of location or setting and on the increasing strangeness of the characters. A golden animal, Miacis, roams, talks, and telepaths: a band of wild children communicate through song; winged Slaker beings search for an end to Dustland and their despair; a cyborg, Celester, and a stupendous computer, Colossus, go about saving civilization.[21]

By uniting their varied powers, along with those of their friend Dorian, the children mind-travel to Dustland—its name is descriptive of its ecology—where they meet a host of fantastic life forms. Justice begins to sense the unit's mission: "What matters is that they get a free chance to see what they can do."

On the children's second mission, as described in *The Gathering*, they lead the inhabitants of *Dustland* on an unknown trek to escape the evil influence of a force called Mal. They are impelled toward a domed city (called a "domity"), where they are taken under the wing of Celester and meet the brain, Colossus, which each of the four children sees in a different image.

Virginia Hamilton has a powerful imagination, but in *The Gathering* it

21. Hamilton, 640.

is almost uncontrolled. In straight, typical, didactic science fiction manner, the children learn in the domity that they are in earth's future—an earth that has been plagued by natural disasters but that has also been brought to destruction through the rape of its natural resources, wars, and the lack of concern by the have-nations for the have-nots. The result is a computerized, artificial society where the weather and crops can be controlled and people can be either cloned or drugged. The scenes with the computer resemble many from the famed television series "Star Trek." However, allied to this kind of extrapolation from present events is the highly mystical return of the children's minds to earth as they battle against Mal. Back in their own time and place and with their loving father and mother, the conventions of fantasy are both broken and sustained. The children have actually been away in real time, while their inanimate bodies lay propped up against the riverside trees. However, both Thomas and Levi have been changed: Levi becoming more physically healthy, and Thomas overcoming his mean disposition and therefore his stutter. While some fantasies fail because they have the ingredients without the flavoring, in both *Dustland* and *The Gathering*, the flavoring overwhelms the ingredients.

Animal Fantasy and Beast Tales

Stories of talking and intelligent animals provided the most cohesive group of the decade. While writers such as Robert Westall in *The Devil on the Road*, with its original mixture of accurate history and witchcraft, showed the diversity that is possible in such a basically stable form as past-time fantasy, those concerned with the animal world propounded only one major idea, and they did so almost simultaneously. Their voices rise in a chorus proclaiming that animals are superior to humankind.

The most compelling voice is that of Richard Adams as he persuades his readers of the humanness and humanity of rabbits. He also draws on folklore, myth, satire, and the study of a naturalist—R.M. Lockley's *The Private Life of the Rabbit*—to enrich his thesis.

Adams slings fewer arrows at modern society than did Russell Hoban in *The Mouse and His Child*, but his concentration on only a few targets—such as mankind's inferiority to animals and the flaws in its social systems—makes Adams's marksmanship all the more telling. In its simplest form, *Watership Down* (it takes its title from the Berkshire Downs in England) is a political novel. It begins with a rabbit warren (a society) that to all outward appearances is secure, comfortable, and satisfied with itself. However, the rabbits replicate, in essence, "the decline and fall of the Roman Empire"; all warnings of impending disaster go unheeded. When a small band of rabbits sets out on a quest for a better life, they meet the extremes of societal living, ranging from a dictatorship to a seeming lotus land. Their own newly established warren (won after a battle of epic proportions) is based on Jeffersonian principles—all rabbits are created equal. Individuality and eccentricities are not only tolerated but appreciated; the only limitations on freedom are those that are needed for the common good, and a head of state is chosen by common consent. Hazel, the leader, is neither aggressive nor ambitious; he has an instinctive understanding of rabbit nature, and in his judgments, he stands somewhere between a Solomon and a Solon.

What separates *Watership Down* from other beast tales of the seventies, such as Robert O'Brien's *Mrs. Frisby and the Rats of Nimh* (1971) and John Donovan's *Family* (1976), is its mythology. Like any body of immigrants from a foreign land, Hazel and his band carry with them a tradition, a culture, and a religion—all of which gives them a community spirit and a sense of worth, as well as hope and stability when things go wrong. There is always a story, indeed a parable, in the tales of El-ahrairah, who is their folk hero and who has the characteristics of a Brer Rabbit and a Beowulf—a combination of trickery and nobility. Even over this folk hero there broods a figure who is benign and mystical —one who suggests that even for rabbits there is a dimension beyond the naturalistic.

At the end of his *Private Life of the Rabbit*, Lockley makes a statement and poses a question: "Rabbits are so human. Or is it the other way round—humans are so rabbit?" Certainly Adams makes his readers eventually forget that they are not reading about people. It is a triumph that he can do so while keeping to the essential nature of rabbits:

> The story over, the demands of their own hard, rough lives began to re-assert themselves in their hearts, in their nerves, their blood and appetites. Would the dead were not dead! But there is grass that must be eaten, pellets that must be chewed, hraka that must be passed, holes that must be dug, sleep that must be slept.

Adams joins Jonathan Swift in believing that animals are superior to humans, especially his little band of freedom-seekers. For example, Hazel and a companion visit another warren, which is run on fascist lines, to ask for help in securing does for their own all-male group, but they are violently repulsed. Hazel reports the results:

> "Well, I'd rather say no more about the end of that meeting. Strawberry tried all he could to help me. He spoke very well about the decency and comradeship natural to animals. 'Animals don't behave like men,' he said. 'If they have to fight, they fight; and if they have to kill, they kill. But they don't sit down and set their wits to work to devise ways of spoiling other creatures' lives and hurting them. They have dignity and animality.'"

As well as well-crafted arrows, Adams frequently hurls darts at poor, benighted human beings:

> The rabbits mingled naturally. They did not talk for talking's sake, in the artificial manner that human beings—and sometimes even their dogs and cats—do.

Humans appear rarely in *Watership Down,* but when they do it is as destroyers of animal life.

In its readership, *Watership Down* became almost as great a publishing phenomenon as Tolkien's *The Lord of the Rings* but with the results in reverse. Tolkien conceived his epic for an adult audience, but its style and theme was in no way inhibiting to the young; therefore, it was (and still is) read by many children who were delighted with *The Hobbit.* Certainly no well-stocked children's library today would be without copies of the trilogy. By contrast, *Watership Down* was first published in England as a children's book, and within a year it made its way into "Puffin Books," the elite paperback publishing company of children's books. However, British adults fell on the book as eagerly as the young. In the United States, the novel was advertised in its publisher's adult list, a policy that in no way prevented it from reaching a North American child audience. Perhaps, in the final analysis, Adams's greatest achievement has been to single-handedly restore to the animal story the shared audience of children and adults that existed in the past. This shared audience has lasted through Aesop's Fables, the realistic tales of Ernest Thompson Seton and Charles G.D. Robers, Kenneth Grahame's *The Wind in the Willows*, George Orwell's *Animal Farm*, and E.B. White's *Charlotte's Web*, and it has certainly been reconfirmed by *Watership Down*.

Because of this story's mythic quality and the character of Fiver, the visionary young rabbit whose foretelling seizures the others learn to trust, *Watership Down* resembles the more traditional animal fantasies, such as Grahame's *The Wind in the Willows*, than does Adams's second book, *The Plague Dogs* (1977). The latter is strictly in the tradition of the beast tale, and Adams assumes the role of an Old Testament prophet thundering out his disapproval of humans and of their injustice and cruelty toward the animal world, as well as their even more cunning manipulation of it.

The book opens with descriptions of torture inflicted upon animals in an experimental laboratory that are so painful to read that one can hardly contemplate ever wanting to re-read them. The dogs cannot even be allowed a pure, simple hatred of their scientist masters, for as Rowf says:

> "A dog stands firm. . . . A dog never refuses whatever a man requires of him. That's what a dog's for. So if they say the water—if they say go in the water, I'll—" he broke off, cowering . . . "I can't stand that water any more."

The two dogs make their escape into the Lakeland District, in which they find themselves ill-suited for survival. As Rowf says: " . . . you'd wonder why we take so much trouble to stay alive." Soon their life becomes more than a matter of a search for food, shelter, and warmth. A whole population joins in the search for the two dogs, for the experimental scientists have deliberately spread the rumor that they are infected with the plague. It is a veritable relief, although rather surprising given Adams's viewpoint of human nature, when the story ends in a scene as heartwarming and sentimental as that from either Anna Sewell's *Black Beauty* or Marshall Saunders's *Beautiful Joe*.

Although *The Plague Dogs* has a strong plot, it is also fragmented. This fragmentation results because of Adams's rather old-fashioned authorial interventions. In *Watership Down*, we receive only the thoughts and comments of the animals themselves. In *The Plague Dogs*, on the other hand, there is a whole range of voices—human and animal. There are also constant philosophic asides and digressions that have many echoes in literature. Adams is very well-read indeed. Among others, there is the musical eloquence and ruminations of a Sir Thomas Browne, the seventeenth-century sermons of a John Donne, and, most of all, the biting wit and sarcasm of a Jonathan Swift. This style and the use of heavy dialect make *The Plague Dogs* far less accessible to children, of course, than is *Watership Down*.

The American writer Robert O'Brien has much the same pessimistic view of the human race as Swift and Adams. He has expressed this view in speech as well as in writing:

> I had been, and still am, concerned over the seeming tendency of the human race to exterminate itself. . . . I have wondered: if we should vanish from the earth, who might survive us? . . . I began to speculate: rats are tough, highly adaptable and . . . prolific . . . What would a rat civilization be like? . . . Once I got started, the rats took charge, and they turned out to be much saner and pleasanter than we are.[22]

The rats in O'Brien's *Mrs. Frisby and the Rats of NIMH*—the initials stand for National Institute of Mental Health—are not cruelly treated in an experimental laboratory; but they are prisoners, and they are subjected to injections that over time increase their intelligence and life span. The rats outwit the scientists, escape, ultimately settle in a farm close to an animal reserve in a mountainous area, and set up a technological society that they manage by tapping into a farmer's electricity and stealing his food in typical rat-like style. However, as a result of their research (they have learned to read and write), the rats have discovered the chief reason for the age-old human dislike of rats and are determined to set up a self-sufficient society. There is to be no more stealing.

This aspect of the story resembles science fiction rather than fantasy. It is Mrs. Frisby of the title who gives the story the aura of animal fantasy. She is a mouse and a devoted mother. When her youngest son, Timothy, falls seriously ill—a disaster that will prevent the family from

22. Robert C. O'Brien, "Newbery Award Acceptance Speech," *Horn Book* 48 (June 1972):344.

moving at the required time to escape the farmer's preparatory bulldoz-ing for the spring planting—she goes for help. In a somewhat folklore pattern, she finally reaches the rats of NIMH. Here Mrs. Frisby discovers that she has a talisman in her late husband, who had also been at NIMH and whose ingenuity had been a major factor in the rats' escape. Mrs. Frisby, lacking the gift of superior intelligence, is the true heroine of the story as she risks her life for her children and in so doing saves the rats from annihilation.

The apes in John Donovon's *Family*, who are being used in transplant experiments for the betterment of the human race, also escape from a laboratory. As with rabbits and rats, the apes also feel superior to humans. As Sasha, the commentator, says:

> They are taught at the youngest age to see progress in change. It is why they get their education, and subsequently set their minds to improving the world. I dearly love their innocence, it is so sweet and short-sighted. And their great intelligence, it makes them the most stupid of all animals. This is another sad truth that all apes know.

Like Adams's rabbits and O'Brien's rats, the apes also make a break for freedom; and like them, too, the apes set up their own form of an ideal society—here a close family group. However, unlike the small animals, the apes are defeated by the weather and ravaged by hunters, and the two remaining apes are forced to return to the experimental station.

All three writers generate emotion on behalf of the animals, but the closer the stories come to fantasy, the more successful they are in com-pelling the Secondary Belief that (contrary to the natural law) animals act in a rational rather than in an instinctive manner. It is interesting, too, that rabbits—who are not the intelligentsia of the animal world— and rats—who are hardly lovable in reality—should make a more suc-cessful story on the same theme than do apes—who are so much higher on the evolutionary scale and who bear more of a resemblance to humans. Adams's and O'Brien's art of storytelling seems simply to be greater than that of Donovon.

It is perhaps inevitable that today's animal fantasies and beast tales are compared to Adams's *Watership Down,* and chiefly to their detriment.

Few writers have Adams's probing scalpel into human nature or his command of language. Perhaps also we are now all too accustomed to harshness in books for the young. Colin Dann's *The Animals of Farthing Wood* (1978) is a soft, even sentimental version of Adams's epic. The plot is identical—animals are forced to seek a new home through the depredations of the bulldozer and through humans' lack of concern for other creatures of the earth. The animals have no strong personalities beyond their ordinary animal ones and are characterized only by their generic names—Toad, Fox, Badger, etc. Although Dann's plea for conservation is admirable and his nature lore is impeccable, his dialogue is flat to the point of monotony. In its way, *Watership Down* is as original a piece of work as Grahame's *The Wind in the Willows* and cannot be imitated.

Some Thoughts on the Seventies

As with every period that follows one of sudden change, the 1970's are difficult to categorize. In regard to fantasy, this decade appeared to embrace every type of fantasy much as society accepted all manner of living—ranging from the conventional to the unconventional—and reflected this acceptance in its literature—ranging from the outrageous use of fantasy by Stephen King to the sensitive, realistic novels of Joyce Carol Oates and Joan Didion. Nevertheless, the wheels of change are never completely reversed. Despite the breadth of this period's offerings, they reinforced and even advanced many of the trends of the 1960's.

The age of the protagonists continued to be a factor—most were teenagers rather than children; and with Patricia Wrightson's "Wirrun" trilogy, Robert Westall's *The Devil on the Road*, Penelope Farmer's *Year King*, and Alan Garner's *Red Shift*, we see the arrival of the adult protagonist in books written for the young. In a kind of tandem with writers of fine realistic fiction who were concerned with the emotional development of their teenage protagonists rather than with a strong plot (Jill Paton Walsh with *Goldengrove* and *Unleaving* is an example here), many fantasists followed the same route. William Mayne, Alan Garner, Penelope Farmer, Penelope Lively (with *A Stitch in Time*) and Nancy Bond did their share to shift fantasy from a story with a strong adventure component to one that probed into the psyche of their central character. While the fantasy component certainly enriched the realism, making psychology much more palatable, the chief result was much less distinction between the two types of fiction than in the past. In general, "introverted fantasy" (as Penelope Farmer described it) became much more the order of the day and continued into the 1980's, although at times with major modifications.

It is probably because of these writers' emphasis on the personalities of their characters or on their personal problems that, again as in the 1960's, the realistic aspect of the stories is both more satisfying and more memorable than is the fantastic. In Nancy Bond's *A String in the Harp*, it is modern Wales (although still steeped in the past) and a modern family that linger in the mind rather than the rift in the curtain of magic. No matter how skillfully many modern writers use some aspect of the supernatural or set their stories in a landscape that has mythic resonances, they do not clothe their stories in an aura of enchantment (Susan Cooper is a major exception). Therefore, disbelief is not willingly suspended. When the supernatural is held up to the cold light of day as is the witch from the past in Robert Westall's *The Devil on the Road*, or when the inanimate bodies of the children in Virginia Hamilton's *The Gathering* lie on the riverbank for four days of real time, the spell is broken before the story ends. However, the novels' weaknesses in the creation of a Secondary Belief have compensations in such strong characterizations, innovative plots, and stylistic brilliance.

In the period under review, the writers of the gentler stories of enchanted realism—Eleanor Cameron in *The Court of the Stone Children*, Natalie Babbitt in *Tuck Everlasting*, Penelope Lively in *A Stitch in Time*, and William Mayne in *A Year and a Day*—display both the gift of creating atmosphere and the ability to suggest the passing of real time in far-from-lengthy books. Other writers who kept to narrow perimeters and who were most successful within them were Leon Garfield with his shivery ghost stories and Penelope Lively with her humorous ones. Both writers managed to show the range of this subgenre of fantasy as they moved away from the equivocal short stories of Walter de la Mare.

Also, because so many modern fantasists begin with a problem rather than an image (C.S. Lewis has recorded that he created the *Narnia Chronicles* as a result of his inner picture of a faun carrying an umbrella), they tend to concentrate on only one or two main characters, with little or no emphasis on minor ones. These latter characters are included only to advance the plot. While mothers and fathers are necessary in these stories—they cause many of the problems—they are rarely clothed in flesh. An exception is certainly the modern Tom's narrow-minded parents in Alan Garner's *Red Shift*, but then, the majority of Garner's characters in this book are adult. Entirely lacking in fantasy since the 1950's are minor but memorable creations such as C.S. Lewis's cocky Reepicheep and dour Puddlegum or even the witch, Miss Smith, in Beverley Nichols's *The Tree That Sat Down*, who is more the product of a beauty parlor than of magic. One cannot imagine any modern minor character being worthy of an entry in a "Who's Who in Children's Literature." Animals are an exception. Because they come in groups and because there is so much interaction among them, these characters have to have strong personalities; therefore, we remember the mystic Fiver of Richard Adams's *Watership Down* as much as the leader Hazel.

As the decade of the 1970's came to an end, there became noticeable one major distinction between writers of the past and the present. From the Victorian Age to the 1950's almost every major fantasist had been a successful writer for adults before turning mind and talent (often in special circumstances) to a book for the young. Such a roster is composed of John Ruskin, Charles Kingsley, George MacDonald, Oscar Wilde, Walter de la Mare, Kenneth Grahame, A.A. Milne, and many others, perhaps less distinguished, up to E.B. White and James Thurber. In all their works, one senses a breadth of vision and a knowledge of life that the writers deliberately held within narrow boundaries to make their stories more applicable to and acceptable to children. The few fine writers, such as Philippa Pearce and Lucy Boston, who directed their talents exclusively to the young, showed much the same qualities. However, since the 1960's, most fantasists have made a career of writing only for children and/or young adults, and they appear impatient with the restrictions of childhood, seeking instead—in tune with the times— to extend their works further and further into the complexities of adult life but without illuminating it. This trend was to continue into the 1980's.

Most major fantasists of the 1970's used various strands of myth, legend, and folklore in their works. British writers clung chiefly to their own backgrounds, drawing on their landscape, history, and racial memories of Arthurian, Celtic, and Scottish lore. However, as shown in Nancy Bond's *A String in the Harp*, "the matter of Britain" is available to everyone and can be reinterpreted with originality and sensitivity even by an outsider.

However strongly the works of the 1970's remained close to the roots of fantasy, it can be seen in retrospect that signals were abroad that heralded a major change. For example, in *The Gift* (1973), by the English writer Peter Dickinson, we meet the first young hero in children's literature to be endowed with special powers that do not come through a talisman or through some other form of magic. Whereas Nesbit's children had a wish or an amulet, Susan Cooper's Will Stanton was the seventh son of a seventh son, and the sensitive teenager in K.M. Peyton's *A Pattern of Roses* gained his empathy with a boy of the past by handling old drawings, Dickinson's Davy Price has inherited second sight through his grandmother; and he finds his gift a burden rather than an asset. When, in a climactic scene, Davy uses his gift both sensitively and heroically, he is rid of it forever. In thus closing the story, Dickinson is a traditionalist. Davy's special powers have been used as a literary device and not as a cultural belief. On the other hand, Virginia Hamilton, in *Justice and Her Brothers*, basically changed the rules. Her premise of children with awesome supernatural abilities, untouched by magic, was to become a dominant feature of the 1980's. A mythic sense was almost to be replaced by a psychic one.

Chapter 10

Possibilities and Plausibilities:
Fantasy of the 1980's

A fter its beginnings as social and scientific satire, fantasy became chiefly the property of the young, much as folk- and fairy tales were relegated to the nursery. There were some exceptions, of course. Fantasy for adults had a brief blossoming in the long Victorian era with such works as George MacDonald's *Phantastes* and *Lilith* and William Morris's *The Well of the World's End*, and in the 1920's with the fantastic novels of American writers James Branch Cabell and H.P. Lovecraft. But whatever fantasies there were (and in the early twentieth century, many had aspects of science fiction), none captured the imagination of a large body of adult readers until the publication of Tolkien's trilogy *The Lord of the Rings* in the 1950's. In the 1970's, the publishing company of Ballantine Books capitalized on this built-in audience by republishing most of the almost forgotten fantasies of earlier times and seeking out modern ones for their adult fantasy series. Other publishers noted the increased readership, and soon a stream of fantasy writing directed at an adult market became a flood.

Most of these new writers appear to consider themselves modern Tolkiens. Their books are filled with the traditional "matter" of fantasy. They are set in imaginary lands and are peopled with kings and queens, lords and ladies, witches and warlocks, sorcerers and sirens. Magic is abroad. The ambience is one of prophecies and portents, transformations and tests, riddles to be solved, kingdoms to be saved, and quests to be fulfilled. There is also an attempt to emulate Tolkien in providing a background for these feudal-type lands, often with quotes from pretended historical, religious, and mythical sourcebooks. Good and evil are clearly delineated; the vision is binary or Manichean. There is little evidence of the subtlety of characterization, theme, or plot that has always been associated with an adult novel as opposed to one for children. In such works as Michael Reeves's *The Shattered World,* Stephen Donaldson's *Thomas the Covenant* series, or David Eddings's *The Belgariad* series, one can certainly see imagination at work, but it is often overworked, resulting in an impression of writers who cannot control their material. At any rate, some stories need more than 400 pages of small type to accommodate their huge casts of characters, and even more spread themselves over three to seven volumes of somnolent prose.

The age-old charge against fantasy as an escapist literature has some validity here, but it is not one that can be brought against the new fantasies for the young. There is a distinctive stream of fantasy for children and young people that is different from that for adults, as well as, in most cases, different from children's fantasies of the past. One significant aspect of it, however, has not changed, and it is doubtful that it ever will. Like writers in other genres for children, the new fantasists still hew to the traditional purposes of children's literature—to instruct, to enlarge horizons, to make moral judgments, and, in particular, to help the young come to terms with themselves and with the situations in which they find themselves. This basic approach gives children's fantasy a more serious goal than that for adults, and it also offers a greater scope for variety in themes, plots, and style.

Nonetheless, within this range, there are noticeably strong trends and patterns. In the dominant group of the new fantasies, the supernatural is used only as an adjunct to reality, rather than as a new vision of it and thus gives rise to the seemingly contradictory but explanatory phrase, "the fantasy of reality." Within this spectrum, there are several concentrations. There is the concept of "possession"—children and young people (chiefly through unhappiness) develop, for a brief time, powers beyond the normal. Then there are a host of protagonists who are endowed with ongoing supernatural powers, perhaps better described as paranormal, that can range from extrasensory perception, and its allied phenomena, to witchcraft. The use of fantasy as therapy (psychofantasy) also continues as a strong motif from the 1970's. In many such works, the lines cross to embrace two or more of such characteristics. However, in all of them, the scenarios are played out in the real world with an intensity of emotion that gives them an explosive force. They are in no way gentle worlds of the imagination.

Psychic Fantasy

Robert Westall's *The Scarecrows* (1981) is a powerful example of the fantasy of reality combined with "possession." Fourteen-year-old Simon is devastated by the death of his father, whom he adored, and is even more outraged by his mother's rather quick remarriage to a cartoonist, who represents to Simon all that his military father despised. Simon's anger not only (on one occasion) gives him physical strength beyond the normal but leads him to cruel acts of harassment against the newlywed couple. Finally, his mental emanations cause him to create three scarecrows. They wear clothes of two murderers and their victim—clothes that Simon has briefly donned—and night after night, the scarecrows move inexorably toward his stepfather's house. The ending comes in a burst of supernatural terror that Simon has anticipated but cannot control. However, he does save his family—even his despised stepfather. One presumes that Simon will go on to conquer the devil inside himself.

The plot bears some resemblance to Walter de la Mare's short story *Crewe,* in which a servant who is discharged for theft dies, becomes a scarecrow, and night after night moves inexorably toward the house where his false accusers live. The difference between the two stories lies in de la Mare's creation of atmosphere; the supernatural hovers in the air without an explicit resolution, as in the Westall book.

Patrick Little in *A Court for Owls* (1981) appears to turn more deliberately to a literary antecedent, that of the Gothic tale. The English village of Heriot has a ruined abbey, a recently excavated medieval tomb, an astrological sign over the pub, and even a village idiot. Over it all broods the symbol of the owl as a hunting bird. In this setting and atmosphere, Mike, a young teenager who is seemingly only mildly unhappy with his enforced sojourn with his country relatives, has his being taken over by an evil medieval monk who sold his soul to the devil. Like Westall's Simon, Mike has to garner all the decency within himself to withstand the force of evil.

In *The Shadow Guests* (1980), Joan Aiken rejects the spooflike tone of her *The Wolves of Willoughby Chase* and of her anti-historical novels, such as *Nightbirds on Nantucket,* to use one of the great ploys of the Gothic tale—the family curse. Cosmo Courtoys is an Australian child, living in exile with his aunt, an Oxford don. Here Cosmo finds his life invaded by beings from the past—his ancestors. They are eldest sons who have died under a curse that has been in force since Druidic times, and they demand compensation for their untimely deaths. Cosmo finally learns that his mother and his elder brother went out voluntarily into the Australian desert to die in order to lift the family curse, but it is Cosmo who bears the burdens of persecution and who wins the final battle.

In these three books, the young protagonists are displaced and unhappy, and in this state they summon up supernatural powers—either interior, as in *The Scarecrows* and *A Court for Owls,* or exterior, as in *The Shadow Guests.* However, in all cases, their writers give them the fortitude and understanding they need to overcome their grievances (sometimes unformulated) and their emotional distress.

The works of these British writers are deeply premised on a sense of place in that the landscape assists in sensitizing the emotions of the protagonists: the old mill of Robert Westall's Gloucestershire, the English village steeped in the past of Patrick Little's *A Court for Owls,* and the Oxford of Joan Aiken's *The Shadow Guests,* a place that calls for rational discussion—even of the supernatural.

The young people of Anthony Horowitz's trilogy—*The Devil's Doorbell* (1984), *The Night of the Scorpion* (1985), and *The Silver Citadel* (1986)—do not have to draw on their own integrity and inner strengths to overcome psychological disturbances within themselves; instead they are endowed with supernatural powers. Theirs is not a struggle for self-control but one for the good of the world. This aspect of the plots might seem to put the trilogy in the company of the epic fantasies of C.S. Lewis, Lloyd Alexander, or Susan Cooper, as does their wide geographical range. However, there are major differences.

Horowitz does not root his stories in myth nor create a cosmology nor offer levels of interpretation. They are also devoid of a sense of wonder and enchantment. His "Old Ones" are evil; they seek to control others not through some amorphous design, as in Susan Cooper's *The Dark Is*

Rising quintet, but through specific dangers that beset today's society—nuclear power and drugs. The "Old Ones" are always defeated in their nefarious ends by the superior mind-thrust of the young heroes, who can, under pressure of danger, cause an awesome avalanche of destruction (in *The Devil's Door-bell,* that of a nuclear power plant that has been reactivated by the "Old Ones" through magic, and in *The Silver Citadel,* that of a huge high-rise built in the shape of a hypodermic needle). In spite of their serious subject matter, the pace of the events and their cliff-hanging situations give these stories more the feeling of a Superman movie than of epic fantasy.

Psychic powers, of course, are to be expected in a book titled *Prisoner of Psi* (1985) by American writer Annabel Johnson. Tristan Morgan is a young teenager who flees from his role in his father's famous televised mind-reading act, but he returns when his father is kidnapped by Libyan terrorists who do not believe that the ruination of their plans was caused by Mr. Morgan's power of foretelling. They think that he is a spy.

Tristan rescues his father, and he is, in turn, captured and left to die in a tin hut in incredible heat. He escapes when his father, by mind-thrust, taunts him into shattering his prison with the mental strength that Tristan has tried to avoid using. Both Tristan and the girl he meets and comes to love have developed at least some of the violent aspects of their special abilities (such as a kind of raging poltergeist destructiveness) through a dislike of their domineering fathers. Neither Johnson nor Horowitz suggest, as did Virginia Hamilton in her *Justice* trilogy, that there has been a change in genes that could affect the whole human race. Nor do they intimate that these powers will cease once the personal crisis is over, as does Robert Westall in *The Scarecrows.*

It now seems almost a convention that psi powers are connected with violence, as unhappy young people seek to protect themselves. Shea, in Irma Walker's *Inherit the Earth* (1981), feels that she has been saved from a death by fire by an unknown guardian who continues to protect her and to punish (even by burning to death) anyone who crosses her. But again, like Simon in Westall's *The Scarecrows,* Shea finally realizes that there had "never been anything except her own tormented, suppressed, self-serving id." Shea's powers will continue; she is one of a new breed, even ahead of other people who have developed ESP because she can also move her body through space.

Almost every ill that is known to society is forced upon the boy, Cat, in Joan Vinge's *Psion* (1982)—poverty, slavery, homelessness, torture, and much more. Cat's telepathic powers are of value to those individuals in the world of 2417 who seek to control far-flung planets. However, Cat, like Shea and other modern protagonists of fantasy, will survive. Cat says: "Nothing's changed—yet. But it will. I got a few lives I ain't even tried yet."

Ardath Mayhar's *Soul-Singer of Tyrnos* (1981) has a far more mystical quality than *Psion,* but it also involves people with special powers. Tyrnos is a planet without armies, police, judges, or courts of law. Instead, it has soul-singers—young women trained in a convent-like atmosphere who can sing the image of a soul, whether bad or good, on to a wall for every-one to see. Thus, the singers act as the conscience of the nation. Yeleve is such a soul-singer but one with abilities beyond her training, and it is she who must seek out and destroy the evil that is infecting Tyrnos.

Inherit the Earth and *Psion* resemble Virginia Hamilton's *Justice* trilogy with their rather vague science fiction components that are in no way based on science. Such writers postulate a new type of human being rather than a new type of society. They do not even adhere to the Lamarckian theory that adaptive responses to the environment cause structural changes that are capable of being inherited. Instead, they ap-pear merely to agree with Morris Berman's vague supposition that "In the last analysis, the present species may prove to be a race of dinosaurs and ego-consciousness something of an evolutionary dead end."[1]

Although psychic protagonists know or come to know love, affection, trust, friendship, generosity, and many other heart-warming characteris-tics, the chief impact of such stories is one of violence. This tone lessens, however, when writers give their characters lesser powers, such as simple extrasensory perception. In *The Watcher in the Garden* (1982), by Aus-tralian writer Joan Phipson, the minds of two unhappy teenagers make an enforced and distasteful contact. Catherine has the vague ills of the adolescent, but she is finding peace in a beautiful garden where she is a welcome guest of its blind owner. Terry hates the owner, Mr. Lovett, because Mr. Lovett has refused to sell part of his land to Terry's father for the construction of a gasoline station. Catherine finally senses that Terry is going to murder Mr. Lovett, and she climbs a steep and dangerous hillside in the midst of an earthquake (somewhat of a pathetic

1. Morris Berman, *The Reenchantment of the World* (Bantam: 1984), 303–4.

fallacy) to find that Terry has saved the old man's life. Both young people come to realize the duality of good and bad in their natures.

The American writer William Sleator (probably best known for his chilling futuristic novel *House of Stairs*), also makes use of ESP and possession in *Into the Dream* (1979) and *Fingers* (1983). In the former book, two children, who are at first averse to one another, share the same dream and use the powers they develop to try to save a little boy named Noah. All the children have been subjected to rays from a UFO, but Noah has the greatest potential. He can already move a Ferris wheel cart through the air without benefit of machinery. *Fingers*, to a large extent, resembles the Alan Alda movie "The Mephisto Waltz." At age fifteen, a child-prodigy musician begins to lose his musical capabilities. He plays better than ever, however, when his eighteen-year-old brother writes original music for him, but the music soon is proclaimed to be the undiscovered work of a dead composer. Together, the boys appear to be the reincarnation of the musician.

Two Canadian writers, Cora Taylor with *Julie* (1985) and Janet Lunn with *Shadow in Hawthorn Bay* (1986), have used the extrasensory perception theme with the greatest credibility and literary skill of any authors so far who have published novels in what can now be called a subgenre of fantasy. By the age of three, Julie Morgan (her father calls her his "little Celtic child") is seen to be precocious and imaginative. In a short book (101 pages) and in a short time in Julie's life (until she is about ten), Cora Taylor conveys the feelings a young child experiences in learning how to handle her special gift. Julie is surrounded by happy, normal brothers and sisters, but she feels estranged from her mother, who does not want to acknowledge Julie's second sight. At the climax of the story, Julie's gift saves her father's life but with a sudden addition to her power—that of psychokinesis (she is able to overturn a tractor). The inclusion of this second ability is somewhat of a flaw in an otherwise gentle and moving story, because it seems an unnecessary intrusion into what could have been a more natural rescue.

Mary Urquhart in Janet Lunn's *Shadow in Hawthorn Bay* also has the Celtic second sight. When she is fifteen, Mary hears her cousin Duncan calling to her across the three thousand miles that separate Scotland from Upper Canada. The cousins have been apart for four years, but they have pledged to be together for always. Mary responds to Duncan's voice and, alone and in poverty, makes the long arduous journey to be with him, a journey that makes most recorded pioneer emigrations seem easy in comparison. Mary arrives at her destination only to find that Duncan has died and that her aunt and uncle are already on their way back to Scotland. She is then, in essence, adopted by the practical Yankee Loyalists, who had adjusted to Ontario by 1815. Almost in the Edwardian tradition of the idealization of the young, Mary makes her way into the Loyalists' hearts through her willingness to work, her practicality, and her goodness. However, the mood changes because Mary's Scottish belief in ghosts and boggles disturbs the community. As her patroness Mrs. Colliver says: "Seems to me God's got plenty on his hands taking care of us living, without sending us the dead to deal with." Even more alien to her neighbors are Mary's warnings of ills to come.

The dead Duncan still haunts Mary, and night after night by the water in which he drowned, she hears his voice calling to her to come to him. He is a demon lover, as selfish and black-hearted in death as in life. Finally Mary can break her link with him. However, her gift does not leave her, and she clings to her lot in life even when her neighbors (showing their superstition) avoid Mary because her prophecies have come true. She marries the young Ontarian who has loved her since he first saw her and who comes to accept Mary's special gift. With considerable acumen, he points out, however, that Mary may be so caught up in her "ghosts and fairies and strange critters" that she does not look at the natural world as he does. However, at the end of the story, a mythic sense conquers such practicality. Mary and Duncan are seen as the vessels through which ancient beliefs will become rooted in a new world that has been devoid of them.

Like Justice of Virginia Hamilton's *Justice and Her Brothers*, both Julie and Mary receive help and understanding from women who also have the gift and who use it well, although their powers are not as strong as those of their young neophytes. Both books also have a strong local coloring, one that is quite typical of Canadian novels for the young. In *Julie*, the broad Albertan prairie fields merge into "tall ships with rows and rows of full, fat sails tossed as though the black summer fallow field were ridged with waves and not furrows." In *Shadow in Hawthorn Bay*, Mary feels threatened by the huge, sunless forest of Upper Canada that is so different from the gentle banks and braes of her native Scotland with their benign spirits.

Witches, Wizards, Magicians, and Ghosts—
Modern Style

Witches, magicians, ghosts, and various combinations thereof also abound in modern fantasy; but unlike their counterparts in the past, they now flourish in the clear light of day and within powerful doses of realism. Among their strongest proponents is New Zealand writer Margaret Mahy with *The Haunting* (1983), *The Changeover* (1984), and *The Tricksters* (1987).

In *The Haunting,* eight-year-old Barney senses that his being is being intruded upon by a dead boy—Barney's uncle as a youth. The sympathy evoked for Barney is strong indeed, for much like Cosmo in *The Shadow Guests,* he is a quiet, sensitive, loving child, who hardly deserves such a fate. Barney is, however, under some stress because his step-mother, whom he dearly loves, is about to have a baby. Barney fears that she will die in childbirth as did his own mother. Under this unexpressed torment, Barney's mind lies open to his uncle—who turns out to be alive—who has been rejected by his own mother and who wants Barney for his companion and apprentice magician. We also discover that there have always been men in Barney's family who have had "powers and peculiarities most people just don't have . . . ." However, the real surprise comes at the end, when it is discovered that the new magician in the family is Barney's hitherto self-effacing older sister.

Except for Barney's view of the dangers of having a baby, the family life portrayed in *The Haunting* is a very happy one. By contrast, life is more stressful for fourteen-year-old Laura in Mahy's *The Changeover.* Here a single-parent family struggles along on a limited income. Laura resents her father's defection; when he left, she had already received an inner warning that something terrible was about to happen. Now she senses that her three-year-old brother, Jacko, is in danger. He falls seriously ill, and Laura's misery is increased when she discovers that her mother is turning to a newly acquired lover for support rather than to her. Because of her special powers, Laura realizes that Jacko's life is being sucked dry by an "incubus" or a "lemure" who preys on the life force of others in order to ensure his own immortality. In real life, the incubus is a junkman named Carmody Bracque. Laura's powers have been almost latent, but with the help of a witch family—especially the boy witch, Sorry—she enters them fully and is able to defeat Carmody Bracque.

The use of the supernatural in this book is something of a puzzlement. At times it could be argued that Laura is in a psychic trauma, caused by her resentment against her father, her brother's illness, her mother's friend, and her attraction to Sorry. However, the ending does not support this interpretation. Carmody Bracque turns up outside of Laura's school, pleading for mercy since he is now being drained of his life force. Laura annihilates him; only his clothes are left on the ground, to be pilfered by a tramp. This same fate overtook the Wicked Witch of the West in Baum's *The Wizard of Oz*, but then, Oz is a fantasy land. In *The Changeover*, even more so than in *The Haunting*, Margaret Mahy appears to be claiming that the supernatural is not only a part of the real world but that it is the real world. At least the supernatural is so for people with special powers; and Laura and Sorry have ongoing ones.

A modern witchcraft cult, complete with the Black Mass and ritual killings, provides the core of the plot of *Witchery Hill* (1984) by Canadian writer Welwyn Katz. (As in Mahy's works, family relationships are a major secondary theme.) At the heart of the cult is an arcane, unwritten book whose secrets can be passed on only through death, resulting in a form of "possession." After committing murder and attempting more murder, the coven is finally brought to justice by a teenage boy who defeats evil through his ingenuity and courage. The witch step-mother is evil incarnate, thus producing scenes of such violence that the reader is grateful for the author's lack of stylistic ability. (If scripted, the book would be an excellent candidate for a late, late night television horror show.)

In their portrayal of witches—whether good, as in *The Haunting* and *The Changeover* wherein both girls could be considered "white witches," or wicked, as in *Witchery Hill*—Mahy and Katz have moved a long way from the folktale-type novels of earlier writers. John Masefield's governess in *The Midnight Folk*, Beverley Nichols's more modern Miss Smith (she visits a beauty parlor) in *The Tree that Sat Down*, and C.S. Lewis's "white witch" in the *Narnia Chronicles* all operated within Secondary Worlds—under the cover of night, in an enchanted forest, or in a land where it is "always winter but never Christmas." Mahy and Katz have made such worlds as these seem old-fashioned. However, while combining witchcraft with modern realism and thus opening up new possibilities for plots and characterizations, these two authors have also tried to give rational explanations for the irrational. This approach creates fantasy chaos, unless, of course, one really believes in witchcraft.

While Mahy and Katz do not at all attempt to surround their stories with an aura of the supernatural, Louise Lawrence in *The Earth Witch* (1981) tries very hard indeed. Lawrence's novel begs for comparison with Alan Garner's *The Owl Service*. In both, an alienated Welsh youth is contrasted with two English young people from a well-to-do family who are regarded as intruders in a modern Welsh valley. In both, too, the valley operates as a Secondary World. In this realm, forces are abroad from the past. However, while Garner used a well-known and complete excerpt from the Mabinogion as the basis for his story, Lawrence turns to what may well be historical fact in ancient times—the sacrifice of a handsome young man for the propitiation of the land and the renewal of the crops. Such rites have been acknowledged in myths such as that of the Corn King, Adonis, and in adult novels such as Naomi Mitchison's *The Corn King and the Spring Queen* (set in primitive times) and Thomas Tryon's *Harvest Home* (set in modern times).

The Welsh boy, Owen, is ripe for some gesture that will show his alienation from his lot in life. He is a foster child who is bitter at being abandoned by his mother and chafing at his lowly position. He meets an old woman who is really an "untamed spirit" of the Welsh hills and is subtly pressured into doing jobs for her at the cost of his schooling, his relationship with his foster parents, and his friendship with the two English young people. Literally before his eyes, the old woman is transformed into a beautiful young one. Owen falls in love with her— not from a distance nor with the formality of courtly love—but passionately and sexually. He is bewitched, both through magic and through his own nature. Owen is, of course, the intended victim, but he is saved by the young English girl in the closing violent scenes.

In essence, Lawrence destroys the basic meaning of the ancient ritual, since the "earth witch" appears to have a grudge against men in general and Owen in particular. Nor does Owen receive the perquisites that, in the past, the knowing victim received as his payment.

Diana Wynne Jones's *The Time of the Ghost* (1981) uses the combination of a ghost story and witchcraft. It is a brilliant and unusual story of four sisters (all talented) who live a neglected and chaotic life in a boys' boarding school that is run by their parents, who give all their attention to their students. In one of their games, the girls create a doll whom they name Monigan (a derivation of the evil Morgan Le Fay of the Arthurian legend) and invent rituals and sacrifices for her. Seven years later, one of the sisters is injured and becomes a ghost. She senses that she has two tasks—to find out which sister she is and to prevent Monigan from claiming a life. L.P. Hartley would approve of Wynne Jones's concept of a ghost. Some of the most humorous scenes in an otherwise most dramatic story come when the ghost tries to find out what it can or cannot do in its ethereal state.

The Time of the Ghost has a highly intellectual quality. With its English boarding school setting, eccentric parents, and brilliant conversational exchanges, it is sometimes reminiscent of Jones's contemporary, Jane Gardam, with her realistic novel, *Bilgewater,* about a girl who lives with her father in a boys' school.

Margaret Mahy's *The Tricksters* has the ambiguity of a ghost story by Walter de la Mare while lacking his delicate aura of the supernatural. In Mahy's story, a New Zealand family spends Christmas at their large rambling beach house, which was once owned by the Carnivals—whose eldest son is presumed drowned. On the surface, all is well as the family prepares to celebrate Christmas with all the trappings of the northern hemisphere. However, tensions exist beneath the surface, exacerbated by the arrival of three look-alike brothers who claim to be descendants of the Carnivals. But who are these young men who, when the family skeletons come to light, suddenly disappear? Or, do they instead disintegrate? Are they ghosts—a composite of the young man who is presumed drowned but who really was murdered by his father? Or are they a composite of the imagination of the chief protagonist, seventeen-year-old Ariadne, who has been secretly writing an old-fashioned but lurid love story? If ghosts, the young men are, to paraphrase L.P. Hartley, given a great deal of freedom, since there is a fairly explicit sexual scene between one of the young men and Ariadne. As a story about complex family relationships, the novel's plot, setting, and characters are brilliantly conceived and detailed, so much so that they approach the perimeters of a novel for adults. However, the role of the Carnival brothers remains too much of an enigma to be satisfying with respect either to reality or to fantasy.

Few writers soften their apparitions from the past as does Phyllis Naylor in *Footprints at the Window* (1981). Trudi, a modern young teenager who is upset by her parents' move from a large English town to a village, makes a link with an unknown child who has peered through Trudi's bedroom window and whose grave and diary Trudi eventually

eventually discovers. Thus, Trudi is able to solve the mystery of a nineteenth-century fire in the village poorhouse for which the child was blamed. It is a simple but satisfactory ghost story.

Most good wizards in children's literature have been modeled on Merlin, the mentor of King Arthur (Alan Garner's Cadellin or Susan Cooper's Merriman). These wizards played the role chiefly of surrogate parents in the children's adventures, helping out with some magic in times of crisis. In Diane Duane's *So You Want to Be a Wizard* (1983) and *Deep Wizardry* (1985), it is two young teenagers, Nita and Kit, who have the supernatural powers and the responsibility of saving the world from the Prince of Darkness. The first book is highly eclectic, resembling most epic fantasies in its portrayal of a struggle between good and evil. It also has echoes of Joy Chant's *Red Moon and Black Mountain* in its presentation of evil as the fallen angel, Lucifer, and of science fiction in its personification of machines in a parallel world. Nevertheless, this mixture works better than does the more innovative *Deep Wizardry*, in which Nita and Kit are transformed into whales to help prevent the Lone Power from erupting a volcano under the Atlantic Ocean near New York City. In a final—and long—outburst of ecstasy (à la Madeleine L'Engle), twelve whales (including Nita and Kit) sing the "Song of the Twelve" to offset the destruction.

Nita's discovery that she has unwittingly contracted to give her life to the cause creates considerable dramatic tension but is not as moving as is Oliver's free sacrificial choice in Joy Chant's *Red Moon and Black Mountain*. There is a strong ecological theme to the plot; the ocean is being destroyed by human waste and wantonness. However, with blame attached also to a supernatural power, the edge of the message is confused as well as blunted. A more cogent message of human responsibility for the state of the world is expressed in Susan Cooper's *Silver on the Tree*, even though the evil is consistently attributed to the forces of the Dark.

Fantasy Based on Myth, Legend, and Folklore

The propensity of many modern writers to endow their young protagonists with extraordinary powers and to mix a strong dose of realism with the supernatural constitutes a "new wave." Others have still found inspiration in the oral tradition—in its atmosphere, its familiar figures, its images, and in its inner core—and their works have been strengthened thereby. While not as daring as many of their contemporaries, when they succeed, the latter writers illuminate some aspect of reality rather than confusing the real with the unreal; and, perhaps most importantly, their heroes and heroines are just like us, that is, lacking in special innate powers.

Meredith Ann Pierce's *The Dark Angel* (1982) is too complex a novel merely to be described as a vampire story (here spelled Vampyre), but it does keep to the basic themes of the old legends, those so well described in Bram Stoker's *Dracula* or Sheridan Le Fanu's long short story "Carmilla." In *The Dark Angel,* this Vampyre, too, renders his victims bloodless and mindless, and they cannot be saved. However, it is also a story of love and selflessness.

The chief protagonist, Ariel, is a true heroine—not merely a girl with a problem—and she does not struggle against her lowly lot in life, nor is she hemmed in by it. When her young mistress of a rather sketchily portrayed feudal household is abducted by the Vampyre to become his bride, Ariel sets out to rescue her mistress in true fairy tale style. In her attempt, Ariel herself is abducted and becomes the Vampyre's servant and eventually his fourteenth and final bride. Now he will have the power to destroy the world. Ariel is aware of the Vampyre's cruelty; she has served his thirteen wives, who are now helpless wraiths, and she therefore knows that she has to destroy the Vampyre in order to save herself. Nevertheless, Ariel is attracted to him as well as repelled; the tall winged figure has a certain majesty and beauty, much like Milton's Satan. When she decides not to kill him, Ariel learns that the Vampyre has come from mortal blood and has been under the spell of an evil witch. As in "The Frog Prince," Ariel's compassion transforms the Vampyre into his former self.

It is unfortunate that Pierce's second volume, *A Gathering of Gargoyles* (1984), of a projected trilogy lacks the dramatic unity of the first book. In this sequel, Ariel again goes on a quest, but this time to save the Vampyre, now her husband Irrylath, who is still under the power of the witch. It is a tedious journey (both for Ariel and for the reader) in which exotic names and creatures and a vague mysticism are substituted for the clear lines of *The Dark Angel.*

Ursula Synge has long been known for her adaptations and interpretations of such legend and folklore as *Weland Smith of the Gods* and *The Giant at the Ford.* In her *Swan's Wing* (1981), she borrows characters and motifs from Hans Christian Andersen's "The Wild Swans" and "The Snow Queen." *Swan's Wing* is not set in a "once upon a time" world but in the historically satisfying one of a medieval countryside, city slums, churches, and inns. However, the Other World is not all that far away. As the teller of the tale warns us:

> Enchantment is confined to fireside tales and if we chance to meet it in our waking lives we say nothing, knowing that such treasure is spoiled by daylight. But mostly we see only what is in front of us—wood and stone, cobwebs and dust and, if we are lucky, the play of light among the leaves. Nevertheless, we should be wary—things are not always what they seem.

Matthew, a wood-carver, recalls his journeyings with Lothar, the prince who has a swan's wing in place of one arm, and Gerda, the goose girl, who wants to release Lothar from his enchantment. Like Pierce's *The Dark Angel,* this is a story of sacrifice and unselfishness. Matthew subordinates his quest for perfection in his art to Gerda's obsession with Lothar. Gerda is the Gerda of "The Snow Queen" and the princess, Elise, of "The Wild Swans," an ordinary girl without magic powers. When Lothar is seduced by the "White Lady" (Andersen's "Snow Queen"), Gerda can only wait for him to break the spell himself. Gerda does manage to release Lothar—only to see him turn into a real swan. "Things are not always what they seem."

Patricia Wrightson continued to make use of Australian aboriginal motifs in *A Little Fear* (1983). Mrs. Tucker is a senior citizen who has been shunted off to a retirement home against her wishes. When she inherits a remote, run-down cottage, Mrs. Tucker determines to live in it without telling her relatives. The problems surrounding her daily existence, perhaps minor for someone younger, are very well detailed. They would have been serious enough without the harassment of the Njimbin, who is annoyed at the invasion of his territory and the erosion of his food supply. Mrs. Tucker never sees him, but she senses that she is up against something "small and fast and tricky and ancient." The Njimbin wins the battle, and Mrs. Tucker returns, more reconciled, to Sunset House. This is a slighter work than Wrightson's *The Nargun and the Stars* and *The*

Ice Is Coming, but the story is perfectly conceived, and one's sympathies are equally divided between the two protagonists.

Virginia Hamilton's *The Magical Adventures of Pretty Pearl* (1983) has the feeling of a black folktale, but it is combined with history, encompassing the capture of the black people from their homes in Africa, their enslavement in Georgia, and the march of a community to their freedom in Ohio and Illinois. Pretty Pearl is a god-child who lives with her older brother, John de Conqueror, on Mount Kenya. However, she wants to try her wings among the humans, even though her brother is not in favor of "truck" with them:

> " . . . they got winnin' ways. They grow on you," he said. "You can't fool around de human bein's too long, else you commence actin' human youself."

Of course, that is precisely what happens to both Pretty Pearl and her other brother, John Henry, of steam drill fame. John de Conqueror demotes them as gods as a punishment for acting like humans, but as John Henry says: "To be human is about worth de whole world, to my mind." This is a story of freedom. In lesser hands, it might be rather heavy; but in those of Virginia Hamilton, it is wise, witty, and contains a touch of mythology in the making.

Gregory Maguire's *The Dream Stealer* (1983) is set in a Russian village of the not-so-distant past (it has a train service), and Maguire weaves into it the famous tale of "The Baba Yaga" along with echoes of "The Firebird" and "Vasilissa the Beautiful." He also creates two charming and courageous children who, without magical powers, unlock the riddle of how to defeat the demon wolf that is plaguing the village. However, it is the peasants—shrewd, humorous, and practical—who keep the folktale quality to such an extent that one feels the story should begin, "Once upon a time in the village of Miersk."

Diana Wynne Jones is perhaps the most versatile of modern writers for children. She has produced a fascinating past-time story in *The Spellcoats* and an equally fascinating one with overtones of science fiction and myth in *The Homeward Bounders.* In *A Charmed Life* (1977) and *The Magicians of Caprona* (1980), Jones plunges into magic with lighthearted gusto. Both books deal with magicians' skills, witches' brews, sudden transformations, and spells as an ordinary way of life. Both are also held together by young boys who are serious and responsible and whose magical powers are at first underrated. As delightful as these books are, they now seem but preludes to Jones's full flowering as a humorist in *Howl's Moving Castle* (1986).

The wizard Howl is cast somewhat in the Merlin tradition, falling somewhere between his less-than-omniscient position in Malory's *La Morte d'Arthure* and his bumbling ways in T.H. White's *The Sword in the Stone*. Although Howl gets star billing in the title and his moving castle (much like a merry-go-round) has some effect on the plot, the book really belongs to Sophie, a true heroine in the folktale tradition. She is a combination of Mollie Whuppie in her ingenuity and Cinderella (although a feisty one) in her duties as Howl's servant.

The complicated plot, with its spells and transformations and the undoing of them, works very well but comes to be of less interest than the characters. Even a fire demon has a distinct personality. Diana Wynne Jones has a precise understanding of light fantasy, one also exhibited in her earlier works, such as *The Magicians of Caprona*. She makes good-natured fun of the form she is using—the folktale. Seven-league boots, those marvelous means of locomotion, can cause as much frustration as assistance. If the boots move only a league at a time, how does one stop at the right point? What about a suit that becomes smaller and smaller, but then suddenly becomes bigger and bigger? Also, as the oldest sister in the story, Sophie should not succeed, yet she does.

However, Howl does not possess the extraordinary powers that Duane's modern wizard children do; and, with one humorous anachronism—an excursion into the twentieth century—he is firmly contained in a familiar, semi-folktale world and one in which things are not always as they seem. Perhaps Jones's greatest achievement has been to create a fully sustained and fast-moving light fantasy. Most other such fantasies in the past have been brief or episodic.

Legends of underwater cities have existed since Plato first mentioned Atlantis. In recent science fiction, such as Monica Hughes's *Crisis on Conshelf Ten* (1975), such cities have been promoted as practical solutions to the various problems of the land. Legends of mer-people have also fascinated people since earliest times and have been a part of children's literature since Hans Christian Andersen's "The Little Mermaid." However, a combination of folklore and scientific concepts makes for uneasy bedfellows in Ruth Park's *My Sister Sif* (1986).

Beneath the waters of a small Pacific island lies a city built by mer-people, who have high (but unexplained) technological skills. The island is inhabited by a race of dark-skinned dwarves called menehunes, a few ordinary people, and two girls who are the products of a marriage between a landsman and a mermaid. The narrator, fourteen-year-old Erika, moves easily among these three worlds—the sea, the land, and that of the menehunes—until her private world is disturbed. At first, Erika fears that her sister Sif will fall in love with a young American shell-collector who has come to the island. However, an even greater crisis develops when Erika learns that the mer-people are leaving the environs of the island. The mer-people must flee to distant, more inhospitable yet safer waters. The message is strongly ecological—the oceans are being destroyed by the greed and carelessness of the landspeople. Sif, whose lungs and body chemistry are more closely adapted to underwater living than Erika's, may elect to go to live with her mother and brother, who are completely mer-people.

In its theme and aquatic lore, *My Sister Sif* is somewhat of a companion piece to *Deep Wizardry*, but it is much more stylistically competent than is Diane Duane's work. It is also seriously flawed in its realism as well as in its fantasy. Randall Jarrell, in *Animal Family*, gave a folktale quality to the love that exists between the hunter and the mermaid and their strangely assorted adopted family. Park, unfortunately, asks us to believe in a bizarre marriage resulting in greatly differing types of progenies, in ESP, and in an ancient race of dwarves—all in a semi-scientific atmosphere and occurring in the near future. After her explicit account of the depredations of the oceans, it is difficult to believe in Park's mistily conceived conclusion that the world has been or will be saved from its follies.

It takes a very special skill to make effective use of the material of myth, folklore, or legend in fantasy. Not only must writers know their sources intimately, but, in selecting just the appropriate details for their own purposes, they must recall to the reader the qualities that made these old tales unique in the first place. In using the Andersen tales with consummate skill, for example, Ursula Synge reminds us most of all of their emotional depths while extending them symbolically.

Writers who fail in this area do so for a variety of reasons. Some, such as Patrick Little in *The Hawthorne Tree* (1980), strain credulity by simply replaying an old theme in modern dress without creating a viable modern premise. When a young teenager takes an ancient nail from a hawthorne tree, the forces of faerie are unlocked; and these forces take away a young girl in the "Tamlane" or "Thomas the Rhymer" tradition and also substitute a changeling for her. The story has an occasional effective moment, such as the magnificent ride of Herne the Hunter, but such moments as this are also ones that have little to do with the plot. Little's retelling is far less memorable than Dahlov Ipcar's simple, novelistic retelling of the Tamlane story in *The Queen of Spells*.

Gloria Dank's *The Forest of App* (1983) offers a host of folktale characters—a witch-child, a dwarf, Nob the Fool, a unicorn, and a werewolf, among others—but they are basically name-tagged. In a short book there is little opportunity to give these creations the genuine characteristics of their folktale prototypes. The theme of the story is the depredation of the forest of App and the banding together of its denizens to protect it, but the author breaks another rule of fantasy by making her message didactic rather than subtle.

Pat O'Shea's *The Hounds of the Morrigan* (1986) exemplifies either the author's lack of selection in using folk material or her obsessive love and knowledge of such material. In 469 pages, O'Shea introduces almost all the figures of Irish mythology, with the exception of the tragic ones of Deirdre and the children of Lir. The end result is a mishmash of Irish folklore and legend, which becomes more than tiresome. The story is partially saved by its hero, a modern ten-year-old Irish boy (Pidge)—who is a conventional fantasy child in his innate goodness, obedience to rules, and childlike charm—and by his spirited five-year-old sister (Brigit), who acts and speaks older than her age.

Pidge has unwittingly released the serpent Olc-Glas (contained by St. Patrick) from the pages of a book, and now he and his sister Brigit must find and control Olc-Glas before the serpent is used by the evil witch— the Morrigan. In a journey that is lent spice by traditional folktale prohibitions, and pursued by "the hounds of the Morrigan," the children are aided by a host of creatures, by a great deal of magic, and by Irish legendary figures. In its early pages, the story is given considerable humor by the Morrigan and her witch sisters and by a juxtaposition of modern life and ancient witchcraft.

Past-Time Fantasy

Since past-time fantasy, by reason of its historical subject matter, has less of a magical quality to it than other types, the method of entry to the past and the return to the present become of major importance; this method is the chief, and frequently the only, fantasy device in the plot. Writers of the 1980's still use the conventional means of entry—a talisman or a shift in reality or perception—but just as in the 1970's, the stories also have their entrants to the past spurred by unhappiness.

A combination of these three methods is used brilliantly in *Playing Beattie Bow* (1980) by the Australian writer Ruth Park. Abigail is a young teenager who hates her father, whom she feels deserted her when he divorced her mother. Abigail even refuses to use her father's pet name for her. When her mother decides to remarry her ex-husband and move from Sydney to Sweden, Abigail erupts into violent rage. However, Ruth Park keeps this typical bit of modern realism under control and adds a rich strand of Australiana to the plot. In the street outside Abigail's apartment building, some children are playing "Beattie Bow." It is a game actually played by children in Australia for the fun of scaring themselves to death, although the game has a name other than the one given here. At the appearance of a white-sheeted figure, the children scream: "It's Beattie Bow—risen from the dead!" A spectator of the game is the real Beattie Bow, a ten-year-old child drawn by her name across a hundred years of time.

Curiosity, along with an old piece of lace sewn into the "granny dress" she is wearing, impels Abigail to follow the little "furry" girl in a headlong chase that takes Abigail back to Victorian Sydney and into the lives of the Bow family. The Bows are among the most endearing of families in children's literature. There is lame Dovey, whose name suggests her nature; spoiled Gibbie, who is expected to die; handsome Judah, the young sailor son with whom Abigail falls in love; tempestuous Beattie, whose one wish is for education—an impossible dream for a girl in her station in life in nineteenth-century Australia; and the father, a pathetic figure due to his war injuries, but one who is lovingly tended by his family and his understanding neighbors. Above all, there is Granny, the head of this motherless family who has "the Gift"—inherited from her Orkney Island ancestors. However, Granny's powers of second sight are failing, and Abigail is seen as "the Stranger" who is intended to help the family in this time of difficulty and to play her part in the prophecy, "one to be barren and one to die." Abigail tries to escape back to her own time but fails because she is missing her talisman—the piece of lace. However, she comes to love her adopted family and to feel a warmth and security that lately have been missing in her relationship with her mother.

Playing Beattie Bow is an exciting, finely crafted novel. As a piece of historical writing, it has the liveliness and the surefootedness of a Leon Garfield moving through the eighteenth century in such books as *Black Jack* or his "Apprentice" series. There is the daily life of the Bow family—which is very strange to a modern girl—the smell of the candy shop (the Bow's livelihood), and outside, the larger, bustling, and frequently dangerous flow of the city. Ruth Park also obeys the dicta of fantasy, especially that of "things are not always as they seem." The prophecy is eventually fulfilled, but not as Granny had expected it to be.

Abigail, of course, does get back to her own time, and "The Rocks" of Sydney act as a Secondary World or as a magical bridge; it is down these rocks that Abigail first stumbled into the past. Abigail returns refreshed and more able to cope with the complexities of the adult world. Her apprenticeship is over.

The American Civil War, rather than Ruth Park's type of social history, gives a strong focus—and symbolism— to Janet Lunn's *The Root Cellar* (1981). Nonetheless, the emotional pattern is the same. Twelve-year-old Rose Larkin is distanced from her personal turmoil when she finds her way into the past and so is able to reconcile the conflict within herself. Through her friendship with Susan—the girl of the past—and their search for a young Canadian who has joined the Union Army, Rose sees the aftermath of the war in the military hospitals of Washington and in the plight of those who are wounded in spirit as well as in body. Here the story bears some resemblance to Stephen Crane's *The Red Badge of Courage*. Although she is happier in the past than in the present, Rose comes to realize that she belongs in her own time and that she cares deeply for the noisy casual family of relatives with whom she was placed after the death of her grandmother. She is no longer "a house divided."

Lunn uses several well-blended motifs for transition to the past. There is the root cellar itself. When the shadow of a hawthorn tree falls exactly between the cellar's two doors, Rose can escape from the life she hates.

Talismans also play a part in the time switches. However, the chief supernatural influence is that of the old house in which Rose's relatives live. Since it is a Canadian house, it is in no way as old as Alison Uttley's Thackers or Lucy Boston's Green Knowe, but it has been a happy one and this atmosphere lingers. Rose is given glimpses of the house in its former well-cared for state. She also meets and converses with an old woman who gives her name as Mrs. Morrissay and who assures Rose that she is not a ghost; Mrs. Morrissay instead is occasionally "shifted" out of her own time. The ground is thus well prepared for Rose to be shifted.

At the end of the story, reality and unreality, and the past and the present commingle. Lunn tries to convince her readers that Rose's experiences have been as real as the Civil War itself. Here are no metaphysical questions on the nature of time, reality, ghost-lives, and dreams, as in the relationship between Tom and old Mrs. Bartholomew in Philippa Pearce's *Tom's Midnight Garden*. Susan is Mrs. Morrissay, the house was hers, and Mrs. Morrissay returns again to give Rose some very practical help. In a burst of familial feeling, Rose insists on cooking the Christmas dinner by herself, and she ruins it. She then prepares her typical meal of sausages and mashed potatoes. However, when she flings the kitchen door open to admit the family, the goose is perfectly cooked, the table set with old-fashioned dishes and table linens, and the room is appropriately decorated. Such a transformation scene has not occurred since the fairy godmother waved her wand over Cinderella.

Catherine Storr's *The Castle Boy* (1983) is well crafted, but it is less engaging than either *Playing Beattie Bow* or *The Root Cellar,* chiefly because the time that the young teenager spends in the past is completely described in narrative style. One misses the conversations that enliven the two former works. The castle of the title is a medieval English one, now renovated as a modern hotel. To it come Robert and his family, Robert reluctantly because the vacation is being paid for by his uncle. He is also under the strain of being an epileptic—a source of shame to Robert just as it is to his father, who has been a war hero but who is now a failed businessman subject to the bounty of his younger brother.

Robert finds a piece of the castle's original stonework, and it becomes his entrance to a time long past. In this past, Robert is invisible and can wander at will in a world that is at once both alien and comforting. He sees the deformities of many of the lower classes as a greater burden than his own. Storr here develops a plot linked to social background. In his wanderings, Robert becomes conscious of a spy who plans to admit the enemy to the castle and thus slaughter its inhabitants. Robert determines to kill the traitor, but then discovers that he cannot take a human life— even for a good cause. Since the past cannot be changed, the pillage occurs, and the castle and the hotel are set on fire. In the present, Robert's father dies a hero's death. Like Lunn's *The Root Cellar,* the message of *The Castle Boy* has a broader application and is not simply about the protagonist's own problems.

Belinda Hurmence's *A Girl Called Boy* (1982) is a straightforward "message" fantasy. Blanche Overtha Yancey, called "Boy" for short, is a spoiled, modern black girl who takes no interest in hearing about the struggles of the blacks who have made her pleasant existence possible. On a vacation in North Carolina and with just a hint of magic in the presence of a "conjure bird," Blanche is transported to the past, where she has to struggle to escape the bonds of slavery. It is a simply told story that lacks the dramatic impact of Paula Fox's *Slave Dancer,* but still it succeeds by virtue of its subject matter. No account of slavery can be less than important and moving.

Park's *Playing Beattie Bow* is a look into both family history and the stresses of a modern family. So too are *A Handful of Time* (1987) by the Canadian writer Kit Pearson and *Sweet Whispers, Brother Rush* (1982) by the American Virginia Hamilton. Both writers look back on only a short time span from the present, and in both stories also, unhappiness is the spur for the events. But there the similiarities end. Pearson is very conventional in her use of a talisman that takes twelve-year-old Patricia back into her mother's life to a time when her mother was her age. The stage is set very carefully with a duplication of place (a summer cottage in northern Alberta) and a reunion of the main characters. Through an old watch, whose magic works with Nesbit-like precision, Patricia comes to understand the family situation that has formed her mother's character and ambitions. An added bonus is a view of children's holiday activities, both in the present and the past.

Whereas the magic in *A Handful of Time* clearly separates the past from the present, in Hamilton's *Sweet Whispers, Brother Rush,* there is no specific magic or use of the supernatural. The entry to the past "implies the supernatural" (to use E.M. Forster's phrase), "but in no way states it." *Sweet Whispers, Brother Rush* could aptly be described as enchanted realism were it not for the fact that the harsh realism of the story negates any feeling of enchantment.

When fourteen-year-old Theresa (called "Tree") first sees Brother Rush, it is his clothes that attract her. She thinks he is "the stone finest dude she had ever seen." He leans against the stoop of an apartment building—with his right hand cupped around his ear. When she sees Brother Rush in the little room of her bedroom

> The hand that had been cupped around his ear now held something. It looked like an oval mirror, but it was not a mirror. What Rush held was an oval space shaped like a mirror, and it glinted at her. In it was a scene of life going on. Rush held the oval space wrapped in a sheet from her ream of paper, as if he thought he might cut himself on the space's edges if he didn't hold it in the paper.

Tree is very much like Clare in Penelope Lively's *The House in Norham Gardens*—she has too much responsibility for her age. However, her problems are even more severe than Clare's. Her mother is away from home almost all the time, and one begins to suspect that it is more by design than because of the exigencies of her job—that of a practical nurse. Tree is in charge not only of herself and the apartment, but also of her sickly older retarded brother, Dabney. Through Brother Rush's nonexistent mirror, Tree enters her own past as a small child and her mother's past. She discovers that her mother hates her retarded son and has treated him cruelly and that her uncle Rush committed suicide under the torment of a rare disease that afflicts the males in this black Southern family. Her mother returns (with a lover) as Dabney is dying of the same disease. Tree explodes in rage, not only at her mother but because she is not allowed to be at the bedside of her dying brother.

Virginia Hamilton does not shy away from complex characterization, particularly that of Tree's mother. The mother's dislike of her son is still apparent at the end—she never calls Dabney by name. The mother's excuses to Tree regarding youth and inexperience do not ring true because she neglects her children even as a mature woman. Nonetheless, she has managed to attract a very wise and kind man, and Tree loves her very much.

The detailed descriptions of Tree's daily responsibilities give the book its main strength, especially since there is no plot. These include Tree's caring for her brother (she has to make him take a bath); her preparation of meals with food running low (how to cook spaghetti sauce with frozen meat); and her household chores (she criticizes the cleaning lady). So absorbed have we become in Tree's life and in her comments on it that the ending comes as almost a letdown when Tree quickly adjusts to her brother's death and to what we know will be her new family—a stepfather, a stepbrother, and a reformed mother. Nevertheless, its touch of something beyond the real enriches the book, for it offers a wider vision of life "as it is lived, and as it might be lived and as it ought to be lived."[2]

The most unusual of recent past-time fantasies is Emily Hanlon's *Circle Home* (1981). Here, a Stone Age girl named Mai awakens in the body of a twentieth-century child who has been pronounced dead. Will she be Mai or Isabelle? Will she return home or live as a stranger in modern suburbia? We see Mai in her primitive era as well as in the modern one that is so strange to her. While modern writers have almost overused emotional distress as the chief premise for time travel to the past, *Circle Home* lacks impact simply because there is no premise, no reason in the lives of either child as to why such transfer has taken place.

Despite its concentration on the troubles of its chief characters, this subgenre of fantasy has remained quite stable and conventional and indeed meshes with much of earlier fantasy in general. Like Bilbo Baggins of *The Hobbit,* the young go "there and back again." However, their journeys are more difficult and dangerous than in the past; theirs are roads from innocence to experience, and so they leave their childhood behind them. Although the creators of such stories frequently put aside the quality of imagination for an undue emphasis on reality, they still abide by one of the chief dictates of fantasy—the need to return their characters, and so their readers, with a greater perception of themselves and of others and with a determination to take hold of life fully.

Epic Fantasy

In epic fantasy, modern writers are borrowers rather than subcreators in the Tolkien sense—that of making a Secondary World based on its

2. Ursula K. Le Guin, *The Language of the Night* (Putnam's: 1979), 58.

own inner logic yet "derived from Reality" or "flowing into it." Most of the newer works that are set in Other Worlds can be taken only at face value. These include Geraldine Harris's four-part "Seven Citadels" series,[3] Nancy Springer's three-part "Isle" series,[4] Jane Louise Curry's *The Wolves of Aam* (1981) and its sequel *Shadow Dancers* (1983), Paul Fisher's *Mont Cant Gold* (1981), and Stephen King's *The Eyes of the Dragon* (1987), all by American writers. To describe one book is almost to describe them all. These writers move their characters through mistily formulated feudal or primitive lands that are touched by magic. Landmarks are rarely named; there is only a progression of hills and valleys, mountain passes and trails, caves and camps. The cast is one of princes and lords, sorcerers and magicians, birds of the air and beasts of the forest. Occasionally, there is a fittingly invented name, such as the "Tiddi" of Curry's *The Wolves of Aam,* who are long-toed, pointy-eared little people who hunt wild horses. The plots are complex (convoluted in the case of Harris's "The Seven Citadels"), and there is a plethora of incidents. Harris especially has an over-luxuriant imagination, but her work succeeds the best of this group chiefly because of its stronger characterization (there is constant tension between the hero and his half-brother) and because there is some variety in the lands the characters visit to find the seven keys that will save an empire.

King's *The Eyes of the Dragon* is in no way a children's version of his surrealistic novels for adults (although these are simplistic enough to be popular with some young readers). While the opening pages of King's first venture into a deliberately conceived fantasy for children contain some gratuitous and crude sexual references, the story quickly develops into a fairly conventional fantasy, with a wicked magician (Flagg); a prince (Peter) who is charged with his father's murder, deposed, and imprisoned; and his weak younger brother, (Thomas), who inherits the throne and is Flagg's minion. As the *deus ex machina,* Flagg bears more than a superficial resemblance to Flay, the manipulator in Mervyn Peake's *Gormanghast* trilogy, except that Flagg has been alive for four hundred years. King has an inventive mind, which can be seen in several

---

3. Geraldine Harris, *Prince of the Godborn* (1982), *Children of the Wind* (1982), *The Dead Kingdom* (1983), and *The Seventh Gate* (1984).

4. Nancy Springer, *The White Hart* (1979), *The Silver Sun* (1980), and *The Sable Moon* (1981).

aspects of an otherwise mundane plot. Chief among these inventions is Peter's plan of escape. Through his inherent kingly sense of worth and command, Peter is able to have his three meals a day served with linen napkins. These he unravels, using the threads on a toy loom from his dead mother's dollhouse to weave a rope by which he can escape from his prison at the top of a tower that is three hundred feet high. With only a slight use of the fantastic, *The Eyes of the Dragon* reads more like a Gothic tale than a fully fledged fantasy. King is so old-fashioned here that he has re-invented the authorial intervention. However, unlike writers of the past, he does not introduce these comments to offer additional information to children—remarks that do not really affect the plot—but instead uses them to explain the plot. He does not trust his readers.

Like these American writers, Austrialian author Victor Kelleher makes no attempt to combine fantasy and modern reality in his *Master of the Grove* (1982) nor in his earlier work *Forbidden Paths of Thual* (1979). *Master of the Grove* appears to hover within a world that is vaguely primitive and vaguely feudal—fighting is done with spears and bows and arrows; but farmhouses have glazed windows, and potatoes are a staple food. However, it does have a strong storyline—the boy, Derin, sets out to find his father, rid the land of autocratic rulers, and fullfill his destiny. *Forbidden Paths of Thual* is also a quest story, but one that is more firmly set within a primitive society. The evil Mollags who conquer Quen's village have an alien science fiction touch, and their pursuit of Quen through the forest has many harrowing moments. The ending is somewhat similar, though, to that of Tolkien's *The Lord of the Rings* in that a talisman that gives power can also destroy the individual who carries it. The boy's growing attachment to the forest in which he hides is well described, and the conservation theme is not obtrusive.

In Robin McKinley's *The Blue Sword* (1982), neither the time nor the place of the action is specified. However, with the book's references to Governors and Residencies, Outlanders and Homelanders, native people and white people, and its scenario of desert and hills, northern borders and mountain passes, the story might take place in northern India under the early British Raj. Nevertheless, the setting is different enough to give the suggestion of an imaginatively created Other World supported by concrete details of a nomadic way of life that is touched by magic. Its tone is reminiscent of Kipling's *Plain Tales from the Hills*, E.M. Hull's novelette *The Sheik,* and the high adventure tales of Rider Haggard. These literary antecedents suggest romance, and indeed *The Blue Sword* is a love story that is unique in fantasy written for the young.

Harry, short for Angharad, has come from what one presumes is England after the death of her father in order to live with the Resident and his wife, who are fond of Harry's older soldier brother. At age sixteen, Harry is tall for her age, has been brought up to ride and shoot, and has little interest in parties and young men. She is somewhat like (in the book of the same name) Caddie Woodlawn before Caddie was introduced to women's work and women's ways. Harry develops an immediate affinity for her new country, where the ability to ride is a real as well as a social necessity.

To the Governor's Residency comes Corlath, chief of a Hill-tribe, to ask for military help against the Northerners who, his spies tell him, are ready to invade his lands and perhaps those of the Outlanders. Corlath is refused.

The magic begins almost immediately as Corlath and Harry's eyes meet for the first time:

> It was though a thousand desert suns beat down on her. Magic? She thought from inside the thunder. Is that what magic is?

Corlath possesses *kelar,* the gift of second sight, and he recognizes the same power in Harry. He kidnaps her, sensing that she will be of use to his tribe in its time of need. Harry is not treated like an ordinary prisoner, however, and she does not try to escape, feeling quickly at home in her nomadic life. We are not surprised to learn eventually that Harry's great-grandmother was a Hill-woman. Harry is trained in warfare for single combat, much like the knights of old. She is superior in all that she does, and everyone loves her—her horse, her desert cat, the King's Riders, and the people of the outer tribes who flock to her *kelar.* The climax comes when Harry, with the aid of the magic sword Gonturan, brings a mountain crashing down upon the enemy—who possess evil supernatural powers—and in so doing saves the land of Damaria, both for Corlath's people (now her own) and for the Outlanders. The story ends with marriages and reconciliations all around, but then, so does *Pride and Prejudice.*

The Hero and the Crown (1985) is a precursor in Damarian time to The Blue Sword. It is the story of Aerin (Harry's great-grandmother), the daughter of the King of Damaria by his second wife, who was never crowned queen and who was considered by popular verdict to be a witch from the North. The King's second wife died giving birth to Aerin, and now, in Aerin's sixteenth year, Damaria is again threatened by strange happenings among the Northern tribes.

Physically, Aerin is much like Harry—tall, athletic, and interested in riding and sword-play. She is handsome rather than conventionally beautiful. Uncomfortable with her equivocal station at court, even though she is a "sol"—that is, noble—Aerin avoids social functions as much as possible and spends her time retraining her father's injured war-horse and in perfecting an ointment against dragon-fire. She becomes famous and beloved of the people as Damaria's dragon-slayer. However, Aerin is not invincible. When she slays the arch-dragon Maur, Aerin is wounded unto death, while he continues to exercise his evil magic over Aerin and over the Damarians through his severed, dried skull.

Aerin is cured of her illness by Luthe, the magician, from whom she also receives knowledge, consolation, the experience of sexual love, and, as a parting gift, the magic sword Gonturan. Then her quest begins, and she climbs through time to face her wicked uncle, who has caused the chaos in Damaria. Aerin defeats her uncle, retrieves the lost crown of her country, and returns home to save her people in their final battle against the Northerners. She then marries the heir-apparent, who has long loved her and who will now be king, although he recognizes Aerin's prior claim to the throne.

The difference between the two books lies chiefly in the use of the "matter" of fantasy. In The Blue Sword, it is so muted that the power of Gonturan at the end comes with something of a shock. The Hero and the Crown, on the other hand, is filled with the fantastic—dragons and other sentient animals, witches and magicians, spells and enchantments. Each book, however, has its own merits, thus proving that what material of the supernatural is used is of less importance than how it is used.

There also are resemblances between the two works—the landscapes; Harry's and Aerin's affinity with animals, especially horses; the links with Gonturan; and the love interests (although less romantic in The Hero and the Crown than in The Blue Sword). The styles are also similar, smooth-flowing and leisurely, with an apt but restrained use of invented words—*kelar* (second sight), *malak* (a beverage), *mik-bar* (a treat for horses), and *sol* (noble).

Overall, it is the portrayal of the heroines that gives some pause for thought. Like the heroes and knights of old, the heroines undergo rigorous training for their trials and quests; they win their spurs and ride off to conquest and fame. However, unlike their prototypes—King Arthur, Roland, and Beowulf—they do not go down to defeat. It may well be that Robin McKinley has created these skillful and courageous young women as an ideal for young women of today; the aura of enchantment and romance is no barrier to such an interpretation. The title, *The Hero and the Crown,* is certainly of some significance. Aerin is the hero, and perhaps we are meant to feel that the word *heroine* is as passé as are the words *authoress* or *poetess.* Yet despite Aerin's and Harry's innate abilities, as well as their supernatural gifts, there is a strong intimation at the end of the books that both young women will revert to traditional women's roles. It is as if the struggle with adolescence were over and the time to settle down had come.

Susan Cooper's *Seaward* (1983) is a nightmarish world that has two violent and basically unexplained entrances to it. For the young teenager, Westerly, entrance into it entails an escape through a door at the urging of his mother, who is then killed, one presumes, by the police of a military state. Cally, in a burst of violent rage against the illnesses that have deprived her, in turn, of her father and mother, presses her strange, rough, and thickened hands against a mirror and is jerked into another dimension. Both young people find themselves in a world that is even more bewildering than the ones they have left. Westerly and Cally eventually meet and make their way to the sea—a symbol of safety, hope, and renewal because "the sea links all worlds." Just as in Cooper's *The Dark Is Rising* quintet, the book teems with mythic references—especially Celtic ones. In addition, there are a live chessboard (somewhat similar to Lewis Carroll's); moving, gigantic, stone people; a snake; a spider; and the ever-recurring figure of the Lady Taranis, who has a double face. The landscape is best described as surrealistic rather than enchanted. So helter-skelter are the events and the symbolism that the various episodes, unlike Cooper's epic fantasy, lose all impact. It is difficult to believe that both works are by the same author.

Allan W. Eckert's Twilandia in *The Dark Green Tunnel* (1984) is an attempt to emulate The *Narnia Chronicles* (the book is dedicated to them). However, the story is a pale reflection of C.S. Lewis's epic, and the children are almost caricatures of Susan, Lucy, Peter, and Edmund. Even the entrance to Twilandia is incongruous—a turnstile in the midst of a Florida swamp.

British writer John Gordon creates a parallel world in *The Edge of the World* (1983). It is a terrifying one for two young teenagers, especially because of the skeleton horsehead that pursues them in both worlds. The plot also involves ghosts, a witch, and a love triangle stemming from World War I. There is an epic quality to the plot, since the protagonists are striving to save a young man's life and an old man's happiness. As in many modern fantasies, the supernatural leaves a definite imprint on the real world—the old man's sweetheart is released in fantasy and is restored to him in reality.

"The Town" is the Secondary World in Ursula Le Guin's *The Beginning Place* (1980). It is a vague place, not least because it is always in twilight; it has a kind of feudal lord and a kind of mage at the top of a vague feudal society. The peasantry appear to be engaged in cottage industries, and all the inhabitants are under an undefined spell; they cannot leave the Town.

There is nothing unsubstantial about the events that begin the story. Here is stark reality as Le Guin recounts the serious and sordid problems of two California young people. Hugh is overweight and apathetic. His days are spent as a clerk in a supermarket, and his evenings with his widowed, selfish mother in a sterile round of watching TV and eating TV dinners. However, there is a divine spark in Hugh, and it is this spark that leads him through a fence and into a magical dell where time is suspended, the water is pure, and the air is invigorating. Here he undergoes a gradual transformation—an energizing of his character in the real world.

Irena has had even more serious problems than Hugh. She has been sexually harassed by her stepfather, and her one refuge (that of living with friends) has been destroyed. She has been a visitant to the Town before Hugh; and when they meet, she is jealous of him since Hugh is to be the Town's savior. Although he is a most reluctant hero, Hugh and Irena set out on a quest to fight something they know little about and for a reason that is unknown to them. Hugh manages to kill a nameless horror but is almost undone by its chill, which enters his whole being. By virtue of a strength she did not know she possessed and through her burgeoning love for Hugh, Irena forces Hugh on and out through "the beginning place" and into the real world—with real time unchanged—where, it can be assumed, all will be well since Hugh and Irena now have one another.

The Beginning Place is an exemplar of much of modern fantasy. Its strength and chief interest lie in its portrayal of a slice of reality (the fantasy of reality), and the fantasy component is used to bring about a change in the minds of the protagonists (psycho-fantasy). However, in its lack of a clear delineation of the fantasy world (the reader can believe only that such a lack was deliberate on the part of the creator of *Earthsea*), this novel shows a shift in purpose. Modern writers either cannot create a viable Other World, as is shown by *The Dark Green Tunnel,* or they consider an Other World secondary to reality, as is shown in *The Edge of the World* and certainly in *The Beginning Place.*

Science Fiction Fantasy

Although they have an opportunity to create fresh and viable future worlds, it is of some interest that writers of the 1980's in the genre of science fiction fantasy have not done so, at least not to date. Austar IV in Jane Yolen's *Dragon's Blood* (1982) is a future feudal planet, first settled by convicts and guards in the year 2303. In the year 2485, the planet's economy is based on dragons. The best dragons are trained for the fighting pits, and the poorest and weakest are slaughtered for meat and leather. The society is divided between the masters who own the dragon farms and the bond slaves who can earn their freedom by filling the bags they wear around their necks with their minimal wages. "I will fill my bag" is a phrase that echoes throughout the book with boring repetition. Jakken, a bond boy in a dragon nursery, determines to take a shortcut to freedom by stealing a red baby dragon from his master and raising and training it secretly in the desert for the fighting pits. Jakken comes to love his dragon, and they develop a touching of minds (ESP) so that in the dragon's first fight, Jakken can direct it by mental communication. The fighting scenes are violent indeed. Here the fighting is not only representative of nature "red in tooth and claw," but also of a society that feeds off violence.

Neither the blessings nor the problems of a democratic society seem to have any attraction for modern writers who take us into the future. Joan Vinge's world of *Psion,* for example, is violently autocratic; in Mayhar's *The Runes of the Lyre,* the threat of evil and destruction comes from the side that has "the bomb"; and even Mayhar's *The Soul Singer of Tyrnos* envisions a society where power is in the hands of a very few superior people.

In *The Green Futures of Tycho* (1981), William Sleator avoids any necessity for unveiling a future by instead concentrating on character. Here a young boy finds a talisman that takes him into his own future. He does not like himself there, but he finds that he has the ability in the present to make choices. The message of all such science fiction fantasy appears to be that we do indeed carry our past into the future.

Doll and Toy Fantasies

Dolls and other miniature models continue to add a supernatural touch to various types of fantasy. Sylvia Cassedy's *Behind the Attic Wall* (1983) combines a doll theme with what can now be described as "modern traditional"—an unhappy and disturbed young teenager brought to terms with herself and her life. The result is a most compelling story, and although it leaves several major questions unanswered, the suspense conquers all. Maggie arrives at her great-aunts' home "whose huge stone house looked like a prison." Because Maggie is an orphan— and a difficult one to handle (she is no Anne of Green Gables)—we hope desperately (within a few pages) that now everything will be love and kindness for her with, of course, a few incidents for the sake of dramatic tension. However, as Maggie enters the house of the Misses Green

> Something stirred at the far end of the hall, and Maggie stepped back. Two figures, one in brown, the other in green, suddenly emerged. They grasped one another, as though each would fall if the other let go, and stopped at a distance from Maggie, holding her in a long fixed gaze. She had been looked at like that before, always on her first day at a new place and always by the headmistress. These then were the headmistresses—*two* of them this time!

Maggie is right in her estimation of her new situation: although her aunts are not cruel to her, they are authoritarian and make no effort to understand her. Maggie has her own defenses—her constant rudeness and rebellion, and her imaginary companions, "The Backwoods Girls," whom she scorns—doing to them as she has been done by. However, there are also mysteries in the house—her great-uncle Morris, who is kind to her but who also puzzles her, and strange voices that become louder and more alluring. "Behind the attic wall," she finds two dolls and a toy dog and many of the appurtenances of housekeeping. The dolls talk, but they cannot move, and at first Maggie responds to their requests with rage. Then she comes to love them. There is a link between the dolls and a picture in the parlor—one of Mr. and Mrs. Green, who had been in charge of a boarding school many years ago. Uncle Morris dies, and Maggie is to be sent away. In saying farewell to the dolls, however, she sees that there has been an addition to the group—an Uncle Morris doll. Maggie is happy in her new home, but we never know with whom. She tells the story of her life to two young children, but she never tells them about her profound experience with the dolls. *Behind the Attic Wall* is one of those rare books that combines suspense with a vivid style.

Dolls and dollhouses also play important roles in Reby Edmond Mac-Donald's *The Ghosts of Austwick Manor* (1983) and Betty Ren Wright's *The Dollhouse Murders* (1983). MacDonald's book revolves around a curse on the eldest son that is discovered when family journals and a doll's house arrive from England for a young Canadian teenager who is now heir to the English branch of his family. The doll's house is a model of the Tudor home in England called Austwick Manor, and with it are sets of dolls dressed in various period costumes. Donald's two young sisters find that the doll's house lights up at night and that through it they can enter different periods in the past. The sisters hope to find the period during which the curse was first uttered and thus avert it. They do so in a scene that resembles the ending of *The Exorcist*.

The Dollhouse Murders is not quite what the title suggests. The dolls do not commit murder. The dollhouse is a replica of the house in which the action takes place, and the dolls are replicas of real people—the grandmother and grandfather, who were murdered, and their two grandchildren. Now the grandmother doll, through her actions, is able to reveal the true murderer of herself and of her husband and thus release her now grown-up granddaughter from personal torment. The great-granddaughter, Amy, is the catalyst who releases the magic of the dollhouse, and, in so doing, she learns to be more patient and loving with her younger, retarded sister.

Both books bear a strong resemblance to the ghost story "The Haunted Doll's House," by the famous writer of the supernatural M.R. James; in this, a crime is re-enacted every night. Both tales also are simply told, The Dollhouse Murders even flatly so. Although Cassedy's Behind the Attic Wall is the furthest removed from M.R. James in regard to plot, it comes closer to his story in atmosphere and memorableness.

Richard Kennedy has long been noted for his sophisticated fantasy picture-books with their echoes of folklore and for his honed, controlled style as exhibited in The Porcelain Man. In Amy's Eyes (1985), Kennedy spends 437 pages unfolding the most complicated plot in children's literature; and, with the exception of Pat O'Shea's The Hounds of the Morrigan, his book has one of the largest casts of characters ever to be found in a single volume. Dolls and toys come alive and are engaged in a search for gold, with pirates as their antagonists. They are all as motley a crew as ever sailed the Seven Seas. Robert Louis Stevenson's Treasure Island seems mild in comparison.

There are several switches and jarring notes played out on old themes. The child Amy, in her loneliness and while undergoing a mysterious per-secution at the hands of one of her teachers (Amy's letters are intercept-ed) in the orphanage where she has been left by her father, loves her sailor doll into life. Here one thinks of Margery Bianco's The Velveteen Rabbit. However, the actual transition has less than a magical quality. Amy accidentally jabs her doll in the head with a needle. The toy animals are eventually brought to life by the same means, while Amy, miserable under the loss of both her father and her sailor, dwindles into a doll her-self. The book's theme of oppressed children calls to mind Maria in T.H. White's Mistress Masham's Repose and the young heroines in Joan Aikens's The Wolves of Willoughby Chase, but Amy has none of their feisti-ness; instead, she is but a pawn. The teacher, Miss Quince, is surrounded by the same ambiguity of the governess in Henry James's novel The Turn of the Screw. Each chapter is headed by a Mother Goose rhyme (Amy has read the rhymes to her doll), and there are numerous and obscure references to Mother Goose throughout the story, as well as to numerol-ogy and to the Bible (particularly the Book of Revelations), along with the introduction of symbolic figures—such as the white albatross and the black seeress who claims Mother Goose as her sister.

The moral of the story is plain enough: the mark of the Beast will be on "those who clutch and grasp at gold." However, the journey to this conclusion is a tedious as well as a cloudy one. C.S. Lewis once stated that he wrote a children's story when he considered it "the best art-form" for something he had to say.[5] The difference between these two writers is that Lewis's secondary level of meaning is within the comprehension of children, while Kennedy's calls for an annotated edition of *Amy's Eyes* even for the literate adult.

Kennedy makes no attempt to bolster his Secondary Belief that dolls and toys can come alive with the talismans of magic. On the other hand, British writer Lynne Reid Banks in *The Indian in the Cupboard* (1981) and in *Return of the Indian* (1986) follows the Nesbit rules of magic with complete success.

Among the presents given to Omri on his birthday are a plastic toy Indian (which he thinks he has outgrown) and an old medicine cupboard (which delights him, especially when his mother provides a key for it—one that she had been given as a child). The Indian comes alive in the cupboard and is later joined by a tiny cowboy—the prototype being provided by Omri's friend, Patrick. How does one provide for a proud, demanding Indian brave and an equally troublesome cowboy—especially when the traditional anatagonism breaks out between them, sparked by a typical television show of "cowboys and Indians" ("another Redskin bit the dust")?

Although Omri has more of an initial sense of responsibility than had Maria of T.H. White's *Mistress Masham's Repose,* he comes to a realization that he has too much power over a human being smaller than himself; and so both Little Bull and Boone, the cowboy, are sent back to become their own size in their own time.

Return of the Indian is a more explosive book as Omri and Patrick (who have brought their plastic toys back to life again) face the problem of Little Bull—who has returned, wounded in battle, from the wars of the Iroquois and the English against the Algonquins and the French. Little Bull is an Iroquois. Omri and Patrick finally decide to send Little Bull

5. C.S. Lewis, "On Three Ways of Writing for Children," in *Of This and Other Worlds,* ed. Walter Hooper (London: Collins, 1982), 57.

back to his own time with modern weapons. In an extension of the magic, Omri is a helpless witness to the results of this decision. Both books work because of the precision of the magic and the writer's imaginative powers, which are never out of control. The boys' efforts—and successes—in finding plastic toys to abet their scheme (even including a hospital matron to attend to the wounded) are always kept within the limitations and the cunning of ten-year-old boys. Lynne Banks also proves how an old idea—that of the inanimate coming alive, as in Pauline Clarke's *The Twelve and the Genie*—can be used with originality and the complete suspension of disbelief.

Epilogue

S tories such as *The Indian in the Cupboard* survive, and survive well, on the Nesbit tradition. Nonetheless, there is sufficient evidence to show that since the 1960's, the concept of fantasy has almost been reversed from that of the past. In earlier fantasies, once the major premise had been accepted—that children could fly (as in *Peter and Wendy*) or that people could be only six inches tall (as in *The Borrowers*)—writers made the fantasy world as real as possible. The fabulous gradually became the ordinary. When the children in *Peter and Wendy* are approaching Never-land, delighting in their flying acrobatics, Peter says to John, "Do you want an adventure now, or would you like to have your tea first?" When, in *The Hobbit,* the dwarves keep pouring into Bilbo Baggins's house, he worries about the state of his larder like any good host. When Arrietty, in *The Borrowers,* goes to bed, she fixes her candle on a pin that serves as a candleholder. Lewis Carroll's Alice—that polite, unflappable Victorian child—serves as our hold on the real world while she moves through the extravaganza of Wonderland. Therefore, no matter what the type of fantasy, neither the protagonist nor the reader felt a stranger in a strange land. Moreover, the magic was under tight control and worked logically. In Rumer Godden's *The Dolls' House,* for example, it is made very clear that there are some things the dolls cannot do for themselves. Charlotte, the spider in E.B. White's *Charlotte's Web,* may be able to talk and write, but still she dies in the way that all spiders do in the cycle of nature.

Almost conversely, most fantasists in modern times ask for the suspension of disbelief by concentrating on events and details in the real world. We know a great deal about the protagonists in their daily lives—their homes, their parents, their schools, their looks, and especially their problems. Moreover, the premises on which many modern fantasies are based are rarely magical. To hate one's stepfather so much that one becomes possessed, like Simon in Robert Westall's *The Scarecrows,* is not magic; to be so overburdened with responsibilities that one enters the past, as does Tree in Virginia Hamilton's *Sweet Whispers, Brother Rush,* is not magic; and to have evil defeated by psychic powers or to have extrasensory perception as a springboard for a plot is far from magical. In these and in many other works, it is the psychological tensions of the protagonists that create the supernatural events. Like Ida in Maurice Sendak's fantasy picture-book *Outside Over There,* the young must go "outside over there" to preserve themselves.

It is worth noting, however, that Sendak's psychological picture-book is set in an Other World, one that is complete with goblins and changelings. Lloyd Alexander, Ursula Le Guin, and Ruth Nichols also take us to other dimensions of time and space while giving us insights into the minds and problems of their heroes and heroines. With such writers, as with Sendak, magic is a natural part of the worlds they have created, and it is not dependent on a belief that strange events could happen or had happened in real life. Again almost conversely, the majority of writers who take "outside over there" to mean a supernatural experience in the real world because of emotional distress ask their readers to accept the supernatural literally, thus leaving readers with little room for maneuverability and the opportunity to use their own imaginations.

Alexander, Le Guin, and Nichols also represent the few modern fantasists who have constructed two-level fantasies—those stories that satisfy on a plot level, yet lend themselves to interpretation on another level. These writers are the heirs of George MacDonald who, in his *Princess* books, was the first to tell a fast-paced adventure story while leaving to the reader the rich experience of sensing the inner truth contained within the external events. Those writers who do create another time and setting—such as Victor Kelleher in *The Master of the Grove,* Patricia McKillip in the *Hed* trilogy, or Stephen King in *The Eyes of the Dragon*—

are content with a strong story line, simple characterization, and a semi-feudal or semi-folktale setting. Of course, much of the new fantasy of reality gives somewhat the feel of a two-level story because it is rife with symbolism, which is particularly apparent in such works as William Mayne's *A Game of Dark,* Alan Garner's *Red Shift* and *Elidor,* Penelope Farmer's *A Castle of Bone,* and many others. However, in such cases, the symbolism is integral to the action, and the various levels of meaning are combined. Such an approach in no way makes such works lesser in literary skill or in portraying various aspects of the world we inhabit; but it does make the stories more complex on a primary level and certainly different from the past.

Many modern writers appear deliberately to flout some of the traditional conventions of fantasy. Chief among such conventions is that the magic ends when the story is over. In William Mayne's *Earthfasts,* evidences of the strange happenings remain in the real world; and in Margaret Mahy's *The Haunting* and *The Changeover,* the young people will keep their witch powers as will those who have psychic abilities. Another convention has been that in the passage between two worlds, physical objects have a natural place in the real one. As late as 1965, Alan Garner, in *Elidor,* hewed to this kind of magical practicality. When Garner's four children bring four splendid and bejeweled artifacts from Elidor into Manchester, the artifacts keep their magical qualities yet become pieces of junk. How else would the children explain the objects to their parents? In the recent *The Ghosts of Austwick Manor,* the youngest child brings back a piece of marzipan from Tudor times that is sprinkled with gold leaf. The parents check every bakery in the city to find the origin of the marzipan, and when they are unsuccessful, they speak of taking the child to a psychologist. Once magic is made too real, it is destroyed. Parents and adults in general now play a much greater role in the supernatural events than they did in the past; magic is no longer seen as only the imaginings of childhood, but as a force to be reckoned with in the rational world for all ages.

Other changes are noticeable by default, as it were. Modern fantasists are not image-makers. Once presented to the mind's eye, who can forget a faun carrying an umbrella, Mary Poppins sliding *up* the bannister, or North Wind with her black hair streaming out behind her in the storm but with little Diamond snuggled safely among its strands? Such sharply etched images—the result of juxtaposition, incongruity, or sheer playfulness—have disappeared from modern fantasy, again perhaps because of an emphasis on reality that tends to limit the writers' imaginations. It is more difficult to account for a lack of memorable and quotable phrases, but the reason may be much the same as for a lack of imagery. Modern fantasy is filled with everyday conversational matter that is often highly intellectual but not applicable in other situations. Lloyd Alexander has some fun with words, and Ursula Le Guin displays profundity, but neither can match: "Bother! O blow! Hang spring-cleaning"; "Spit spot into bed!"; "SOME PIG"; or "You have to run twice as fast to stay in the same place."

Why is modern fantasy so different from that of the past? One answer may be simply that the old wellsprings have dried up. Perhaps there can be only one Narnia, one Middle-earth, one Earthsea, and one Wonderland. These lands grew out of their creators' solidly based personal beliefs; each is a vision created by a unique imagination. The making of a Secondary World, as Tolkien has pointed out, takes a special "elvish craft." Modern fantasists are far from elfin in their approach to fantasy; instead, they are realists, interested in the supernatural or attracted to it in a specific aspect. Modern fantasists sometimes copy the matter of fantasy without being concerned with its inner substance.

Other reasons for these differences may be that the new writers simply became tired of the older types of fantasy or that they felt the older conventions to be irrelevant for the modern child. In any case, like writers in other genres—realistic, historical, or science fiction—these fantasists sought to give literature for the young a "new look." The realists found a "new look" in Stendahl's "mirror" concept, that is, art reflects life as it is. Writers of historical fiction concentrated on young people caught in the web of history rather than on history's sweeps and battles and momentous events; and science fiction writers turned from an extrapolation of science and technology to its sociological effects on individuals and communities or introduced a fantastic element into a futuristic novel. However, most of them, including the fantasists, found new blood in presenting adolescents rather than children as chief characters. Because adolescents were the problems as well as the ideals of the 1960's, they quickly made their way into literature almost en masse. The result was that the concept of childhood and that of the generic child— one who stood for "Everychild"—was eroded.

However, all these reasons are probably minor ones in comparison with the overriding one of societal change. The new fantasists are as much a part of their time and its fabric as were those of the past—ranging from Charles Kingsley to Lucy Boston. Artists' visions come, at least in part, from what they see or sense around them. It may well be that the writers who now endow their protagonists with paranormal insights and strengths are compensating for a spirit of helplessness that is abroad in a world under the threat of nuclear destruction, and one in which our vaunted science and technology cannot cure or assuage the major ills of war, poverty, and disease. It is noteworthy that these powers—psychic, extrasensory, or second sight—are all vehicles of communication. In an age of ever-increasing electronic communication, the personal is still the most important and yet seemingly the most difficult to achieve. Most of the young people in these recent books suffer from some form of alienation; however, this form of malaise is not present in the few books that have child characters at their center.

Also in tune with the new social mores in recent decades has been the introduction of a love interest. Here the age of the protagonists gave many writers a chance to exercise a freedom that was certainly close to reality. Romantic love is portrayed in Robin McKinley's *The Blue Sword,* Ruth Park's *Playing Beattie Bow,* and Margaret Mahy's *The Changeover* (among many others), and sexual encounters, in Louise Lawrence's *The Earth Witch,* Robin McKinley's *The Hero and the Crown,* Ursula Synge's *Swan's Wing,* and Margaret Mahy's *The Tricksters.*

While writers' concerns and therefore their messages to their audience have changed throughout the three hundred years of children's literature, basically moving from the expression of an external morality to an internal one—personal fulfillment—there is one cause that links the present to the past. This is the theme of conservation. In novels ranging from Charles Kingsley's *The Water-Babies* to Kenneth Grahame's *The Wind in the Willows* to Alan Garner's *The Moon of Gomrath,* George Seldon's *Tucker's Countryside,* Peter Dickinson's *The Weathermonger* and more recently, Richard Adams's *Watership Down,* Diane Duane's *Deep Wizardry,* and Ruth Park's *My Sister Sif,* warnings have been issued about the destruction of the environment. In the latter two cases, in keeping with recent knowledge, attention has been focused on the pollution of our oceans rather than the land.

That the young are still interested in fantasy is beyond doubt. This interest is shown by their attendance at fantasy films, playing "Dungeons and Dragons," playing video and computer fantasy games, and reading the "Choose Your Own Fantasy" series. All of these are based on the epic or quest fantasy, even if it is watered down to almost nothing. Fantasy has also appeared in commercial, patterned series books, such as "Dark Forces" and "Twilight." Such works as Les Logan's *The Game* (1982), Bruce Coville's *Eyes of the Tarot* (1983), and Sarah Armstrong's *Blood Red Roses* (1982) are as superficial as the "Baby Harlequin" romances and have the same page-turning appeal. They were ostensibly published for teenagers but are simple enough to be read by even the reluctant child reader. In most of these books, the mind of a teenage girl is taken over by an evil spirit through her obsession with the Tarot cards, a Ouija board, or another artifact such as a mirror. Supernatural horrors break out, but the girl is saved by either a devoted boyfriend, a sister, or both. It can be presumed also that children and young people read the fantasies of their own time; publishers are not noted for pouring books into a void. Many young people are also attracted to the romantic quest and epic fantasies written and published for adults. Indeed, if only numbers of publications were to be considered, then certainly the 1980's would be fantasy's "Golden Age."

By the early 1980's, the amount of fantasy literature produced and, by extrapolation, an increase in its readership had come to the attention of some cultural historians, psychologists, and sociologists who, as reported in an article in the *New York Times Magazine*,[1] viewed the phenomenon with dismay. Said one critic:

> In a modern era shaped by science and technology, it is startling to see this fascination with mystical symbols and motifs that hark back to notions of an enchanted universe and to the hierarchical social order of the Middle Ages.

Other experts on behavior spoke of the increasing interest in fantasy as "a profound malaise" in society, as "a symptom of a profound crisis in Western thought," as a "disillusionment with science," and as a society in a state of fragmentation without a common agreement "on standards of morality or the nature of reality."

Unfortunately, the article took most of its examples from space opera movies such as "Star Wars" and from such adult fantasies as Frank Her-

1. Kathleen Agena, "The Return of Enchantment," *New York Times Magazine* 27 (Nov. 1983): 664.

bert's *God Emperor of Dune,* Doris Lessing's less than successful quintet of science fiction fantasies, and Zimmer Bradley's revisionist retelling of the Arthurian legend *The Mists of Avalon.* The article makes no distinction between fine fantasy and poor fantasy, but more seriously, it shows a misunderstanding of the nature of fantasy. Indeed, the *Times* article is filled with every misconception that has plagued the genre since Roger Ascham first raged against *La Morte d'Arthure* in the sixteenth century.

The article appeared in the same year as the English translation of Michael Ende's *The Neverending Story,* first published in Germany in 1979 as *Die Unendlich Geschichte.* The translation arrived, almost as if by magic, to refute the above charges against fantasy and even more, to praise fantasy as a healing of the soul.

On the surface, *The Neverending Story* is a traditional fantasy quest set in an imaginary land called Fantastica, but its protagonist from the real world is typical of modern fantasy. Bastian Balthazar Bux is a fat, bespectacled, unhappy ten-year-old. His mother has just died, and his father is too plunged into his own misery to give Bastian any more than token attention. Bastian steals a book from an old bookseller—a book bound in copper-colored silk with a picture on the cover of two snakes eating one another's tails—and he begins to read about a land called Fantastica that is dying of "Nothing" because no human has visited it for a long time. Then the lines of print become fluid and Bastian finds himself a character in the book he is reading. In Fantastica, he becomes a handsome prince (just as the ordinary children in the *Narnia Chronicles* become kings and queens); and, eventually, armed with his magic sword, Sikanda, he begins his quest to find a cure for a dying world. However, like the wife in the old folktale "The Fisherman and His Wife," Bastian becomes more and more arrogant and wants more and more power. As his desires in the fantasy world increase, his memory of his real world fades. At the end of the story, Bastian's worried Fantastican friends persuade him to go back, through the Water of Life and the encircled snakes (symbols of wholeness), to his own world, where he finds that his father loves him after all.

The Neverending Story is a long book (377 pages in paperback), and it has a cast of thousands. All the standard figures and creatures of faerie are in it, while from a seemingly bottomless imagination come such bizarre figures as "Shlamoofs" (butterfly-clowns), luck-dragons (which are not like ordinary dragons), rockchewers, tinies, wind giants, and a host of others. Ende's vision of the reality of unreality sparked a cult in Germany much like Tolkien's *The Lord of the Rings* in the English-speaking world, and it is easy to see why this novel can be attractive to adults. References from all types of literature abound: ranging from the serious to the trivial; from the Bible to national epics; from fairy stories and science fiction to the comics. Ende plays with topics and motifs from such sources as Wagner's "Ring" cycle, the "Tales of Hoffman," James Hilton's *Lost Horizon,* and Goethe's *Faust.* There is even a reference to an early traveler to Fantastica "who was called Schexpir or some such name."

Viewed solely as a literary effort, Ende's epic has some fairly serious flaws. Its length allows for some monotonous repetition and an excess of subplots. However, as a statement about fantasy and as a defense of the genre, it ranks with J.R.R. Tolkien's essay "On Fairy-stories." To Michael Ende, as to Tolkien, fantasy offers "recovery, escape, and consolation." Ende goes further than Tolkien in his vision of the world of the imagination dying because the rational mind refuses to exercise visitation rights. The result of such avoidance is "NOTHING." Fortunately, there have always been people such as Hoffman, Goethe, and Shakespeare who have helped in the past to keep Fantastica flourishing and healthy. As the old bookseller says to Bastian at the conclusion of the story:

> There are people who can never go to Fantastica, . . . and others who can, but who stay there forever. And there are just a few who go to Fantastica and come back. Like you. And they make both worlds well again.

Ende neither preaches escapism nor creates dangerously simplistic worlds that are drawn only in black and white. Instead, he wants to encourage his readers to incorporate fantasy and poetry into their everyday lives, to apply their wishes and dreams to reality instead of drifting off into enticing replacement worlds. A journey to Fantasia, therefore, is to be seen as an enrichment of life and a medication against the "delusion and dazzlement" of reality. There are few writers for the young, in the English-speaking world of the present, who have Michael Ende's faith in the power of fantasy and his understanding of the easy entry to it. In *The Neverending Story,* the reader is asked only to believe in a book, a story, a fiction. Ende equates fantasy with the imagination, not with the paranormal.

As with all other forms of literature, fantasy must change or else stagnate; it cannot depend only on old motifs and patterns. Many of the new writers have shown new possibilities in the genre, and, indeed, those who have not broken out of the fixed mold seem dull by comparison. Many writers have also striven hard for plausibility by an emphasis on reality. Paradoxically, this approach has often resulted in a negation of fantasy, a raising of disbelief rather than its willing suspension. Perhaps even more significantly, the modern writers who endow their young characters with supernatural powers (that is, beyond the momentary use of talismans) deprive us of a chance to deal with our own humanity. The best fantasies remind us of our humanity, not allowing us to fantasize beyond our innate capabilities, but encouraging us to use these capabilities to the utmost.

Once upon a time, "worlds within" meant the release of the imagination that could then be applied externally; now the phrase all too often means the internalization of emotional problems and an alienation from the external world.

As in real life, people can change, move on, explore, and gain new insights without losing their roots. It is to be hoped that future fantasy will not stray irrevocably from its distinct and distinctive path. It will be a sad state if modern fantasists totally reject the traditional matter of fantasy, its ancient and accepted forms, and its familiar goals—the affirmation of moral and emotional truths, the opening of the inner eye of the imagination to look beyond reality, the understanding that things are not always as they seem, and the creation of imaginary worlds and their inhabitants who, like C.S. Lewis's Puddlegum, can have faith in the midst of disaster. Such fantasies keep us close to our ancestors—to a time when there was a spirit in every river, a demon in every cave, a life force in every tree, when animals spoke to people and people spoke back. But as yet, in the present, it appears as if children will have to go to the literature of the past to partake of the enchantment of the world.

Bibliography

CHAPTER 2

Bunyan, John. *The Pilgrim's Progress.* New York: Airmont, 1968.

Dorset, Mrs. *The Peacock at Home.* London: J. Harris, 1810. o.p.

Fielding, Sarah. *The Governess; Or, Little Female Academy.* London: Oxford Univ. Pr. 1968. (A facsimile of the 1791 American edition; first pub. 1749)

Roscoe, William. *The Butterfly's Ball and the Grasshopper's Feast.* London: J. Harris, 1807. o.p.

Sherwood, Mrs. Mary. *The Rose; A Fairy Tale.* Boston: Samuel T. Armstrong, 1824. o.p.

Swift, Jonathan. *Gulliver's Travels.* Illustrated by Aldren Watson. New York: Grosset & Dunlap, 1986.

Trimmer, Sarah. *Fabulous Histories.* London: T. Longmans, 1786. (Later republished as *The History of the Robins*) o.p.

CHAPTER 3

Allingham, William. *In Fairyland.* Illustrated by Richard Doyle. London: Longmans, 1870. o.p.

Andersen, Hans Christian. *The Complete Fairy Tales and Stories.* Translated from the Danish by Erik Christian Haugaard. New York: Doubleday, 1974.

_____. *Wonderful Stories for Children.* London: Chapman and Hall, 1846. o.p.

Baum, L. Frank. *American Fairy Tales*. New York: Dover, 1978.

_____. *Dorothy and the Wizard in Oz*. New York: Dover, 1984.

_____. *The Marvellous Land of Oz*. New York: Penguin, 1985.

_____. *Ozma of Oz*. New York: Dover, 1985.

_____. *The Wonderful Wizard of Oz*. Illustrated by W.W. Denslow. New York: Morrow, 1987.

Browne, Frances. *Granny's Wonderful Chair*. Illustrated by Kenny Meadows. Harmondsworth, Middlesex: Penguin, 1985.

Carroll, Lewis [pseud.]. *Alice's Adventures in Wonderland and Through the Looking-Glass*. Illustrated by John Tenniel. London: Macmillan's Children's Bks., 1984.

_____. *Alice's Adventures Underground*. Illustrated by Martin Gardner. New York: Dover, 1965.

Cox, Palmer. *The Brownies*. New York: Dover, 1965.

De Morgan, Mary. *On a Pincushion*. London: Seeley, Jackson & Halliday, 1877. o.p.

Ewing, Juliana Horatia. *The Brownies and Other Tales*. Illustrated by George Cruikshank. London: Bell & Daldy, 1870. o.p.

_____. *Timothy's Shoes*. In *Lob Lie-by-the-Fire*. Illustrated by George Cruikshank. London: Bell & Sons, 1874. o.p.

Farrow, G.E. *The Wallypug of Why*. Illustrated by H. Furniss. London: Hutchison, 1895. o.p.

Harris, Joel Chandler. *Uncle Remus: His Songs and Sayings*. Illustrated by A.B. Frost. New York: Schocken, 1966.

Hood, Thomas, the Younger. *Petsetilla's Posy*. Illustrated by F. Barnard. London: Routledge, 1870. o.p.

Ingelow, Jean. *Mopsa the Fairy*. London: Longmans, 1869. o.p.

Kingsley, Charles. *The Water-Babies: A Fairy-Tale for a Land Baby*. Illustrated by Rosalie K. Fry. London: Dent, 1982.

Lang, Andrew. *Prince Prigio*. Illustrated by Gordon Browne. Bristol, England: J.W. Arrowsmith, 1889. o.p.

_____. *Prince Ricardo*. Illustrated by Gordon Browne. Bristol, England: J.W. Arrowsmith, 1893. o.p.

_____. *Princess Nobody*. London: Longmans, 1884. o.p.

Lear, Edward. *A Book of Nonsense*. Illustrated by the author. London: J.M. Dent, 1983.

Lemon, Mark. *Tinykin's Transformations*. Illustrated by C. Green. London: Bradbury, 1869. o.p.

MacDonald, George. *At the Back of the North Wind*. Harmondsworth, Middlesex: Penguin, 1984.

_____. *Dealings with the Fairies*. London: Strahan, 1867. o.p.

_____. *The Golden Key.* Illustrated by Maurice Sendak. New York: Farrar, 1976.

_____. *The Light Princess.* Hertfordshire, England: Lion Publishing, 1981.

_____. *The Princess and Curdie.* Harmondsworth, Middlesex: Penguin, 1970.

_____. *The Princess and the Goblin.* Harmondsworth, Middlesex: Penguin, 1984.

_____. *The Wise Woman.* Hertfordshire, England: Lion Publishing, 1981.

Molesworth, Mrs. Mary. *The Cuckoo-Clock.* Illustrated by C.E. Brock. New York: W.H. Smith, 1980.

_____. *The Tapestry Room.* Illustrated by Walter Crane. London: Macmillan, 1879. o.p.

Mulock, Dinah Marie. *The Adventures of a Brownie.* London: Sampson Low, 1872. o.p.

_____. *The Little Lame Prince.* London: Daldy, Isbister, 1875.

Paget, Francis Edward. *The Hope of the Katzekopfs.* 1844. Reprint. New York: HBJ, 1968.

Paine, Albert Bigelow. *The Arkansaw Bear.* New York: R.H. Russell, 1898. o.p.

Parry, Edward A. *Butterscotia.* Illustrated by A. Macgregor. London: D. Nutt, 1896. o.p.

Pyle, Howard. *Pepper and Salt.* Illustrated by the author. New York: Harper, Junior Books, 1886. o.p.

_____. *The Wonder Clock.* Illustrated by the author. London: Dover, 1966.

Ruskin, John. *The King of the Golden River.* London: Dover, 1975.

Stockton, Frank. *The Casting Away of Mrs. Lecks and Mrs. Aleshine.* New York: The Century Co., 1886. o.p.

_____. *The Griffin and the Minor Canon.* Illustrated by Maurice Sendak. New York: Harper, Junior Books, 1986.

_____. *Ting A Ling.* Illustrated by E.B. Bensell. New York:: Hurd and Houghton, 1870. o.p.

Thackeray, William Makepeace. *The Rose and the Ring.* London: Smith, Elder & Co., 1855. o.p.

Wilde, Oscar. *The Happy Prince and Other Tales.* Harmondsworth, Middlesex: Penguin, 1985.

CHAPTER 4

Barrie, Sir James. *Peter Pan: The Complete Book.* Illustrated by Susan Hudson. New York: Tundra Books, 1988.

_____. *Peter Pan in Kensington Gardens*. Illustrated by Arthur Rackham. London: Hodder and Stoughton Ltd., 1983.

Bianco, Margery Williams. *The Velveteen Rabbit*. Illustrated by William Nicholson. London: Heinemann, 1970.

Burgess, Thornton W. *Old Mother West Wind*. Illustrated by Harrison Cady. Boston: Little, 1968.

De la Mare, Walter. *The Three Royal Monkeys*. Illustrated by Mildred E. Eldridge. London: Faber, 1929. (First pub. as *The Three Mullah Mulgars*, 1910) o.p.

Grahame, Kenneth. *The Wind in the Willows*. Illustrated by E.H. Shepard. London: Methuen, 1908.

Hudson, W.H. *A Little Boy Lost*. Illustrated by A.O. M'Cormick. London: Duckworth, 1905. o.p.

Jefferies, Richard. *Wood Magic*. London: Rex Collings, 1969.

Kipling, Rudyard. *The Jungle Book*. Illustrated by M. Wilson. London: Macmillan's Children's Bks., 1983.

_____. *Just So Stories*. London: Macmillan Education Ltd., 1984.

_____. *Puck of Pook's Hill*. London: Macmillan, 1983.

_____. *Rewards and Fairies*. London: Macmillan, 1983.

_____. *The Second Jungle Book*. London: Macmillan Children's Bks., 1984.

Lindsay, Norman. *The Magic Pudding*. Illustrated by the author. Sydney, Angus & Robertson, 1984.

Lofting, Hugh. *Doctor Dolittle in the Moon*. Illustrated by the author. Harmondsworth, Middlesex: Penguin, 1970.

_____. *The Story of Doctor Dolittle*. Illustrated by the author. Harmondsworth, Middlesex: Penguin, 1970.

_____. *The Voyages of Doctor Dolittle*. Illustrated by the author. London: Cape, 1966.

Milne, A.A. *The House at Pooh Corner*. Illustrated by E.H. Shepard. London: Methuen's Children's Bks., 1974.

_____. *Once on a Time*. Illustrated by Susan Pearl. London: Hodder & Stoughton, 1917. o.p.

_____. *Winnie-the-Pooh*. Illustrated by E.H. Shepard. London: Methuen's Children's Bks., 1973.

Nesbit, Edith. *The Complete Book of Dragons*. New York: Dell, 1986. (First pub. as *A Book of Dragons*, 1900)

_____. *The Enchanted Castle*. Harmondsworth, Essex: Penguin, 1979.

_____. *Five Children and It*. Illustrated by H.R. Millar. Harmondsworth, Middlesex: Penguin, 1984.

_____. *Five of Us—and Madeline*. Illustrated by Peter Freeman. London: Ernest Benn, 1958. o.p.

_____. *Harding's Luck*. Illustrated by H.R. Millar. London: Hodder & Stoughton, 1909. o.p.

_____. *The House of Arden*. Illustrated by Clarke Hutton. New York: Viking-Penguin, 1986.

_____. *The Magic City*. Illustrated by H.R. Millar. London: Ernest Benn, 1910. o.p.

_____. *Nine Unlikely Tales*. Illustrated by H.R. Millar and Claude A. Shepperson. London: Ernest Benn, 1901. o.p.

_____. *The Phoenix and the Carpet*. Illustrated by H.R. Millar. Harmondsworth, Middlesex: Penguin, 1984.

_____. *The Story of the Amulet*. Illustrated by H.R. Millar. Harmondsworth, Middlesex: Penguin, 1971.

_____. *Wet Magic*. Illustrated by H.R. Millar. London: Ernest Benn, 1913. o.p.

Potter, Beatrix. *The Roly-Poly Pudding*. London: Frederick Warne, 1908.

_____. *The Tailor of Gloucester*. London: Frederick Warne, 1902.

_____. *The Tale of Ginger and Pickles*. London: Frederick Warne, 1909.

_____. *The Tale of Jemima Puddle-Duck*. London: Frederick Warne, 1908.

_____. *The Tale of Mr. Tod*. London: Frederick Warne, 1912.

_____. *The Tale of Mrs. Tiggy-Winkle*. London: Frederick Warne, 1905.

_____. *The Tale of Peter Rabbit*. London: Frederick Warne, 1902.

_____. *The Tale of Squirrel Nutkin*. London: Frederick Warne, 1903.

_____. *The Tale of Tom Kitten*. London: Frederick Warne, 1907.

_____. *The Tale of Two Bad Mice*. London: Frederick Warne, 1904.

Stewart, Mary. *The Way to Wonderland*. Illustrated by Jessie Wilcox Smith. London: Hodder & Stoughton, 1920. o.p.

Tarn, W.W. *The Treasure of the Isle of Mist*. Illustrated by Margery Gill. London: Oxford Univ. Pr., 1919. o.p.

CHAPTER 5

Brooks, Walter R. *Freddy and the Perilous Adventure*. Illustrated by Leslie Morrill and Kurt Wiese. New York: Knopf, 1986.

_____. *Freddy Goes Camping*. Illustrated by Kurt Wiese. New York: Knopf, 1986.

_____. *Freddy Goes to Florida*. Illustrated by Leslie Morrill and Kurt Wiese. New York: Dell, 1980. (First pub. as *To and Again*, 1927)

_____. *Freddy the Detective*. Illustrated by Leslie Morrill and Kurt Wiese. New York: Knopf, 1979.

————. *Freddy the Pilot.* Illustrated by Leslie Morrill and Kurt Wiese. New York: Knopf, 1986.

————. *Freddy the Politician.* Illustrated by Kurt Wiese. New York: Knopf, 1986.

————. *Wiggins for President.* Illustrated by Kurt Wiese. New York: Knopf, 1939.

Buchan, John. *The Magic Walking Stick.* Illustrated by Morton Sale. Edinburgh, England: Canongate, 1985.

Coatsworth, Elizabeth. *The Cat Who Went to Heaven.* Illustrated by Lynd Ward. New York: Macmillan, 1967.

De la Mare, Walter. *Animal Stories.* London: Faber, 1939. o.p.

————. *Broomsticks and Other Tales.* London: Constable, 1925. o.p.

————. *Collected Stories for Children.* Illustrated by Robin Jacques. London: Faber, 1947. o.p.

————. *The Magic Jacket and Other Stories.* Illustrated by Irene Hawkins. London: Faber, 1943. o.p.

————. *Mr. Bumps and His Monkey.* Illustrated by Dorothy Lathrop. Chicago: J.C. Winston, 1942.

————. *Told Again.* Illustrated by A.H. Watson. Oxford: Basil Blackwell, 1927.

Farjeon, Eleanor. *The Little Bookroom.* Illustrated by Edward Ardizzone. London: Oxford Univ. Pr., 1979.

————. *Martin Pippin in the Apple Orchard.* Illustrated by Richard Kennedy. London: W. Collins, 1921. o.p.

————. *Martin Pippin in the Daisy-Field.* Illustrated by Isobel and John Morton-Sale. London: Michael Joseph, 1937. o.p.

Field, Rachel. *Hitty; Her First Hundred Years.* Illustrated by Dorothy Lathrop. New York: Macmillan, 1969.

Gibson, Katherine. *Cinders.* Illustrated by Vera Brock. New York: Longmans, Green, 1939. o.p.

Hatch, Richard. *The Curious Lobster.* Illustrated by Marion Freeman Wakeman. New York: HBJ, 1937. o.p.

Housman, Laurence. *The Field of Clover.* Illustrated by Clemance Housman. New York: Dover, 1969.

————. *Moonshine & Clover.* London: Cape, 1922. o.p.

————. *What-O-Clock Tales.* Illustrated by J.R. Monsell. Oxford: Basil Blackwood, 1932. o.p.

Hughes, Richard. *Don't Blame Me.* Illustrated by Fritz Eichenberg. London: Chatto & Windus, 1940. o.p.

————. *The Spider's Palace and Other Stories.* Ilustrated by George Charlton. London: Chatto & Windus, 1931. o.p.

Joy Street. Oxford: Basil Blackwell, 1923–38. o.p.

Lawson, Robert. *Ben and Me.* Illustrated by the author. Boston: Little, 1939.

Lewis, Hilda. *The Ship That Flew.* London: Oxford Univ. Pr., 1939. o.p.

Lynch, Patricia. *The Turf-Cutter's Donkey.* Port Laoise, Co. Laoighis, I.R. Dolmen Press, 1984.

———. *The Turf-Cutter's Donkey Goes Visiting.* Illustrated by George Altendorf. London: Dent, 1935. o.p.

Masefield, John. *The Box of Delights; or, When the Wolves Were Running.* Illustrated by F. Jacques. London: Heinemann, 1984.

———. *The Midnight Folk.* London: Collins, 1984.

Milne, A.A. *The House at Pooh Corner.* Illustrated by E.H. Shepard. London: Methuen Children's Bks., 1974.

Parrish, Anne. *Floating Island.* Illustrated by the author. New York: Harper & Brothers, 1930. o.p.

Sandburg, Carl. *Potato Face.* New York: HBJ, 1930. o.p.

———. *Rootabaga Pigeons.* Illustrated by Maude and Miska Petersham. New York: HBJ, 1974.

———. *Rootabaga Stories.* Illustrated by Maude and Miska Petersham. New York: HBJ, 1974.

Seredy, Kate. *The White Stag.* Illustrated by Helen Sewell. New York: Viking, 1937.

Tolkien, J.R.R. *The Hobbit.* Illustrated by Michael Hague. London: Allen & Unwin, 1984.

Travers, Pamela. *Mary Poppins.* Illustrated by Mary Shepard. London: William Collins, 1982.

———. *Mary Poppins Comes Back.* Illustrated by Mary Shepard. London: William Collins, 1958.

———. *Mary Poppins in Cherry Tree Lane.* Illustrated by Mary Shepard. New York: Delacorte, 1982.

———. *Mary Poppins in the Park.* Illustrated by Mary Shepard. New York: HBJ, 1976.

———. *Mary Poppins Opens the Door.* Illustrated by Mary Shepard and Agnes Sims. New York: HBJ, 1982.

Uttley, Alison. *Mustard, Pepper, and Salt.* Illustrated by Gwen Raverat. London: Faber, 1938. o.p.

———. *The Squirrel, the Hare, and the Little Gray Rabbit.* Illustrated by M. Tempest. London: Heinemann, 1929. o.p.

———. *A Traveller in Time.* Harmondsworth, Middlesex: Penguin, 1977.

CHAPTER 6

Bailey, Carolyn Sherwin. *Miss Hickory.* Illustrated by Ruth Gannett. New York: Viking, 1946.

Dickinson, William Croft. *Borrobil.* London: Cape, 1944. o.p.

Du Bois, William Pene. *Peter Graves.* Illustrated by the author. New York: Viking, 1950. o.p.

_____. *The Twenty-One Balloons.* Illustrated by the author. New York: Viking, 1947.

Field, Rachel. Hitty: *Her First 100 Years.* New York: Macmillan, 1969.

Gannett, Ruth. *My Father's Dragon.* Illustrated by Ruth C. Gannett. New York: Random, 1986.

Godden, Rumer. *The Dolls' House.* Illustrated by Joanna Jamieson. Harmondsworth, Middlesex: Penguin, 1971.

_____. *Home Is the Sailor.* Illustrated by Jean Primrose. London: Macmillan, 1964.

_____. *Impunity Jane.* In *Four Dolls.* Illustrated by Pauline Baynes. London: Macmillan's Children's Bks., 1983.

_____. *Mouse House.* Illustrated by Adrienne Adams. New York: Viking, 1957. o.p.

_____. *The Mousewife.* Illustrated by H. Holder. London: Macmillan, 1983.

Goudge, Elizabeth. *The Little White Horse.* New York: Avon, 1985.

_____. *Smoky House.* Illustrated by C. Walter Hodges. London: Duckworth, 1940.

Lawson, Robert. *Rabbit Hill.* Illustrated by the author. New York: Viking, 1944.

Linklater, Eric. *The Pirates in the Deep Green Sea.* Illustrated by William Reeves. London: Macmillan, 1949. o.p.

_____. *The Wind on the Moon.* Edinburgh, England: Canongate, 1986.

Nichols, Beverley. *The Mountain of Magic.* London: Armada, 1975.

_____. *The Stream That Stood Still.* London: Armada, 1975.

_____. *The Tree That Sat Down.* London: Armada, 1975.

Sauer, Julia. *Fog Magic.* Illustrated by Lynd Ward. New York: Penguin, 1986.

Thurber, James. *The Great Quillow.* Illustrated by Doris Lee. New York: HBJ, 1975.

_____. *The White Deer.* Illustrated by the author and Don Freeman. New York: HBJ, 1968.

Watkins-Pitchford, Denys [B.B., pseud.]. *The Little Grey Men.* Illustrated by the author. London: Methuen Children's Bks., 1978.

White, E.B. *Stuart Little.* Illustrated by Garth Williams. New York: Harper, Junior Books, 1945.

White, T.H. *The Ill-Made Knight.* London: Collins, 1941. o.p.

_____. *Mistress Masham's Repose.* Illustrated by Fritz Eichenberg. New York: Putnam, 1946. o.p.

_____. *The Once and Future King.* London: Collins, 1977.

Wilkins, Vaughan. *After Bath.* Illustrated by Audrey Pilkington. London: Cape, 1945. o.p.

CHAPTER 7

Bond, Michael. *A Bear Called Paddington.* London: Collins, 1958.

_____. *More About Paddington.* London: Collins, 1959.

Boston, Lucy. *The Children of Green Knowe.* Illustrated by Peter Boston. Harmondsworth, Middlesex: Penguin, 1975.

_____. *The Chimneys of Green Knowe.* Illustrated by Peter Boston. Harmondsworth, Middlesex: Penguin, 1976.

_____. *An Enemy at Green Knowe.* Illustrated by Peter Boston. Harmondsworth, Middlesex: Penguin, 1977.

_____. *The River at Green Knowe.* Illustrated by Peter Boston. Harmondsworth, Middlesex: Penguin, 1976.

_____. *The Stones of Green Knowe.* Illustrated by Peter Boston. Harmondsworth, Middlesex: Penguin, 1979.

_____. *A Stranger at Green Knowe.* Illustrated by Peter Boston. Harmondsworth, Middlesex: Penguin, 1977.

_____. *Treasure of Green Knowe.* Illustrated by Peter Boston. San Diego, Calif.: HBJ, 1978. (First pub. 1958 as *The Chimneys of Green Knowe*).

Briggs, Katharine. *Hobberdy Dick.* London: Kestrel Books, 1978.

Clark, Catherine Anthony. *The Diamond Feather.* Illustrated by Clare Bice. Toronto: Macmillan, 1962. o.p.

_____. *The Golden Pine Cone.* Illustrated by Clare Bice. Toronto: Macmillan, 1950. o.p.

_____. *The Hunter and the Medicine Man.* Illustrated by Clare Bice. Toronto: Macmillan, 1966. o.p.

_____. *The One-Winged Dragon.* Illustrated by Clare Bice. Toronto: Macmillan, 1955. o.p.

_____. *The Silver Man.* Illustrated by Clare Bice. Toronto: Macmillan, 1958. o.p.

_____. *The Sun Horse.* Illustrated by Clare Bice. Toronto: Macmillan, 1951. o.p.

Eager, Edward. *Half Magic.* Illustrated by M.M. Bodacker. San Diego, Calif.: HBJ, 1985.

_____. *Seven-Day Magic.* San Diego, Calif.: HBJ, 1985.

Kendall, Carol. *The Gammage Cup.* Illustrated by Erik Blegvad. San Diego, Calif.: HBJ, 1986. (First pub. 1959 as *The Minnipins*)

Lewis, C.S. *The Horse and His Boy*. Illustrated by Pauline Baynes. London: Collins, 1980.

———. *The Last Battle*. Illustrated by Pauline Baynes. London: Collins, 1980.

———. *The Lion, The Witch, and The Wardrobe*. Illustrated by Pauline Baynes. London: Collins, 1983.

———. *The Magician's Nephew*. Illustrated by Pauline Baynes. London: Collins, 1980.

———. *Prince Caspian*. Illustrated by Pauline Baynes. London: Collins, 1980.

———. *The Silver Chair*. Illustrated by Pauline Baynes. London: Collins, 1980.

———. *The Vogage of the Dawn Treader*. Illustrated by Pauline Baynes. London: Colllins, 1980.

Norton, Mary. *Bonfires and Broomsticks*. Illustrated by Mary Adshead. London: Dent, 1946. o.p.

———. *The Borrowers*. London: Dent, 1975.

———. *The Borrowers Afield*. London: Dent, 1975.

———. *The Borrowers Afloat*. London: Dent, 1975.

———. *The Borrowers Aloft*. London: Dent, 1975.

———. *The Borrowers Avenged*. Harmondsworth, Middlesex: Penguin, 1983.

———. *Complete Borrowers Stories*. Harmondsworth, Middlesex: Penguin, 1983.

———. *The Magic Bedknob*. Illustrated by Joan Kiddell-Monroe. London: Dent, 1945. o.p.

Pearce, Philippa. *Tom's Midnight Garden*. London: Heinemann Educational Bks., 1979.

Sharp, Margery. *Miss Bianca*. Illustrated by Garth Williams. New York: Dell, 1974.

———. *Miss Bianca and the Bridesmaid*. Illustrated by Eric Blegvad. Boston: Little, 1972. o.p.

———. *Miss Bianca in the Antarctic*. Illustrated by Eric Blegvad. Boston: Little, 1971. o.p.

———. *Miss Bianca in the Orient*. Illustrated by Garth Williams. New York: Dell, 1978.

———. *Miss Bianca in the Salt Mines*. Illustrated by Garth Williams. New York: Dell, 1978.

———. *The Rescuers*. Illustrated by Garth Williams. Boston: Little, 1959. o.p.

Sleigh, Barbara. *Carbonel*. Illustrated by V.H. Drummond. London: Kestrel Books, 1975.

_____. *Carbonel and Calidor.* Illustrated by Charles Front. Harmondsworth, Middlesex: Penguin, 1980.

Tolkien, J.R.R. *The Lord of the Rings.* London: Unwin Paperbacks, 1983.

White, E.B. *Charlotte's Web.* Illustrated by Garth Williams. New York: Harper, Junior Books, 1952.

_____. *The Trumpet of the Swan.* Illustrated by Edward Frascino. New York: Harper, Junior Books, 1973.

CHAPTER 8

Aiken, Joan. *Black Hearts in Battersea.* Illustrated by Pat Marriott. Harmondsworth, Middlesex: Penguin, 1968.

_____. *The Cuckoo Tree.* Harmondsworth, Middlesex: Penguin, 1973.

_____. *Night Birds on Nantucket.* Illustrated by Pat Marriott. London: Cape, 1966.

_____. *The Stolen Lake.* Harmondsworth, Middlesex: Penguin, 1983.

_____. *The Whispering Mountains.* Harmondsworth, Middlesex: Penguin, 1970.

_____. *The Wolves of Willoughby Chase.* Illustrated by Pat Marriott. London: Puffin, 1971.

Alexander, Lloyd. *The Black Cauldron.* New York: Dell, 1969.

_____. *The Castle of Lyr.* New York: Dell, 1980.

_____. *Coll and His White Pig.* New York: Holt, 1965. o.p.

_____. *The High King.* New York: Dell, 1980.

_____. *Taran Wanderer.* New York: Dell, 1980.

Clarke, Pauline. *The Twelve and the Genii.* Illustrated by Cecil Leslie. London: Bodley Head, 1985.

Cresswell, Helen. *The Night-Watchmen.* Illustrated by Gareth Floyd. Harmondsworth, Middlesex: Penguin, 1976.

_____. *The Piemakers.* Harmondsworth, Middlesex: Penguin, 1976.

Dahl, Roald. *Charlie and the Chocolate Factory.* Illustrated by Joseph Schindelman. New York: Knopf, 1964.

_____. *James and the Giant Peach.* Illustrated by Nancy Ekholm Burkert. New York: Knopf, 1961.

Dickinson, Peter. *The Changes Trilogy.* Harmondsworth, Essex: Puffin, 1985.

_____. *The Devil's Children.* Illustrated by Robert Hales. Harmondsworth, Middlesex: Penguin, 1970.

_____. *Heartsease.* Illustrated by Robert Hales. Harmondsworth, Middlesex: Penguin, 1971.

_____. *The Weathermonger*. London: Victor Gollancz, 1984.

Farmer, Penelope. *Charlotte Sometimes*. Illustrated by Chris Connor. London: Bodley Head, 1985.

_____. *Emma in Winter*. London: Chatto & Windus, 1966. o.p.

_____. *The Magic Stone*. Illustrated by John Kaufmann. New York: Harcourt, Brace, & World, 1964. o.p.

_____. *The Summer Birds*. Illustrated by James J. Spanfeller. London: Bodley Head, 1985.

Garner, Alan. *Elidor*. London: Macmillan Education, 1982.

_____. *The Moon of Gomrath*. London: Collins, 1972.

_____. *The Owl Service*. London: Macmillan Education, 1982.

_____. *The Weirdstone of Brisingamen*. London: Collins, 1971.

Harris, Rosemary. *The Bright and Morning Star*. London: Faber, 1972.

_____. *The Moon in the Cloud*. London: Faber, 1968. o.p.

_____. *The Shadow on the Sun*. London: Faber, 1970. o.p.

Hoban, Russell. *The Mouse and His Child*. Illustrated by Lillian Hoban. New York: Avon, 1986.

Jarrell, Randall. *The Animal Family*. Illustrated by Maurice Sendak. New York: Knopf, 1987.

_____. *The Bat-Poet*. Illustrated by Maurice Sendak. New York: Macmillan, 1964.

_____. *Fly by Night*. Illustrated by Maurice Sendak. New York: Farrar, 1976.

Juster, Norton. *The Phantom Tollbooth*. New York: Random, 1961.

Le Guin, Ursula. *The Farthest Shore*. Illustrated by Gail Garraty. New York: Atheneum, 1972.

_____. *The Tombs of Atuan*. Illustrated by Gail Garraty. New York: Atheneum, 1971.

_____. *A Wizard of Earthsea*. Illustrated by Ruth Robbins. Berkeley, Calif.: Parnassus, 1968.

L'Engle, Madeleine. *A Swiftly Tilting Planet*. New York: Farrar, 1978.

_____. *A Wind in the Door*. New York: Farrar, 1973.

_____. *A Wrinkle in Time*. New York: Dell, 1986.

Mayne, William. *Earthfasts*. London: Hamish Hamilton, 1966. o.p.

Moon, Sheila. *Knee-Deep in Thunder*. Illustrated by Peter Parnall. San Francisco, Calif.: Guild for Psychological Studies, 1986.

Selden, George. *The Cricket in Times Square*. Illustrated by Garth Williams. New York: Farrar, 1960.

_____. *Tucker's Countryside*. Illustrated by Garth Williams. New York: Farrar, 1969.

Sendak, Maurice. *Higglety-Pigglety Pop*. Illustrated by the author. New York: Harper, Junior Books, 1967.

CHAPTER 9

Adams, Richard. *The Plague Dogs*. Harmondsworth, Middlesex: Penguin, 1978.

————. *Watership Down*. Harmondsworth, Middlesex: Penguin, 1983.

Babbitt, Natalie. *Tuck Everlasting*. New York: Farrar, 1975.

Bond, Nancy. *A String in the Harp*. New York: Atheneum, 1976.

Cameron, Eleanor. *The Court of the Stone Children*. New York: Dutton, 1973.

Chant, Joy. *Red Moon and Black Mountain*. London: Unwin Paperbacks, 1982.

Cooper, Susan. *The Dark Is Rising*. Illustrated by Alan Cober. New York: Atheneum, 1976.

————. *The Dark Is Rising*. Boxed Set. New York: Collier Bks., 1986. (This set does not include *Over Sea, Under Stone*.)

————. *Greenwitch*. New York: Macmillan, 1986.

————. *The Grey King*. New York: Macmillan, 1986.

————. *Over Sea, Under Stone*. Illustrated by Margery Gill. San Diego, Calif.: HBJ, 1979.

————. *Silver on the Tree*. New York: Macmillan, 1986.

Dann, Colin. *The Animals of Farthing Wood*. Illustrated by Josephine Tettmar. London: Pan Books, 1980.

Donovon, John. *Family*. New York: Harper, 1976. o.p.

Farmer, Penelope. *A Castle of Bone*. Harmondsworth, Middlesex: Penguin, 1979.

————. *Year King*. London: Bodley Head, 1984.

Garfield, Leon. *The Ghost Downstairs*. Illustrated by Anthony Maitland. Harmondsworth, Middlesex: Penguin, 1975.

————. *Mr. Corbett's Ghost & Other Stories*. Illustrated by Anthony Maitland. London: Kestrel Books, 1982.

Garner, Alan. *Red Shift*. London: Collins, 1985.

Hamilton, Virginia. *Dustland*. New York: Greenwillow, 1980.

————. *The Gathering*. New York: Greenwillow. 1981.

————. *Justice and Her Brothers*. New York: Greenwillow, 1978.

Hunter, Mollie. *The Bodach*. Illustrated by Gareth Floyd. London: Blackie, 1970. o.p.

————. *The Haunted Mountain*. London: Armada, 1974.

————. *The Kelpie's Pearls*. Illustrated by Charles Keeping. London: Magnet Books, 1984.

————. *A Stranger Came Ashore*. London: Collins, 1983.

————. *Thomas and the Warlock*. Illustrated by Charles Keeping. London: Blackie, 1967. o.p.

_____. *The Wicked One*. London: Magnet Books, 1985.

Lively, Penelope. *Astercote*. London: Pan Books, 1973.

_____. *The Driftaway*. Harmondsworth, Middlesex: Penguin, 1985.

_____. *The Ghost of Thomas Kempe*. Illustrated by Antony Maitland. Bath, England: Chivers Press, 1986.

_____. *The House in Norham Gardens*. London: Heinemann, 1974.

_____. *The Revenge of Samuel Stokes*. Harmondsworth, Middlesex: Penguin, 1983.

_____. *A Stitch in Time*. Harmondsworth, Middlesex: Penguin, 1986.

_____. *The Whispering Knights*. London: Heinemann, 1971.

_____. *The Wild Hunt of Hagworthy*. Harmondsworth, Middlesex: Penguin, 1984.

McCaffrey, Anne. *Dragondrums*. Illustrated by Fred Marcellino. New York: Atheneum, 1979.

_____. *Dragonsinger*. New York: Atheneum, 1977.

_____. *Dragonsong*. New York: Atheneum, 1976.

McKillip, Patricia. *The Forgotten Beasts of Eld*. New York: Atheneum, 1974.

_____. *Harpist in the Wind*. New York: Atheneum, 1979.

_____. *Heir of Sea and Fire*. New York: Atheneum, 1977.

_____. *The Riddle-Master of Hed*. New York: Atheneum, 1976.

Mayne, William. *A Game of Dark*. London: H. Hamilton, 1971.

_____. *IT*. London: H. Hamilton, 1977. o.p.

_____. *A Year and a Day*. Illustrated by Krystyna. London: H. Hamilton, 1976.

Mazer, Norma Fox. *Saturday, the Twelfth of October*. New York: Dell, 1986.

Nichols, Ruth. *The Marrow of the World*. Illustrated by Trina Schart Hyman. Toronto: Macmillan, 1972. o.p.

_____. *A Walk Out of the World*. Illustrated by Trina Schart Hyman. New York: Ace Books, 1986.

O'Brien, Robert C. *Mrs. Frisby and the Rats of NIMH*. Illustrated by Zena Bernstein. New York: Macmillan, 1986.

Peyton, K.M. *A Pattern of Roses*. London: Oxford Univ. Pr., 1984.

Walsh, Jill Paton. *A Chance Child*. Harmondsworth, Middlesex: Penguin, 1985.

Westall, Robert. *The Devil on the Road*. Harmondsworth, Middlesex: Penguin, 1981.

_____. *The Watch House*. Aylesbury, Bucks.: J. Goodchild, 1984.

_____. *The Wind Eye*. Aylesbury, Bucks.: J. Goodchild, 1986.

Wrightson, Patricia. *The Dark Bright Water*. Harmondsworth, Middlesex: Penguin, 1983.

_____. *Down to Earth*. Harmondsworth, Middlesex: Penguin, 1973.

_____. *The Ice Is Coming*. London: Hutchinson, 1977.

_____. *Journey Behind the Wind*. New York: Ballantine, 1986.

_____. *The Nargun and the Stars*. London: Hutchinson, 1974.

_____. *An Older Kind of Magic*. Illustrated by Noela Young. London: Hutchinson, 1972.

CHAPTER 10

Aiken, Joan. *The Shadow Guests*. Harmondsworth, Middlesex: Penguin, 1982.

Armstrong, Sarah. *Blood Red Roses*. New York: Dell, 1982.

Banks, Lynne Reid. *The Indian in the Cupboard*. London: Dent, 1980.

_____. *Return of the Indian*. Illustrated by William Geldart. London: Dent, 1986.

Cassedy, Sylvia. *Behind the Attic Wall*. New York: Crowell, 1983.

Cooper, Susan. *Seaward*. New York: Macmillan, 1983.

Coville, Bruce. *Eyes of the Tarot*. New York: Bantam, 1983.

Curry, Jane Louise. *Shadow Dancers*. New York: Macmillan, 1983.

_____. *The Wolves of Aam*. New York: Atheneum, 1981. o.p.

Dank, Gloria. *The Forest of App*. New York: Greenwillow, 1983.

Duane, Diane. *Deep Wizardry*. New York: Delacorte, 1985.

_____. *So You Want to Be a Wizard*. New York: Delacorte, 1983.

Eckert, Allan W. *The Dark Green Tunnel*. Illustrated by David Wiesner. Boston: Little, 1984.

Ende, Michael. *The Neverending Story*. Translated by Ralph Manheim. Illustrated by Roswitha Quadflieg. New York: Doubleday, 1983.

Fisher, Paul. *Mont Cant Gold*. New York: Atheneum, 1981.

Gordon, John. *The Edge of the World*. Ipswich, Suffolk: Patrick Hardy, 1983.

Hamilton, Virginia. *The Magical Adventures of Pretty Pearl*. New York: Harper, 1983.

_____. *Sweet Whispers, Brother Rush*. New York: Putnam, 1982.

Hanlon, Emily. *Circle Home*. New York: Bradbury, 1981.

Harris, Geraldine. *Children of the Wind*. New York: Greenwillow, Seven Citadels, 1982.

_____. *The Dead Kingdom*. New York: Greenwillow, Seven Citadels, 1983.

_____. *Prince of the Godborn*. New York: Greenwillow, Seven Citadels, 1982.

_____. *The Seventh Gate*. New York: Greenwillow, Seven Citadels, 1984.

Horowitz, Anthony. *The Devil's Door-bell.* Cambridge, England: P. Hardy, 1983.

―――. *The Night of the Scorpion.* Cambridge, England: P. Hardy, 1985.

―――. *The Silver Citadel.* London: Methuen's Children's Bks., 1987.

Hurmence, Belinda. *A Girl Called Boy.* New York: Houghton, 1982.

Johnson, Annabel and Edgar. *Prisoner of Psi.* New York: Macmillan, 1985.

Jones, Diana Wynne. *Charmed Life.* Harmondsworth, Middlesex: Penguin, 1979.

―――. *Howl's Moving Castle.* London: Methuen's Children's Bks., 1986.

―――. *The Magicians of Caprona.* London: Macmillan, 1980.

―――. *The Time of the Ghost.* London: Macmillan, 1981.

Katz, Welwyn. *Witchery Hill.* Toronto: Groundwood, 1984.

Kelleher, Victor. *Forbidden Paths of Thual.* Illustrated by Antony Maitland. Harmondsworth, Middlesex: Penguin, 1983.

―――. *Master of the Grove.* Harmondsworth, Middlesex: Penguin, 1983.

Kennedy, Richard. *Amy's Eyes.* Illustrated by Richard Egielski. New York: Harper, 1985.

King, Stephen. *The Eyes of the Dragon.* Illustrated by David Palladini. New York: Viking-Penguin, 1987.

Lawrence, Louise. *The Earth Witch.* London: Collins, 1982.

Le Guin, Ursula. *The Beginning Place.* New York: Harper, 1980.

Little, Patrick. *A Court for Owls.* London: Macmillan, 1981. o.p.

―――. *The Hawthorne Tree.* London: Macmillan, 1980.

Logan, Les. *The Game.* New York: Bantam, 1986.

Lunn, Janet. *The Root Cellar.* Toronto: Lester & Orpen Dennys, 1981.

―――. *Shadow in Hawthorn Bay.* Toronto: Lester & Orpen Dennys, 1986.

MacDonald, Reby E. *The Ghosts of Austwick Manor.* New York: Atheneum, 1983. o.p.

McKinley, Robin. *The Blue Sword.* New York: Greenwillow, 1982.

―――. *The Hero and the Crown.* New York: Greenwillow, 1985.

Maguire, Gregory. *The Dream Stealer.* New York: Harper & Row, 1983.

Mahy, Margaret. *The Changeover.* London: Dent, 1984.

―――. *The Haunting.* London: Dent, 1982.

―――. *The Tricksters.* New York: Macmillan, 1987.

Mayhar, Ardath. *Runes of the Lyre.* New York: Atheneum, 1982. o.p.

―――. *Soul Singer of Tyrnos.* New York: Atheneum, 1981. o.p.

Naylor, Phyllis. *Footprints at the Window.* New York: Atheneum, 1981.

O'Shea, Pat. *The Hounds of the Morrigan.* London: Oxford Univ. Pr., 1985.

Park, Ruth. *My Sister Sif.* Victoria, Australia: Viking Kestrel, 1986.

―――. *Playing Beattie Bow.* Harmondsworth, Middlesex: Penguin, 1982.

Pearson, Kit. *A Handful of Time.* Toronto: Viking Kestrel, 1987.

Phipson, Joan. *The Watcher in the Garden*. Harmondsworth, Middlesex: Penguin, 1984.

Pierce, Meredith. *The Dark Angel*. London: Collins, 1984.

_____. *A Gathering of Gargoyles*. Boston: Little, 1984.

Sleator, William. *Fingers*. New York: Macmillan, 1983.

_____. *The Green Futures of Tycho*. New York: Dutton, 1981.

_____. *Into the Dream*. Illustrated by Ruth Sanderson. New York: Dutton, 1979.

Springer, Nancy. *The Sable Moon*. New York: Pocket Bks., 1986.

_____. *The Silver Sun*. New York: Pocket Bks., 1983.

_____. *The White Hart*. New York: Pocket Bks., 1979.

Storr, Catherine. *The Castle Boy*. London: Faber, 1983.

Synge, Ursula. *Swan's Wing*. London: Bodley Head, 1981. o.p.

Taylor, Cora. *Julie*. Saskatchewan, Canada: Western Producer Prairie Books, 1985.

Vinge, Joan. *Psion*. New York: Delacorte, 1982.

Walker, Irma. *Inherit the Earth*. New York: Atheneum, 1981.

Westall, Robert. *The Scarecrows*. London: Bodley Head, 1984.

Wright, Betty R. *The Dollhouse Murders*. New York: Holiday, 1983.

Wrightson, Patricia. *A Little Fear*. Harmondsworth, Middlesex: Penguin, 1985.

Yolen, Jane. *Dragon's Blood*. New York: Delacorte, 1982.

Index

Sheila Egoff is professor emeritus in the School of Library, Archival, and Informational Studies at the University of British Columbia in Vancouver. Earlier in her career, Egoff worked as a children's librarian in Toronto. Egoff is the author of *Thursday's Child: Trends and Patterns in Children's Literature* (ALA, 1981) and is a highly regarded speaker and writer on topics in children's literature.